EXTRAORDINARY PLACES BY BICYCLE

EXTRAORDINARY PLACES BY BICYCLE

Pauline and Hugh Symonds

Hayloft Publishing Ltd

First published in the UK by Hayloft Publishing Ltd.

ISBN 978-1-910237-75-5

Copyright © Pauline and Hugh Symonds, 2023

The right of Pauline and Hugh Symonds to be identified as the authors of this work has been asserted by them in accordance with the Copyright, Designs and Patents Act 1988.

All rights reserved. No part of this publication may be reproduced, stored in a retrieval system, or transmitted, in any form or by any means (electronic, mechanical, photocopying, recording or otherwise) without the prior written permission of the publisher.

A CIP catalogue record for this book is available from the British Library.

Printed and bound by Short Run Press Ltd, Devon

For every new book published, Hayloft commits to plant a tree, chosen by the author, in a new 'Wood of Words'. For this book the author has chosen *Syringa vulgaris*, the wild white lilac tree. The woodland will capture carbon throughout its life and help to replace the carbon and paper used in the production and printing process.

Maps created by Andrew Symonds

Hayloft Publishing Ltd,
Low Cairndoon, Whithorn, Wigtownshire,
Dumfries & Galloway, DG8 8NF
www.hayloft.eu
Tel. +44 (0) 7971 352 473

Visit www.hayloft.eu to read more about our books.

*Dedicated to Martin Symonds, Hugh's brother and fellow
'crazyguyonabike'
13th January 1959 to 2nd April 2021*

*Martin's heart stopped suddenly, without warning,
at the end of a family bike ride in Penarth, South Wales.*

EXTRAORDINARY PLACES BY BICYCLE

CONTENTS

1. How a decade of adventure began
    - Lost on the Altiplano — 9
    - Tandems and Tricycles — 20
    - Cyclists' Paradise — 25
2. The Land of the Patagarang — 37
3. How far can we get from home in a year?
    - Heading South into a European Winter — 58
    - You can't cycle to Divriği — 77
    - The visa nightmare — 102
    - The worst road in the world — 115
    - The Pamir highway — 145
    - Yurts, high lakes and mare's milk — 166
4. Chemo for Cancer before Cuba — 191
5. Cancún to Cornville – C2C — 205
6. Chengdu to Phnom Penh
    - No Aliens allowed — 221
    - Into the Cauldron — 239
7. Where the bikes are upside down — 255
8. Back Roads in unacquainted Europe — 263
9. Through the Rif and the Sierras of Spain — 303
10. Carlos' Colombia before Covid — 323
    - Epilogue — 388
    - Index — 390
    - Reviews — 398

EXTRAORDINARY PLACES BY BICYCLE

1
How a decade of Adventure began

I am on a lonely road and
I am traveling, traveling, traveling, traveling
Looking for something, what can it be?
Joni Mitchell, 'All I Want' from the album, *Blue,* 1971

Lost on the Altiplano
Pauline:
The wind was fierce, cold, and coming from the north. The force tried to thrust us to one side as we headed west, too far west, across the dead pan flat surface of the dusty salar. It had been a struggle to find the route south out of San Juan with only tyre marks in the salt and sand to indicate the way. There was nothing that could be called a road, or even a track. We were lost; our only navigation tools being a compass, a ridiculously large scale (1:1,300,000) paper map and photographs of tourist information taken ten days previously in Oruro.

We decided to stop, put more clothes on and wait, hoping for a vehicle to pass by so that we could ask for directions to San Agustín, the place we hoped to reach. After ten minutes or so, we saw a figure on wheels, heading towards us from the east. At first we thought it was a motorcyclist but it was going too slowly. After several minutes we recognised the particular shape that front and rear panniers give to a bicycle. Astonishing; another cyclist in this dusty, wind battered, corner of south-west Bolivia! After greetings and embraces, we asked Hervé where he was going. The Frenchman, brimming with enthusiasm, spoke in a bizarre mix of French and Spanish. In the strong wind it was tough to decipher what he was telling us. We saw 'Villa Alota' written on his pencilled notes and thought, great, we are going there too. We rode on as a threesome, his large figure giving me some shelter from the crosswind.

We realised our mistake when we reached the military base of Chiguana a couple of hours later. We sheltered in the lee of a scruffy building at the entrance to the base and ate crackers with *dulce de leche*. Looking at our maps we realised we were now well off our intended route. Hervé, an ex-army man who had served as a mountain guide, had different plans and carried provisions for several days. We knew nothing of what lay in the direction he was heading. We had provisions for the next 24 hours at most, and just a couple of litres of water. When the men at the military camp told us they had no water to give, that clinched it. We decided that it was too risky to follow this wild Frenchman with his hand-drawn directions. Sadly we had no choice but to go our different ways.

We knew that our road should cross the nearby railway line, so we followed the north side for the best part of 20km, blasting along at high speed with the wind now at our backs. This turned out to be a good plan. On reaching a track crossing the railway line, we decided to wait and hope that the time would come when we could ask someone the way. We were in luck. Within five minutes a 4x4 arrived from San Agustín. The driver confirmed our route and told us that the village was only ten kilometres away. The distance turned out to be 30km. We made another 24km by dusk, with lots of pushing in deep sand on the way. It was too dark for me to see, and Hugh only had one functioning eye; a contact lens had become displaced in the wind. We pitched camp on a raised sandy spot close to scrub and cacti. Taking no notice of Hugh's inclination to just lie down and go to sleep, I cooked by torchlight – pasta with tuna and oregano.

The previous day we had been mightily relieved when we reached the tiny settlement of San Juan. For much of the day the wind had blown us along on a hard sandy track which was lovely, but once we turned west on a rough road to San Juan, frequent heavy gusts brought clouds of grit into our faces, sand blasting any bare flesh and forcing us to stop. Hugh was very glad he had tinted goggles to help keep grit from his eyes. We were low on food, as the village of Manica, where we expected to find a shop, was deserted. We were saved, also by a Frenchman with the unlikely name of Dallas, travelling in a 4x4. He gave us a choice of quality cereal bars from France – wonderful. We must have looked hungry.

So how did we come to be pedalling through this surreal landscape in a remote corner of Bolivia? A region where ramshackle villages are linked by rutted and often loose gravel tracks, water sources are scarce and the chances of getting supplies hit and miss? We had ridden bikes for almost all of our lives and been on tours lasting several weeks in the UK, France and parts of Spain. We had taken our children along on a handful of little adventures. However, we had never before flown our bikes to another continent with eight months of riding ahead, frequently at high altitude (our highest point was 4,800m) and much of it on rough gravel roads.

In 2005 our son Andrew cycled down the length of Chile with his girlfriend, now his wife, Carole. He sent us CDs full of enticing pictures of mountains, deserts and glaciers. That was where we wanted to go; we wanted to do that too. The seed was sown. We simply had to do a grand cycling tour before our bodies started to fall apart. Then I stumbled on 'crazyguyonabike.com' and found a whole world of captivating journeys by bike. What really caught my eye were entries by a Swiss guy, Christian Bomio. He had taken, what appeared

Flying along a near empty Pan American highway in Peru.

to me then, to be an improbably desolate route across the high Bolivian plateau. I asked myself, 'could we do that?'

We gave up our teaching jobs in July 2010 and moved to a smaller house which was easier to lock up and leave. After a flight to Santiago de Chile we took a bus north to Arica, just 20km from the Peruvian border. This is where our ride began and we were hoping to reach Ushuaia at the tip of South America. We were thrown in at the deep end, setting out along the Pan American highway, heading for Arequipa in Peru where we planned to spend a few days acclimatising. For the first five days we were covering around 100km a day, passing through a waterless, barren landscape; mountains in shades of greys, pinks and browns, sometimes ground down into multi-coloured sandy hills sprinkled with fine white dust which looked almost like snow. We traversed high plains where the road stretched for miles into the distance, before descending into the next green valley where the rivers fed irrigation channels allowing the people to grow crops and provide grass for a few cows. Food stops and watering holes were far apart.

On day two we approached Moquegua, desperately trying to outrun the snarling dogs as we entered the town in the fading light. We left the following morning with seventeen litres of water on board, which was intended to last us for two days. At the end of that day we pitched our tent in a hidden sandy valley in the middle of nowhere. We heated up a pan of hot water for a face cloth wash; not as good as a shower but much better than nothing. Such were the first few days of our first major tour. This felt like adventure. We were coping with the challenges and we both felt good.

The only form of communication we had with us was a basic mobile phone, purely for emergency use. It was by this means, that on day four, in the miserable, poor, dusty town of La Joya, I received the news of my father's death. He had been suffering from a chronic disease, deteriorating gradually over several years. I had said my goodbyes before I left, not knowing if he would still be around when I returned. In the months prior to departure we had agonised about what we should do, discussing whether to cancel or postpone the flights. The situation caused tension between us and I found it impossible to work out what was the right thing to do. We had built up to this trip for so many years. It was what we had given up our jobs to do and neither of us wanted to abandon it. My mother told me to go; but was that what she really wanted? I was not at all sure. I can't say I know what my father would have wanted. We didn't return for his funeral either, and I don't think that my mother ever forgave me for it. Thoughts of what I didn't do, but probably should have done, still haunt me.

I realise that most people would willingly drop everything to support the family at such times. How could I behave in such a way you may ask? A question I ask myself to this day. Yes, I had three siblings to deal with things who all supported my decision, but that wasn't any excuse. To give any sort of answer I have to put myself back in time. The way my mum dealt with my father's illness made it virtually impossible to help or sympathise. There was so much anger, and discussion of constructive ways of dealing with things was often met with scorn and derision. It sounds harsh but at the time it was so difficult. I didn't know what I would do if I stayed and delayed our adventure; I wasn't sure I could really help; so we left. There were so many complications now that my father had died one week after the start of the trip. Would we return with our bikes or leave them in Peru? We had no car at home as we had lent it to our son. Should we both go back or just me? Would we abandon altogether or return to South America after a few days or weeks or months? Also, my relationship with my mum was not in a good place and this wasn't a time when I could deal with it. My dad was slipping away as we were on the flight to Santiago from London, but we hadn't known that. If we had, I doubt that we would have got on the plane.

So it was with a heavy heart that I set out with Hugh on the ascent to Arequipa where we planned to have a short period of rest, recuperation and acclimatisation. I rang mum as often as I could from the phone booths in towns and she seemed to be coping.

Our feelings were a heady blend of challenge, fear and excitement as we set out to cross the Mirador de los Volcanes at 4,800 metres heading for Chivay and views of the mighty condors in the Colca Canyon. Irish Pubs turn up in the most unlikely places! In Chivay, American Peace Corps volunteers were meeting at the bar for their weekly music session. It was thrilling to be able to get out my whistle and join in the rapid medley of jigs and reels.

It was after Chivay that we had our first taste of the rough stuff, leaving the paved comfort of the main highways. It felt quite ridiculous to be using a 1:500,000 scale map to navigate our way along a vaguely defined network of tracks; sometimes smooth dirt, sometimes rocky and sometimes loose sand. We quickly realised that we would soon wear ourselves out if we tried to go too far on this terrain at this altitude; it wasn't a race after all! However, after a period of five days at over 4,000m the blood cells were multiplying and we found we could even put a spurt on up a short steep section.

We were fast learning the art of spotting a hideaway for the night, looking to the right and left of the road at around 4pm onwards. Under a clear sky at an altitude of over 3,000m, the temperature plummeted at around 6pm when the sun set, dropping from over 30°C to several degrees below zero. Sometimes we camped near a stream or lake, but often we had to carry water long distances. Nearly 1,000km into the journey in Peru, we found what we thought to be a near perfect spot for our tent: wide scenic views capable of late sunset and early sunrise plus a river to wash in and take water from. There was also a small stone ruin to give us some cover from the road, which in the event turned out to be very fortunate.

Hugh described what followed in our blog, Wednesday, 8 September 2010: Imata to Santa Lucía:

> We should have noticed that there were no grazing animals, no small houses and more importantly there were large areas of black scorched scrubland in the neighbouring area. We offloaded our kit from the bikes and prepared to establish camp while Pauline went down to the river to wash and collect water for cooking. It is very strange that only that morning we had unusually been talking about shocking moments in our lives
>
> Well – from perfect peace to near disaster in a few seconds this was for me a living nightmare for the best part of half an hour. Pauline had disappeared out of

sight down the steep river bank and I was in the process of unpacking our kit and assembling the stove when I smelt smoke and saw fast burning grass rushing towards me. My immediate reaction was to stamp on flames and squirt water from our bidons but it was useless. I was instantly activated into high altitude pandemonium where on my own I had to frantically pick up as many bits and pieces as I could and throw them beyond a nearby line of flames. Then I saw flames lapping at the tyres of our bikes. They were already double locked, so after a quick scramble for the keys I rushed the bikes to a stony track 20m away hopefully safe from the racing flames. I returned to find flames lapping at the tent bag, a petrol canister and two of our bike bags. I threw the petrol can as far as I could beyond the flames and lifted the tent and bags away to the same spot as the bikes. Meanwhile about five acres of ground was burning in a strong wind and the smoke was billowing high. After more frantic movements of kit I reached a stage where I thought I could run to the river to get Pauline's help. We filled two dromedaries (strong ten litre flexible bags) with roughly eight litres of water each and chased flames in a completely pointless exercise. I kept trying to ignore my constant gasps for breath.

The fire and ourselves must have been clearly visible from the road but to our amazement no one stopped to help. We simply thought that the camp was now useless and we had to get the hell out of the area with all the stuff we could get and check its condition later. We did just that whilst I was in a state of some sort of shock. Another five kilometres down the road we checked into The Hostal Los Andes in Saint Lucía at a cost of ten Soles each per night (just over £2 each). We discovered scorched straps, sandals, mitts and holes in the tent bag. I was astonished that we had not lost anything significant – not even a hole in the ground sheet of the tent. If the tent had been up then it would have certainly disappeared. Our recovery was rapid as the small town of Santa Lucía was calm and friendly but surrounded by hills also partially blackened by previous scorched earth fires.

We were very surprised not to be asked by anyone about the incident. We left with a feeling that such events must be commonplace. Two days later we camped close to a lake with no scorched areas in sight and were grateful to find the tent and all our kit fully intact. The only remaining evidence is scorched bungees and other such things – oh – my camera strap has melted and is useless but the camera is fine!

So, how did the fire start? This was the bit we left out of the blog in fear of being chased by the police for arson. Noticing a small piece of toilet paper on the ground Hugh took it into his head to burn it, never thinking that he was about to incinerate several acres of land. The vegetation was sparse, but as it turned out, tinder dry. Fortunately the fire was contained at a point where the river met the road. The experience left us very shaken and ever since we have been super cautious with the use of a naked flame.

In the following days we noticed many burnt patches on the mountainsides and several fires. We never found out if they were started accidentally or deliberately. Still feeling shocked after the fire, we found ourselves on a lovely gentle downhill route on fast tarmac through a valley populated with small settlements. Alpacas roamed over a landscape scattered with shepherds' huts, dry stone walled enclosures and eucalyptus trees.

As we approached the small town of Deustua we were followed by a young guy on a bicycle. After a few questions he became our guide for the next bit of rough stuff – an off the beaten track route to Puno on the shores of Lake Titicaca. He rode a single speed bike with one brake and a rusty chain but he was fit. At one point he pushed his bike up a shortcut, and we rode the track; we were chuffed to beat him to the top. We met lots of young children riding home from school in the next village, Vilque, which had a huge, blue painted smart looking school.

We were looking to camp by Lago Umayo hoping for a bath and a scenic camp. We reached the lake but the water was way below us down a steep rocky slope. It was a great spot with fantastic bird life including lots of flamingos, but no chance of camping on the shore. I climbed down to the lake with a dromedary to supplement our water supply with five litres of lake water. Just as we were settling into our warm sleeping bags to admire the stars in comfort, a bright light shone into my eyes. We had ridden and pushed our bikes some way off the nearest motorable track, so we were very surprised to see that a young man had arrived on a motorbike. He repeatedly asked to see our passports but there was no way we were handing them over. Hugh showed his driving licence but struggled to hold on to it.

Shortly afterwards he was joined by an old man, slight, a little stooped and dressed in a loose shirt tucked into baggy pants, secured with thick, knotted cord around his waist. His missus arrived looking angry, waving a pointed finger – witch like we thought! They were the couple we had seen as we rode past an old stone house on the way to the lake.

What followed was a curious conversation, involving a lot of messy Spanish on our part and probably a lot of misunderstanding on both sides. The gist of it was: the old couple didn't want us there; they wanted to know what we were looking for (peace and birds) and what we were doing. We tried to explain but it was difficult in our rusty Spanish. Slowly, they warmed to us when we showed them pictures of our family and our journey. They were fascinated by our kitchen kit and tent. The old man's deeply lined, sun-hardened features broke into a detectable smile and they both began to express worry about our welfare. We picked up the words, *gringo frío* and they seemed to be suggesting that we should stay in their house; an offer we politely declined. Just before they left, the old missus waved a stick at us and we were left wondering what it was all about. As a precaution we moved the bikes right next to the tent; partly in the tent in fact, as the young man had taken far too much interest in the *bicicletas bonitas* and what they might cost.

We reckon that the old couple may have been frightened of us; what were these old gringos on bikes doing camping on rough ground high above a lake near their house? We had another visit from the young man in the morning, but he went when I politely suggested that we were about to have *desayuno* (breakfast).

After Puno, our journey took us along the shores of Lake Titicaca (the largest lake in South America at an altitude of 3,812m) and across the Altiplano, landing us in the chaotic far flung traffic ridden town of Oruro which was in the throes of one of Bolivia's infamous demonstrations. As we worked on our jour-

Morning after the night before. The old man was still puzzled why two 'gringos fríos' would want to camp high above Lago Umayo (Peru).

nal in the internet café, our senses were hit by the sound and smell of gunfire (hopefully blanks) permeating from outside. Travellers are advised to keep well away from such events! Oruro was the last place that could be called a town before we set out on the last bit of paved road we would see for a while, launching into that increasingly remote, wild and wonderful terrain that had caught my imagination so many months ago.

So: how did it go from there? I wrote this summary in our blog on Wednesday, 13 October 2010:

> Looking back on our journey across SW Bolivia from the comfort of San Pedro de Atacama
>
> The tarmac ended at Quillacas and we would not see a good surface again for sixteen days with the exception of the tracks across the Salar de Uyuni worn smooth by the countless Toyota 4x4 'gringo carts' (Hugh's expression). For six

weeks we didn't go below 3,500m and we found we were able to get away with putting in more and more effort in the rare air.

We rode, and often pushed, south over sandy, rocky and rutted tracks, never sure of how far it was to the next place, and never sure of what we would find there. The maps were basic, contradictory and often wrong so we had to ask the locals planting quinoa, and the drivers of lorries and tourist cars, how far it was to the next place – or more usefully how long would it take by car? Then we had to allow for the distance being more than double and the possibility of not making it to the next pueblo. As a result we carried water when we didn't need to or found ourselves short when we needed it. Twice we went wrong and struggled over extra kilometres against violent winds and impossibly bumpy tracks – very frustrating.

We passed through isolated villages, with dusty streets. The school would often be a fine new building and the school children dressed in smart uniforms. Many of the villages appeared quite dead when we arrived and there would be few clues as to which of the mud brick buildings was a shop – possibly a Coca-Cola sign outside the door. The locals were always happy to help. As we went further into the wilderness, the shops became more and more bare, sinking to the lowest common denominator of fizzy drinks, biscuits, crackers and tins of fish. Locals made their own bread and two lovely 'profesoras' in San Agustín sold us some bread and bananas as neither bread, fruit nor vegetables were for sale in the shop. When we stayed in hostels, we sunk to scavenging left over pancakes from the tour group's breakfasts.

As we moved into the far south-west, beyond the last pueblo of Mallku Villamar, we had a feeling of being on another planet, where the volcanic mountains are multi-coloured with copper red and the white of borax, and pink James's flamingos wade in red waters. The wind became more vicious and cold. We recorded temperatures of -18°C outside our tent (only -10°C inside) – our water bottles and Dromedaries froze in the night and ice crystals fell on our sleeping bags from the walls of the tent in the morning. Without the radiant heat of the sun the only place to be was inside a sleeping bag, and we perfected the art of making breakfast without getting out of bed.

Bolivia was wonderful but harsh to the end. As we headed for the very southwest tip and the ramshackle Bolivian border post, the wind kept up the fight. Several steep undulations in the road sapped our last breaths at this great height before we finally hit the summit (4,600m) of the main asphalt route from Argentina to San Pedro. A two hour descent of around 35km took us into another world, a warmer, kinder world. Yes – San Pedro de Atacama is a tourist hot spot – just what we need right now. This is our localised Utopia. We need some good 'nutritious' food (no more chips and rice) and our cracked fingers and brazed bums need to heal after hours of being jolted around in the cold. We are fit and lean – the clothes are loose (most of them are now in the washing machine).

We are pleased and happy that we made it – Hugh said it was harder than his run over the mountains of Britain or doing a two day mountain marathon. It is certainly the hardest thing I have ever done but astonishingly rewarding. Our biggest problem was probably the lack of accurate information followed closely by the state of the roads. Our bikes are great – they have taken us, luggage and sometimes eight litres of water each over the roughest tracks – no breakages or punctures.

EXTRAORDINARY PLACES BY BICYCLE

Our trust in The Roberts bikes is now very high after a month in Peru and a month in Bolivia and all we have had to do is tighten the chains occasionally. It is fairly unbelievable not to have punctured as yet, particularly when you see so many shredded car and lorry tyres by the sides of the tracks and roads and the amount of shattered glass near towns. The Rohloff oil will need changing in another 2,500km and we wonder where we will be by then – exciting.

Our route had taken us on a north to south line, directly across the Salar de Uyuni; at over 10,000 square kilometres, the largest salt flat in the world. The hard crust sits over a pool of brine which harbours over 15% of the world's lithium reserves. What better way to travel across the dead pan flat surface than on a bike, driven by the strong wind at our backs. However, it is not a place to be in the rain. We had planned this trip so that we reached this point in the dry season! We were heading for an island in the middle of the Salar, but it wasn't visible from the edge. Setting out in a dead straight line using a compass bearing, we watched in amazement as a small black blob, hovering over the salt in the distance, grew, eventually taking the form of a small hill. As the island grew larger we realised that this was the Isla Incahuasi, an oasis of cactus forest surrounded by the salt sea. What can compare with putting up your tent on the rock hard, dazzling white surface and watching the crusty ridges of the polygonal tiles brought into sharp relief as the sun goes down?

The first of two camps on the Salar de Uyuni (Bolivia).
Just leave no trace and carry everything out.

Carlos and Hugh 'high' (4,000m) on the Altiplano in Chile.

This was one of the highlights of our South American trip.

Reaching San Pedro de Atacama was a major feat. We headed straight for one of the cool cafés serving delicious juices. And who should roll in? Yes, Hervé! It was just awesome to meet again after a week on different routes. We compared notes on how many times we had been blown over and how far we had pushed bikes. His home is a rotating dome in the Écrins National Park near Gap in France. Almost a year later we delighted in a visit to his home – by bike.

Tandems and Tricycles

Life is like riding a bicycle.
To keep your balance you must keep moving.

Albert Einstein

Hugh:

Pauline and I met at Durham University in 1972. We shared a taste for adventure and in the first summer holiday we hitch-hiked around Scandinavia on £50 each taking all the muesli we needed for eight weeks. The highlight was hiking from Norway to Finland in Arctic Lapland. We loved traveling together and for two summers we worked for Dick Phillips' walking holidays in Iceland guiding and sorting out provisions. After graduating we taught mathematics at a school in the foothills of the Indian Himalaya. From that base we completed several self-sufficient treks one of which took two weeks and crossed the mountains from Kargil to Kishtwar. We enjoyed traveling under our own steam and rarely travelled by car. We have always had a dislike for motoring. In 1978 we returned to my home town of Manchester after a long overland journey home through Pakistan, Afghanistan, Iran, Turkey and Europe. It was an adventure but we became tired of long bus journeys.

The following summer in 1979 we hiked the length of the Outer Hebrides from Barra to the stone circle at Callanish. On the final afternoon before taking the ferry to the mainland from Stornoway, we met a couple on a tandem. They had followed a similar journey to us from Barra. We admired their freedom and pace of travel. A catalyst had been sown. We returned home and the following week bought an off-the-peg tandem for £400. We knew very little about bikes and nothing about cycling with camping gear. The Gitane tandem was fun and we spent many long weekends exploring the nearby Peak District. We learnt that Gitane meant gypsy woman. However we had a really scary moment when in heavy rain one day the brakes simply would not work. We were learning as we raced headlong towards the back end of a car. Rim brakes and steel rims don't work in the wet. We returned to the bike shop in Timperley where we had bought the Gitane and they arranged for us to have a new rear wheel with a weatherproof drum brake. It worked!

The following summer we took a ship to northern Spain and cycled back to the north coast of France sleeping in our tiny tent on the way. It was great except that after we had crossed the Pyrenees the rear wheel started to fail under the strain and we were snapping spokes daily. The wobbly wheel struggled to get north of the Loire but we made it to the Gitane factory at Machecoul near Nantes and bought a non-drum brake rear wheel. We made it home without rain but we were now determined to buy a tandem with decent equipment. We wanted one which would go, stop and not break in bits.

It takes knowledge to make decisions and in owning the Gitane we had learnt a lot. With a little bit of research we found Mercian Cycles in Derby, not too far from Manchester. We booked an appointment and went for what turned out to be a consultation lasting more than two hours. We ended up spending three times as much as the Gitane and more than twice as much as we had spent on our old car. Six months later the custom built bike was ready so we took a train to Derby and cycled back. Pauline was now eight months pregnant so we had to turn the rear handlebars upwards to ride home. The guy at Mercian said this happens to people who ride tandems!

The bike was, and still is a beauty, but now very much in the retro style with downtube changers, cut-out lugs and chrome forks and dropouts. It is an outstanding bike for light weight fast touring and we have travelled with it many times on credit card tours in France. The wheels have forty spokes each and there are double Mafac cantilever brakes at the back so it stops in the rain. However, when we first bought it we thought it was a bit precious for traveling with a new born baby and also perhaps a bit wobbly.

We found the perfect solution in a second hand Claud Butler tandem tricycle. This turned out to be a terrifically versatile machine for a growing family. With the addition of 'kiddy cranks', which enable a child with short legs to ride on the back, Andrew, our first born, was able to pedal his own weight from the age of six. Within a space of another four years, Joseph and Amy were born and we were determined to continue cycling. Pauline had a custom designed George Longstaff tricycle built and with ultra-low gears she was able to pedal it with two youngsters on the back.

We did some short camping trips in the Yorkshire Dales and in 1987 when the children were six, four and not quite two, we went trike touring in the south of France. I had it easy on the tandem trike, turbo charged by Andrew so we carried the two tents, the stove and sleeping bags. Pauline had no such pedal assistance so her extra baggage was kept to a minimum with articles like disposable nappies. Gradually the children could ride their own bikes but one addition which helped the transition was a pink second hand Freddie Grubb Rann trailer. This single-wheeled extra attached to the rear of either of the trikes and enabled another child to pedal.

In the summer of 1990 none of us rode bikes for three months. I took a sabbatical term away from my work teaching mathematics at Sedbergh School. I had been a competitive runner since a teenager. Races had been on the track, road and cross-country but after moving to the Yorkshire Dales in 1981, my favou-

France. Hugh on the way to a race in the Pyrenees. Andrew, Joe and Amy on the way to another campground and place to play

rite form of racing had been on the fells. Combining my love of mountains with the hill fitness I had gained, I set about running the Munros (Scottish mountains of over 3,000 feet) in one continuous traverse. The five of us went to live in a campervan for three months. Pauline supported me and educated the kids along the way. The event ended up being a massive fundraiser for Intermediate Technology (now Practical Action) – the third world development charity introduced to us by adventurer, Richard Crane. Over a period of just less than one hundred days, I ran over and in between 303 high mountains of Scotland, England, Wales and Ireland taking motorised transport just once for the ferry between Holyhead and Ireland. The story of this adventure is recounted in my book, *Running High*.

By the time Amy was ten we were all riding solo bikes. The summer holiday was spent cycling from Bilbao in Spain to Cherbourg in France. The tricycles had been really practical but they took up a lot of space so we sold them and we hoped that they would continue lives of adventure. In their teenage years the children began their own cycle adventures and gradually Pauline and I returned to trips where there were just the two of us. Looking back now, the total fivesome family era seems short. Now we are buying Isla bikes and Chariot trailers for grandchildren and watching them or joining them on their cycle tours.

For eighteen years Pauline commuted to work by bike ten miles each way. For many of these years she was on a cheap old bike. In 2000, Andrew had left home and was working in London for a year. We visited him for a long weekend and he and I ran the London Marathon together. Pauline and I had become aware of Roberts Cycles in Croydon so we took the opportunity to pay Chas a visit. This was like the Mercian consultation all over again. Within a year we were both riding Roberts audax bikes and Pauline's commute had become faster and easier. In the summer of 2007 we toured on these bikes on a circuit starting and finishing from our home in Cumbria. The tour took us to the Isle of Man, Belfast, across Ireland to County Clare returning to Fishguard in South Wales. All the cycling was good, even the Sustrans route through the centre of Manchester.

Our thoughts were now turning to retirement and long term travel by bike. Andrew had cycled the length of Chile following his gap year in London. The photos he showed us of deserts, waterfalls and glaciers were inspirational. Whilst riding across Ireland we had time to fantasise about future journeys and how we would go about long term cycle travel perhaps for periods of up to a year. Clearly we had to be able to carry a lot of gear and the bikes would have to be tough. The Mercian tandem would not carry enough kit and for long term travel we preferred the idea of separate bikes. The Roberts audax bikes were very comfortable but only had rear racks and were probably not robust enough for some of the world's wild places.

We returned from Ireland and gave Chas Roberts a call. We were enthused by his ideas for building us Roughstuff bikes so we travelled to London again to order expedition bikes. It was so good to have the knowledge of Chas. His experience of building bikes for travellers was invaluable. We were now convinced of the usefulness and practicality of the fourteen speed Rohloff internal hub gears. We were persuaded to have mechanical disc brakes and with flying the bikes to many destinations we had the frames built with S&S couplings which enable the frames to be split and the bikes to be packed well in small boxes.

All we had to do now was pay deposits, wait eight months and fantasise more about wild places. By the spring of 2009 we were itching to go wild and in the one week half-term break we ventured to Scotland and Glen Tilt. It was a great test for the Roughstuffs and their ability to carry a lot of kit and cope with rough tracks. The circuit took us to Britain's highest permanent settlement at Fealar Lodge before we returned to civilisation at Blair Atholl. A few weeks later we were on our last summer holiday of our working lives. We left home on the Roughstuffs and headed east. We adored travel like this. Serendipitous travel where each day is different and unplanned. We followed the Elbe River in Germany as far as Dresden and onwards to eastern European countries before crossing into Ukraine. It was time to go back to work for another year. We turned a corner and returned to Leeds on a cheap flight from Krakow. Our appetites had been truly whetted so it was not long before we were booking flights to Santiago in Chile.

Cyclists' Paradise

'That's Living'
Brian of Roberts Cycles (Croydon)
when we phoned to say the Roughstuffs
had been fault free in South America.

Pauline:

For 4,270km the improbable shoe string strip of land known as the country of Chile sits squeezed between the vast expanse of the Pacific Ocean and the ice-capped chain of the Andean mountains. South of Puerto Montt, the sea eats its way far into the mountains along the lines of what were once deep valleys between peaks rising to over 3,000m, breaking up the coast into a multiplicity of islands. Water is in abundance; the powerful, turquoise torrents of some of the world's last untamed rivers, and wild windswept lakes. Icy rivulets emerge from the hanging glaciers which drip over the edge of the mountain chain draping the crags with fine threads of spray. This is a land where nature's powerful armour defends itself against the invasion of man; where glaciers meet with the sea and precipitous craggy mountainsides block the way around every corner. Lush impenetrable rain forests clothe the lower slopes.

In 1976, Augusto Pinochet took on the battle and began one of the most ambitious construction projects of the 20th century; a road to link the tiny, disconnected, remote communities of this region known as Aysén. Routes going east through the mountains into Argentina already existed, but a north/south route presented much more of a challenge. More than 10,000 soldiers worked on the construction of the road which opened to traffic in 1988. Little did they know at the time that the Carretera Austral was to become one of the world's iconic cycling routes. This is a journey that just cries out to be travelled on a bicycle and not surprisingly, we found it to be the most sociable experience we have ever had in our ten years of bike touring. One evening there were ten of us sat around the table at the campsite on Laguna Chaguay.

The cyclists we met were on journeys of many different kinds. Nadja, an Austrian living in Barcelona, had begun her cycling journey in Lima. Having tired of bus travel she had bought a bike and arranged for the cyclists' favourite Ortlieb panniers to be sent to her from Germany. Her first cycle tour took her straight up into the Andes; she caught us up cycling out of San Martín de los Andes. Nadja became our adopted daughter for almost two weeks, but sadly had to leave us on day two of the Carretera as her wheels were in the process of collapsing.

Maz and Pob (Marion and Oliver), from London, were on their honeymoon. Their journey had begun in Salta, Argentina and would end in Ushuaia. We had met them a few days before joining the Carretera, in a curious bit of Wales lodged in Argentina. In Trevelin we ate scones and *torta galesa* (bara brith) at Nain Maggie's tea room where you could also buy Welsh dolls and the Welsh Dragon flag. Many of the streets and houses have Welsh names. Along with Nadja we became a *grupetto* of five for a few days. We camped together on the beach by Lago Yelcho – absolute paradise in the warm sunshine with clear blues skies above and strands of cloud hovering atmospherically along the lower slopes of the snow patterned mountains across the water. Nadja gave us both much needed haircuts.

For us the Carretera Austral was part of a continuous six month journey from Arica in Chile to Ushuaia in Argentina which had begun on the high, dry and cold of the Altiplano, the most extensive area of high plateau outside Tibet. The contrast with the southern Andes of Patagonia couldn't be more stark. The legendary Ruta Cuarenta, Argentina's longest road, took us much of the way south, following the eastern edge of the Andes. However, there were times when the traffic built up and we had to look for alternatives.

South of Mendoza we found the classic cyclists' gift – the old road. From Pareditas to El Sosneado a new stretch of R40 had been constructed further to the east. The old road, now renamed R101, had been helpfully abandoned by all the traffic, for good reason. There were no villages and no shops on this 160km stretch of rough dirt track – only *puestos* which may be 20km or more from their nearest neighbour. These are simple farmsteads where people live and keep animals – goats, cows and hens. They were easily spotted in the distance as a clump of green, tall trees standing out from the surrounding dry bush. Small tracks led off the main route out into the middle of nowhere. We had thought we could ride it in two days but it took us three.

On the first day we saw no cars – just the occasional gaucho on horseback. We set up camp by a river and then an old school bus rocked up. The drivers set up a *parrilla* a few yards from our tent. José and Oscar threaded a long thin cut of ribbed beef onto a metal stick and after half an hour over the hot wood embers it was done to perfection. They offered it to us served with bread, and wine from an improvised glass cut from a plastic Pepsi bottle. Away from the *parrilla* it was surprisingly cool – and then we looked at the altimeter and realised we had climbed to over 2,000m.

The next day we arrived at Escuela la Jaula – in a big river valley, over 60km from the nearest *pueblo*. It serves the children from the surrounding *pueblos*. They board for 20 days and then go home for ten days to help on the farms. These *albergues*, as they are called, are essential. There is no way parents could get their kids to school each day. Jessica, one of the teachers, showed us round the school. José and Oscar, drive a school bus around collecting the pupils from remote *puestos*. They have a crazy job driving around in a Renault Trafic van over rough tracks with amazing views. They were full of fun and laughs – they appeared to enjoy their work. It really brought into focus how spaced out the country is. The view from our camp that night looked across the arid scrub to the full moon rising over a distant volcano.

After months in arid lands we left the Ruta Cuarenta and crossed over the Paso de Pino Hachado into Chile once more, and a land of plentiful water. We crossed between Chile and Argentina seven times, each time having to take care with the restrictions on food stuffs allowed. At one frontier we had to eat most of a jar of honey to save it from being wasted. Our first sight of the monkey puzzle trees came as a complete surprise – we rounded a bend and there they were, set against a bright blue sky on ridges of folded basalt columns. More scientifically known as *araucaria*, these incredibly alluring trees were unlike the ones we see in gardens in England. Their trunks were bereft of leaves until high above where the scaly snake-like branches spread out like umbrellas.

This was also the land of volcanos – many of them active. We pedalled through the Conguillío Park on a stony track with dark, jumbled lava fields on either side, and tantalising views of the steaming Volcán Llaima framed by the thick dark green fronds of the *araucaria.*

We took the Ruta Interlagos dirt road through Mapuche country. The Mapuche are the indigenous inhabitants of the region and the largest ethnic group in Chile constituting 10% of the population. The land is a magical world of pristine lakes and streams; waterfalls shooting over high crags; and lush forest where we found idyllic camping spots.

An ashy track took us through the Parque National Villarrica narrowing to little more than a footpath, twisting and climbing through dense forest. Occasionally bird sounds from the woods came alive and we spotted brilliant red-headed magellanic woodpeckers playing in the trees. We had to push our bikes around deep muddy puddles and sections of short, sharp, water-worn ravines. It was very useful to be in the company of experienced Adelaide mountain bikers Alister and Anna – they gave us some confidence in dealing with the challenging terrain.

It was the height of summer, December, but we found ourselves pushing the bikes through snow. We camped together on a family small holding – Pamela, Patricio, Matias (13) and Nicolas (9) – much assisted in our communication by Anna's excellent Spanish. They offered us their *ruka* (a traditional mapuche house) for shelter, cooking and a fire; their home for a meal of eggs, fresh bread, hot milk straight from the cow and succulent honey from their bees. For the first time I had a go at hand milking a cow. Pamela filled the buckets in no time but I only managed a few drops! The next night we reached the small town of Coñaripe, overlooked by the symmetrical, snow white nipple of Volcán Villarrica; when it blows its top the lava heads straight for the town.

Near San Martín de los Andes, we dipped back into Argentina again, here more verdant than the arid country we had left further north. Now travelling with Nadja and joined by Dave Moser from Portland, Oregon we set out on 'La Ruta de los Siete Lagos' – a beautiful section of the Ruta Cuarenta which runs from San Martín de los Andes to Villa la Angostura. With blue skies and a quiet and paved road it was simply gorgeous riding in what now really felt like Patagonia – lush trees, powerful *cascadas* and occasional well-built wooden *estancias*. That was our vision of Patagonia – an enchanting land where nature is queen.

Patagonia is the name given to the tapering southern tip of South America which separates the Atlantic Ocean from the Pacific. The northern boundary is ill defined but we had certainly crossed it! Argentinian Patagonia, away from the slopes of the Andes is an arid region of steppe-like plains but our route was still within the grip of the Andes. Chilean Patagonia is for the most part that narrow strip of land where Pinochet built the Carretera Austral.

We moved south in Argentina through a marvellous mountain landscape. Vast areas of pink and purple lupins covered the fields in the valleys and bright yellow broom lit up the roadsides – all making for a pretty picture. However in reality the picture isn't too pretty as both are damaging invasive species. *Lupinus polyphyllus* is native to North America. Broom, is a prolific seeder, native to Europe and North Africa. It has escaped from cultivation all over the world – we went on to see much of it in New Zealand and it is common in Australia. At least the noisy black-faced ibis prancing around the campsite fields were in their native land.

We avoided a busy section of R40 from Villa La Angostura to San Carlos de Bariloche by taking a beautiful single track ride through the Parque Nacional los Arrayanes. We had to carry our bikes up suspended wooden stairways. The Arrayanes is a low growing tree with flaky, cinnamon coloured bark, which likes to have its feet in water. This rare tree is protected within the park. An expensive tourist boat then took us across the Lago Nahuel Huapi to Llao Llao, giving us a delightful alternative view of the mountains around.

Back on the R40, heading for El Bolsón we passed the sign giving the distance to Ushuaia, 1,953km – the year of our birth. We would ride another 3,095km before reaching the end of our journey! There was another Pauline staying at the campsite in town. Pauline Symaniak from Portobello in Edinburgh was on a two year trip on her Thorn Sherpa. She had cycled through Europe and then taken the boat from Valencia to Buenos Aires – a great experience on an MSC cargo ship she said – *muy despacio y muy carro y muy tranquilo*. She was then heading for the United States and New Zealand. She is living proof that appearances can be deceptive – this small and slight woman was

CYCLISTS' PARADISE

Lago Yelcho (Chile), just before joining the Carretera Austral.

pedalling around the world with the same load as many big, strong looking guys.

Just over a year later we were heading down R6 on the west coast of the South Island of New Zealand. It was a dripping wet day. There was no one else at Punakaiki – the place of pancake rocks – a curious formation of finely layered limestone looking like towers of diminishing pancakes. On reaching Greymouth we received a message from Pauline – she was camping at Hokitika. It wasn't an exciting ride and it was busy with traffic – trucks, milk tankers, cars and campervans – so we pegged it along the road, taking it in turns to break the wind. Hokitika is famous for its driftwood art, displayed on the beach. The raw materials are in plentiful supply. It was a whacky place for two Pauline cycling Syms to meet.

In 2014, just before setting out to Cuba we bumped into her again – this time by pure accident on the beach at Portobello!

We joined the Carretera Austral in Villa Santa Lucía, 315km south of its start in Puerto Montt and headed south.

Two weeks down the Carretera we met Tim and Tina at the campsite near Puerto Río Tranquilo. Subsequently we discovered that Tim was the author of an iconic book titled *A Long Ride for a Pie*, telling the story of his journey back home to New Zealand from London, a book we had really enjoyed reading. We were later to meet Tim and his German wife Tina in Christchurch, New Zealand, where they were living close to our daughter Amy, and Tim would visit us in the Yorkshire Dales when he came over to ride the famous Three Peaks cyclocross race.

For some a brief visit was not enough to satisfy their needs! Thomas and Katrin from Germany had not been to their home country for over ten years when we met them at Campo Alacaluf, their spiritual home in the rainforest 45km from Puerto Río Tranquilo up the Exploradores Valley, where they now live with their daughter Danielle.

We had been encouraged to explore this valley by Andy Weston. We were introduced to him in the nick of time by a friend who knew exactly how valuable his advice would be. Much of Patagonia is well known to Andy as he had spent several years teaching at a school in Santiago de Chile. Being a keen cyclist himself and a lover of rough rides, he had taken the school children on many intrepid trips in Patagonia. When we arrived in Chile he put us up in his flat, stored spares to be used at our half way point in his *bodega* and introduced us to the best of Chilean craft beer – like us he loves a 'quiet' beer. Needless to say he is now a good friend.

We made our way up the steep sided valley – waterfalls tumbling down everywhere over the cliffs in a series of steps. There were tantalising views of the glaciers above. A 4x4 drove up alongside us and opened the window to say hello. Astonishingly the passenger was an Indian tourist who had been a pupil at the Lawrence School Sanawar in the Indian Himalaya foothills, where we had taught from 1976 to 1977.

Thomas and Katrin had the courage to make the lifestyle they aspired for a reality. For five years they worked twelve hour night shifts as taxi drivers near Munich and saved enough to buy 50ha of land in the Patagonian rainforest. They built Campo Alacaluf from their own trees. It was a brave and monumental shift. Their beautifully built home is clad in the traditional shingles – 9,500 of them on the outside and 4,500 on the inside – all carefully cleaned and shaped by Katrin and Thomas. For two and a half years they lived in a pickup truck whilst working with local carpenters.

Around every two weeks they visit Puerto Río Tranquilo, to get provisions. However, to do some serious shopping they must go to Coyhaique, the only significant town on the Carretera and a seven hour drive mainly on dirt roads; they do this about every two months. When we arrived, Katrin was waiting for Thomas to return from a shopping expedition of several days, and he returned with the car stuffed to the roof.

They had just bought a water turbine from Coyhaique and installed 45 twelve metre long pipes to drop water a height of 110m over a distance of 548m, to generate a regular 220volts – that is until the silt blocked the input after heavy rains. We went with Thomas on the rough climb up the hillside, which he has to do every eight days to inspect the system. The pipes had come all the way from Antofagasta in the North of Chile, at a cost of two million pesos (a lot of money) and it took four men to carry each section up the hill. They chose a damp place to live with three times as much rain as Puerto Río Tranquilo. In this part of the world there can be three climatic zones within 200km. Dinner was a plate of wild mushrooms gathered from the rainforest (*morillas*) cooked in a creamy sauce – a rare treat as each year there are only enough to supply about 20-30 meals.

The road up the Exploradores valley will eventually reach the spectacular Laguna San Rafael at the Bahía Exploradores, a national park of *lagunas* and glaciers. Right now the road doesn't quite reach, but tourists can get there by boat, plane or possibly on foot or horse. So much of the spectacular scenery of Patagonia is inaccessible. We went up the valley to see the Glacier Exploradores where on a good day you have a great view of the glacier and Monte San Valentín, the highest mountain in Chilean Patagonia (4,058m) – we only caught fleeting glimpses of the heavily glaciated lower slopes.

On the recommendation of Thomas at Alacaluf we deviated 10km west of the Carretera to the tranquil setting of camping *refugio* Río Ñadis close to the mighty, turquoise waters of the Río Baker. The story goes that Lilli from Germany was riding on her horse through Patagonia when she met Rosendo – and so began a life on a Patagonian farm. We arrived ten minutes before a group of 20 Italians arrived. Lilli apologised profusely for the lack of peace, but we profited from their lively company and a share of their Asado al Palo – a whole *cordero* (lamb) stretched over a vertical spit and slow roasted over a fire.

Traditionally men unsheathe their knives and slice the meat – beautiful, golden, and crispy on the outside, soft and juicy on the inside – right off the bones. A leather drinking bag full of wine was passed around, and when everyone was done, they all shared a communal cloth napkin. Our meat was carved by Rosendo and the Italians shared their bottles of wine. The Italian team were on an adventurous journey, also making a film about the issue of the proposed *represas* (dams).

All along the route we had seen huge billboards displaying pictures of the free running Río Baker, topped and tailed with the lines, Patagonia, *sin represas*. HidroAysén, the company pushing the mega project, responded with *energía más limpia, para Chile y las región de Aysén* (cleaner energy, for Chile and the region of Aysén); the benefits to Aysén were far from clear! At Río Ñadis a book on the subject included disturbing images of glaciated mountains and turquoise lakes viewed through a shroud of electricity cables strung between monstrous lattice steel pylons. Contrasting views showed, *cómo es ahora* (how it is now) and *cómo sería* (what it would be like) – the change was too disturbing to contemplate. The farm was destined to be 18 meters underwater if the dam was built. It was truly heart breaking to think of their wonderful home, the product of so much work, slowly sinking under the waters of the gigantic lake. The lake would flood some of the Parque Nacional de San Rafael, making it an illegal move, so Lilli was hopeful that this would put a barrier in the way. However, other people we spoke to didn't seem too hopeful that the Sin Represas movement would succeed.

We exchanged our bikes for horses and went with Lilli to El Saltón, a narrow point on the Río Baker close to a point at which a *represa* was planned. For the last stretch, we tethered the horses and took the Corte San Carlos, a narrow path cut into the riverside cliff which once served as the route to the

Heading for Laguna Amarga and Torres del Paine (Chile).

village of Tortel. Horses could be taken along this route, but not when mounted. It was a novel experience for us to be pushing through floods, with our feet in the stirrups almost in the water and moving up and down narrow muddy paths putting total faith in the sure footedness of the steed. We learnt that our Brooks bike saddles are more comfortable than horse saddles – for us, anyway!

Multitudes of waterfalls feed the Río Baker flowing alongside the route to Caleta Tortel, a village close to where the mighty river meets the sea. People living on the opposite bank have to cross the fast flowing water to get to the road. Until 2003 Tortel itself was only accessible by boat or plane – virtually cut off from the outside world. For us it was a 22km detour off the Carretera. The villagers harvested the cypress trees and built their homes on stilts – above the damp vegetation along the shoreline and spilling over into the shallows of the sea. Boardwalks and wooden staircases substitute for streets – the only way round most of the village is on foot.

Leaving Tortel, we crossed paths with 22-year-old Swinde, from Germany, travelling on her own, along the length of the Americas from Tierra del Fuego to Alaska, a journey which commonly takes two years by bike and tempts many cycle tourists. Earlier on we had met another couple also heading for Alaska. Matt (English) and Sylwia (Polish) were hoping to get there by the summer – not the next summer but the one after in 14 months' time. They gave us many useful tips on the journey south beyond the Carretera.

We took their excellent advice on taking a continuous route through the Torres del Paine National Park – we hadn't known it was possible to do this. A camp on the fringes of the park gave us a deep rose view of the Torres at sunrise. We rode on the beach alongside Laguna Amarga, with a view of the glaciated summits and sheer rock towers on our right and *vicuña* – a slighter relative of the llama – grazing by the roadside. A helpful receptionist at the Hotel Las Torres showed us a room where we could leave our bikes and panniers for the night. After packing overnight kit into the rucksacks that we had been carrying for just such an opportunity, we followed a busy path to the campsite at Campamento Torres.

Rising at 4.40am reminded Hugh of the atmosphere at two day mountain marathons – there were people with headtorches shining in all directions and a peaceful and purposeful sense in the air as everyone at the camp got their act together and ascended to the Mirador de los Torres before sunrise. The Torres stood grey against a clear blue sky, and then faint wisps of cloud behind turned a pale pink. The sun climbed and the light on the rock descended, reflecting first in a pale glow then gradually changing to a sharp gold. The sharp line of the shadow sank to almost the surface of the lake below as the towers emerged into daylight – the golden sheen gone for another day. It was magical.

We rode out of the park, the irregular, jagged shapes of Los Cuernos (horns) del Paine at our back, in sharp relief against a faintly clouded sky. Nature's sculpture was all the more striking for the sharply contrasting bands of rock in the massif – close to black at the base, a thick band of pale grey granite in the middle and the black points of the horns reaching for the sky. The view in our mirrors constantly beckoned us to stop for another look round.

The Carretera Austral comes to an abrupt end 7km beyond Villa O'Higgins, a tiny town of less than 500 people. We exchanged stories with Steve and Stephanie from Battersea – at the end of their speedy three week tandem ride down Ruta 7 (the official, boring name for the Carretera Austral).

The exit is the *pièce de résistance* for the travelling cyclist. In Villa O'Higgins we secured a precious place on the boat across Lago O'Higgins, the first stage of an ingenious route into Argentina, only possible for walkers or cyclists. The boat is primarily for taking tourists to visit Glacier O'Higgins and there were many Chilean and Argentinean sightseers alongside the nine cyclists aboard that day. We were lucky; some wait days to get a place. We went on to camp closer to the jetty, with fellow cycle tourists from Austria – Philipp and Valeska. They had been on the road for four years travelling in India and Africa and had spent the last two and a half years travelling southwards from Alaska. A couple of days earlier we had met them in Puerto Yungay at a point where the Carretera comes to an abrupt halt. Here the fjord penetrates long and deep into the mountains. We were waiting for a boat across and I was feeling very weak and sick. Across the water at Puerto Bravo, we all bedded down in the luxury waiting room – complete with spotless loos. I got straight into my sleeping bag and went to sleep. Philipp and Valeska had been so kind to me.

We had to off-load our bikes on the far shore of Lago O'Higgins at Candelario Mancilla so that everyone could get a good view from the front of the boat on the out and back glacier trip. The three kilometres wide, 80m high snout, plunges into the lake in an impressive display of calving ice blocks. The glacier is 38km long and shrinking fast; it was twice as long in 1920.

One kilometre out of Candelario Mancilla our passports were stamped denoting our exit from Chile; our seventh crossing over the Chile/Argentina border. We then returned to the *zona acampar* where a charming man offered us a horse to carry our luggage in the morning. We all politely declined, hooked on the purity of self-propelled travel; over land at least! Here, a family lived; two brothers and an old grandfather. A young woman and her child were also staying there for the summer. We were offered a welcome hot shower at the house and we bought eggs and bread. The farm runs on solar panels and water power, using a turbine which was made at a workshop on site.

Living at the far end of the shoe string, beyond where even Pinochet was unable to push the road, these people have a three hour boat ride to get across

CYCLISTS' PARADISE

the lake to the diminutive town of Villa O'Higgins where at least there is a shop. In the other direction a rough gravel road climbs up to the border with Argentina. From there seven kilometres of single track footpath leads to Lago del Desierto where we camped in the shadow of the Argentinean border post. We pushed the bikes through countless streams laced with fallen logs and over rotten, broken bridges. The mud caked our tyres and our low slung front panniers snagged against the sides where the track was deeply rutted. I put this snippet of advice on our blog:

> How to tackle a narrow and deep path with low rider panniers: stand astride the bike with your feet on the top of the rut. When it is too narrow for the panniers, lift up the front end and edge the bike forwards until the rut widens.

Pauline, Maz and Pob in paradise.

There was a lot of pushing involved and we often had to take our panniers off. From Lago del Desierto another boat takes you underneath hanging glaciers and alongside spectacular waterfalls to the road leading to El Chaltén, the first town en-route in Argentina.

In 2007/8 we had taken a trip to Antarctica followed by a trek in the area of Cero Fitzroy. We had coffee at the Hostería El Pilar, 17km from El Chaltén along the route to Lago del Desierto. We had dreamt of returning one day to ride the route that led to this place from Chile. Sometimes dreams come true. We were lucky to find a room available in the hosteria; a transport strike had prevented guests getting there. Not just any room; one with a view of Cero Fitzroy from the window.

There is something deeply satisfying about using this extraordinary mix of boats, paths and gravel roads to render the route continuous and we have to admit, rendered even more satisfying in that it is only an option for self-propelled travellers. The road we travelled was mostly gravel but much was in the process of being 'improved'. The most tedious sections for us were those in the process of being prepared for paving. It will no doubt become a much more comfortable ride before long, but traffic will surely increase and the sense of adventure will diminish. Within the following four weeks we moved on through El Calafate, Torres del Paine, Puerto Natales and Punta Arenas.

Such is serendipity that good friends of ours were passing through Punta Arenas at the same time on an adventure of their own. Anne was at university with us back in the early 1970s. She studied a mysterious language and used it in her profession for many years at GCHQ where she met her husband Martyn. Because Anne has flight phobia, they were travelling the world by sea and had just arrived from a trip to Antarctica. When we realised that we would be in the same place at the same time, we arranged to meet by the monument to the Portuguese explorer Hernando de Magallanes.

We crossed Tierra del Fuego to the journey's end in Ushuaia having pedalled the 9,264km from our starting point in Arica. We hadn't known what was possible when we set out – we had tested our strength and resolve to the full – we were hooked. This would be the first of many journeys by bike – of that we were certain.

2
THE LAND OF THE PATAGARANG

In the land of the Patagarang the murkies are dreaming
In the land of the Patagarang the stars are upside down

'The Land of the Patagarang' from Patrick Street's album, *Irish Times*, 1990. It was inspired by the book, *The Fatal Shore* by Robert Hughes. What we call the kangaroo is the patagarang in aboriginal languages.

Pauline:

We filled the supermarket trolley with as much food as we thought we could carry and hoped that it would be enough. Roadhouses along the way would supplement our supplies but we weren't sure what we would find there. We were told that groceries were limited and expensive. It was said that they can

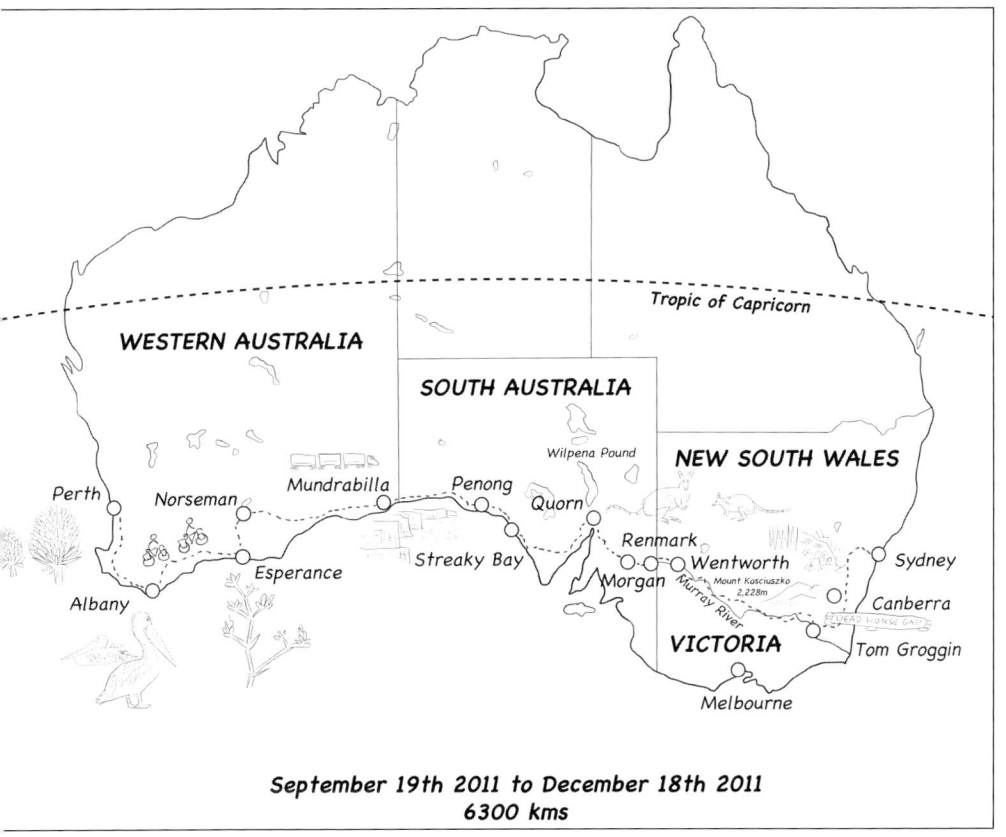

September 19th 2011 to December 18th 2011
6300 kms

charge a fortune for bottles of water and that the tap water is often brackish and undrinkable. So we added nine more litres of water to our combined load. The road ahead was long and barely inhabited. However, unlike the Altiplano of Bolivia it was almost flat and well surfaced so the bikes would roll along nicely. We would ride 1,185km before we reached the next shop, a village store in the tiny settlement of Penong, population 285.

The Eyre Highway is the only sealed road linking the states of Western Australia and South Australia. Two lanes of asphalt stretch far into the distance across the arid, treeless plain known as the Nullarbor; named from the Latin, *nullus* 'no' and *arbor* 'tree'. Edward John Eyre was the first European to cross the Nullarbor by land, in 1840-41. We were to follow the highway from its start in the small town of Norseman where we did our shopping, to Ceduna the next place of any size – another 1,263km of pedalling. It is a wonderfully straightforward and speedy way to cross a huge section of southern Australia – no navigation needed and very direct. So direct in fact that at one point there is no change of direction for 90 miles (146.6km).

However, many Aussies regard the journey across the Nullarbor as an adventure, a 'rite of passage', a major undertaking; and this is in a car or a campervan. To pedal across it you must be foolish/fit/crazy or probably all three, so they said.

We had done some research and we anticipated heat! Temperatures can reach 50°C in the summer and fall below freezing in winter, but we assumed October would be kind. We expected the land to be waterless and empty. We knew where we would find roadhouses, generally a day's ride apart but sometimes further or closer. We knew about the 'road trains', articulated trucks with 2, 3, 4 or more trailers that thunder along the road, take forever to stop and need miles of road to execute any kind of manoeuvre. As cyclists, we shouldn't take the risk of expecting them to get out of our way. We took the advice of an Australian government website and attached mirrors to our handlebars. Ever since, mirrors have become an essential item on all our bikes.

So, why Australia? What is the draw that takes cycle tourists to different places? For our first trip with the world at our feet, South America stirred our enthusiasm the most. We love mountains and we revel in the thrill of climbing them on our bikes. We live in the hills; small hills but often very steep. We know that with low gears we can slowly gain height and enjoy the effort. So we headed for the Andes! We love empty country where there is freedom to pitch a tent on our own little patch in the wilderness and we can ride lonely dirt tracks or thin ribbons of tarmac without a stream of cars threatening us and disturbing the peace. We love exciting landscapes; rocks, cliffs, gorges, forests, waterfalls, wild rivers, lakes, deserts and more. Our journey from Peru

THE LAND OF THE PATAGARANG

Penetrating the bush on the Munda Biddi trail.

south to the tip of the continent exceeded our expectations. At the end of it we were totally addicted to cycle touring, convinced that it was the way to feel and breathe a country.

A very different avenue took us to Australia. Our daughter Amy and her partner Steve had decided, as so many medics do, to spend a year working in New Zealand. We were thinking about where we could tour for a few months before visiting them in Napier and cycling around New Zealand too. Australia was an obvious candidate but we had reservations! Australia is mostly very flat. That may sound good for cycling but, we enjoy the thrill of climbing. Some friends warned us that places of interest are very far apart, linked by long monotonous roads where the scenery changes slowly – very slowly on a bike. In places there are huge distances between food and watering holes. Water is very heavy! Others told us that they loved Australia. We realised that this was going to be completely different from our last tour but we had gained experience in dealing with rough back roads, remote regions and arid conditions. We decided to give it a go, very much attracted by the obvious end to end journey of Perth to Sydney.

EXTRAORDINARY PLACES BY BICYCLE

The start of the trip was very special, down to two keen cyclists, Caroline and Wayne who live in Perth. We chanced upon them at Perth airport. They put us up for three nights whilst we recovered from the long flight and helped us get information, maps and supplies for the start of our journey.

Munda Biddi means 'path through the forest' in the Nyoongar Aboriginal language, a perfect description of our chosen route out of Perth. Eleven days of riding on trails, sometimes single track, stony in patches, occasionally steep and often surprisingly muddy, took us through the 'bush'. It was a wonder world of extraordinary vegetation; grass trees with dark, thick, branching trunks topped with heads of long spiky hair, huge curling ferns, enormous fungi and a host of unfamiliar colourful flowers. We passed curious kangaroos with their babies peeking out from their pouches. Squawking red tailed cockatoos and colourful parrots flew over our heads.

We stayed in camp shelters in the heart of the forest. They provided the basics: toilets, a place to lay our sleeping bags and tanks of water collected from the corrugated iron roofs of the shelters.

We always had the shelters to ourselves. Fallen, rotting eucalyptus trees often blocked our path and rocky descents tested our riding skills. We loved it. It was nothing like anywhere else we had ever been with its utterly unfamiliar natural environment – perhaps as you might expect on an island on the other side of the globe from home. We met only one other cycle tourist, Vanessa from New Zealand going north.

On day twelve we hit the tarmac and it was welcome as we needed to make faster progress across this vast country if we were to cross the Nullarbor without frying in the summer heat. Our route around the far south-western corner of Australia was surprisingly undulating. The roads were good and the traffic minimal.

We travelled through miles of forest, beautiful unfamiliar forest; tall, straight karri trees with smooth grey trunks, rough barked tingle trees with hollowed out bases sometimes big enough to drive a car through, and as we went further south, shorter eucalyptus, the tree that keeps its leaves and loses its colourful bark. We passed cleared areas for grazing sheep, cattle and occasionally, alpacas – pockets of a past homeland created by farmers originally from the other side of the world. Scatterings of European trees made them feel more at home.

The roadside flowers were bizarre; bottlebrush trees with bright red flowers which look just like – well – bottlebrushes, banksia with their enormous, yellow, cone shaped flower clusters, deep red and dark green kangaroo paw atop their long, slender stalks. We saw tiny, luminous blue fairy wrens in the grass, large long beaked pelicans on the stunning white beaches and foraging emus, a bird exceeded in height only by the ostrich. Bobtails with their bulky armoured bodies and short legs ambled dangerously and slothfully across the roads.

We passed through some charming little towns, often with superb bakeries and attractive colonial style timber built hotels and pubs. Shopping was so easy – so much variety, but expensive due to the poor exchange rate. The towns are far apart, sometimes more than a day's ride, so we were already beginning to rely a little on roadhouses, but often there were farms, wineries, houses offering bed & breakfast and caravan parks dampening that sense of isolation.

Approaching the small town of Esperance – population 12,000 – we experienced a typical example of the small world that is Western Australia. About 10km out, an approaching car came to a halt, a head poked out of the window and said 'Dorothy is waiting'. Jenny and Hazel had just left our destination for the day and were able to give us helpful directions. We were heading for the home of a family that we had never met before; they are friends of friends of ours who live in Kendal.

We were made extremely welcome by Dorothy and Mike at their beautiful home overlooking Lake Warren, on what is known as a 'lifestyle' plot, a large home in a rural location surrounded by a generous portion of land. We stayed in the bothy which in our book was a very comfortable bungalow. They may not be flattered by this, but we remember them for the saying, 'if it's brown, wash it down, if it's yellow, let it mellow', referring to how to minimise your use of water when the supply depends on what falls upon the roof and into a collection of huge drums! On a more charming note they directed us towards the gorgeous, deserted pristine white beaches of the area populated by mini dinosaurs, goannas; large predatory lizards with sharp teeth and claws, camouflaged against the intricately weather carved sandstone rocks. And, as so often happens, one thing led to another. Dorothy and Mike put us in touch with a feisty family living right in the middle of the wide expanse of the Nullarbor at Mundrabilla Station.

We rode out of Norseman, past its roundabout festooned with white corrugated iron camels and heading for the void, the next stop sign posted being Balladonia, a roadhouse 189km away. It was the day before my 58th birthday. For much of the journey we had the company of delicately branched, scented eucalyptus lining the roadside, their ribbons of peeling bark forming a dense grey mat on the ground below and leaving stripped trunks of fine shades of reddish brown and pink. Their branches are prone to spontaneously splitting from the trunk and roadside signs warned of the danger of being struck on the head. So – not exactly treeless then! The land to the north where the railroad crosses is much more barren.

The temperature rose to 38°C, more in the sun. Not the hottest we have experienced by some margin, but enough to exert a strong pull towards getting off the bike and slumping in the shade of the roadside trees. On our first day on the Nullarbor, we were nearly caught out. The nine litres of water was running low and was now nearly hot enough to make a cup of tea. A couple driving a campervan came to our rescue. Manna from heaven arrived in the form of two cups of cold water from a fridge.

I was finding the ride quite hard so it was fortunate that we didn't need to get all the way to Balladonia; 100km along the road from Norseman we arrived at Fraser Range Station. No, not somewhere you can catch a train, but a station being a large farm, sometimes exceedingly large, for rearing livestock. Fraser Range offers the essentials of somewhere to put a tent and a kitchen along with more luxurious accommodation for those who prefer. It was a perfect setting to celebrate my birthday evening in the company of a group of amiable Aussies who shared their wine, peaches and chocolate with us. It felt like a proper party!

The next day we carried twelve litres of water and set out at 7am, not taking the risk of trusting the forecast for cooler weather. However, the powers that control these things gave me a good birthday present of cool air. The temperature dropped by 13°C and we had water to spare.

We passed a decaying kangaroo lying by the roadside next to a smashed up overturned bulk of a 4x4, presumably trying to avoid the creature when it could still jump. We saw a kettle and fan plugged into a socket on a tree. Then at Balladonia museum, a replica piece of NASA's Skylab. In 1979 motel guests were treated to a stupendous fireworks display as chunks of the space station fell to earth. The solitary phone line caused a fight amongst the reporters rushing to get their story out. Such are the eclectic sights of the Australian outback, somewhat whacky and thinly spread.

On day three we found ourselves riding on an airstrip! A reassuring emergency landing strip for the flying doctor service, so long as we had warning of their arrival. We were learning to admire the subtle changes in the landscape, enjoy the huge sky above and at times an almost 360 degree view to the horizon. The day's pictures show eucalyptus or gum trees as those 'down under' call them, standing tall or lying dry on the ground, flattened by tornados. Yes, we were coming to appreciate the many differing forms, hues and patterns of these ubiquitous gum trees. The start of the '90 mile' straight was a novelty but generally we appreciated the subtle turns and miniscule undulations that kept some of the road stretching to infinity out of our view. We spotted Aussies busy making a 'boot' tree. Several days ago I had seen boots hanging from a bush and I had thought, 'how odd'. So here was the explanation – or was it? They are also fond of 'pot' trees, and sexy 'bra' trees! Something to give humour to the day's photos when nothing much changes.

At the end of 151km of riding that day, we arrived at, well, nowhere – a wild camp amongst the hooting owls that inhabited the low bushes (no boots) and grassland around us. We were totally reliant on our own resources, including water. We had carried 24 litres in two dromedaries (strong ten litre flexible bags) and four bidons (plastic water bottles for use on the bike). Aided by an uncommon south-west tailwind, with cloudy skies and even a bit of light rain cooling us down, we had made fast progress following a start soon after first light at 5:40am.

The thrill of the next morning on day four was the excitement of hitting the first bend in the road for 90 miles, just before Caiguna roadhouse. For lunch we had our first taste of a 'steak burger with the lot', 'the lot' being a huge pile of healthy vegetables: carrots, onions, beetroot, tomatoes and lettuce along with bacon and eggs. 'The lot' was my favourite bit. It was a superb lunch for a hungry cyclist and it helped us to eke out our supplies.

We cruised along in pleasant T-shirt temperatures watching the world go by; grassland, gum trees, bushes, grassland, road train, motor bike, grassland, road train, caravan, gum trees, bushes, burnt grass, bottle, can, grassland, rusting car, dead owl, dead kangaroo… and on and on to infinity! Tight flocks of bright green budgerigars shot through the huge blue sky above us along with pink and grey galah cockatoos and magpies.

Then, near the end of the day we slipped into the peculiarity that is the Central Western Time Zone, where the roadside instruction says, 'advance clocks by 45mins'. This trip was before we became dependent on a smart phone, but even if we had possessed one it wouldn't have recognised this weird time warp which is really only relevant to the couple of hundred people who live along this 350km stretch of highway.

Our home for the night was, Cocklebiddy, population eight, budgies 25, quails seven, dogs seven and kangaroos 1,234,567! Like many of the roadhouses it was possible to buy some useful provisions but not much. Junk drinks and sweet snacks are no problem but nourishing groceries were pretty rare. We spent $4.70 on half a litre of fresh milk for our breakfast muesli.

On day six we enjoyed the novelty of a freewheel descending an escarpment curiously known as the Madura Pass, giving us a far reaching view of a dead pan flat land dotted with small trees. The sign called for trucks to 'use low gear'. March flies, or what we call horse flies, attacked us for most of the way. They hitched a ride on our backs, their painful bite piercing through our jerseys and also our socks and shorts. Luckily we found an insect free camp spot on the edge of a picnic site.

We were approaching the mid-point of our journey across the Nullabor, fighting against a headwind for the second day running, on our way to Mundrabilla homestead – home literally in the middle of nowhere to the enterprising family of Brie and Colin and their three children, Duncan, Sophie and Ben. Although they had never met us, being friends of friends of friends of ours, they wholeheartedly welcomed us feeding us up on a scrumptious dinner of roast chicken with roast vegetables followed by chocolate, raisin and rum bread and butter pudding. It was quite a marvel for us, especially after days of simple camp food – plus the odd burger.

The family lives in a charming confusion of around 20 rooms, many added over time to the original stone building dating back to 1873. Colin told us that it will soon have to be demolished as it is virtually impossible to restore the poor quality building, a pity as it is so charming and antiquity is rare in Australia. Around our home in the Yorkshire Dales many buildings centuries older are standing strong but they are built of solid stone.

Living so far from all services, and 600km in either direction from the nearest shop, they have to be totally self-sufficient. Power comes from wind and solar energy, supplemented by a diesel generator when necessary. All the household water is provided by bore water run through a de-salination plant which can treat up to 300 litres an hour.

Sophie and Duncan had daily lessons in their little school house in the

The Great Australian Bight

garden, via the Kalgoorlie School of the Air using a speedy satellite internet connection which uploaded our photographs in no time at all. Jenny, their Kiwi governess, was there to help them and keep them on track throughout the long school day, starting at 7:30am and finishing at 3pm (is that Western Australian time or Western Central time?) We met her on the day of the World Cup Rugby Final – New Zealand v France and she was all dressed up for the occasion in her black and white kit. She went off to see the game on the TV in Eucla, just 100km up the road and came back very happy after a tense match giving NZ the victory by one point, at the time the slimmest margin to decide a world cup final. The delightful school room was crammed with materials, books and educational posters. With the help of the kids we were able to make our daughter Amy a 26th birthday card which we put on our blog. Despite their seemingly isolated life, the children were very comfortable in the company of strange adults.

Mundrabilla is a farm of enormous proportions supporting 2,000 cattle and 500 sheep on a million acres. In our native Cumbria one acre can support two or three cows but out on the Nullarbor two or three hundreds of acres are needed for just one animal. I pondered how they managed to find their animals grazing in this vast expanse. The answer is – water – trapped by rainwater dams for the animals to drink. Unfortunately for the farmer this water is also handy for the wild kangaroos, camels and dingoes. Colin had a night time job, shooting the kangaroos which he stacked in a huge fridge by the roadside. He was paid $2 a kilo for the meat which is used to feed dogs. It was not a job he liked. He told us that dingoes can kill a lot of sheep but cattle put up more of a fight.

Brie and Colin took us up onto the plateau above the station to explore down under proper. A hidden, narrow opening between limestone boulders took us into an underworld festooned with stalagmites and stalactites. Kelly's cave is just one of many in the area. Moving on we gazed down into the Snake Pit, a cylindrical shaft open to the sunlight, where snakes can be seen basking on the hot rocks below. There was no way for us to get down and probably no way for the snakes to get out. Death adders are common in the area. As the name suggests, it is highly venomous using its sharp bite to catch and poison its prey, which fortunately it does mainly at night. They lie in wait camouflaged, ready to ambush their victims. Before the development of anti-venom, the mortality rate was around 60%. We were told that after a bite you have around two hours to get help before you are in serious trouble. That landing strip could come in handy after all; the family didn't look too worried as the children ran across the grassland.

Whilst we were out they showed us the trucks with water tanks, used to fight a fire which had spread over 40,000 acres of farmland the previous week. Fires are frequently caused by lightning. Back at Cocklebiddy we had seen a Kiwi couple using a helicopter to survey the area for fires so they could relay information to ground crews. Eleven year old Duncan enjoyed himself driving the truck back to the house even though he could barely reach the pedals. He also loved to buzz around the place on a trail bike – such wonderful freedom.

Our day ended with a night out at Eucla, which gave us a preview of our next day's ride. The two Lukes, award winning performers on guitar and vocals, were doing a gig. It was a pity that the audience was so small, but then Eucla only has a population of 50. This was a chance for the kids to get together with some of their nearest neighbours, and they loved it.

The next day we headed for Eucla again, this time on the bikes in cool, damp conditions with a strong cross wind. Shortly after getting into the tent I was startled by something small scampering around – eek – a mouse. Yes, I actually shrieked! This was a first for us. At least eradicating one mouse from our small space was easy. Those staying in the rooms at the roadhouse were not so lucky. The little creatures were running all over the walls. They were also scampering all over the camp kitchen. Luckily the roadhouse restaurant provided an excellent T-bone steak.

Unlike the railway which crosses the Nullarbor further inland, the Eyre highway gently curves around the appropriately named, Great Australian Bight. Beyond Eucla, the sea is close by, the land cut sharply at the great Bunda cliffs – part of a 200km long precipice on the edge of the world's greatest lump of limestone covering over 200,000 square kilometres. It is true, the scenery doesn't change in a hurry. When we reached the cliffs we were travelling alongside them for three wonderful days, the time it takes for the Indian Pacific train to take you from Perth to Sydney. It would take us 90 days to cross the continent.

The edge is abrupt and badly eroded which together with a strong wind discouraged us from venturing too close. Getting down to the shore is impossible. The next two nights we camped amongst the bushes, sand dunes and mating lizards with views out to sea. It was a rare treat to savour.

Our road then left the coast. Some 51km before reaching the Nullarbor roadhouse we found some roadside water tanks. We had used a few along the way, one pointed out to us by a passing cyclist going in the opposite direction. It is risky to rely on these as it is some people's idea of fun to take a pot shot at them with the obvious result. Also some are filled from rainwater and others from tanks and you can't be sure of the water quality. We usually treated such water with our Steripen which uses ultra violet light to create drinkable water out of reasonably clear water in just 90 seconds.

At the roadhouse we set up camp under an interesting low slung tree in an otherwise rather dull setting. However the tree was also home to a colony of large, orange, flying wasp like insects which appeared to be quite benign until I made the mistake of sitting on one – ouch! I thought it wise to ask the friendly guy at the roadhouse if these were creatures with a deadly sting requiring immediate attention. He reassuringly told me that the last person to be stung by them was fine. They were a type of large wasp, often called hornets in Australia although true hornets don't live that far south.

THE LAND OF THE PATAGARANG

The following morning, Dez and Marie who we had befriended the night before, gave us muesli, fresh milk and apples for breakfast. We left with five apples and eight oranges in our panniers – another gift. Together with eight litres of water each, it made for a heavy load. Once on the road I was selfishly thinking, it would be lovely to have some bananas, and then Marjory stopped in her campervan and offered us some. All this fresh fruit was such a treat and these gifts were so typical of Aussie generosity. They were usually absolutely fascinated and amazed by what we were doing although not infrequently they considered it to be completely nuts. 'Haven't you heard of the combustion engine?'

The end of the day gave us our first experience of the dark side of the country. We put up our tent under a tree in the bush, on the edge of securely fenced off land 25km beyond a boarded up and burnt out roadhouse. We had to clear away a little rubbish but the outlook was pleasant enough. We had just passed a turn off to the left marked by a sign saying, 'WARNING, RESTRICTED AREA, NO ENTRY – NO CAMERAS, NO ALCOHOL, ALL PERSONNEL REPORT TO CO-ORDINATOR, by order Yalata Council.' A less intimidating sign by the side of our road said, 'You are now travelling through Yalata Aboriginal Lands. Permits are required by all visitors to assist in the protection and management of this arid coastal environment…' Rather unsettling when you plan to spend the night there. So, who are these Yalata people who need to be fenced off in a remote and secret location, not to be visited by others? Why are they living there?

Yalata is a community of Aboriginal people. The British Government moved them away from their land at Maralinga to the north, a place where the British were secretly testing nuclear weapons in the 1950s. Many Aboriginal people were not adequately warned about the tests' dangers and were blinded, affected by radiation poisoning and left with an ongoing legacy of radiation-related health problems. The Australian government was curiously unaware of what was going on. There was an inquiry and documents were unearthed from Aldermaston in England. Millions of pounds of compensation came their way but will the people ever recover? The land will probably never recover. It was left contaminated with radioactive waste. Even after two clean-up operations in 1985 and 2000 there was still debate over the safety of the land. However, the Aboriginal people continued to fight for the right to manage this land and it was returned to them in 2009. The whole sorry story is a complex mix of secrets, lies and abuse of Aboriginal rights.

This was the story that we uncovered in 2011 when we passed through. Now, in 2020, a search for information on these people brings up a sunnier picture. In 2013 the Yalata Indigenous Protected Area (IPA) came into being, covering 456,300 hectares of coastal dunes, limestone cliffs, sand plains and mallee shrub lands. The idea is that in declaring their land as a protected area, the owners can enter into an agreement with the Australian government and work to protect and pass on their intimate knowledge of the environment. Hopefully this is addressing some of the injustices of the past, providing work for the people and enabling visitors to understand the delicate landscape through knowledgeable Yalata rangers. Work is going on now to help those from all sides of the story to understand and come to terms with what happened in the past, but the Maralinga Tjarutja people will not forget the injustice done to them.

We had travelled half way across Australia without, to our knowledge, setting sight on any of the country's original inhabitants. Moving on from our camp across a landscape of open grassland, still fenced on either side, we came to the scruffy roadhouse at Nundoo. Aboriginal people, very dark and looking very miserable were hanging around the place. It was a sad sight. At one point we had thought we would make it there for a night's stay but we had no regrets about camping in the bush instead.

The landscape had become rather dull and the Eyre Highway had become busier, so we took a turn off to Fowlers Bay, which was formerly known as Yalata. The deserted dirt road headed towards a distant range of soft, pure white sand dunes peeking out of the dark green bushes growing along the shores of salty lakes. It was a little reminiscent of parts of the Bolivian Altiplano, altitude excepting. The wind creates sharp, ever changing ridges and intricate wavy patterns on the leeward sides. As we walked along the slopes, admiring the open views of the bright blue bay, our footprints were instantly removed by the wind.

In days gone by the bay provided shelter for many explorers and now it is popular with whale watchers and fishermen. We stayed in a very pleasant little campground where we met Sue and Paul. They were taking a weekend break from their work with the Aboriginal community at Oak Valley, four hours drive to the north, in the outback. This was one of the communities that people from Maralinga were relocated to when the British began their nuclear testing. Sue and Paul were the only white people living there in a community of 300. Paul was a community development officer and Sue a nurse and midwife. From them we gained some insight into the life of the community and the problems resulting from this presence of two very differing cultures in the same land. It is a complex issue which has no easy answers. They told us that the community is 'dry' (no alcohol) and that the health problems are huge; children as young as ten were becoming diabetic. When you think of the sudden, extreme change of lifestyle which has been forced upon these people it isn't surprising that they can't adapt any more than the European settlers could have adapted to a nomadic life in the outback. Their land was taken from them and even worse, their children were taken from them. It was a deliberate policy to wipe them out. Now so much is being done to redress the balance but it is an uphill struggle.

Our final two days into Ceduna were something of an anti-climax. We were riding into headwinds across a somewhat dull farming landscape – grasslands

THE LAND OF THE PATAGARANG

168km day on the Eyre Peninsula. Only a handful of vehicles all day.

and wheat fields. On the fourteenth day since leaving Norseman we arrived in Penong – a place with a general store, about 300 inhabitants, a caravan park where we stayed and a pub which served excellent T-bone steaks with Cooper's beer on tap.

The roadhouses had been good for beer, steaks, fish and 'burger and the lot', but we had found little in the way of standard groceries. Sometimes we had found milk, bread and some tinned stuff. All along the route our diet was nicely supplemented by gifts from the ever amiable Australians – fresh fruit which couldn't be taken across state borders, lunchtime sandwiches from the doors of their huge, luxury campervans and cold drinks from their fridges. Many were taking advantage of the several months of leave often given to loyal workers after seven to ten years of hard graft, some doing the round of the whole island.

For us Penong felt like the end of the adventure across the Nullarbor. Ceduna is usually given that title, the name being a corruption of the local Aboriginal Wirangu word, *Chedoona*, meaning, appropriately in this case, 'a place to sit down and rest'. However, we postponed our resting for a couple of days until we reached Streaky Bay where we found a gorgeous colonial style hotel with a sea view balcony and incredible seafood on offer at a bay side restaurant.

EXTRAORDINARY PLACES BY BICYCLE

Here we bought a dongle, a device to connect our laptop to mobile internet. By this time we had realised that the stories of it being unusual to find wifi in Australia were actually true. This neat little USB stick enabled us to upload our journal and Skype our kids even in the middle of the bush.

From Ceduna the Eyre Highway continues across the Eyre Peninsula to Port Augusta. We crossed the peninsula by a quieter route further south, following the coast for a while. Pelicans gathered in large numbers on the beaches, preening themselves with impossibly long pink beaks. The dark shadows of dolphins leapt across the white surf out to sea. The Australians were there for the fishing – a stunning variety of fish can be caught – there are rules about how big a fish you can catch and how many crabs, squid, 'tommies' (herring), snapper, garfish, whiting and many more. Fishermen like to camp by the jetty, where there are special fish cleaning and scaling areas.

Doug and Val were travelling along this rugged coast in their 'Wildcat' home – extremely spacious living on the move! It must have been as long as a bus and with pop out sides that turned it into a monster – probably bigger than many people's houses; mind you, for some Australians their RV is their only home. It was pure luxury inside – a spacious living room complete with comfy sofa, hifi and big screen television. Their Australian adapted 'fifth wheel' was made in the USA, weighed five tons and was towed by a beefy Ford F250 (USA) which consumed 20 litres per 100km. We wondered what they made of our travelling home – carried by two human powered engines needing three hearty meals per 100km.

It was easy riding across sparsely populated farmland to Port Augusta; we covered more than 100km each day. In many countries a settlement is marked out by a church tower or minaret – the equivalent here is the huge grain silo. We took a day's rest in the pretty little town of Quorn where some distinctly Aussie delicacies were on offer – kangaroo mixed grill and quandong pies. The mixed grill was delicious and we couldn't help wondering why Australians didn't eat more of this native animal which having been robbed of its natural predators, is now over abundant and decimating the native plant life. It is said to be a healthy meat and could be a sustainable alternative to beef and lamb. We were told that wild kangaroo meat is full of worms – it needs to be cooked well. However, Australians do have a problem with eating their national emblem; the meat is generally only eaten by curious tourists like us. The quandong is a fruit unique to Australia, which grows in arid saline environments – described by the restaurant manager as having a taste like a cross between rhubarb and peach.

A detour took us into the Flinders Ranges – once as high as the Himalayas but now worn down into a 430km long stretch of rugged peaks and gorges. We

THE LAND OF THE PATAGARANG

followed the dirt roads of the Mawson trail to the Warren Gorge where we set up camp. A group of yellow-footed rock-wallabies were tucking into the vegetation at the foot of the red sandstone cliffs. These creatures, smaller and prettier than kangaroos were almost hunted to extinction by humans and foxes, but now the population in the Flinders is stable. They have a very long reddish brown tail with a hint of lighter rings along its length and a predominantly grey body with markings of white and orange brown on their face, ears, chest and limbs.

We ventured into the range, far enough to ride and hike up to the Rawnsley Buff for a view of a remarkable feature known as the Wilpena Pound – an elliptical crown of serrated mountains enclosing a shallow, sunken bowl, seventeen long by eight kilometres wide. Hardy early settlers farmed in the pound but abandoned their attempts after a disastrous flood in 1914.

Usually ours was the only tent on the campsite – or caravan park as they were usually called for obvious reasons. However, there was another tent at Rawnsley Park. Phil and his brother may have been camping in a similar style, using the camp kitchen as we did, but their mode of transport couldn't have been more different. They were on a flying tour in a small Cessna. Before they left, in order to save weight, they donated some of their spare food to us – the baked beans and beetroot went down well with our sausages.

We were sorely tempted further into the Flinders Ranges and enticed by an outback route taking us further east but we had to abandon the idea as we had no information on water sources and couldn't risk being marooned in the sand.

We headed south east to the Murray River, passing through the copper mining town of Burra, a State Heritage Area – now mainly a centre for merino sheep farming. In 1845 a shepherd discovered copper ore here leading to the development of a monster mine. He got £10 for his trouble. For fifteen years it was the largest copper mine in Australia and one of the biggest in the world. The population of the town grew to 5,000 – more than three times what it is today. It was then the largest inland settlement in Australia. The names of villages which merged into the town of Burra – Redruth, Llwchwr, Aberdeen with street names to match – reflect the areas from which settlers came. Muleteers came from Chile and gardeners from China. Temperatures were hitting 40 degrees so we took a day of rest in one of a little row of cottages built for Cornish copper miners in the 1850s, now renovated for tourist accommodation; the thick stone walls kept it cool.

The next day the temperature dropped by fifteen degrees and we arrived at Morgan on the Murray River at the end of a day of drizzle following the night's storms – the river was in full flow. Our fingers were white at the end – we were damp and cold having neglected to don our waterproofs, thinking it was too warm.

We camped on the river bank where the ferry constantly moved traffic across. The Murray is the third longest navigable river in the world, after the Amazon and the Nile – yes – a real river with boats, water skiers, fishermen and houseboats. Morgan was once the largest inland port in Australia, taking goods from the barges working upstream and transferring them to the rail line taking freight to Adelaide. Now the river is a playground and nature park. It also supplies water via pipelines to many Australian towns. The river flow is often very low so a series of locks had to be built to keep it navigable, creating a kind of cross between a river and a canal.

We were in Renmark, two days on, looking for a way to avoid the busy main road going east and noticed an alternative on the opposite side of the Murray. We sought advice from Lara in the Royal Automobile Association office in town – she phoned a ranger to find out about the state of the road – a dirt surface but fine. We decided to go for it. On our way out of town we stopped at a fuel station to buy a new lighter. The conversation went like this:

Local lady: 'Where are you cycling to up here – don't you know it goes into a dirt road?'

Hugh: 'We're heading for Wentworth – it's a nice place, Wentworth?'

Local lady: 'It's a small place. Wouldn't go there – wouldn't send a tourist to Wentworth. Wouldn't go cycling up there – the road's full of ruts – very sandy – no way I'd cycle up that way.'

Hugh: 'The lady at the Royal Automobile Association centre in Renmark said the road was good – just a little rutted in places.'

Local lady: 'Well, you can take notice of a big national organisation or listen to a local. I say it's no place for a bike.'

We were committed having already loaded up with water for a night or two and we were several kilometres out of the town centre. In any case, the alternative, the busy Stuart Highway was just not palatable. We carried on and hoped that she was overly pessimistic about what we could ride. The sign read, Wentworth 143km, unsealed. We turned on to a nicely paved road taking us past vineyards – emus strutting between the rows of vines. The surface turned to dirt and the landscape with the vines turned to GAFA – the Great Australian Fuck All – as the inhabitants call it; there's a lot of it in Australia. Far into the distance the flat expanse was covered in bluebush – a low growing shrub with musty blue-grey leaves; only the occasional outcrop of eucalyptus penetrated the skyline. Slight undulations in the road gave views of distant saline lakes. We loved the simple beauty of this nothingness – not 'fuck all' at all, but a very special landscape known as *mallee* country; we were entering a biosphere reserve. Mallee is an aboriginal term applied to a group of eucalyptus species, small trees with numerous slender trunks growing from an underground tuber which can resprout very quickly after bush fires.

That day we had ridden 103km before we set up camp next to a copse of eucalyptus – not such a bad road then. Kangaroo bones were scattered on the red earth all around us – ribs with bits of fur still attached. Later a truck driver told us it would be the work of 'roo' shooters who only keep the hind quarters and leave the rest to rot.

The next day we met tarmac again after only ten kilometres. A little further on, we crossed a river just downstream from a lovely old wooden bridge. Eucalyptus grew on the banks; many lying on their side, their higher branches now half submerged in water. This was the 'Great Anabranch of the River Darling', a branch of the River Darling but not a tributary because it flows out of and not into the Darling. A true anabranch returns to the same river, but this one joins the River Murray upstream of the confluence with the true River Darling in Wentworth. The anabranch – a new term for us – only flows when the flow of the Murray exceeds 10,000 mega litres a day. Just west of Wentworth loch number ten spans the Murray. Here it is only 31 metres above sea level although the water has 830km to go to reach the sea. Old paddle steamers and houseboats cruised gently along the River Darling. Spoonbills and long necked darters perched in the riverside trees.

This little excursion on the Old Wentworth Road had been a mini-adventure within an adventure – a taste of the Australian outback and a much lonelier experience than the Nullabor. Our route was close to the line of the Murray for seventeen days until we reached the Tom Groggin rest area on the Alpine Way. The now much diminished river provided clear water for bathing – also a pastime enjoyed by the snakes.

🚲   🚲   🚲

The Alpine Way then turned sharply east to cross the Great Dividing Range through the 1,582m pass known as Dead Horse Gap. The Great Dividing Range is a substantial mountain range separating the east coast from inland Australia. It is the fifth longest land-based range in the world stretching for 3,500km, from the pointed northern tip at Cape York to the far south in Victoria. A series of hills, mountains and plateaux make up the range, including the Snowy Mountains, the Blue Mountains, the Grampians and the Victorian Alps. Dead Horse Gap is only a few kilometres from the highest peak, the 2,228m Mount Kosciuszko in the Snowy mountain range; there were one or two small white patches high up on the rocky ridges. Some of the ranges are rugged but erosion over time has produced gentle slopes and virtually all of the summits can be climbed without mountaineering equipment.

The climb up to the pass took us up through trees devastated by the fires of 2003. Crimson rosellas, starkly bright red and blue parrots perched in the charred eucalyptus. For the first time in Australia, Hugh broke the law in riding without a helmet; it's so much cooler on the climbs. Apparently the Australian police are quite vigilant about this law but there were not many police around or much traffic. We saw very few cyclists too – an iconic climb in Europe in the equivalent of June would attract hundreds of riders on their carbon fibre bikes.

We descended to the ski resort of Thredbo and then moved on to Jindabyne where we were going to stay with Syd. Sydney had sent us a message: 'I've been enjoying following your travels and wanted to say that if you are following the Murray into the Snowy Mountains and want somewhere to stay in Jindabyne just let me know.'

It made a pleasant change to converse with someone who understands why we travel as we do. Syd had a stunning picture of the Salar de Uyuni on his wall; he is a photographer of some repute. He must have one of the world's largest collections of cycle travel books, including a copy of *Me and my Hero*. Hugh had just reviewed this book about a ride across India on a bog standard bike of the people, the book written by Tim Mulliner, the Kiwi we had met in Chile.

Six days later, we left Goulburn – pronounced 'Goalbun' – Australia's first inland city and the biggest place we had been to since Perth. It was a ride lacking in inspiration – rather indifferent farming country – sheep and cattle grazing with the occasional alpacas. Sporadic patches of gum forest were a reminder of what the land once was. Patches of brambles, clover and dandelion like flowers made me feel uncomfortable – they shouldn't be here! The bush of the Munda Biddi at the start of the trip had been so unlike home – that's how it should be. Such is the tragedy of the transformation of this far away land by white Europeans, turning the most fertile and habitable parts into a copy of home and devastating the unique native flora and fauna – much of it deliberately introduced.

The history of the introduction of the rabbit tells the story. It was introduced for hunting in 1859 and then allowed to run free. It took only 50 years for them to spread across the whole continent, adapting so well to this new environment. In the process they have wreaked havoc on Australian croplands, and contributed to the decline of native plant and animal species. Attempts have been made to get rid of them using fences, poisons, and pathogens. The government even commissioned the construction of a fence that stretched across Western Australia, from the north to the south, the Rabbit Proof Fence. Foxes introduced for the same reason have preyed on native species unable to deal with this unfamiliar predator.

Heading for Australia's most impressive limestone caves, we descended to the Abercrombie River and for the only time on a paved road in Australia were nearly defeated on the steep climb out, even in our super low bottom gear. The Jenolan caves are in the Blue Mountains, part of the Great Dividing Range – not really mountains at all but a plateau which gradually slopes upwards towards the east. A tangle of steep valleys and rocky escarpments drop off to the level of the coastal plain below. This complex jumble of steep inaccessible forest formed an effective barrier to the interior in the early days of colonisation. The drama of the landscape is in the escarpments, not so much in the peaks.

THE LAND OF THE PATAGARANG

We camped by the car park just above the caves where there were toilets and free hot showers.

The Jenolan caves are thought to be 340 million years old and possibly the oldest open caves in the world. Our guide for the trip down the Orient Cave started out by saying it is one of the most beautiful caves in the world – at the end of our trip we thought he was probably right. Whilst it is sad that a certain amount of destruction results from providing public access, it is wonderful that so many people can enjoy the carefully lit formations of an astonishing variety. Thin, wavy sheets of calcite suspended at an angle from the rock face, known as 'shawls', were lit from behind bringing out the delicate shades of the banding – deep orange browns and beiges blending into each other. So many intriguing formations – wide curtains of closely packed thin stalactites; gravity defying helictites, bending stalactites named from the Greek word helix meaning twist; and 'cave corals' reminding me of some of the corals on a shelf at home which my sister sent from the Bahamas.

The road out of Jenolan took us through a cave – the appropriately named, Grand Arch. We were now in the end-game, trying to find a low traffic route into Sydney through the densely populated area around it. We had arranged to meet an

The end of our Australian journey.

old school friend of Hugh's in Windsor. Rob had been living in Sydney for forty years. He had offered to guide us into the city and to his house in Neutral Bay.

We did well at first finding a delightful dirt road short cut via Cox's River, including some fine climbs, but it landed us on the A32, the Great Western Highway where I had a complete sense of humour failure. The traffic was the worst of its kind – fast cars, and huge trucks. OK there was a hard shoulder but it vanished on steep climbs and bridges leaving us stranded in an inferno. It was only six kilometres to Mount Victoria but it was six kilometres too far. There was no choice. In Mt Victoria we booked into the Imperial Hotel – one of those typical Australian country or small town hotels with attractive wooden balconies – a little bit historical. We enjoyed beer, food and the great live music of Jack Pledge and his band in front of a cosy warm open fire – summer in the Australian mountains.

From Victoria there was one other option – it had to be better than the A32. We headed north along the Darling Causeway which follows a railway line, heading for Bell. The road is lined with yellow daisies, said to be the result of a woman throwing the seeds from the train, in a mission to make the countryside prettier. We joined the B59, curiously known as the Bells Line of Road.

As we passed through the fruit growing region we treated ourselves to fresh cherries and apple pie sold by a Frenchman. We flew down Bell Bird Hill to the metallic ring of the bell minor bird, losing 1,000m of altitude. I wouldn't particularly recommend this route either traffic wise, but it was certainly a better option and the view of the rugged eastern escarpments was impressive. The back route to Windsor near the Hawkesbury River, took us past one of the largest turf farms in Australia – the inhabitants of Sydney love their lawns.

A plate of curry from the Curry Hut followed by a pint in the Macquarie Arms in Windsor, the oldest pub in Australia, rounded off the day nicely. The Poms had transferred the English pub tradition to Oz more or less intact. The only thing missing was the hand operated pump supplying the real ale. We were not whingeing though – there was plenty of good beer about.

Rob guided us along a varied, scenic and very hilly 68km into the heart of Sydney taking us through the Galston Gorge and over its old bridge. He told us it was the longest ride he had ever done. A swift one in the Hornsby Inn replenished our fuel and we soon found ourselves gazing over a six lane highway taking in our first view of the Harbour Bridge – huge – and the Opera House – looking unexpectedly small; a magic moment. A roast lamb dinner was the ultimate treat for two Cumbrians missing the Sunday roast. As you would expect near any city there was plenty of traffic but we didn't feel threatened and it was well worth pedalling the whole way – from Perth to Sydney in 90 days – we had crossed a continent.

On our blog we answered the question,
'so, what does Australia bring to mind most of all?'. Laughing kookaburras, screeching galahs, brightly coloured parrots shooting across the road in front and

magpies attacking from above. An orchestra of bird song. Kangaroos and wallabies hopping around the camp in the early morning, and stinking by the roadside in various states of decomposition. Massive wheat fields, huge gum forests, expansive vineyards and orchards. Tall trees, spindle trunked trees, ancient old woman trees and trees with dripping bark. Long straight roads reaching far into the distance. A long way to the next town, water, place to buy food. Arid lands, lazy rivers which split and re-join, muddy waters disturbed by alien carp. Road trains, monster winnebagos with cars and boats in tow and UTEs. Cosy country pubs with delicately decorated verandahs and tin roofs. Crazy native flowers and imported roadside weeds. Tasty beer, big steaks and incredible sea food. And above all good mates wherever you go.

The Nullarbor had been kind to us. After the heat on the first day, temperatures dropped and at one point we even began to feel a little cold in light rain! Crossing in October kept us ahead of the summer heat as we had planned. We hadn't realised that the predominant south-south-easterly wind direction would not be in our favour and we had several days of headwind which we managed with our usual technique of taking it in turns to do the 'work' in front whilst the other slipstreams.

The road trains were also kind to us, pulling out to give us room when we stopped by the roadside to let them pass. We were told that they give warnings of cyclists to other drivers down the road. There were too few of them to be a problem; in general traffic wasn't a problem at all until we neared Ceduna. However, the road trains were not the only crazy large vehicles to look out for. Trucks transporting giant silos, enormous water tanks, outsize tractors and other miscellaneous super-scale agricultural machinery took up the entire width of the road.

Our ride across the Nullarbor had opened our eyes to the wide, expansive, emptiness that is much of Australia, something that hits you even more when flying over the country – four hours with virtually no sign of human intervention on the ground. The people mostly live round the edges, but there are gaps in the ring where the land is too inhospitable for significant habitation. This serves to accentuate the remarkable nature of the Aboriginal way of life, using their intimate knowledge of where to find the essentials for life; knowledge built up over perhaps as many as 50,000 years. Australia – 'The Lucky Country' – for some.

3
How Far can we get from Home in a Year?

Heading South into a European Winter

The journey of a thousand miles starts with a single step
Lao Tzu

Hugh:

It was a special feeling thinking that we could and should be on the road for a year. Unlike the two previous major trips, there was no 'getting to the start'. Our home was the start. The plan was to arrive in Central Asia in spring, before the heat would boil the water in our bidons, but this meant we would have to cross Turkey early in the year when snow blocks mountain roads. At some points we would surely wilt in the heat and shiver in the cold. Right now we were protected from the elements in our comfortable home, soon to be exchanged for a small tent. But, we love our tent. We love the simplicity of life with the bare necessities, just what you can carry on a bike. However, it is pretty amazing what you can carry on a bike, and the list appeared to be growing!

So, where were we going? We weren't sure – where the road took us! We had thoughts of reaching China or Mongolia. What happened would depend upon encounters on the road, the whim of the embassies that deliver visas to aspiring tourists and our own health and fitness. We proceeded with optimism, eagerness, a thirst for exploring the unknown and a love of wandering through the world.

We cycled away from our home in late September 2012. Cycling through our town of Sedbergh on a Wednesday, the day of the weekly market, we waved 'bye' to friends and market stall holders we had come to know over the years. To my acute embarrassment I hit the curb with my front panniers and keeled over in front of Kevin, the fruit and vegetable seller. He must have thought – 'how the hell do they expect to make it to Kazakhstan?' We left home in a gathering North Atlantic storm.

Going east was the way to go. As we turned off on a tiny road to Hardraw, we asked ourselves 'is this the way to Mongolia?' In fact we were heading for the English east coast port of Hull. Riding down the track to the Jonas Centre, hoping that this was the campsite marked on our map, we were intercepted by Simon (the director of the centre) in his car. The centre offers subsidised

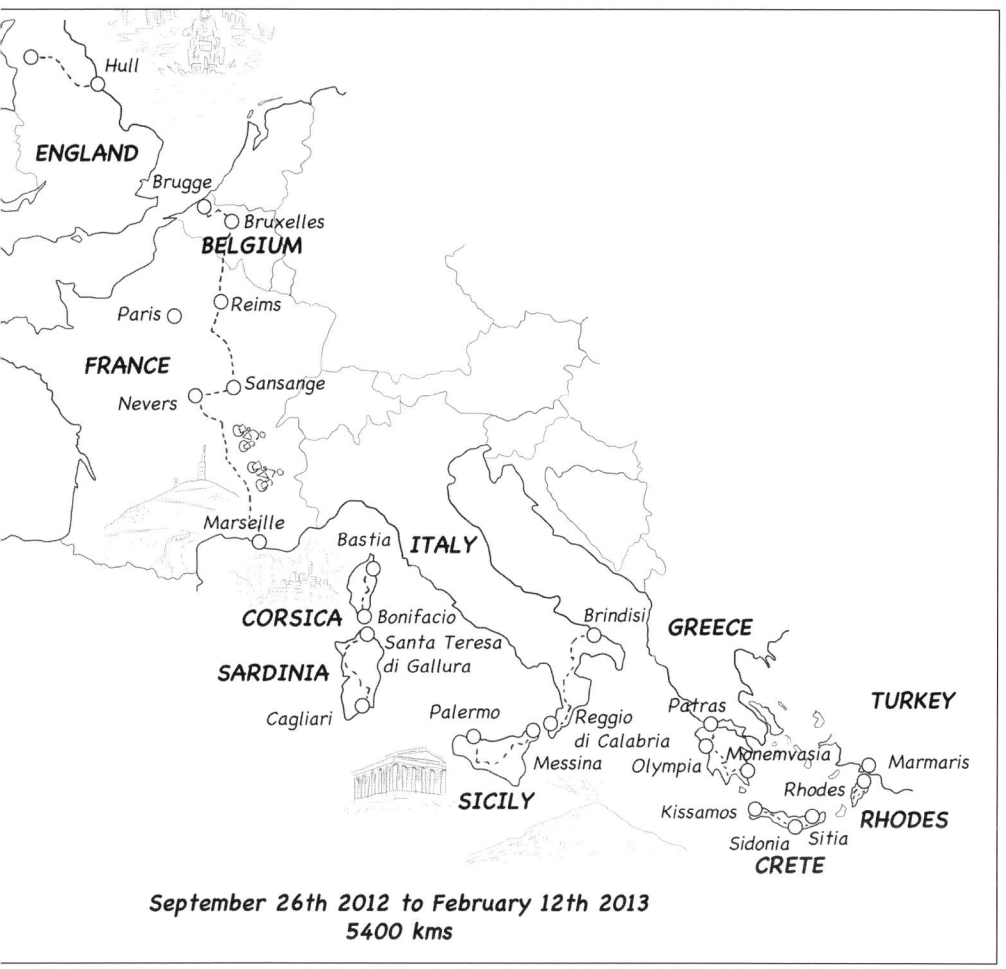

September 26th 2012 to February 12th 2013
5400 kms

holidays for those in need, children of Chenobyl, carers needing a break, people with Alzheimer's disease and the terminally ill to name but a few. Simon offered us the luxury of 'Garsdale', one of the many cosy wooden cabins set amongst huge ash, beech and sycamore trees. We felt that it was a wonderful chance encounter, to receive such kindness at the very beginning of our journey, but Simon felt there was more to it than luck! Instead of a wet tent in a soggy field we were able to wallow in a hot bath and spread out our gear in the luxury of a heated room. We offered a donation for our stay and we were so impressed by the Jonas Centre that we have continued to donate ever since.

On Thursday the flood waters continued to rise. The rivers Swale, Ure, Nidd and Ouse were all bursting their banks. Some roads were blocked, bridges closed for danger of them collapsing and houses were having bags of sand put against their doors. We found comfort and shelter at the Bay Horse of Green Hammerton and a supportive landlord at the Hope and Anchor of Blacktoft who let us camp by the pub by the river Humber. The Trans-Pennine cycle trail led us to Hull and the King George dock where we boarded *The Pride of Bruges* which sailed us overnight to the Belgian port of Zeebrugge. It was the first of ten ferry journeys which aided our low traffic route through to east of the Caspian Sea. Little did we know that the eleventh ferry would be a whole year later from Rotterdam to Hull when we retraced our wheels home via Blacktoft, Green Hammerton and the Jonas Centre, baking in a September Indian Summer in 2013.

It is a great feeling riding straight off a boat, especially at the start of a trip, so much better than waiting for bags on an airport carousel. We immediately found a cycle track leading alongside a canal to Brugge. Avoiding traffic is easy for the cyclist in Belgium. The Fietsnet, a vast network of cycle tracks links most places in Belgium. We call it 'cycling by numbers'. In the old city of Brugge, we were entertained by charming architecture, street musicians and the tastiest beer in the world. It was great to pass through a country which gives so much respect to the cyclist. We followed minor roads and canal paths, passing between huge fields of leeks and ripening corn, cabbages and patches of lettuce and fennel. We crossed the waterways on swing road bridges and cycle bridges with long gently sloping ramps. For a country of eleven million people in an area only half as big again as Wales, it is surprisingly peaceful to cycle through. Where the route follows a major road there is always a dedicated cycle path and most motorists seem to give way to cyclists.

We enjoyed a very sociable time on our six day passage of Belgium. At Meulebeke we were invited to the home of two Belgian cyclists we had met earlier in the year whilst in the Alps watching le Tour de France. Michel and Vera gave us a tasty lunch and in the afternoon guided us on their bikes to Gent where we stayed with Celien and Jeroen, two other cyclists we had also met earlier in the year, this time on the Otago Rail Trail in New Zealand. In Bruxelles we stayed with runner, childhood friend and politician, Chris Davies. To us, it feels so sad to be writing this exactly when our country is leaving the European Union. Chris had worked tirelessly for fifteen years as an MEP and was well known for his commitment to the fisheries, environment, and the climate and energy policy sectors. We were privileged to be given a tour of the European Parliament.

Our route continued south alongside the Canal du Charleroi. It is good to see that so much haulage is done off-road. Belgian canals achieve altitude differences by interesting means besides simple locks. The Plan Incliné at Ronquières is a railed ramp with weighted cables which transports barges in enormous dripping baths with gates at either end. We watched in awe from the vantage point of the adjacent cycle track.

Negotiating floods on day two of the one year trip, near Boroughbridge.

Our sociable cycle continued into France. A few years earlier Claire, from Paris, came riding up to our house in Sedbergh, looking for a non-existent campsite marked on her map. She was on a tour from Paris to the four corners of Britain. We offered her the garden, a shower, a bottle of wine and all the bike maintenance kit she could need. A friendship had been formed. Now Claire was able to spend a couple of days cycling with us through what she calls *la France profonde*. Claire is one of those really hard core riders who does the Paris-Brest-Paris self-supported ride which happens once every four years. She has completed it twice, once on a recumbent. In order to finish within the 90 hour time limit you need to survive with minimum sleep. Easy days for her and good days for us of 97km and 142km and we reached Romilly-sur-Seine. On the way we passed through the centre of Reims and its incredible thirteenth century cathedral. We sort of learnt how to pronounce Reims by practising 'Rrrrrrrrainzz' again and again as we wandered through the vineyards of champagne country.

France doesn't have the sort of network of cycle routes that both Belgium and the Netherlands have, but the whole country has so many tiny roads that as long as you make time to navigate, then it is wonderful to cycle through. We followed a labyrinth of D roads and the Canal de Bourgogne and reached the home of English friends living in Bourgogne. Bob and Colleen had moved to Sansange two years earlier after retiring from working at Casterton School where Pauline taught for eighteen years. Bob had been a mystery to me as I couldn't believe his age of 92. Bob had been lucky to survive the Second World War. Over dinner he told me a story from the war. Working as a navigator in a plane, he was shot down over the Mediterranean and spent nine days floating in the sea with little food or water. He was picked up by a British ship after it was confirmed that he was not German. The mission had been to bomb Reggio di Calabria in Italy, a city at the foot of Italy which we would cycle through nine weeks later.

After a day's rest, we deviated from our route south and headed west to Nevers, the city closest to the centre of France. Here we stayed with the parents of our daughter-in-law. Our son and his family had driven north from their home in Provence. A weekend of fine dining and lots of attempts at talking French fuelled and educated us for our remaining four weeks in French speaking territory.

After visiting the Loire valley our route became more directly south until we reached Sicily in the last week of November. It was now the middle of October and we spent nine days chasing the tail end of summer to Provence. At Nozières, west of Valence, we caught a glimpse of the snowy peaks of the Alps on the horizon. We had now ridden over 1500km and we felt a real sense of travel as we crossed the Rhone to the region of La Drôme to camp wild on a warm evening. We had left cooler damper conditions behind and we held a belief that heading for southern Europe would work.

This was how we hoped it would be, summer stretching into November, riding in short sleeved shirts and shorts. The vista was glorious, hilltop villages piled up on the slopes, distant views of a snow-capped Mont Ventoux, the craggy defiles of the Luberon and the vines shedding their last leaves in the valley bottoms. After a ten day break at the home of our son and his family, we were now heading for the port of Marseille and the overnight ferry to Bastia.

I remember a time when we were a little in fear of visiting the island of Corsica. It was known for its bandits, a little insecure, a place where bad things may happen. Indeed the island's motif shows a bandana clad rogue and there seems to be a certain pride in the historical wild characters who are seen in pictures sporting long beards and holding rifles. This was where Napoleon Bonaparte was born. It feels very different from the rest of France, but it is undeniably beautiful and a great playground for biking and hiking.

The forests were beautiful with golden leaves clinging to the trees and lying on the roads. The landscape has a look of wild emptiness at first sight, but much of it is grazing land of a kind, for pigs, goats, cows and sheep, which trample the undergrowth out of existence and roam across the roads with impunity. The island's charcuterie and cheese are special. Descending towards Ponte Leccia, an interestingly decorated gate enclosing a field of goats caught our eye and we stopped to look. Phillipe, his brother and Luciene (referred to

The citadel at Corte, Corsica

as 'the Italian') were cooking mutton ribs on an open fire. They invited us to share their meal. Phillipe had the ribs on the end of a long metal fork and every now and then he took them off the fire and pressed them between two huge chunks of bread. It looked like he was making a sandwich for a giant, but he was soaking up the meat fat with the bread to make the bread more moist. He handed us each a huge tasty rib, a chunk of fat-soaked bread and a tumbler of weak rosé to wash it all down.

We gathered that they were inviting us to spend the night in a caravan with a comfortable bed, but it was difficult to be sure of anything because the Italian spoke mainly Italian, and Phillipe, French with a fair smattering of Corse. It all sounded like a mixture of Italian and French. Both were probably well lubricated with wine. Their hospitality was wonderful and the mountain location under a rich blue sky was truly splendid, but the wonderful weather was too good to waste. They gave us a parting gift of mandarins, and we left them with their 350 goats and an enormous flagon of wine.

It is a land of spectacular mountains and beautiful coastline. We kept to the heights where the quiet roads are, only touching the coast at the start in Bastia and the end in Bonifacio. It wasn't all up and down. Sometimes the roads follow the contours giving great views of the picturesque hilltop villages. After six Corsican days we pedalled into Bonifacio or Bunifaziu in Corsu language. The small town sits between a beautiful natural harbour and chalky white cliffs on which a medieval citadel stands and other old buildings cling. This southerly point lies just 12km from the Italian island of Sardinia.

Fifty minutes on a ferry across the straights and we landed at Santa Teresa di Gallura, the northernmost point of Sardinia. We had reached our southernmost point of familiarity. Except for a couple of places in Turkey, everywhere from now on was going to be new to us. It wasn't that the adventure hadn't begun seven weeks earlier when we had left Cumbria. It was the gradual evolution of more faraway places and the leaving of family and friends for perhaps a year. We missed people we knew, but when travelling, new people arrive, people come and go for an hour or two, or maybe a day or two or more.

In Santa Teresa di Gallura we were studying a map whilst waiting for our washing in a lavenderia when Filippo introduced himself to us. He was surprised to find travellers near his home so late in the year. Typical of many beautiful places in Europe, tourists only come for a handful of peak months a year. Filippo invited us to stay with him in the small village of Aglientu. After spending the night in Santa Teresa, we cycled 30km and finally uphill to meet Filippo in a bar in the village. Not knowing what the arrangement was, things were now out of our hands. As a cyclist, you become used to being in control of your day-to-day existence. Now, suddenly, the rest of our day was in the hands of a stranger.

Filippo offered us a tour of the area in his 4x4. We soon regretted it as we were sat in the back of a car for seemingly ages seeing nothing through the now thick mist. Somehow, it just feels wrong to be in a car sightseeing on a bike tour. We began to get feelings of guilt and angst because we now didn't want what we were being given. He was developing an *agriturismo* business after cutting through two years of red tape. He offered us a free night at his place just for the pleasure of meeting travellers out of season.

Filippo had been an advertising executive, from Milan, but he was now a small scale farmer trying to set up a holiday letting business. He had seven dogs which ran wild and free, ten cats used to going in and out of the little house we stayed in, two rescued horses, two donkeys, one sheep, one goat and several chickens which supplied him with eggs. This lifestyle doesn't come cheap at €400 a month on animal feed. He lit the rusting stove for us in the little house and having evicted the cats we made ourselves very comfortable. Filippo lives in a lovely old stone house with a great view out to sea. He took us back there for a tasty meal of pasta with squid which he cooked after he had remembered to feed the seven dogs.

The dogs bounded into the house, one peeing on the floor and one pooing in the bathroom. There was lots of leaping around and barking and one dog tried to lick my face. We enjoyed a comfortable night in his *agrituristico* once we had learnt to dodge all the many piles of cat excrement. It was an experience, but one which we were quite happy to ride away from the following morning.

We descended to the coast again, this time in sunshine and temperatures reaching 21°C. Crazy jagged mountains were silhouetted against the eastern sky and a blue sea stretched out from a rocky coastline to the west. The road climbed here and there but with a wind behind us we went quickly. The road to Osilo turned into gravel winding up and down through the green hills. We lost all traffic and sharpened our rough riding skills. Finding water in a valley bottom stream not long after 3pm we decided to stop in time for a wash with pans of hot water and to have dinner before dark. Dogs barked from a distant farm, stars came out in abundance in a pollution free sky, the odd vehicle made its way along the hill tracks and we settled in our tent feeling reasonably clean, full and satisfied with a good day's ride on a warm November day.

Our route passed through the medieval fortified town of Alghero and along the wild western coast to the south. The road weaved a route up and down through the rocky, bush-clad mountains of the coast leading to the colourful town of Bosa. Some say Sardinia is 'not quite Africa and not quite Italy'. It certainly felt different to Corsica. Sardinia has three times the area of Corsica and our transit took twice as long.

We now headed for the interior in search of the Bronze Age ruins of Su Nuraxi di Barumini. Dating from 1500BC Su Nuraxi is the most important Neolithic site in Sardinia. The special type of defensive structure known as nuraghi (for which no parallel exists anywhere else in the world) developed on the island of Sardinia. The complex consists of circular defensive towers in the form of truncated cones built of dressed stone, with corbel-vaulted internal chambers. Barumini is the finest and most complete example of this remarkable form of prehistoric architecture. There are so few tourists in late November that when we asked whether we could put our tent in the adjacent olive grove they suggested that we used the site reception room for our overnight stay. In our remaining eleven weeks in Europe, we frequently wanted to camp near archaeological sites to give us more time to explore. In most cases we ended up in an olive grove at some distance from the site as guardians were often worried about security.

Passing more unguarded ancient ruins we cut along the top of the wild Fumendosa gorge with its rough rocky edge strewn with prickly pears. Carrying water onwards from a village fountain, we enjoyed one more remote camp before arriving in the capital Cagliari. The boat to Sicily was delayed, so we explored the colourful colonnades of Cagliari and tasted authentic Sardinian cuisine. A friendly man at a shop selling local delicacies told us of a special place to eat. We found the rather rough looking Ristorante Stella Marina di Montecristo and booked a table. As soon as we entered we knew it was different. We were shown swiftly to our table and asked one simple question – *rosso o bianco*? Then we just waited to see what happened. Prompt service with no frills. Wine and water arrived. Then a delicate arrangement of seafood morsels, served on their shells, whetted our appetites. Then a pasta dish – simple pasta al dente, flavoured with prawns and basil. Finally on a cork platter, seafood tasted as if it had just been landed.

Then we were asked what we would like to drink – as if we had not drunk enough wine already. *Mirto* (myrtle spirit) was poured into our glasses and before we knew it the bottle was emptied and another brought out. Oh dear. We were grateful that the boat had been delayed for a day. We wandered slowly back to our room in Hotel Italia, feeling we had tasted the real food of Sardinia – the food that the people eat – not the standard dishes offered to tourists. No menu boards outside, no sophisticated exterior. A simple bill – €30 for the meal on offer – no choice, just great cuisine from the local *cucina* – simple and amazing.

Another overnight ferry took us a little bit further south and four degrees east to Palermo, the capital of Sicily, the Mediterranean's largest island. Is this the beginning or the end of civilisation? Whatever the answer on this Sunday, in late November, it was full of families enjoying themselves – out and about in the city on foot, on bikes, on skate boards and scooters. The sun shone warm and bright and the streets were alive to the chaos of time that is Palermo. For the most part the people are Sicilian and Italian but there are odd concentrations of Bangladeshi and African people. Like Cagliari – the city was heavily bombed in the Second World War. Nevertheless, the scruffy, and sometimes very narrow streets are full of life and interest for the casual onlooker to enjoy and marvel at. This is like no other European city that we had ever visited. We spent the day wandering the streets of the old town, intrigued at the turn of every corner, fascinated by the hotch-potch mixture of ancient, modern, crumbling and dilapidated buildings. It is a city we had considered pedalling straight out of – particularly on a quiet Sunday morning, but we think it is a city not to be missed.

We threaded our way out through the back streets, paved with huge stone slabs, alive with market stalls on a Monday morning. Passing piles of rubbish, dodging scooters and continually distracted by the mesmeric views of historic churches down narrow washing-draped alleyways we made our way to the Palazzo dei Normanni and the Cappella Palatina. The palazzo is a mesh of tenth-century Norman and seventeenth-century Spanish structures and now houses the Sicilian parliament.

Sicily was our stepping stone to the Foot of Italy and we wanted to make something of it and to discover something of the island. Heading upwards and south we stopped for an hour to admire the enormous twelfth century Duomo di Monreale. The inside is decorated with vast glass mosaics created by local and Venetian artists around 1300AD. The cloisters are recognised as amongst the finest in Italy with their 216 pairs of white marble columns completed in 1200AD.

We continued higher and higher on small roads away from the densely populated area surrounding Palermo. Sometimes passing under high flyovers, by mid-afternoon, we had escaped the metropolis and were heading for the interior of the island. We stopped for a picnic in the piazza of Altofonte, where the old men sat around as usual, smoking and conducting their business, taking no notice of the two foreign travellers on bikes, although we got plenty of encouragement from passers-by as we climbed out of the town. We put our tent in a communal viewpoint/picnic spot/playground having got water from an outside tap by a nearby house. It was a peaceful camp where we were hidden by a wooden cabin and we could enjoy a magnificent view overlooking the city of Palermo in the distance.

We had been slow to use digital navigation on our tours. It had been a chance meeting with a Swiss cyclist in Arizona in 2016 that changed our ways. Ever since December 2016, when we were touring in China, we have used Pocket Earth on our phones and found it really good. Here in Sicily we were using a 1:200,000 paper map of the whole island and it wasn't very reliable in terms of the roads and tracks which it showed or didn't show. However, an advantage of not having good mapping is that you are more inclined to ask local people for advice. This can be fun but you have to be careful as many people want to send you the quickest way to the nearest main road. We knew where we wanted to go and we knew what sort of roads we wanted to travel on but we didn't always know how to find the best routes. In heading towards the south side of the island we took some chances and found a remote route learning some Italian on the way. A sign by the side of the road read, *strada priva de segnaletica ed opere di protezione - proceda con prudenza.* Was it something to do with being a private road and road works, we thought after a warning we had been given? It actually meant, 'road without signs and protective structures – proceed with caution.'

After three days we arrived at the hilltop town of Agrigento. Nearing the centre, we were approached by a man clutching a small model of a Greek temple. He didn't need much discouragement when we told him that we really didn't want to buy the rickety piece of white expanded polystyrene. However, his local knowledge came in handy in helping us find an excellent place to stay while we took a look at the real Greek temples. The man was probably one of many migrants from Africa who have fled to Italy via Lampedusa, its most southerly island. Not only was it unlikely that anyone would want to buy his souvenir but, besides us, there didn't appear to be any tourists in town. One of the star attractions of Sicily is the inappropriately named 'Valle dei Templi'.

The Greek temples dating from the fifth and sixth centuries BC were built upon a rocky promontory bound on one side by a steep escarpment. We had the place almost to ourselves on a cool, grey morning. As the rain came down, the lightning flashed and thunder roared, we wondered if the gods were angry.

Our direction was now the far north east of the island and on the way we would just chance upon what we passed. It seems that in Sicily you are never far from food or something Greek or Roman. Just south of Piazza Armerina lie the finest Roman floor mosaics in existence. We had never seen anything quite like the nine bikini-clad girls working with weights preparing for the Olympic Games.

Just before we reached the ancient Greek settlement of Morgantina, we caught our first glimpse of Mount Etna towering in the distance. With snow covering the giant half-way down to the surrounding landscape, the mountain was the dominant force in our remaining days in Sicily and for the first two days in Calabria at the foot of Italy. My plan of escaping the winter's worst by going south was faltering. The closer we got to Etna the colder it got. We sought salvation in cafés where we clutched cappuccinos and cannolis. Like Guinness outside Ireland, it is almost impossible to find a good cannoli outside Sicily. A cannoli is a crisp tube of fried pastry filled with creamy ricotta, cherries, grated chocolate and in this region pistachios.

Riding too high in December across 'the foot of Italy'

SOUTH INTO A EUROPEAN WINTER

Our route skirted the north-west of Etna, Europe's largest active volcano and at 3,329m Italy's highest mountain south of the Alps. From Castiglioni di Sicilia we watched in awe at the constant eruptions and plumes escaping from the summit 20km distant. We descended to Taormina and stopped for a night to take time to admire what is regarded as the most dramatically situated Greek theatre in the world. Perched on the side of a mountain, now covered in snow, the third century BC amphitheatre overlooks the Gulf of Naxos and Mount Etna.

Now there was no escape. For the final 50km to the port of Messina we were trapped between the autostrada and the railway line, all running pretty close to the sea and the grey beaches. It was built up pretty well all the way in a tacky sort of way, the paint often peeling off the monotonous apartment blocks. My plan for keeping warm in the south had fallen apart. Rain and even hail lashed down in temperatures down to 3°C. We dived into a beachside café to warm up with some hot chocolate – not the thin stuff made with powder, but thick liquid chocolate that you can eat with a spoon – awesome therapy at €1,50 a cup. We reached Messina by mid-afternoon and caught a ferry for the half hour crossing to the tip of the big toe of the boot of Italy.

After some rough and wild cold camps and more to come, now and again there is a time and a place for a hotel. The promenade at Reggio di Calabria was perhaps the place, and what about the smartest hotel in town? Always a little nervous of walking in dressed in lots of lycric red and blue, looking like a man from Mars, although this is normal in Italy, I walked towards reception and in my worst Italian asked for a room and was shown one with a view of a brick wall. Our tent doors always have views so why downgrade? I asked whether they had a room with a view and we were upgraded to a balcony suite with marble columns overlooking the straights to Etna.

In the approach to Christmas, we spent two weeks in the regions of Calabria, Basilicata and Puglia. The boot of Italy is an area of rugged mountains and dramatic coastline and, as was to be a theme for the next two months, we were constantly posed with the dilemma of whether to stay low or aim high. In summer we would have no difficulty in opting for the mountainous route but in winter it is oh so tempting to try to keep as warm as possible. In practice we did a bit of both all the way to Fethiye in Turkey.

We soon got tired of the busy coast road along with the scruffy urban developments. After a comfortable camp away from the road and next to a beach, where we enjoyed the sound of the waves and kept warm by a fire of drift wood, we took the first opportunity to leave the coast. It took some time for the effects of the coast road to wear off, like the after effects of a bad dream. We ascended up to a paradise of fresh air, birdsong, and wonderful mountain views. We passed someone chopping up their firewood, and he said something about *névé, montagne*.

As we climbed the temperature dropped, finally reaching zero as we hit the snow. It was now fifteen degrees cooler than it had been at our beach camp. There had clearly been a time recently when this route would not have been a good idea on a bike. It must surely have been blocked by not only snow but landslides. We were keen to get over the top at 1,100m before camping as we didn't want to get trapped on high. We put up the tent on the snow in the forest, getting water from a nearby stream, just 3km before Fabrizia. It snowed in the night and the road was treacherous first thing in the morning on the descent. Calabrians engaged with our adventurous riding and exclaimed 'mamma mia'. Just before Fabrizia, a lady popped her head out of her house window to ask where we were going. Next thing we knew, we were invited in to warm our toes by the wood stove, enjoy hot coffee and a bite to eat. As we warmed up, the snow outside was thickening, falling rapidly and covering the road. We left the lovely lady who, like many Italians at this time, appeared to be in an all-day dressing gown. The road was now completely white but fortunately the local drivers were cautious as we slipped along the 20km to the old town of Serra San Bruno where we found a warm and comfortable *albergo*.

The temperature oscillated on our journey through the foot of Italy, but the hospitality never wavered. We met lots of people who were universally charming. We passed through fascinating villages and whenever we stopped to buy fruit we were simply given it, mainly oranges. Before leaving home we had not heard of Matera, Alberobello or Ostuni. They were simply other places on the way. Now they are places which we will never forget.

People have lived in the hilltop town of Matera since Palaeolithic times. Troglodyte homes were carved out of the sides of the ravines. The so called Sassi people lived with their animals in caves. In the 1950s, the area described as 'magnificent and splendid' in the twelfth century, became a national disgrace. Carlo Levi in his famous novel *Christ stopped at Eboli*, published in 1945, saw the place as the symbol of the misery of peasants. Ironically large families suffering from a 50% infant mortality rate were forcibly moved from their humid homes in the rock to newly built homes on the cliff top, an area once reserved for animal grazing. For a period of around 30 years, until 1980, the area of the Sassi was deserted. Now young couples wanting homes and entrepreneurs running cafés, restaurants and hotels are being encouraged to renovate the dwellings. Many areas are difficult to access by bike, let alone by car as we found when we had to lug our loaded bikes up 88 stone steps to reach our beautiful hotel carved in the cliff.

On our cool 70km ride to Alberobello, we moved into a different landscape of forests and fields bounded by dry stone walls. The Trulli, little round houses characteristic of the area, began to appear. Old broken down ones by the roadside and others which looked new. Some hidden amongst new farm buildings and others in isolation in the fields. Lots of them, with their lovely conical roofs, sometimes painted white near the top and sometimes with a sculptured stone at the apex. In Alberobello (pretty tree) we found a beautifully preserved concentration of Trulli and a cute one to stay in for a couple of nights whilst we explored and prepared to head for Greece. The small city of Ostuni, famous for its narrow alleys and white-washed walls, was our last stop before taking the overnight ferry from Brindisi to Patras in Greece.

In our one year journey, there were five overnight ferry crossings. It is such a comfortable way to travel, so much more relaxing than flying. Two of the five crossings gave substantial 'sea changes' to our trip. One was yet to come but here across the Ionian Sea the change was dramatic. We cycled away from the port in Patras and were reading signs in the Greek script and seeing beautiful churches and basilicas in Orthodox style. It was Christmas day. We had heard so much about the terrible state of the Greek economy and we wondered what we would find of the lives of the current Greeks. The first impression was that many people were doing quite well and that things were perhaps worse in the south of Italy. There were certainly many smart shops, cars and people but there were also many non-Greeks about on the streets selling the usual array of handbags, umbrellas, hats, gloves and scarves. We had no problem finding good food to eat in restaurants and the street cafés were lively and often full.

After Christmas, when the shops reopened, we had little difficulty finding

Leaving a wild, windy and rocky camp on the Tigani peninsula (Greece)

the basics for camp food. However, a realism from our hotel receptionist was that his monthly wage had dropped from €1000 to €800 and at thirty he had no choice but to live at home with his parents and he could not afford a car or motorcycle.

We departed heading for a mountainous route south through the Peloponnese peninsula. Immediately our way was rough and devoid of traffic, just what we love. The road had lots of evidence of landslides and rockfalls and more so after the first camp where we were awoken to the vibrant force of an earthquake. Lying on the ground, we felt a deep bass rumble through the earth and next thing the earth moved with a shake and sharp jolt. Two more little shudders followed. Luckily we had camped in a very safe place. The shake was probably enough to throw out a few loose rocks here and there. Lying flat on the ground gave us a full earthquake experience.

We celebrated the New Year of 2013 at the ancient site of Olympia. The Olympic Games were held here every four years throughout Classical antiquity, from the eighth century BC to the fourth century AD. Travelling through Greece at the time of year of the shortest days had some advantages. Museums housing magnificent statues and endless giant vases kept us entertained beyond daylight hours and the sites themselves were often devoid of visitors.

We had little idea how long each stage of our journey would take. Many things influenced the route choice and the daily distances which we covered. Sometimes a hundred kilometres could be easy and sometimes 25km tough.

A stormy day on the south coast of Crete.

On The Peloponnese the historical and scenic interest were fabulous and the cycling took us on some of the best routes we ever enjoyed. Our departure from mainland Greece was influenced not only by its splendour but also by the fact that there was only one boat a week from the Mani port of Ghythio to Crete. Crete, the southernmost section of the journey east, had always been central to our thinking behind tackling the northern hemisphere's winter. Like on the Peloponnese, we expected temperatures to be mild at sea level. As for rainfall – well – that is less predictable but in the previous three weeks there had been five minutes of rain whilst cycling. Through the month of January we camped in wild places on almost half the nights. If we were high then it was often below freezing and in the snow, but at sea level the temperature rose to the high teens and we occasionally swam in the sea.

We climbed over a high icy col from the Byzantium ruins at Mystras to the wild Mani peninsula, the middle finger of three protruding at the bottom of the Peloponnese. Mystras was a far western point on the Silk Road which we were to come across so often in the next months. The Mani is secluded, barren, wild, windy and rocky where inland from the turbulent coast stand hundreds of castle towers, some in ruins, some occasionally inhabited but most deserted.

On this one year journey, it evolved that Greece was the country which we spent most time in, a total of seven weeks including time on the islands of Crete and Rhodes. The time spent was often extended due to ferry delays, apparently a common event when travelling between Greek islands in winter. It was whilst we were enjoying some good wining, dining and socialising in Ghythio, waiting for the boat from Athens, we found out that it was too windy to dock so there would be no boat to Crete for at least another week. However, there was a chance that a boat could dock at Monemvasia on the next peninsula further east. The reward was an extra 70km of cycling and a chance to admire the well preserved medieval castle town of Monemvasia, exclusively carved on the slopes of a rock protruding into the sea.

It was impossible to find out when the boat from Athens would arrive at the port, so to make sure of catching it, we camped on the shoreline and spent the night peering out of the tent door to see if we could spot a ship coming. Sure enough, at six in the morning we saw a line of lights approaching across dark waters. We scrambled to pack our kit and made a dash to the jetty. It was a good job that we had, as the boat barely docked for a handful of minutes, a common trait of Greek ferries.

The seven hour sailing eventually gave us enticing views of the mountainous island of Crete. Lying south across choppy waters there were scenes reminiscent of Scotland with hints of the Isle of Eigg and the mountain of Suilven. Through fortune and not good planning, our landing point in Crete was at Kissamos at the far west of the island and our end point ten days later was at Sitia in the far east. Reinforcing our feeling of being even further from home, the first person we met in Crete was Yussef, an illegal immigrant from Morocco looking for a job in Kissamos. Clinging on to life, here was another seemingly cheerful man with no work, passport or papers! He seemed to think that England was some sort of utopia.

In January, both Crete and Rhodes felt like out of season travel destinations. We were frequently asked why we were visiting in the winter. However, we found many places with cafés and tavernas alive with friendly Greeks. Between towns, Crete has a wild mountainous landscape, and on the days when we were by the sea, a savage coastline bashed by high rolling waves. We found good beach camps either wild or using closed camp sites. The ten day transit of Crete felt a little rushed and we promised ourselves to return. We scratched the surface of archaeological Crete, only visiting the Neolithic ruins at Phaestos. We were beginning to feel a draw to the east and a need to reach Turkey before spring. At Sidonia, on the south coast, we were stopped in our tracks by rough seas washing over the road and a violent storm coming from the sky. We found a taverna with a sea view, and being a Saturday night, we were told that there would be music – 10pm was music time we were told. Bit late for us!

The room was pretty empty, the tables set with glasses and with bottles of strong drink in the centre. No raki in sight, but lots of whisky and vodka. We were directed to a small whisky free table at the side of the stage set for the musicians, and we ordered beers. People started drifting in and plates of nuts, carrots, some kind of raddish and apple pieces appeared. A trio started playing at around 11pm and by then the room was full of a happy crowd of families and friends. We felt a bit distant from the party. The music was curious with a Middle-Eastern/North African flavour. At the centre was a man with a lyra – a small pear shaped three stringed instrument, supported on the knee and played with a bow. The instrument has survived in more or less the same form for 600 years. A few lines of song around a few notes and ending in a vibrato tone, alternated with a section melody on the lyra. There was a guitar and a laouto, an eight stringed instrument a bit like a lute played with great rhythm and lots of finger picked melody – a lovely ringing tone.

Feeling a bit tired after midnight we were thinking of bed when two beers appeared on our table – a gift from a happy chap who had spotted us looking rather lonely. Soxorakis asked us to join him and friends at his table, pouring out two whiskys – and then we went into a time warp. The music got livelier, some started singing along, people got up and danced – in a kind of open circle with lots of fancy footwork which reminded us of Irish dancing. Old men and women, young kids and teenage boys all joined in. Fuelled by the whisky and the music of their own island, they got up on the tables and clapped and danced. Totally pissed older men danced looking like they might keel over. More beers appeared, more whisky and then pieces of grilled lamb and chips.

Before we knew it many hours had passed – we wondered how it got to 3.30am? We had a slow start to Sunday morning. With there only being another 100km to the port of Sitia and having four days to ride them, we decided to rest our hangovers and stay another night. Before we left on the Monday morning, Soxorakis found us and gave us a parting gift of three litres of olive oil and three litres of wine. Perhaps we would need all the time we had to reach the port.

We made our way slowly east and broke the journey to camp high by Prophet Helia's church near Sykia. We picked up water from a garage and took it up a little, but very steep hill, with a church on top where there was some flat grass for the tent and shelter in the lee of the church. As we sat down to our dinner of curried lentils and couscous topped with Greek yoghurt and chopped tomatoes, we were surprised to hear a vehicle coming up the hill. The two chaps were pretty bemused to see us sat there tucking into our food and were curious to know where our car was! Hugh showed them the tent and bikes. I think they were still puzzled but they left us in peace. We could see the two seas to the north and south (Libyan and Cretan) from our vantage point and it was great for sunrise and sunset.

For the first time since we left Corsica, a ferry was on time for our eight hour sailing from Sitia to Rhodes. We were glad to alight in Rhodes at an hour before midnight. We had managed to stay intact but we didn't read or eat much and we spent most of the time lying down. Journeys by sea had now amounted to over eighty hours and the latest was by far the roughest. We rode 9km through the midnight hours searching for a hotel bed. The cobbled streets of the old town were dark and produced no luck but we eventually found a welcoming Hotel Lydia in the new town at a quarter to one.

We spent longer than intended on the island of Rhodes, a total of twelve days. Rough seas caused the cancellation of the irregular flat bottomed ferry to Marmaris in Turkey a few times. However, we found the old city of Rhodes to be a really good place to be in winter and we spent a few days on a short bicycle tour of the island. It was interesting to see a mix of antiquity and the mess which tourism can make. The sheer scale of the development for mass tourism and its destruction of some of the coastal environment was a revelation to us – so far removed from the idyllic idea of the romantic Greek island. The coast road from Rhodes city to Kolympia is a line through industrial tourism of a very unattractive kind. However there are some ancient places. We loved the charming village of Lindos with its high acropolis. The coastline near Lindos is beautiful and there appear to be lovely wild headlands to explore.

Inland we found some lovely roads, through interesting wild, rocky, goat grazing hill country, particularly the one from Laerma to Platania. There were plenty of tavernas advertising the usual *souvlaki* and *gyros* but they were mostly closed. Many of them, like the tourist resorts on the coast, have a skeleton population in winter but there was usually at least one shop and a café open.

The roads we travelled were quiet or deserted apart from the main coastal road from Rhodes city down to Kolympia and the bit of the north-west coast road from Kremasti to Rhodes city. Wild camping was easy. There is lots of open wild ground in pine forest and unfenced olive groves. Water is not hard to find in streams in February, and there are often fountains and outdoor taps by buildings. It was warm by English standards and our down bags were too hot.

We returned to the old city and waited five days for the first small boat to Marmaris. Each day we looked longingly across the sea to high snowy mountains confirming that we were about to experience vast changes on our journey ahead as we slowly moved east into Asia.

You can't cycle to Divriği

The road that leads to nowhere for others might just be the road that leads to somewhere for you.

Mehmet Murat ildan (playwright, novelist and thinker from Eastern Turkey)

Pauline:

'You can't cycle to Divriği' was the indisputable opinion of Kemal at our guesthouse in Göreme, Cappadocia. We were carrying the *Lonely Planet* guide to Turkey which stated, 'the quadruplet of 780 year-old stone doorways on Divriği's Ulu Cami and Darüşşifası complex are so intricately carved that some say their craftsmanship proves the existence of god'. The guide also informed the reader that Divriği is a difficult place to reach by public transport and is a 'dead-end' road involving a lengthy out and back detour. However, it was a battered old copy dating from 2006. The 2013 *Rough Guide* describes it as 'being stuck in the middle of a mountainous nowhere'. It certainly didn't look like a dead-end on our map – on this trip, a paper map – although our onward

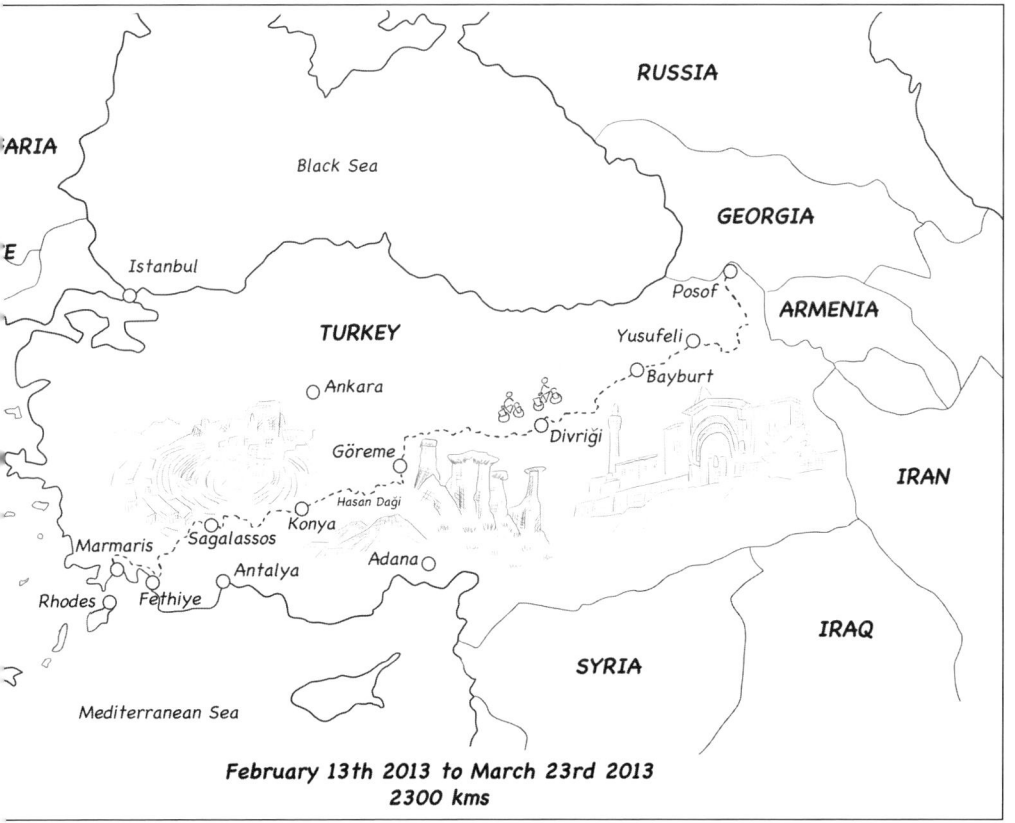

February 13th 2013 to March 23rd 2013
2300 kms

route did look pretty remote. We looked forward with excitement to our ride through the 'mountainous nowhere' to see the work of the hand of God!

We had passed through Göreme in 1978 on the hippy trail heading home from India, overland by bus and train. Then again in 1999 with two of our three children on a visit to see a *güneş tutulmasi*, a total eclipse of the sun. We were so bowled over by the eclipse that we went to Turkey yet again in 2006 to see yet another total eclipse from the coastal town of Antalya, hence the 2006 guidebook. In 2013 the Cappadocian landscape was every bit as wonderful but the whole area had become much more of a tourist magnet with the resulting overblown development.

However, I was about to spend a very special day walking through the fantastical landscape which the erosive hand of nature has sculptured in Cappadocia. The walk from Zelve to Göreme was rated by my family as one of the best walks ever when I spent a day sick in bed in 1999 whilst they all had fun. They had teased me about it ever since, never considering that I would have the chance to put things right! Amazingly, Hugh remembered where to find the narrow gulley that climbs up steeply between rock towers, out of the back

The empty ruins of Sagalassos.

of the Hidden Garden café in Zelve, which took us up to a surreal landscape which we had all to ourselves. Sadly, the Buket Hotel where we had stayed fourteen years previously was no longer the charming little place that we remembered being in a pretty location on the edge of the troglodyte town of Uçhisar. Now it was surrounded by building works and in the process of being swallowed up by the town on all sides. It being the beginning of March when the weather is fickle, Göreme was relatively quiet but the town's excellent restaurants were open and we took the chance to enjoy the amazing varied cuisine before we set out into the great unknown.

We had been picnicking in warm sunshine on our walk, but the day we left, the fairy chimneys of Göreme were coated with a dusting of snow which lay more thickly on the flat ground below. We decided that we were going, whatever the weather. So, how did we come to be heading for the high ground of eastern Turkey, still in the grips of winter?

Nearly three weeks previously we had left the sunshine of the Mediterranean coast at Fethiye and taken a sharp turn to the north and up. It had taken us three days to get to Fethiye from Marmaris, our landing point in Turkey having taken a ferry from the Greek island of Rhodes. Since leaving home four and a half months earlier, we had never been far from the warming effect of the sea, and the rough plan was to stay with it as long as possible until spring arrived!

A good plan, but we didn't like the coast road; it was too much of a proper road which scarred the landscape, having a hard shoulder and sometimes two carriageways. We were enjoying the occasional sea views but we craved something rougher, sparsely inhabited and less developed. Both of us felt ready to take our chance with the cold, high up on the Western Anatolian plateau. So we went up, 1000m above the balmy waters of the Med, into the depths of winter and that night we put up our tent on a carpet of snow in a pine forest. The following morning at dawn, the beautiful varied birdsong was broken by a call from a mullah through a loudspeaker on top of a minaret in the nearby village – a sound which was to become our friend throughout our journey across Turkey. Many gigantic mosques were being built, sometimes in the tiniest of villages.

Riding away from our camp that Sunday morning, we found that the beauty of the white snow had attracted a beautiful bride also dressed in white. She was there for a photoshoot, along with her groom who was smartly turned out in a crisp white shirt and dark suit. Families were up there too, picnicking on rugs laid out on the snow, warming themselves next to roaring fires lit by the roadside, building snowmen and eating Turkish ice cream; in this case fresh snow with sugar syrup squirted on top.

We felt that we had entered a completely different world. In this slower moving place, away from the busy coast road, we were meeting so many more people. They would wave, stop to chat, ask 'where have you come from?' – 'where are you going?' – 'how old are you?' – 'how long have you been married?' and more. It was not uncommon for them to laugh out loud at the answers. We were able to answer these basic questions, getting better as we repeated the same story so many times, but we did find the language very difficult. English speakers were few and far between. At least the written script was generally comprehensible once we had learnt a few extra letters. In times past it would have been much harder.

Up until 1928, Turkish was written in the Arabic alphabet. Mustafa Kemal Atatürk who founded the Republic of Turkey in 1923 following a War of Independence against invading armies and a civil war against the Ottoman Sultan, changed it to the Latin script. However, the Turkish alphabet has 29 letters – six of them modifications of their Latin originals – Ç Ş Ğ İ Ö and Ü; these allow for the particular sounds needed in Turkish, e.g. the squiggly c in çay is pronounced like 'ch'. They don't use Q, W or X. It appears that Erdoğan has been talking about going back to the Arabic script, but this seems like a bad idea if the comment in the Turkish online paper the *Hürriyet Daily News* (secular and liberal or centre-left publication) is anything to go by: 'Going back to the Arabic script seems neither possible nor practical since the literacy rate in today's Turkey is above 93 percent. It is not possible to reset it, unless Erdoğan would like to drag the country down into such a situation while he is talking about taking a scientific jump.'

On and on we went, up and down, along roads lined with snow on the high ground, alongside patchworks of ploughed fields in the flat valley bottoms and all the while, snow speckled mountain tops above us. As we passed through Gölhisar and on to Burdur we soon realised that the white, mountain tops were not snow-covered at all, but huge marble quarries – not much liked by the flamingos living on the nearby Lake Yarışlı. For the first time in 2016 the flamingos did not migrate to the lake because of the activity of construction equipment, dynamite explosions, dust and noise pollution. The more we travelled around the world, the more we were discovering that everything has a price beyond that of the money paid to buy it! So while we can have white marble floors in our homes, the flamingos have to do without their spring home on Yarışlı. Turkey does big business in the supply of marble, travertine and granite and it is growing.

We were heading for an ancient stone construction, the UNESCO world heritage site of Sagalassos which dates back to 1200BC. Way up on the mountainside above the village of Yeşibaşköy a staggering Roman city is being slowly uncovered. This blanket of earth and vegetation along with the remoteness of the location has saved it from looting over the centuries. As a consequence it is one of the best preserved ancient cities in the Mediterranean. We arrived with just enough daylight to explore, which was good, because dense low cloud covered the site the next morning.

That afternoon I sat, in splendid isolation, on the top tier of the immense, circular, Roman theatre, which was built to seat around 9,000 people. My eyes were drawn to the stage so far below me, now a tumble of stone blocks and leaning columns, shaken by the tremors of ages – and beyond, dark, barren mountain ridges extended forever into the distance. This is reputedly the highest Roman amphitheatre in the world, and it certainly felt like it. We couldn't help wondering why the Romans had built their city so high up the hillside at over 1,400m. The enormous site was splattered with snow and icicles hung from the masonry. In mid-February no one else had ventured up the hill apart from the man issuing tickets and Memhet from the pension cum fish farm where we were staying, who had sped us up there in his Hyundai. We had cheated, our excuse being that it would get dark soon and we wanted as much time as possible to look around!

The stones of the stage still lay more or less the way in which they were found. All around the huge site, intricately carved blocks and sections of columns lay on the ground, some gathered into organised piles; 3D puzzle pieces waiting to be put together to form a recognisable structure – each piece being coded to indicate how it might connect with the others. A significant part of the nymphaeum had been rebuilt incorporating new pieces, exquisitely carved in great detail to match perfectly with the partially preserved ancient blocks. The southern street leading into the city had been uncovered and sections of columns were laid out on either side, waiting for the reconstruction of the colonnade. Perhaps by now much more has been rebuilt. The reconstruction has to be very strong in order to withstand the frequent earthquakes which reduced much of it to ruins in the first place.

We were stunned by Sagalassos. We didn't even know it existed until a couple of days before when we noticed a point of interest on the map, roughly in our direction of travel. We certainly weren't expecting a significant ancient Roman site in such an out of the way place. There is something special about stumbling across unexpected marvels; the surprise, the feeling of discovery, the impossibility of it 'not living up to expectations' because we didn't have any expectations. We had visited Roman amphitheatres in Nîmes and Arles in France, and also at Ephesus in Turkey but this one was very different.

As we rode through the slushy snow in the morning, we were invited into the office of the local mayor. He asked some questions which for us, were quite difficult to answer given the circumstances, with the Imam sitting opposite us;

'Do you believe in God?', 'Do you believe in life after death?' In these situations we feel it is unwise to be point blank honest and we responded as usual with some vague platitudes which didn't give too much away. Much to our relief the exchange was very amiable. The mayor was pleased to have much in common with Hugh; the same month of birth, both were mathematics teachers and both have three children. He told us that the town produces cherries for export and Simir bottled water. The Imam was particularly impressed with Hugh's beard which had been left to go its own way for several months.

Following some exceedingly pretty mountain riding and a delightful overnight camp, we landed in Eğirdir on market day, where there was a wealth of fine produce on sale. There were big trays of olives, large and small in a myriad of colours; black, pale brown, reddish brown, muted greens turning a little pink, olive green, some stoned some not and some filled with garlic or chilli. There were goats cheeses wrapped in goat's skin, sacks of grains, monkey nuts and lentils, fresh fish of all shapes and sizes, fruit and vegetables in profusion, heavily sweet Turkish pastries, pots of honey and more. With this wealth of ingredients it is no wonder that the Turkish cuisine is so varied and tasty.

It was tempting to nestle in the warm comfort of Charly's Pension in Eğirdir. We could admire the lake from our room, enjoy the company of the clientele, including two Finns – and we had lots to read. We could tell ourselves that the weather was bad; it was cool and wet. But – it wasn't that bad – it could get much worse for sure. The wind was light and it was above freezing. In view of what may be to come that was good, although we feared that the wet roads might turn to ice. So the next day we moved on, passing through a series of dingy villages, looking all the more dismal through the murky mist. Cows and goats wandered over the wet muddy road and we armed ourselves with stones to deter the chasing dogs.

It was getting late in the day and we needed somewhere to stay, but we had passed by the only possibility. When, on the cusp of darkness it became clear that we were going to have to put up the tent, there was nowhere flat and dry to put it. Then we spotted a small white-washed building not far off the road, with the word, *mescit* written vertically in large, red letters down one side. It had a small wooden door, one window to the side and a tiled roof extending to a small veranda, propped up by rough wooden struts. Hugh went for a look inside and it was evident that this was a mini mosque. It was tempting to squat there and Hugh would have done it without question. However, I had an uncomfortable scenario turning over in my mind – what if one of the local men turned up to pray, and found us lying there in our sleeping bags? How would he react? We wouldn't worry about seeking refuge in a church at home although the situation has never arisen, and we know that Sikh gurdwaras can be places you can stay – but a *mescit*? We discussed it. It was miserable outside and there was barely room to put the tent up near the building but it would be possible. Hugh was still up for sleeping inside the mosque, but I didn't want

YOU CAN'T CYCLE TO DIVRIĞI

Cold and sunny under Hasan Dağı (3253m)

to risk the anger of a Muslim worshipper. We had no idea if it was considered grossly offensive to snuggle down in a place of worship. The rugs inside were nice but we opted for the tent which we erected on the uneven ground to the side, knowing at least that in the event of an emergency there was shelter at hand.

The next morning we headed uphill to 1850m on slushy, slippery roads with snow piled high on the verges. Tantalising glimpses of high, white mountains appeared through gaps in the foggy gloom. We kept warm going up but on the descent we froze and were more fearful of slipping. We entered the village of Kurucaova, a collection of rough stone houses – some with battered ottoman style protruding windows which made them look attractively quaint to our eyes. A small, thin and elegant minaret stood out proudly above the tiled rooftops. There was a café where we took refuge. These little villages would invariably have a café where the men, almost exclusively the men, would drink tea – never beer.

Best of all there would be a very hot, stove – usually a DIY metal construction – a patchwork of assorted metal sheets, boxes and drums with a thick metal pipe heading for an outside wall or roof, and a box of wood to one side. These contraptions had a very hashed together look about them but they certainly blasted out the heat. The men welcomed us in, always eager to share warmth, tea and companionship. I was often the only woman, but I never felt out of place. These rooms were our saviour in the grip of the Turkish winter. In the café in Kurucaova the men sat on their plastic chairs around tables covered with flowery plastic cloths, welcoming us with warm smiles. One of them spoke some French as he had worked there for some time.

Two days ride onwards we reached Konya, the home of the Mevlevi whirling dervishes, but along the way we stayed in Beyşehir, situated on the shore of a large lake of the same name. Beyşehir is one of those lesser known places, often listed as an excursion from places better known, such as Konya, but on a bike we don't generally do excursions unless they are very short. Out and back rides are not very appealing. A young English teacher who we met in the town told us we must go and see the Eşrefoğlu Mosque, a UNESCO site dating from 1296 and noted for its magnificent wooden columns and ceiling. There is no other like it in Anatolia.

The Mevlana museum in Konya, the original lodge of the whirling dervishes, is a place of pilgrimage for many Turkish people. Celaleddin Rumi, known as Mevlana, was their leader and his tomb lies in the museum along with those of 55 other members of his family. He founded a sect within Sufi Islam which insists that love is the centre of Islam. They are known as the whirling dervishes because that is what they do – whirl! As they rotate through a full 360° their long circular skirts rise up and create amazing three dimensional patterns.

We left Konya in kinder weather, wearing shorts and T-shirts as we made our way swiftly across the Anatolian Plateau. It would take us another five days of riding to reach Göreme in Cappadocia by which time we would still be less than half way across the country having done 982km. It took us 38 days to cross Turkey covering a distance of 2,192km. The magnificent mountain, Hasan Dağı (3,253m), rising an abrupt 1000m above the height of the surrounding plain, would be our constant companion for many days to come, much as Mount Etna (3,326m) was in Sicily earlier on in the trip and Pico de Orizaba would be a few years later in Mexico. All are volcanoes and all were coated in white but Hasan Dağı and Pico de Orizaba are now quiet, whilst Etna is not. We would see the shape of these mountains changing as our journey progressed giving us views from different angles. One of our first sights of Hasan Dağı was from our camp after Konya. The silhouette of the mountain was gradually brought into focus as the sun rose a few degrees to the right, scattering its crimson rays across the plains making the thin grasses sparkle. Later in the day as we approached Sultanhani the steep crags and snow fields of Hasan Dağı lay behind a thin veil of mist – a backdrop to the minarets and tiled roofs of the village.

YOU CAN'T CYCLE TO DIVRIĞI

In Sultanhani there is a caravanserai, a roadside inn originally a place for travellers to stay, where they could rest and recover. This one was constructed by the Seljuks in 1229 and they built it well. It is said to be the largest and best of its type. The Seljuks originally came from Iran and they ruled over a large part of Western Asia in the eleventh to thirteenth centuries. How we would have loved to stay there. But now, current day travellers can only visit and marvel at the exquisite architecture – the pointed arch of the main portal, vaulted in the classic Islamic style and surrounded by ornate geometric patterns – the elegant arches surrounding the interior courtyard – and the little mosque in the courtyard supported by carved arches. We explored inside and cycled all around the outside a couple of times admiring its solid construction. The rectangular building is built from large stone blocks in a patchwork of shades of desert sand. While we were there a bus load of British/German/Dutch tourists arrived. They were out for a week in Turkey and many of them were very interested in our journey, and surprised that we were away for a year. One of them hadn't bothered to go inside the caravanserai, thinking it looked rather cold inside, which it was in the sunless side rooms with only a tiny opening for light. In summer this would be very welcome.

It was a frustrating experience finding a back route onwards from the caravanserai. Hugh was navigating and I was getting cross with him for taking too much notice of the signs which often don't indicate the way we want to go. He seemed reluctant to hand over the map and compass. Asking directions resulted in us being directed back to the main roads which we were trying to avoid – a common scenario. Not for the first time, our paper map wasn't matching reality. We cycled in the dark for half an hour before we could find water and a place to camp, not something we like doing. It wasn't the first time we had struggled with navigation in Turkey when trying to follow remote dirt roads. Now I realise that we would probably have got on much better using digital maps. We only had a basic mobile phone with us on this trip although we did also have a netbook computer. We were using the Marco Polo 1:800,000 map (bought in Rhodes) which was frequently wrong. Occasionally, when we had wifi, we used Google maps for further information. We couldn't find any decent maps in Turkey and surprisingly, petrol stations didn't seem to have them.

A couple of days riding accompanied by the ever changing views of Hasan Dağı took us to the southern edge of Cappadocia; once an ancient kingdom stretching over north eastern Turkey as far as the Black Sea – but now understood to refer to the triangle of land that lies between Nevşehir, Niğde and Aksaray which is so popular with tourists attracted by the remarkable landscape. We were heading for the tiny village of Soğanlı which, so far, has escaped the fate of being drowned by the rising tourist tide. Given that this very quality is now being promoted in tourist brochures one can't help wondering how long it will stay that way. In the *Rough Guide* it is described as a 'spectacular diversion' but for us it was simply on the way to Central Asia.

The women in the village square were selling colourful knitted socks and gloves, but they had covered up their stalls, there being few customers. Dressed in their baggy, floral patterned, Turkish pants they were passing the time playing a version of cricket, using a roughly cut wooden bat and a block of wood for a ball. The people keep sheep and use the many hillside caves for storage. Traditional village life goes on but visitors are not neglected. We found lodgings in the charming pension run by a lovely old couple, Fevzi and Müneuver (Mine for short).

We went on an afternoon ramble up the valley visiting churches carved into the rock, many of which were richly decorated with impressive frescos – and one with Greek graffiti. The Kubbeli Kilise (church with the dome) is the most striking of all being a three tiered honey comb carved out of the rock. The dome, being more like a cone, is shaped out of the top of a fairy chimney. There is a huge split in the whole top section where a large part of the church has become detached.

Like so many Cappadocian homes the pension was partly built into the steep hillside and our bed was fitted into an alcove hewn from the rock. Traditional colourful Turkish rugs and cloths covered the beds, the floor and the table top, all kept so cosy and warm by a range in the corner. In the morning we sat by a low table to have breakfast: olives, homemade cheese, homemade apricot jam, warm bread and a spicy omelette made in a clay pot. Before we left, Fevzi showed us his extensive collection of stamps from around the world which included many Victorian British specimens. Mine gave us a doll which she had made and it now has a special place in our home. Travelling by bike means that we can only return with a few particularly meaningful mementos. We gave Mine a postcard of our home town, Sedbergh, which she studied intently. They had made us so welcome in their village home.

Soğanlı is a very special place, and this hit us even more when we arrived in Göreme. In Soğanlı we had found a fascinating fragment of the area just lightly touched by tourism. Göreme is soaked in it and I didn't much like it. It would be the last place we would pass through in Turkey which is frequently visited by foreign travellers. Indeed we met no other foreign travellers along the route to Posof, our final stopover in Turkey another 1,210km away. The eastern half of Turkey has a slightly edgy feel to it for some, bordering Syria and Iraq to the south and Iran, Armenia and Georgia to the east. We had crossed into Turkey from Iran in 1978 on our way back from India. We had decided not to go through Iran this time, it being on the list of countries where UK citizens were advised 'against all but essential travel'. Our route would cross remote eastern Anatolia where the only real urban centre is Erzerum; we didn't go there but we were frequently asked if that was where we were heading.

From Posof we would cross over the border to Georgia, the other countries all presenting difficulties. We were taking, what was for us, one big turn of the pedal into the great unknown. This was the way to Georgia so this was the way

YOU CAN'T CYCLE TO DIVRIĞI

The Ulu Cami (great mosque) of Divriği.

we were going. We knew little of what lay ahead but we knew it would be mountainous, it would frequently be very cold and it would be hard at times, but by now we felt we knew the people well enough to be confident that we would be welcomed wherever we went and we would get help if we needed it.

So, we rolled out of Göreme on a turn of the weather; the falling snow testing our resolve. Within just a couple of days we realised that we were going to need a certain amount of luck to pull off this journey to Divriği – which by now had become almost a place of pilgrimage in our minds – and on to Posof. So far we had crossed high passes either just before or just after heavy snows and as yet the temperatures hadn't turned the wet roads to ice, but it had been a close thing. The roads were surprisingly well cleared and gritted, but we had higher passes – over 2000m – and more remote country ahead.

We pedalled across open roads on wind chilled plateaus where we just longed for the warmth of a tin pot stove in a tea shop – through dull brown, barren hill country and across frozen wastes where icicles hung from the rocks.

We were often wearing over-trousers to keep out the cold wind, shoe covers, thick gloves and buffs. Hugh was wearing his hat with ear flaps so there was no point in talking to him!

As much as we often craved a warm room, it wasn't always possible. We camped in a little wind sheltered hollow, in the protection of a giant rock where our tent left a hexagonal print in the snow and at the edge of a cropped wheat field – all in sub-zero temperatures. We ate our camp dinners wearing our hats and down jackets wrapped up in our sleeping bags. We fell asleep to the sound of calls to prayer from the mosques and dogs barking in the distance.

In Çayıralan we went looking for a warm room, only to be told there was no hotel. However, a helpful local told us there was an *öğretmenevi* – teacher's house. We imagined it was the home of a local teacher who put up occasional guests, but no; it was accommodation for teachers who have been sent off to the back of beyond for their first year in the job. The man in charge of the house spoke no English so he got on his phone and before long the local English teacher arrived to act as translator. We were shown to a warm room, with a hot shower and a comfy bed – for just 40TL (£15). A bargain when temperatures of -8°C were forecast for the evening. We had dinner with two teachers staying in the house. They were quite puzzled as to what brought us there. One was from İzmir where it is warm and nice – she wasn't impressed with Çayıralan.

The route to the pass beyond Çayıralan took us along a rough dirt track where the red brown earth had turned to mud with the consistency of cement. As we rode a wiggly course around the icy puddles, it clung to our wheels and stuck under the mudguards making progress almost impossible. There was a road works depot near the top of the pass where Şambas had a nice warm cosy cabin. We had no idea what he was doing up there as there was no one else around apart from his friendly dog, but we were very happy to accept his invitation to warm up inside his shelter. Before long he produced cups of tea and a table laid with bread, olives, cheese and sliced hard boiled eggs. I relaxed on his mattress in the corner where his gun was propped against the wall – for the wolves perhaps? Later on we found water at a garage and sprayed off the mud with our water bottles!

At every town we were greeted with waves, smiles and calls of *merhaba* (hello) and urged to join the men for tea. Our offers to pay were always rejected. It wasn't uncommon for people to get on their mobile phones in an effort to help us out. On the street men and young boys would often crowd around us puzzled as to why we were there and eager to help. Sometimes they would take our photo so we had no reservations about taking theirs. They found Hugh's bizarre cycling gear pretty funny – it was – particularly the bright blue leg warmers below skin tight cycling shorts. People watched us cycle by with astonished looks on their faces and truck drivers sometimes offered us lifts. That is something we just can't do unless it is the police who insist! At street stalls we were given fruit, vegetables and bread – no payment accepted!

The small towns were pretty drab – the sort of places the teachers would not want to be banished to – but the people were as cheerful as ever. New, characterless blocks of flats were going up all over the place on the outskirts of the towns where there appeared to be no other infrastructure – no shops, no markets, nowhere for people to congregate. They were possibly more warm and comfortable than the old cottages but they lacked any hint of charm. Turkey seemed to be undergoing a building bonanza – new homes and new roads. Often a four lane dual carriageway would take us the last few kilometres into a town – usually empty of traffic and seemingly way over the top for the purpose.

Roughly half way to Divriği we passed through the town of Kangal. At the entrance to the town stands a statue of a fearsome looking beast, the Kangal shepherd dog, looking all the more threatening for the spikey collar around its neck. These were the creatures that barked at us and sometimes chased at our heels. Apparently they can run at speeds of up to 50km/hr – not much point in trying to pedal away from them! They keep the wolves, jackals and bears off the sheep – so in theory they shouldn't have been too bothered about us. I read that they are supposed to be friendly to people who they regard as their flock, so perhaps we need not have worried too much. It is hard to take that attitude when a noisy, pack is hurtling after you at full speed as you pedal wearily along the road at dusk after a hard day crossing mountain passes. A trick we sometimes tried, although it took some nerve, was to stop, turn towards them and look fierce and angry, waving a stick or showing a stone – they usually went away, although now that sounds like very much the wrong thing to do. The dogs need protecting from the wolves, so they wear the spikey collar to protect their most vulnerable point of attack. We noticed that some had a small stone attached covering their throat – possibly for extra protection.

The day we arrived in Divriği it was uphill all the way to the Karasar Geçidi Rakim, a pass at 1,950m, our highest so far. The sign was partially obscured by deep snow banked by the roadside. Caro et Marc had been there before us on their tandem. We knew this because they had left a picture on the sign post – 'Caro et Marc were here'. The deserted road descended through an empty, white wonderland, the clouds casting shadows on the tops of the rounded hills ahead. We descended below the snowline into a complex maze of eroded valleys, not a tree in sight – the slopes carved into a profusion of deep gullies; and then, finally, scattered villages – small single story cottages, some whitewashed and others of bare earth – and lower down, larger, two story homes.

We had cycled to Divriği. Passing the ruined castle tumbling down a craggy promontory and then a glorious ancient Ottoman house in dire need of roof repairs, we entered the narrow cobbled streets in the centre of town. Finding a place to stay after our two nights' cool camping was a challenge. Ninni Otel looked like it might do from the outside but no one turned up at reception, despite help from Mehmet the baker who phoned various contacts; he was in the process of wheeling a barrow of cut wood into the bakery – fuel for the ovens. The Özkanlar Pansiyon appeared to be a place for blokes – rooms with single beds and an off-putting urinal in the shower. At 80TL for a night we decided it was a rip off and Hugh found the proprietor's habit of spitting out nut residue whilst standing right next to him, rather off-putting.

So we set out to head for what was probably a smarter place 1/2/4/6km down the road depending on which of the people we asked. Less than one kilometre down the road we bumped into the Taşbaşı hotel – a pleasant, warm room with a double bed, proper bathroom and a view from the balcony over the citadel and a rocky cleft, into which the train to Erzincan vanishes through a tunnel. We then headed straight to see the wonders of the third century Divriği Ulu Cami ve Darüşşifası (Divriği Great Mosque and Hospital). Standing there, quietly, in the peace of the early evening it was such a treat to infuse the intricacies of the carvings irradiated with the golden light of the early evening sunshine. Never before had we seen such detailed three dimensional masterpieces and we stood there totally in awe.

The Great Mosque is deservedly included on the UNESCO list of the 500 great masterpieces of the world – the only Turkish work included on the list and considered to be one of Turkey's great sights. The hospital attached to it was a mental hospital. Inside, an octagonal water pool drained via a spiral run-off. The sound made by the water soothed the nerves of the patients – sounds like very sensitive care.

Often when travelling you build up a place in your imagination, only to be disappointed by reality. Divriği was not one of those places. The hours of pedalling over a stunning snowy landscape led to a fair bit more than even the promised stupendously carved doorways – for which the place should be much more visited than it is. There are also fascinating examples of nineteenth and early twentieth century Ottoman buildings dotted around the narrow paved streets, some in a state beyond repair and some beautifully renovated.

Little mausoleums were scattered around the town, each with remnants of ancient carvings. The place is a huge, seemingly untapped, foreign tourist destination. The citadel lies in ruins unsafe for exploration; we found no tourist information office to guide us around the place – although it was the middle of winter. Places to stay were not to be found on the web or in our *Lonely Planet Guide*. However, there are information plaques on buildings of interest. The only other visitors we saw at the Ulu Cami were a group of Muslim women on a girls' trip out from the nearby town Iliç. They seemed to be having lots of fun and were more than happy to have their photo taken with us.

As we were walking down the street on our way back to our hotel, we heard a call from above, *çay* (tea). A couple of young women were leaning out of a

YOU CAN'T CYCLE TO DIVRIĞI

All on a pilgrimage to Divriği

third floor window and beckoning us in. We climbed up the stairs and to our surprise, found ourselves in a hairdresser's salon and the three professionals just couldn't wait to tackle our unkempt mops, gone wild after months of travel. The real prize though was Hugh's beard, the beard of a mature man now reaching almost to his neck line. They really couldn't wait to get their hands on that – but – Hugh wasn't having it. He had grown too fond of it. After the neat haircut the beard was much longer than his hair, and yes, there was çay too!

We left Divriği well stocked up with provisions including hot bread from the bakery. There are lots of little shops in the town, all selling virtually the same things and a couple of small supermarkets with an abundance of pasta and bulgur wheat on the shelves. The little vegetable stores sell beautiful peppers, aubergines, tomatoes, courgettes and more. We found plenty of nuts and dried fruits – good for snacks. There are also many shops selling beer and raki, and cigarettes with gruesome pictures on the packets designed to put off smokers.

Our road was virtually traffic free and went through some volcanic terrain which looked interesting in sunlight, but as the clouds came over and rain threatened, the landscape took on an uninspiring dull brown tone. When the time to stop arrived we found ourselves in a dry landscape – the only water courses being full of silt – so we deviated up a short dirt track to a small settlement by a messy barrage development, where we found signs of life at a house. The lovely old couple seemed very happy to give us water from their kitchen tap and they had much to say that we couldn't understand. They must have been very surprised to see us rock up on our bikes!

From Divriği it took us five days to get to Bayburt. The only place of any size on the way was Erzincan, where we stayed in a hotel in the modern centre. We passed through the outskirts of the town built on the bank of a rubbish strewn and largely dry water course – first scattered poor little dwellings and then the inevitable uniform blocks of flats. As we were puzzling how to avoid a motorway which had sprung up on the edge of town, a chap stopped to help us. He described himself as being from Belgium – Turks living in Western Europe usually described themselves in this way. He told us that the centre of town was 'beautiful' which it is if you are looking for a decent place to stay and a huge choice of pretty smart eateries of various types. The Belgium man's business lay in cement – a strength he indicated may be behind Erzincan's growth and 'modernity'.

The other three nights were spent in our tent; in a little sheltered re-entrant a little way off the roadside; on a flat area of rough grass below the embankment of a very quiet road; and in a sheltered little copse near a place with the impossible name of Aşağiozlüce close to a babbling stream where there was plenty of wood for a fire. There was hard rain, there were violent storms, wild winds blew and the winter sun shone. We felt a longing for spring to arrive – looking forward to the earth turning green and leaves appearing on the trees. Bright yellow crocuses gave us hope that warmth would come soon. We had missed the last two winters and this one was feeling long. It felt like we had been crossing snowy mountains for some time – and there were more, higher passes yet to come.

We crossed four mountain passes – Gedikbaşı Geçidi 1,710m, Savas Gediği Geçidi 1,630m, Pelitsırtı Geçidi 1,225m and Ahmediye Geçidi at 2,120m – *geçidi* meaning crossing. It was all mountains – multi-coloured volcanic rock in shades of red, green, grey and white – sometimes bare rock and sometimes eroded to sand. On the treeless passes only low bushes grew – there was snow by the roadside and white peaks above us. Farmers moved their flocks along the road. In a high mountain village hardy children played a game in a circle, moving round the little schoolyard, surrounded by puddles and soggy snow. A little girl outside a ruined house gave us a warm smile as she continued skipping with a makeshift rope.

Near İliç where the ladies at the Divriği mosque had come from, yet another barrage was being built. However, Mehmet and his crew at the Şen Ortanklar garage more than made up for the scenic devastation with their spontaneous hospitality. We couldn't really imagine Close's Garage in our home town of Sedbergh asking a couple of random and very foreign cyclists into their warm workshop, and giving them tea, olives, cheese, yoghurt, bread and mother's homemade biscuits! It was such a tidy place – tools were hung on the wall, all arranged in order of size and the shelves were neatly stacked with boxes, tins, bottles and canisters of all sorts of garage stuff. When Hugh offered to buy the rest of the bread off them they gave it to us and refused any payment, which saved us the trouble of having to go up the hill into the town.

On the day we reached Bayburt our attention was caught by the sight of a group of men slaughtering a cow in a yard near the roadside. They were not happy about us being there and for the first and only time in Turkey we felt uneasy. This feeling stayed with us as we reached the next town of Demirözü where we sat down in a bus shelter to have a picnic out of the rain. A man on a bicycle came to the rescue and invited us join him in the çay shop, where as usual it was as warm as toast.

This section was all about getting to the border with Georgia by the most charming and traffic free route – riding – eating – sleeping. There was little in the way of sights to see. However, we did bump into 'the biggest and most important headquarters of the Roman Empire' – the ancient city of Satala – or so it was claimed on the notice. All that remained were some extremely rough arches or just the legs of the arches – the remains of a legendary fortress. It was set in a field of snow patches and mud which glued itself to our shoes.

An ancient citadel built during Roman times towers above Bayburt – an

'Welcome to our workshop' – in Turkey – one of the most hospitable countries we have cycled through.

historic town which was visited by Marco Polo in the thirteenth century. Once an important centre on the Silk Road, it was a place where travellers restocked supplies, sold their wares and rested before continuing on the long journey. The Silk Road which linked imperial Rome with distant China was once the greatest thoroughfare on earth. Fine silk cloth from China, prized for its softness by Europeans and Asians, was the prime commodity but many other luxurious products were traded along the route – cotton, ivory, wool, gold, and silver. The long trip meant that traders wanted high value for the weight of goods carried. In reality it wasn't just one long road but a network of interwoven routes with branches going off in different directions. Bayburt lay along the road from the Black Sea port of Trabzon to the Anatolian city of Erzerum.

In his fascinating book, *An Adventure on the Old Silk Road* John Pilkington writes: 'For centuries travellers have approached Anatolia with sinking hearts. No easy routes cross its plateau, no natural gaps pierce the ranges to the north and south – a land of scorching summers and biting winters, richly fertile around the occasional volcanoes but otherwise of poor to mediocre grasslands given over to angora goats and the occasional herd of cattle – eagerly bypassed if there had been any obvious alternative.' He talks about approaching this stage of his journey with 'trepidation'. We had experienced our fair share of that 'biting winter' and we would have to admit to a little of that 'sense of trepidation' as we left the Mediterranean coast at Fethiye but perhaps we would disagree with the urge to bypass the plateau as our journey thus far and beyond brought many rewards including the occasional magnificent volcano.

We found a good hotel in Bayburt and the perfect place to eat – in a *lokantası*, that is a modest restaurant for locals – or as Trip Advisor now puts it, 'an authentic home cooking experience.' *Lokantasıs* are to be found in any reasonably sized town and are generally pretty smart. We loved them because you could see what was on offer; it was all laid out on the counter in front of you in heated trays. No grabbling with incomprehensible menus. There were meats, beans, lentils and a myriad of vegetables (of the sort we saw in the markets) swimming in spicy red sauces. You could have soups, kofte, chickpea pilau, rice with green vegetables, salads with lemon and yoghurt.

For pudding we would sometimes move on to a *pastanesi* – like the French pâtisserie or the Italian *pasticceria*. Hugh's favourite was a cheesy sweet called *künefe* made from shredded *kadayıf* noodles stuffed with unsalted cheese and sweetened with syrup. The cheese hung in glutinous strands as you lifted your spoon. All the Turkish pastries seemed to need lots of sticky sweet syrup or honey. Baclava is the famous one – made with filo pastry, chopped nuts and honey. Liking it so much, since Covid lockdown, Hugh now makes this one at home. I liked the *kabak tatlısı* which is made from pumpkin. We also had *kadayıf* which is made from finely shredded filo dough, plus sugar, butter and chopped nuts. It came on a large circular metal tray sprinkled with raw green pistachio nuts and cut into long, thin, radiating slices. There was no beer on sale in the *locantasıs*; we drank ayran, a thin, salty yogurt drink. There was no smoking in restaurants either – or in any other public place – and unlike in Greece, the people stuck to the law. People would go outside to 'light up' even if it was pretty chilly.

All the way from Bayburt, through İspir, to Yusufeli we followed the course of the Çoruh River. The heavy waters running silty with snow melt were hurtling down the valley to meet the Black Sea at Batumi in Georgia. Sometimes it was easy riding right by the river's eroding edge. Sadly we saw plenty of garbage, for the moment trapped in eddies, but soon to be adding to the plastic soup in the sea – soft drinks bottles and take-away trays trapped amongst twigs.

At other times the road could not follow the devious ways of the river whose titanic force had made ways through defiles, cutting narrow channels through the rocks. Sometimes the banks were too unstable to keep hold of the road. Our thin strip of rough tarmac had to snake its way up the hillside, searching out the path of least resistance, only to plummet back down to the river again. Sometimes we looked down on the muddy waters, almost blending in with the surrounding colours of the banks and hillsides were it not for the swirling, foaming, patterns created as the water passed over the rocks on the river bed.

The stretch from Bayburt to İspir threw many challenging steep climbs our way, but it was inspirational cycling, inducing such a high that it gained a place in our list of 'Top Day Rides'. Spring flowers gave us hope of warmth to come – crocuses – yellow, pink and purple. A motor mechanic stopped his Renault and popped out to give us chocolate and cake. There was no traffic – nowhere much for traffic to go.

We rode into İspir, and stopped to think about what to do next. In no time a crowd of kids gathered round all waving and showing the 'thumbs up' sign. We took a day of rest, finding a spacious room with an extensive view of the snowy mountains. As we were settling in a tray of tea arrived. The next day Turkish flags were on display all over the town and a ceremony was going on outside the town hall. Every year on 18 March they celebrate the victory over the allies at Gallipoli, known as Çanakkale Zaferi (Çanakkale victory). We explored the remains of the twelfth century castle and the crumbling, but utterly charming houses in the old town.

As we followed the downward trend of the Çoruh we came upon more and more signs of the horrors being inflicted upon it. This beautiful river, considered by the World Wide Fund for Nature and by Conservation International as a biodiversity hotspot – called 'an eco-tourism gem' and 'Turkey's last remaining wild river' – promoted for its white-water as a wonderland for kayakers – is being destroyed piece by piece. Seventeen large hydroelectric dams are planned as part of the Çoruh River Development Plan and a total of 27 are proposed for the Çoruh River catchment. Some are already operational, some are under construction and some are still at the planning stage. It is in effect the rape, slow torture, and death of a very special ecosystem. There are 104 nationally threatened plant species in the valley of which 67 are endemic to Turkey. The area surrounding the river is rich in wildlife, including threatened red vultures, brown bear, wild boar, wolf, jackal, and pine marten.

It was when we left İspir that we noticed for the first time that the river was not running free. The wide expanse of silty, brown water reflected the mountains and the blue sky in its placid surface. We were on a stretch of new road – a well surfaced two lane highway which crossed an equally tamed tributary on a bridge of fresh white concrete. I now realise that we were witnessing the effect of the Güllübağ dam. Passing through the 605m Güllübağ tunnel we emerged into the cold shadows of a canyon where the waters ran free once more.

As the slopes eased, tiny villages clung precariously to the hillsides amongst the tall grey poplars – the trees still showing no signs of greenery. Narrow terraces were held in place with stone walls. The old houses, two or three stories high, were topped with tin roofs – the gables open to the air and the eaves overhanging wide. Perhaps this space was used for the storage of crops, but at the time it all looked empty. Were these places destined to be underwater or were they high enough up to escape? Would the people want to remain in this changed space anyway?

The valley broadened and flat fields tinged with green lay on the other side of the river. Pink blossom was emerging on low roadside almond trees. And then the valley narrowed once more, forcing the path on the opposite bank to hug the riverside cliff, stretching from ledge to ledge propped up on supports of rock and shaky wooden bridges, just a few feet above the torrent.

The road turned to grit as we approached a construction site; a new road was being built, higher up the mountainside, ready for the rising of the waters. The chaps working there were camping out in a hut, shaped like a polytunnel and perched on top of a small stone building. They had all mod cons – a hot tin stove, TV, gas range, fridge, freezer, roof insulation and ample food supplies. They knocked up a *kahvaltı* (breakfast) for us – an omelette with bread, butter, tomatoes, olives and cups of tea. Inside the place was all very neat and tidy. From the outside terrace we could see rocks disturbed by the construction shooting down the scree covered hillside creating white clouds of dust in their wake.

We followed a tacky dirt road further down the deep, precipitously enclosed valley – the apparatus of construction in action here and there. The bikes gained a coating of grit encased in red mud. Then, we hit the wall – all 114m of the Asku Dam. A dark, dripping tunnel hacked from the rock took us through the neat, steeply sloping wall of smooth concrete and out to a scene of pure devastation – scarred mountain sides and a valley floor filled with gravel works.

We wondered how this would all look when the job is finished.

As we approached Yusufeli the river regained its character, flowing swiftly along a flat valley floor covered in a patchwork of green and ploughed fields. Rickety bridges provided a tenuous link to the villages on the other side. Tall poplars were planted close to the river bank – their bare, pale branches lit up by the low evening sun. High west facing snow fields, ruined castles set against a bright blue sky and the sharp relief of the rocky hillsides glowed in the late afternoon sunshine. It was heart breaking to think of this inspiring scene becoming a watery grave for the plants and creatures living there, as the dam downstream slowly did its work and covered all that would be green in the spring and summer.

Yusufeli will be submerged by 2021 courtesy of the downstream dam of the same name, which at 270m will be Turkey's highest and the fifth highest in the world. The government is building a new town for the displaced – apartment blocks like those we had seen thrown up on the outskirts of many Turkish towns. Was the new-build we saw higher up the mountainside part of this development we wondered? Many people have signed up for the new homes but others are worried about how life might change in the new setting. Some locals say they prefer their current single family houses where they can 'grow every kind of vegetable and fruit in the gardens'. The *Turkish Daily* news of November 2018 quotes an 86-year-old resident of the town as saying, 'we have a nice time here having our meals on our balconies and rooftops. In the new settlements, in the new apartment flats, we will have neither of these.'

The current Yusufeli is relatively new: it was only in 1950 that it was given its present day status as a district of Artvin and a *bona fide* town. The citizens have been moved six times before – mostly because of wars and demarcation. But, it is not only the population of Yusufeli town (around 20,000) who will be affected. The project will directly affect around 15,000 people, mostly ethnic minority Georgians. Another 15,000 could also be indirectly affected. Another seventeen towns and villages around Yusufeli will also be completely or partially submerged and much archaeological heritage will be lost.

The new high level route which will snake around the sheer craggy mountains has been described as becoming one of the most scenic 'drives' in the world. No doubt, the views looking up will be spectacular, but, looking down, visitors will see a paradise lost. It will become a completely different manmade landscape of bare rocky mountains protruding above quiet, dead lakes. For those who previously came to Yusufeli to enjoy a river journey, said to be one of the most spectacular white water trips in the world; paradise was lost in 2011. That was the last year when the rafting and kayaking run from İspir to Yusufeli was possible.

Yes, we need energy, clean energy – but at what cost – and is this really 'clean' energy? All over the world we have seen rivers being messed with. Barrages all along the Mekong are decimating fish stocks on which the local people in China, Laos and Cambodia depend for their livelihoods. In Australia we had passed the Snowy Mountain power station at Khancoban which supplies 11% of the country's power. It is fed by a mammoth pipeline carrying water through the mountains from Jindabyne Lake which traps the headwaters of the south east flowing Snowy River, to the west flowing Murray River, where it is also used for irrigation.

We saw three huge pipes cutting a straight line through the mountainside forest. This really is messing with rivers. Further on the people of Dalgety were not pleased. Their once attractive riverside had become a damp river bed of vaguely connected stagnant pools, blocked by the alien weeds of the willow tree and other foreign plants. Here the Snowy River had been reduced to 1% of its former flow. This was then improved to a healthier 21%, but it was still hardly a vibrant river. In Sichuan, China the river beds are factories for sand and gravel extraction, active with constantly working machinery. However, in 2014 a successful battle was won to prevent dams being built on the Río Baker, one of Chile's mightiest rivers, which were threatening to put the farm where we stayed at Río Ñadis 18m under water. We have cycled along the river Loire which has been called the last wild river in Europe, being the only river in Western Europe that has not been canalised – although there are a few dams on its length, mainly for flood control.

Yes – I have given a very biased view of dam building which gives little weight to energy needs. However, when riding through these dam damaged

Sometimes we found ourselves to be the centre of attention.

regions and seeing first-hand the extent of the collateral damage, we could only feel the extreme loss to the natural world. We asked ourselves many questions. Where will the roads be re-routed – the terrain is so severe that the alternatives to the valley routes often look impossible? Won't it be a nightmare maintaining the new roads clinging to the rocky slopes? Will some villages become cut off or dead ends? What kind of place will the area be when it becomes a series of huge lakes with no flat, arable land – a rocky desert? How does the energy generated compare with the amount of energy that goes into construction and earth movement for building the dam and new roads? What will happen in 50-100 years when the dam has outlived its useful life? Seeing the work in process certainly makes you think about it.

Leaving Yusufeli we descended to our lowest altitude for four weeks – 500m. From here it would be up, more or less, all the way to just before the border with Georgia. At the confluence of the Çoruh and the Oltu Rivers we ascended the valley of the tributary. Machinery was gathered there ready for more re-moulding of the landscape. Ironically, a poster showing white water rafting was on display. The scenery was nothing short of spectacular; layers of rock were on show folded at crazy angles and the mountain ridges were a jumble of intricate cliffs, clefts and gullies; nature's mess is different.

Finally we had left the destruction behind – or so we thought. Our road climbed high for a bird's eye view of yet another dam, this time on the Oltu River. That night we camped in a newly blossoming walnut orchard; on the morning of the spring equinox it really felt like spring was coming. A man from the nearby hamlet, who now lives in İzmir, told us that this land will be flooded too. He said that the land is cheap – the people will be given some money to move elsewhere. He saw the barrage development as a good thing but said the people were sad to have to leave.

The next day our road gained height in a series of gentle undulations. We went in search of a wild mountain route from Paşali but part way up the dirt track a passing mini bus driver warned us that it was *kapalı* (closed). The deviation took us to a ruinous but fascinating little Armenian church – round in shape, views through open arches and interesting carvings on the ancient pillars. A young boy appeared and offered to be our guide. In the tiny village of Penek we were called for çay at the home of a lovely old couple; he told us he was 69 – there seemed to be no taboo about asking age. They offered us food and brought out bread and a type of dry stringy cheese that was extremely tasty.

In Akşar we bought provisions for dinner and went on up to look for somewhere to camp – upwards and back into winter. There was nowhere inviting to camp and what's more, as we neared the top of the pass at around 2,200m the ground was covered in at least a foot of snow. We were chased by a large pack of dogs near a military camp at the summit of the pass. Once clear of the barking we stopped to put lights on our bikes and clothes on our bodies. We found ourselves riding into Göle in the dark – dirty snow lined the streets. We thawed out in the simple but very comfortable Akçay Hotel and felt a lot better after a bit of grilled steak and some Efes (Turkish beer).

The road to Ardahan crossed a frozen wasteland where cracked ice sheets flowed along the river. It was late March – but winter is long in these parts. A sign saying Gürcistan (Georgia) gave us encouragement – we were close to the next country in line. In Ardahan we cleaned our bikes at a garage – but not before we had been treated to a cup of tea in a warm room. They gave us cloths for the job and made sure we got to the high pressure hose in front of a queue of white Ford Transit mini-buses. That sums up the Turkish people – invariably helpful and always ready with a cup of tea. They didn't want any money.

The next morning we got ready for an early start. We had to go. We had almost completed the crossing of Turkey – just one more stop in the town of Posof and then we would be crossing the border into Georgia. This is what we wrote in the blog at the end of the day:

> This was a crucial day, the day we had to get over the highest pass so far, on our final push towards the border with Georgia. Tomorrow the temperatures were forecast to drop and snow was expected – it had to be today or we may have found ourselves stuck in Ardahan – not a place you want to be stuck in.
>
> We got ready for an early start, and looking out of our window saw heavy snow falling – not good – but it stopped. Although the wind was strongly behind us for some of the way the climb was hard – a cross wind had us pushing for around 500m near the top. We passed several little settlements, a couple of small towns and a deserted tourist hotel which gave us shelter for a snack. Harsh places to live at over 2,000m.
>
> After a long, finger numbing descent we saw the town of Posof below us, above the riverbed on the opposite side of the valley. There were Georgian and Iranian lorries on the road and some kind of petroleum plant in a crazy spot high above the snowline. Posof wasn't the warm, green, utopia that we had imagined – it hailed on us as we wearily climbed the steep road up to the centre looking for a place to stay. The two little hotels were not appealing so we rode off down the street where we spotted an *öğretmenevi*. We had stayed in one before – they offer cheap and comfortable rooms. This one, like the other, was spacious, warm and well furnished. The only downside is that you have to wait for half an hour whilst the man in charge fills in a lot of information on-line (using one finger to type), which includes the name of your parents amongst other odd facts. However, tea and a comfortable chair are provided while you wait.

It was a day far too cold and windy for a lunch outside, although we have been known to lay our tarp on the snow for a picnic. We decided to stop at a garage where they often have a nice warm room to sit in, knowing we would be welcome. We were given sweet, milky Nescafé and made very much at

Finding a route past a ruined Armenian church at Penek.

home whilst we tucked into our bread and cheese. As we climbed higher the landscape became increasingly white. The road was clear for most of the way, with some slush here and there, and the high banks at the roadside were handy for parking when we needed to don more clothes. Nearing the top we were beaten by a ferocious cross wind – we had to stop and get off the bikes – and then when we managed to get riding again we were heading into a blizzard with zero visibility. The driver of the snow plough that went by appeared to be offering us a lift – but no – that would ruin the challenge. Finally, fantastically, we made it – up our last high pass and our highest in Turkey before the border with Georgia – the Ilgar Dagi Geçidi at 2,550m. Temperatures were dropping – a day later the pass would have been icily treacherous, snowbound and most likely, impassable. We had crossed the Anatolian Plateau in winter and it had been good.

The Visa Nightmare

*Fools must pretend to be wise,
we've a faith that we use as a heavy disguise.*

'Heavy disguise' from The Strawbs
album *Grave New World,* 1972

Hugh:

We left Posof heading to exit Turkey six weeks after our arrival and now it was so much colder despite being the last week of March. We had been lucky to escape the last of the winter's grip. Icicles hung long from eaves. We watched snowflakes fall and listened to a distant call from a minaret just visible through snow-laden trees. The mysterious sound was like a fond farewell from a country and people we had grown to love. The fields were covered in snow but we were on our way down, into Georgia and hoping for spring. Customs formalities were as easy as they get. One minute to leave Turkey and another to enter Georgia. Except for Kyrgyzstan, Georgia was the last country we would visit without the need for a troublesome visa.

We approached our first overnight stay at Akhaltsikhe through small country villages. We rode past an interestingly dilapidated collection of random and scruffy buildings with plenty of chickens in muddy yards and endless yellow gas pipes untidily positioned at the sides of roads. Churches and crosses replaced mosques and minarets. We had left behind the Ottoman red flag with a white star and crescent and were now frequently presented with the bold new flag of Georgia which was only adopted in 2004. The Georgian national flag is a white rectangle, with a large red cross in its centre touching all four sides of the flag. In the corners there are four small and slightly curved Georgian crosses of the same colour as the large cross.

After the familiar Latin script used by Turkey we now had to cope with an incomprehensible language written in an entirely unfamiliar but beautiful curvaceous script. First we learnt the name for coffee 'ყავას', and after our first night we could just about manage hello, thank you and two beers please.

We waved and called out *gamarjobaht* (hello) as we passed people. Sometimes they would respond and sometimes not – the women were more likely to smile and greet us. There were more women in the streets but the people looked glummer than they had in Turkey. Considering the state of the buildings many people lived in we could see why. Homes had a thrown together look, panes of glass missing, roofs falling apart and a lack of any finishing touches. However, we experienced lots of fantastic hospitality in our two week transit. We came to the conclusion that many people are shy and not quite sure how to respond to two foreign travellers on bikes.

Our route to Borjomi followed the gorge of the Potskhovi River. We passed

THE VISA NIGHTMARE

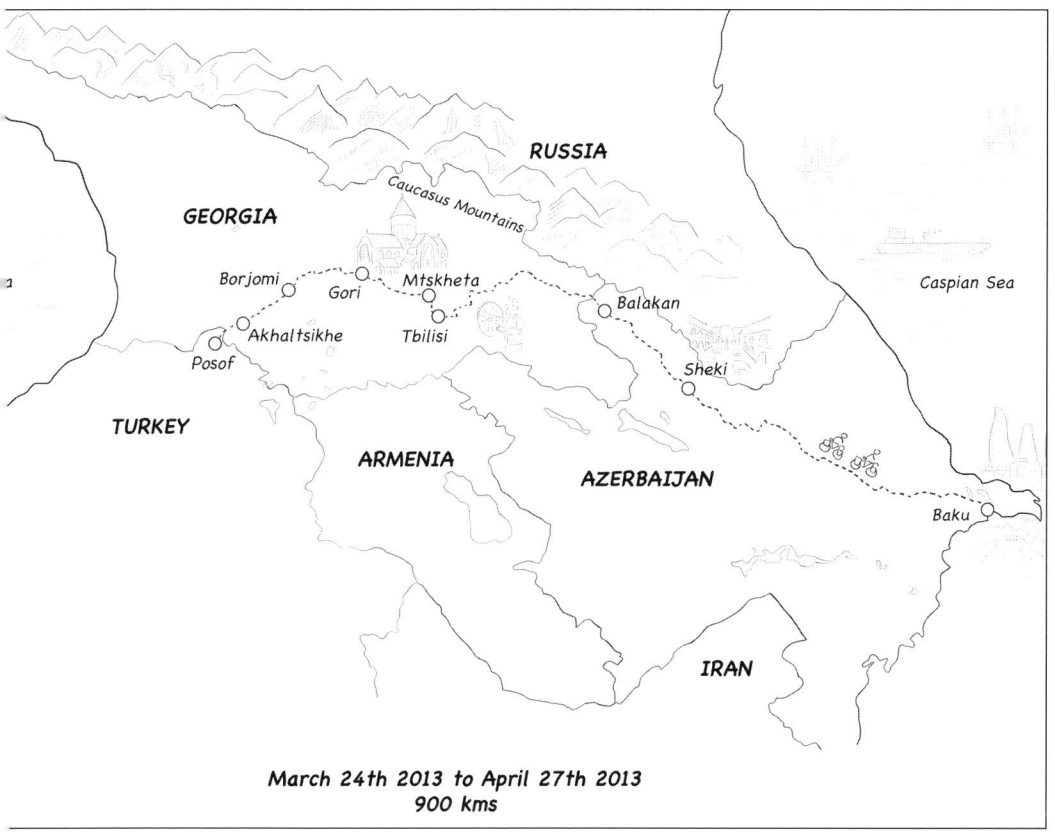

March 24th 2013 to April 27th 2013
900 kms

ruined castles on top of rock outcrops and then a really unusual sight appeared. The first cycle tourist we had met on the road during six months of travel. Jacques, from Paris, was on his way to Hong Kong on a recumbent. We chatted by the side of the road for an hour before parting in opposite directions, our routes being very different. Jacques was heading for Armenia and Iran whilst we were heading for Azerbaijan and the Caspian Sea. We were entering a complicated part of the world. French citizens could visit Iran with no threat to their insurance but that was not the case for British citizens in 2013. If you visited Armenia then access to Azerbaijan would be denied. Turkmenistan is another country which offers an option for transit to Central Asia, but the short term visa can be a nightmare for cyclists.

We cycled into Borjomi in mid-afternoon and were faced with the most dilapidated and depressing looking tower blocks we have ever seen – the Turkish apartment blocks were at least pretty smart. Fortunately we found a cosy homestay in a rustic timber-framed house with a spiral staircase and we were served homemade bread with homemade jam. Borjomi is a resort town, on the strength of its slightly salty mineral water which we filled our bottles with in the water park. The strong smell of sulphur nearly put us off until a nice chap informed us that it was good for health – but 'don't drink more than 300ml'. The canyon has been turned into a park cum playground, where you can take a cable car up to the ferris wheel on the top of the cliff.

Leaving Borjomi we followed the road down a well-populated valley, through rough villages, where cows and donkeys grazed by the roadside. Every so often there would be a restaurant, looking newly built and quite a lot smarter than the average roadside house.

Our road joined the M1 at Khashuri, and a nightmare began. Huge trucks thundered down the road at speed along with cars and vans, few of which took much notice of a cyclist. We got off as soon as we could after about 5km, where a turn off signed Tsromi led to a bridge over the river and a through route to Gori on the other bank. Peace at last and a chance of making it alive to Gori. The road took us through small villages, orchards and vineyards. People were at work in the fields. But then it became apparent that there was another threat to our journey besides fast moving heavy trucks. Looking down at my rear wheel I could see that it was no longer circular. It looked like the tyre had become displaced as it was bulging so we stopped to look and realised that the rim had failed. This is not supposed to happen to disc-braked bikes. There were two splits in the side wall both a few centimetres long. It was obvious that the wheel would not go much further without repair. It was difficult, but we tried to put the problem to the back of our minds until we reached the capital, Tbilisi, less than 150km away.

On arrival in the outskirts of Gori we stopped to ask a group of six teenage boys the way. They wanted one of our bottles but took 'no' for an answer and pointed us in the direction of the Stalin Museum. Gori is the birthplace of Joseph Stalin where he was born to a poor family in what was at the time part of the Russian Empire. Widely considered one of the twentieth century's most significant figures, Stalin was the subject of a pervasive personality cult within the international Marxist-Leninist movement, which revered him as a champion of the working class and socialism. Since the dissolution of the Soviet Union in 1991, Stalin has retained popularity in Russia as a victorious wartime leader who established the Soviet Union as a major world power. Conversely, his totalitarian government has been widely condemned for overseeing mass repressions, ethnic cleansing, deportations, hundreds of thousands of executions, and famines that killed millions.

We found a comfortable hotel near to the museum, parked the bikes in the garage glancing at my split rim and decided that we would pay Stalin a visit in the morning. Stalin – both a hero and a monster among men. Named Joseph Vissarionovich and then Stalin, man of steel, began training as a priest, wrote poetry, dabbled in illustration, and wrote tender caring letters to his mother in her old age. He transformed the Soviet Union into an industrialised society.

THE VISA NIGHTMARE

Having been imprisoned by the Tsar's government, escaping five times, he sent millions to labour camps and death. 'Uncle Joe' was crucial in the defeat of Hitler. In a sense Gori is proud of her hero.

An educated English speaking guide took us on a tour of the exhibits portraying his life, (useful as the explanations are in Georgian and Russian), as we slowly began to freeze in the grand, unheated rooms – perhaps in sympathy with the millions sent to Siberia. A black and white photograph showing the smiling faces of Churchill, Roosevelt and Stalin at the Yalta conference hinted at the esteem with which Stalin was held at the end of World War Two. A brief minute was given to his dark side followed by a short visit to some rough cellar like rooms giving a little of the story of his victims. Finally a visit to his bullet proof railway carriage and the house where he was born completed the tour.

In the afternoon we rode closer to Tbilisi and passed recently constructed homes for internally displaced refugees resulting from the conflict with Russia over South Ossetia in 2008. South Ossetia was only around 50km to the north lying on the southern slopes of the Greater Caucasus mountain range. Only a few countries, most notably Russia, which maintains a military presence in South Ossetia, recognize its independence from Georgia.

Our day became more cheerful as we rode into Mtskheta (მცხეთა) wondering how you pronounce five consecutive consonants. Georgia took to the Christian faith very early, after Rome and Armenia, and today it is very evident

Khvicha replacing Hugh's broken rear rim in Tbilisi (Georgia)

that much of the population of Georgia are practising Georgian Orthodox Christians. The Georgian Orthodox Church is one of the world's most ancient Christian Churches, founded in the first century. In the first half of the fourth century, Christianity was adopted as the state religion. This has provided a strong sense of Georgian national identity, despite repeated periods of foreign occupation. Mtskheta's Svetitskhoveli Cathedral, originally built in the fourth century, has been damaged several times during history, notably by the invasions of Arabs, Persians and Tamerlane, and latterly during Russian subjugation and the Soviet period. The building has also been damaged by earthquakes. Inside the cathedral, we saw a fresco where the faces of the women had been scratched out by Islamic invaders.

The present Svetitskhoveli Cathedral was built between 1010 and 1029. A notable reconstruction was carried out at the end of the fourteenth century after it was destroyed by Tamerlane. The next large renovation came at the beginning of the fifteenth century, when the current dome was built, being subsequently renovated again in the middle of the seventeenth century. The design is based on the cross-dome style of church architecture, which emerged in Georgia and became the principle style after the political unification of Georgia by Bagrat III (978-1014). The characteristic of this style is that the dome is placed across all four sides of the church. We found this and many Georgian churches, which are often built on hilltops, to be extremely beautiful.

Our day ended with a taste of Georgian gastronomy. Mushroom filled *khinkali*, a spinach and walnut paste, yoghurt in some kind of wrap and very garlicky chicken. *Khinkali* is a curious looking juicy type of dumpling traditionally eaten with the fingers. All this for about £8 each including good red wine. We grew to love the rich and deep red Georgian wines, Georgia being one of the oldest wine growing regions in the world.

A short ride along the banks of the river Mtkvari took us to the old centre of the capital Tbilisi. We found a charming room in a so called boutique hotel close to an interesting array of inhabited buildings which looked like they would crumble with a puff of wind let alone an earth tremor. Many of the buildings had washing strung out and ancient rusty cars parked by them often with flat tyres. We looked forward to exploring, but our priorities were to fix the wheel and to get visas for Azerbaijan.

Rezo, a night guard at our hotel embraced the challenge of fixing the wheel. This was incredibly useful as he took us around in his car, acted as interpreter and he knew where to go. The best bet appeared to be Xtreme – a shop specialising in outdoor stuff, including mountain bikes. On the way we spotted the encouraging words 'Bike Shop' above a small outlet, so we gave it a go – a very small place, no sign of a wheel jig and no handy rims with 32 spoke holes. Xtreme sold mountain bikes alright, but that was about it. They had one or two flimsy rims hanging around. Rezo then found us another place where there were lots of bikes on display – but yet again the chaps looked at our cracked wheel with glum, puzzled faces, offering no signs of encouragement. We couldn't even be sure that they knew what we wanted exactly – i.e. a good rim, spokes and someone to rebuild the wheel on my Rohloff geared hub!

So the last resort arrived – to try to mend it. Rezo took us to a garage where they fix cars and used the word 'prophylactic'. Yes, they seemed to know about how to weld an aluminium alloy rim – so far so good. Things didn't look quite so good when a heavy hammer was used in an attempt to realign the split parts. After a bit of grinding and welding we were hopeful. Black spray paint came out in an effort to make it look like new – we weren't too bothered about that, we just wanted it to work. Just as we were about to take it away, feeling rather apprehensive, we noticed fine cracks either side of several spoke nipples. So four of the spokes had loosened – blobs of solder were dropped over the cracks. The result – a bit of a hash of a wheel which wasn't true and which may or may not get us to Baku. There the situation was expected to be more hopeful as we had made contact there with a Warm Showers person who knew a good bike shop and there seemed to be some kind of cycle culture – a national team, cycle routes and the Azerbaijan Cycling Federation. So far in Tbilisi we had seen one cyclist!

It was April Fool's day and being a Monday when the Azerbaijan embassy was open we went to apply for visas. We stood hopefully, in a small queue at the side entrance, behind several Turkish people. At 10am a grim faced security guard appeared at the gate, opened it and dished out four page forms to those that wanted them. We filled one in each whilst sitting on a wall on the other side of the street – fortunately it wasn't raining – and then we went back to the queue. When our turn came, we were let through to the door of the embassy building, and we threaded the forms with our photos, passports and copies of our passports through the bars of the metal grill to the official behind, greeting him with a friendly *salam alaykum*. He looked at our papers and then uttered the dreaded words – LOI – 'letter of invitation'.

Having a very helpful Warm Showers contact in Baku, and a record of our email correspondence with him, we suggested to the chap behind the bars, who seemed to be warming to us, that we print out our exchanged emails. The emails clearly indicated that Cavid was expecting us, happy to host us, and receive our posted parcels and help us find a good bike repair shop. The official seemed to think this would be good so we went off to find a printer. Back at the embassy we were ushered to the front of the queue to hand in our 'LOI'. This time there was a different official behind the bars – unfortunately. However, after initial puzzlement he agreed to take our documents for dispatch to Baku. After five phone calls to the embassy and four days of waiting we got the news we wanted – we could buy visas. All that was needed were two more trips to the embassy – one to pick up a chit for payment of $118 each into the Azerbaijan bank in central Tbilisi and then another back to the embassy to pick up the passports with full page visa stamps.

EXTRAORDINARY PLACES BY BICYCLE

On the way back to our hotel we chanced upon a bike shop with a very helpful manager. Lado was on a mission to give as much help as possible to people such as ourselves travelling through by bike. He told us about Khvicha, the same guru mechanic that Margo Mactaggart had told us about in a message on our guestbook and – yes – we should have chased it up earlier. Such is the benefit of hindsight.

So off we went to the old velodrome. It is where cyclists of Tbilisi hang out. Khvicha told us he could get hold of two second hand rims with 32 spoke holes and if we returned the following day at 11am he could do the job for us. Exactly what we needed to hear. Just in the short journey to the velodrome the cracks around the spoke holes appeared to be increasing.

It turned out that Khvicha had the reputation of being the best bike mechanic in Georgia; in fact the president trusted him with his mountain bikes. He deftly unlaced the wrecked rim and replaced it with one which seemed almost new. Most of the original spokes were reused but it was useful that we had a few spare spokes and nipples. After half an hour the wheel was put on Pauline's bike as her total load was less than mine. Khvicha asked Pauline to do a few laps of the outdoor velodrome, a first! There were a few 'ping' sounds as the wheel settled in and then Khvicha finally tweaked the wheel for the road ahead.

In between visits to the velodrome, bike shops and the Azerbaijan embassy, we found time in our week in Tbilisi to explore and love the old city. Inside one of many churches we visited we heard some very special music. Three young ladies took it in turns to sing words from books in one corner of the church and the chants were handed to a group of young males who sang in harmony before a tall priest dressed in green robes appeared ringing bells and spreading incense whilst singing deeply. The harmonies rang around the church from different corners. It was a very beautiful sound. A little later we discovered how orthodox the Georgian church is. Being a warm afternoon, and having washed my only pair of trousers, I was wearing shorts. We were standing near the doorway of another church admiring the harmonic sounds when a priest came up to me and said 'problem' before physically pushing me out of the doorway. I became very self-conscious when wearing shorts in Tbilisi. They are taboo in churches.

By the river lies the stunning open air flea market at Dry Bridge. The wares were beautifully arranged on the pavements. In addition to great original art, the market has heaps of Soviet-era memorabilia, old costume jewellery, vintage furs, car parts, vases, tableware, wool felt, locally made ceramic beads, children's toys, old clocks, antique maps, original gramophones, out of print books, coins and much, much more. A little frustrating on a bike, that we couldn't take home portraits of Lincoln, Stalin or Putin, but we bought a handful of gifts to post to our children.

THE VISA NIGHTMARE

Picnic in Georgia

It felt wonderful to be back on the road again with our Azerbaijan visas and a working rim on the wheel. We enjoyed our stay in Tbilisi which grew on us over time and it was good to dine well and meet other travellers. Spring had arrived for sure now – lots of blossom, leaves poking out, warm sunny weather. We hoped that we were not too late to cross the upcoming desert without frying! We took the main road out towards the airport, and it wasn't too bad as for most of the way there was a quiet service road alongside it. When it gave up around the turn off to the airport we decided in the interest of staying alive, to get off. It was a delightful ride via back roads, much of it on dirt, to join the main road to Telavi near Ujarma. We savoured the comfort of our tent again having found a quiet off-road camp in the woods.

Continuing east we caught glimpses of the high and hazy white peaks of the Caucasus. Twice in Georgia we were beckoned to the side of the road to join field workers who shared their picnics but the ultimate picnic came just a few miles west of our next frontier. It was a Sunday afternoon and we were invited into a garden for a feast of barbecued kebabs and enormous flagons of wine which were on permanently flowing siphons. It was mid-afternoon and we were invited to camp in the garden for the night. Remembering our extended stay in Crete due to over indulgence we reluctantly decided to move on towards the border with Azerbaijan before we became incapable of riding our bikes in straight lines.

The frontier greeted us with the enormous sign 'Azerbaijan Border – Good

Luck'. Along with several Turkish trucks, we headed for border control. The Azeri border guards greeted us with smiles. They checked out the contents of some of my bags and seemed quite amused at what I had stashed away there. Mmmmm – lots of real coffee. The uniformed man in an enormous wide brimmed hat who took our photographs said welcome to Azerbaijan.

Not far down the road we stopped for a picnic and a young Azeri couple joined us to chat (she spoke good English) and take our photo. As we made our way through busy Balakan and beyond, many people waved, honked their horns and shouted out greetings. We felt very welcome in Azerbaijan. We saw none of the dereliction that had shocked us on our entry to Georgia and possibly coloured our impression of the country from then on. First impressions can indeed be lasting. New building is going on in this part of Azerbaijan – not characterless apartment blocks like those in Turkey, but nice houses. Sadly the drivers seemed every bit as manic as those in Georgia and there were plenty of them about either side of Balakan.

The return to Islam didn't shout out. We only saw a couple of small minarets and heard no call to prayer. We saw one woman dressed in obvious Muslim style. The women seemed less conservatively dressed than those in Georgia. There was no shortage of tight short skirts. The headscarf may be there somewhere around the neck, or tied bandana style around the head but there was no hiding of the hair here.

Both Georgia and Azerbaijan are small countries, similar in size to the Republic of Ireland, and it only took a handful of days to cover the 450km and reach the Caspian. We mixed wild camping with hotel stays and for our first night we found a secluded spot in woods well away from the dirt track road we had been riding. We had the company of tortoises and at dusk we heard frogs croaking and scops owls long hoots gave a luscious haunting sound. Intermittently we heard strange long cries in the distance – perhaps wildcats. It is surprising how often when wild camping in a secluded place, where you think nobody will find you, someone arrives at the apparent scene of stealth. Our immediate reaction when we saw an off-road vehicle approach was that we were going to be in trouble and that we would have to decamp. A man emerged from his car and beamed at us with a huge smile before giving us six litres of bottled water from his spring water plant in the next town. He urged us to enjoy the peace and to make use of a nearby shelter made of mud and sticks if we needed it.

A defining factor of travel east of Turkey is that there is often a predominant car on the roads. Here it was the rectangular Lada. In towns we passed garages full of them for repair along with old and battered buses. Street corners frequently had colourful posters of Heydər Əliyev – Azerbaijan's third President and something of a hero and former communist party chairman. In Sheki we found an old Silk Road caravanserai to stay the night. The huge stone and brick structure had two stories of scores of arches surrounding a quadrangle

THE VISA NIGHTMARE

Old and new in Baku (Azerbaijan)

of peaceful gardens. There are close to 600 individual rooms including the underground storage cells that merchants could access from their sleeping quarters by stepladder if they wanted to check on their goods during the night.

In 1988, after a period of abandonment, a number of these rooms were turned into basic guest accommodation and travellers once again started treading the stone paths of one of Azerbaijan's oldest accommodations. We enjoyed a rare treat of wifi and piping hot water.

Nearer to Baku the gradients became much steeper. We were reduced to gear one for a short spell. The mist robbed us of the views but the many roadside stalls were interesting. They sold honey, tandoor baked bread and fresh lamb, if you selected the one you wanted before the butcher's knife went in.

Just at the top of a long climb, we saw some young lads selling asparagus – dark green and very thin. Was it wild we wondered? Just as I was considering buying some one of the lads stood right in the way of my path and refused to move. I stuck to my line and he shifted but his mate had a go at stopping Pauline, grabbing the back of her bike. No way were we going to buy anything from them. They took their revenge by throwing stones at us as we crawled up the rest of the slope. This was so contrary to the hospitality we had received so far from the people here and the first time on our trip we had been ill-treated.

EXTRAORDINARY PLACES BY BICYCLE

We could feel the enormity of Azerbaijan's capital, Baku, well before we arrived anywhere near the core of the city. This had more than double the population of any other city we had passed through since Bruxelles six months earlier. We felt scared of the traffic but miraculously found our way to the street where Cavid lived. Warm Showers is a non-profit hospitality exchange service for people touring by bicycle. There are hosts in 161 countries. Unusually, the twenty year old Cavid operated his Warm Showers guest room in his mother's apartment. We felt a little uncomfortable at first but Cavid's mother warmed to us after a couple of days, particularly when I had cut back six months of beard growth to something looking a little less terrorist like. Indeed, at times on our one year journey I had been called a terrorist.

The contact with Cavid proved to be extremely helpful in offering a postal address for bicycle parts and for putting us in contact with other travellers who helped us find embassies for getting visas for three of the upcoming 'stans'. Our mission was to start the process of gaining visas. The complexities and misinformation were daunting as is just being in any new city on first arrival. However, the game was simplified enormously through our introduction to Guillain and Anna from France. They had arrived in Baku by bicycle a week earlier having left their start point in the Alps in July 2012.

They had also been introduced to Baku by Warm Showers host Cavid. Cavid didn't know a great deal about embassy locations or visa applications. However, Guillain and Anna were not daunted, and over a period of ten days, they sought out the locations of the embassies of Tajikistan, Uzbekistan and Kazakhstan. Their homework and experience saved us a lot of hassle and time. We met outside the KFC after midday and travelled by bus 88 with them to the top of the main hill above Baku. We changed to bus 5 and jumped off somewhere near the AEF Hotel and went to the embassy of Tajikistan where they collected their completed visas and we initiated the process. Meeting the consul at the Tajikistan Embassy was special. Now this is a polite way to gain a visa. Firstly admire photographs of the country which you want to visit and then write a letter to the ambassador saying why you want to visit Tajikistan and then complete a two sided document and hand over two photos of yourself, a photocopy of your passport and your passport. Return three days later and hope that you will gain the stamp (visa) of approval for a fee.

Following this we walked a mile to the Uzbekistan Embassy where we were given comfortable sofas to sit in whilst waiting our turn to meet the gentle comedian from Tashkent who sees you through the start of the process. An appointment was made for our return a few days later.

On our second visit to the Uzbek Embassy we listened patiently with smiles, whilst the official entertained us with his snippets of English and French literature and made little jokes relating to our names and dates of birth, and the decorations on the pages of our passports to which he added more 'paintings'. He talked enthusiastically about *al-jabr*, which sounded like an Islamic name, but then we realised he was referring to the founder of algebra who was born in Persia. We leant on the sill of the little hatch looking on our man at his desk at the far end of a large, finely furnished office. One must be patient and engage in the process. It wouldn't do to upset the person issuing the visa!

We managed to leave the embassy in time to get to the nearby Tajik Embassy. Once again we were ushered into the room with the huge polished table where the enticing picture books were laid out. By the time the official returned with our passports and visas we were totally enthralled by the beauty of his country. We were able to change the dates on our visas to create more overlap with the Uzbek ones, giving us more flexibility with crossing the border.

The whole affair took us around three hours – and that doesn't count getting the buses out there. There is no way they can process many applications at this pace. We saw only a handful of others at the embassies but each took an age! After all this we had run out of time to get to the final embassy, Kazakhstan. It proved quite easy to get their visa in the morning, but rather boring compared with the others. Not much more than apply, pay and receive. The embassy was extremely smart with some posh cars parked nearby including an Aston Martin. Some money just churns out of the ground in this oil rich state.

The challenge of moving on from Baku was far from over. There was the mysterious boat to Aqtau to catch. To improve our chances of boarding an un-timetabled boat across the Caspian, we had moved close to the boulevard at the sea front. From here we could see boats coming and going and importantly we could move to the port in less than ten minutes with a traffic free ride on the wide promenade fronting the Caspian. Emin, our hotel receptionist at the Old City Inn, was also invaluable in warning us when a boat was loading as he had a friend who worked at the docks. After three days which tested our patience, we heard the news of an imminent boat and not one to Turkmenistan where several foreign motorcyclists were heading.

Like Tbilisi, Baku had been a major staging post for us and we had found time to enjoy some of the city both ancient and modern and time to find a welder to fix a loose pannier rack bolt on my front forks.

The dominant feature of Baku is the Flames. This is a trio of curved skyscrapers with the height of the tallest tower standing at 182m. The three flame-shaped towers symbolize the element of fire – historically resonant in a region where natural gas flares shoot from the earth and Zoroastrian worshippers saw in fire a symbol of the divine. The buildings consist of 130 residential apartments over 33 floors, a Fairmont hotel tower that consists of 250 rooms and 61 serviced apartments and office blocks. The cost of Flame Towers was an estimated US$350 million. Construction began in 2007, with completion in 2012. The facades of the three Flame Towers function as large display screens with the use of more than 10,000 high-power LEDs which display moving flames and the national flag. They were particularly attractive at night.

On a more modest scale we spent time in the gorgeous museum of modern art and took a trip on a bus with Cavid to a large group of natural mud volcanos on the outskirts of the city. There are around 400 mud volcanoes in Azerbaijan, nearly half the world's total. They are usually found in areas rich in oil deposits. A slimy track led us up to a mini range of spluttering mud mountains. Little craters blow big bubbles up and send out flowing rivers of thick mud.

Finally on Friday 26 April after spending twelve days in Baku, we boarded a boat built in Croatia only the previous year. We were puzzled how the large boat could have reached the Caspian until after a bit of research we discovered that there is a canal system which links the Caspian to the Black Sea via the Volga River.

Our cabin was comfortable and the food was tasty. We looked forward to waking in the morning in the middle of the Caspian. We dreamt that the crossing was ultra-smooth until we went on deck before breakfast and saw that we were still staring at the Three Flames. We finally set sail at 8.30, enjoyed a full day on the boat with two other passengers and retired to our cabin for a second night. In the early hours of the morning I heard an anchor drop but we were not in the Kazakh port yet. Seventeen hours later there was a space in the port so we finally docked in Aqtau 55 hours after we first boarded the boat. We had moved 400km in a moving time of twenty hours. There was more officialdom from wide-brimmed hatted men, this time looking decidedly oriental. Having cleared customs at midnight we pedalled 10km in the dark to the centre of the city where we found a quiet corner of a park to put the tent.

The Worst Road in the World

If you don't go to very difficult roads, you will only reach places where everyone reaches.

Mehmet Murat ildan

Pauline:

A cycling blog we had read called our destination for the day 'Shit pee' – so we weren't expecting much. The town is actually called Шетпе (Shetpe). On the way into town a driver stopped to chat and as he left, he put four grand in Hugh's hand (4000 Tenge, around £16), driving off before we could protest! He also told us that there was nowhere to get water between Shetpe and the next town Beyneu, a distance of about 330km – he wasn't the only person who told us that, and it was just as well we didn't take them seriously or we would have been towing a trailer full of it for the next three or four days of hot riding.

Shetpe is a two day ride from Ақтау (Aqtau), the remote Kazakh city on the eastern shore of the Caspian Sea where the boat from Baku had landed us. Aqtau was created by the Soviets in 1961 and named Shevchenko – there is oil and uranium in the area. With the aid of a desalination plant and nuclear power station it acquired the basic necessities to support a fair sized population

April 30th 2013 to June 4th 2013
2600 kms

and around 200,000 people live there today. Its name changed after independence in 1991 – the current name means 'white mountain'.

Aqtau felt like a city on the edge of the world, virtually cut off from all around it including the other 95% of the country – Kazakhstan, the ninth largest in the world. On the west side it is hemmed in by the Caspian Sea, with the only connection by boat being the one we had taken from Baku in Azerbaijan. To the south is the border with Turkmenistan, where a single, very bad road crossing has been closed since 2018. In order to travel overland, to either the Uzbek border crossing to the east, or the rest of Kazakhstan to the north, you must go north east to the town of Beyneu, from where the two routes part. This was our link to the iconic cities of the Uzbek Silk Road. We were soon to find out what a tenuous link this is.

We had struggled to navigate our way out of the busy, sprawling outskirts of Aqtau – lots of new apartment blocks spreading over the sandy flat lands intermingled with newly planted trees to brighten the place up – but when the traffic thinned, shaggy camels and sleek and muscular, shiny coated horses became our roadside companions. We sped along the flat, roughly paved road with a warm wind behind us, little oil drills occasionally nodding at us from

What road?

THE WORST ROAD IN THE WORLD

Kazakh road worker

the land to the side. We had left with eight litres of water and then added five litres more from a shop along the road, ready for a camp in the surreal landscape of the desert where our only companions were tortoises. The next day the temperature rose from the mid-twenties to the low forties; it was fortunate that we passed a roadside café and a shop where we could quench our thirst. The undulating road took us through a landscape of white escarpments, passing through places of little consequence – a few scattered settlements and a larger village of low-lying single story houses. The dense, brick built necropolis on the high ground behind the village had the look of an old town in miniature with its high domed structures built inside walled enclosures and topped with symbolic spikes.

For all its reputation Shetpe didn't seem that bad in the dry sunshine but we couldn't help but wonder what sort of life people led in this far flung place. There were shops for fruit, vegetables and other essentials. We asked if there was a hotel. People gave incomprehensible directions and pointed, and after asking about three people we finally pinned it down. A comfortable enough room, a shower downstairs and a pit loo outside (water is scarce).

We went to the *КАФЕ* (café) next door for dinner. Unable to make much sense at all of most of the menu written in Cyrillic, we caught on to the words *shashlik* (kebabs) and *pilov* and ordered those – with draught beer of some unspecified type. We were really lost when it came to communication. As so often happens, they tried to phone a friend to help us out, but the friend's English wasn't much better than our Kazakh/Russian. We were still a bit peckish after our meal so we looked at the menu and saw a word looking suspiciously like dessert. The young lady seemed to indicate that only one of the three options was on offer – simple I thought – we'll have that. She came out with two Snickers bars!

In the morning we bought *ayran* from the ladies in the curious little bazaar – not like the Turkish version but with a slightly fizzy taste which I found unpleasant. It came in a big bucket which was then decanted into recycled plastic bottles. Such a cheerful bunch of women – some dressed in colourful, patterned tunics and others in velvet coats with golden, appliquéd patterns decorated with sequins around the cuffs and front edges. They wore soft white headscarves edged with lace – wide, etched silver bands and rings – and golden earrings. All such a contrast to the rather drab architecture of the town, meshed in a forest of electricity and telephone cables, lampposts and pylons.

Our first two days in Kazakhstan was a taste of what was to come – but it wasn't the full strength flavour. We had done the easy bit: the road had been paved, if a little broken at times and there had been places to get essentials fairly frequently. The road we were about to follow had a terrible reputation – called 'the worst road in the world' by one blogger and 'the bicycle destruction Derby' by another. We set out for Beyneu, around 350km away, knowing little for sure about where we would find food and water. We knew there would be tea houses but we had no idea where!

We left Shetpe with eleven litres of water and most of the food we would need for four days. After 29km we reached a *chaihana* (tea house) where we found food and we managed to find out that there was another, 40km further on. We didn't know if we would make it that far so we loaded up another ten more litres of water. Our thermometer was reading 47°C, in the sun – and we were riding in the full sun. We did reach the next *chaihana* and took on another six litres of water. In all during that day we took on board 27 litres of water – some to use at camp and some to get us to the next *chaihana* the following morning. That is a lot of water. Fortunately there are few hills on the road to Beyneu.

At our first tea shop on the next day we got chatting to a Kazakh working for Schlumberger. He could speak some English – he had worked offshore from Aberdeen. He taught us how to say, 'how far to the next tea shop?' in Kazakh – essential information in these parts. However, when we tried it out at the next tea shop we were given the distance to Beyneu! Fortunately our friendly Kazakh turned up again and rescued us.

All along the way to Beyneu we bought water – usually in five litre bottles but sometimes in chilled one and a half litre bottles – glorious at the time but they didn't stay chilled for long. Sometimes we filled up from a tap and once from a well. The *chaihanas* supplied water for hand washing at little stand alone basins.

Fifty kilometres out of Shetpe the tarmac ran out. Luckily it was just hard baked earth and dust. By a miracle of good fortune we had hit this route at just the right time – after the tracks have dried out following rain. It doesn't rain much in this part of the world but when it does the route becomes a mud bath, impenetrable on two wheels. A few puddles lingered in the hollows.

The roads became a bit of a free-for-all. Often there was a straight made-up, gravel road, but no vehicles were on it as the surface was a complete nightmare. Vehicles chose their own path, and the result was the equivalent of uncontrolled footpath erosion in our hills at home. A mesh of hard baked dirt tracks twisted like tangled wool by the sides of the actual road and we just looked for the best line – dodging the humps and holes and trying to keep on a different line from the trucks which threw up clouds of fine dust. It wasn't bad at all on two wheels. The road is in the process of being 'improved' and now and again we found short stretches of smooth, dark asphalt stretching across the plain – empty because they were not officially open yet and there was no suitable access for motor vehicles. On a bike we could just dodge around the barriers and enjoy moments of fast, easy pedalling.

On the second day out of Shetpe, the road took us up onto a vast, featureless plain with a sparse carpet of rough, dull green, prickly vegetation – the occasional flower boldly standing out of the hard cracked earth. As with the Nullarbor, the view to the horizon changed only in subtle ways. There was no problem finding a place to put up the tent in this huge empty space where one spot was pretty much like any other – perhaps a little bit of more interesting vegetation here and there. One night we realised we had camped between two of the spaghetti like tracks when we saw trucks passing on either side of us! We loved these camps. As the sun set in the evening, reddened by the distant dust, our shadows stretched across the land and the temperature dropped into the comfort zone.

During the day we could withstand the heat whilst moving. The cooling effect as the bike pushes through the air is enough to make all the difference – we call it 'air conditioning for free'. Once we stopped though, it was very different. How to have a picnic? There were no trees! We found shade at *chaihanas* and once or twice by ruined buildings. At one point we sat in the meagre slender shade of a roadside pylon, shifting as the line moved with the sun. This was not the hottest time of year but it was hot enough!

The *chaihanas* were filled with truck drivers – a great bunch of intrepid workers enabling Eurasian trade. Many were working for the German road haulage company, Willi Betz. Sometimes, when they took a break, we stopped for a chat. One Latvian driver said it would take him eight days from the border of Turkmenistan to reach Riga in Latvia. We knew they wouldn't see us stuck if we got into difficulties and they often threw cold drinks to us.

The Kazakh road workers were equally friendly, although they looked like aliens with their faces completely covered to protect against the dust – a couple of holes covered by dark glasses allowed them to see. When we could see their broad smiles, a flash of gold teeth would sometimes glint in the sunshine.

On the final day's ride into Beyneu there were two surprises. A small boy of around seven or eight popped out of a hole dug into the slope of the hard earth – like a giant animal burrow but with a wooden cage roofed with mesh netting above it. In his hand he held a bottle of *ayran*! Then we crossed the River Manasht – no more than a small stream slimy with green algae, but nevertheless it was flowing – very slowly! We drank our fill of water and poured the rest over our parched bodies before riding into town past a herd of camels and a wedding celebration at some roadside yurts. A little later, in conversation with a Kazakh about our return home for our daughter's wedding in September, we found he was mystified by the small size of our guest list – around 30 close relatives and friends for an intimate celebration in Southern France. A Kazakh wedding typically has around 400-500 guests!

After days of riding through the dusty, uninhabited steppe, it was a relief to get to Beyneu – relief yes, but it came with a sense of achievement. It had been hard work covering around 80km a day as the road was bad – but we had seen worse! There was none of the loose gravel, corrugated by the passage of speedy four wheel drive vehicles that had shaken us to pieces in Bolivia, which at times had made riding impossible. It is incredible that it took us six days to ride to the next significant town that connects with Aqtau on the Caspian Sea – Aqtau's only link with the rest of Kazakhstan. In between there is only Shetpe, a few tiny villages, and the essential *chaihana* which make it all possible.

By the time we reached Beyneu we had been travelling for over seven months and it was the first reasonable sized place we had come to where we were unable to find wifi. However, contrary to what we were told by many people, we eventually found a sort of internet café where we could pay for the use of two computers to update our journal. We were travelling with a small Samsung laptop on which we wrote our diary for the day and selected the pictures for the journal – battery power permitting.

However, there was no shortage of good provisions for the next stage of the journey – dried fruit and nuts in abundance at the local bazaar. On the fruit and vegetable stall there were bags of what looked like lumps of dry, grey clay for sale – was this something to eat we asked? Yes – edible earth! Hugh tried it and found it tasted just what it looked like – mud! It appears to be a traditional practice in many parts of the world – an ancient spiritual and healing system.

THE WORST ROAD IN THE WORLD

Camping on the steppe

We weren't sufficiently convinced to warrant stuffing our panniers with bags of clay! In the supermarket we found all the necessary basics including a huge variety of different oats – our essential breakfast cereal. We also found Guillain and Anna, the couple who had helped us so much with the convoluted process of getting our visas in Baku. It is amazing how often travelling cyclists meet again and again in these far flung, largely empty lands. The route choices are few, as the road networks form a thin mesh, full of huge holes over the terrain so people come together at the inevitable bottlenecks. We went out together for a meal of *shashlik* and *pivo* (skewered meat and beer) which had been a bit of a tradition for us all in Baku.

Beyneu isn't exactly a tourist destination but there were little things that we found interesting, along with the market and edible clay. Walking around town we saw young girls returning from a parade, wearing smart blue, brass buttoned jackets with matching pleated skirts. They wore, startlingly white blouses with frilly collars encircled by a band holding thin blue ties. Sashes with waist bands, decorative tassels, blooms of mesh fabric, knee socks, berets and gloves – also all in white – completed their outfit. They looked so smart with their neatly combed and plaited dark hair. A musician dressed in a baggy grey, collared jacket sat on a stone covered by a cushion of sacking, playing haunting tunes on the two stringed dombyra. His beautifully decorated lute had a long, thin neck which he rested upon his knee as he played. A herd of mud coated camels strode through the town in the late afternoon.

The hotels in the centre of town were most unappealing but we found a large, comfortable room with extravagantly decorative curtain hangings in a place on the edge of town.

After Beyneu we would soon cross the Uzbekistan border, heading for what we hoped would be some of the great gems of our journey. Way back in 1974 Hugh had given me a book for Christmas – *To the Back of Beyond* by Fitzroy Maclean. I had never read it, until shortly before this journey, when I took it from the bookshelf and was soon transfixed by tales of eastern lands I knew so little about. Sometimes there is a 'right time' for a book – I was inspired.

I thought to myself, wouldn't it be just wonderful to set out from home one day on fully laden Roughstuffs and see where we could get to? Travel across the greatest land mass on earth through those mysterious Central Asian kingdoms of the Silk Road – the land of Genghis Khan and the Golden Horde. Ride through four 'stans', the ex-Soviet republics where The Great Game was played out. Visit the ancient oasis cities of Samarkand, Tashkent, Bukhara and Khiva, once centres of great riches. Travel the lofty Pamir Highway on the edge of Afghanistan and reach the wild rolling empty lands of Mongolia.

For sure, it wouldn't all be so romantic. Problems with border crossings, visas, possible unrest and extreme temperatures would all make for a challenging trip with its dull, desperate and uncomfortable moments but surely it would all be worthwhile – providing we made it to the other side! Hopefully the days of snatching travellers to sell as slaves and displaying the heads of the enemy on sticks around the city walls were now over. People had ridden out there – I had read about them on *crazyguyonabike*.

And so, here we were in Beyneu, 224 days after leaving home, having triumphed over the challenge of crossing Turkey in winter snows and the complexities of securing visas for our route through Azerbaijan, Kazakhstan, Uzbekistan and Tajikistan. We had coped with, and perhaps even enjoyed, the isolated, dusty, hot road over the steppe and we were just over a day's ride away from Uzbekistan, home to the remarkable blue tiled cities of Khiva, Bukhara and Samarkand all of which we intended to visit. It would take us four days to reach the next place, Kungrad in Uzbekistan. This road also came with a health warning. A fellow blogger talked of ferocious headwinds, horrendous sandstorms, impossible road surfaces, over-zealous customs officials, huge physical demands and mental torture.

Why would we ride this road, particularly when we could get there on a train in a painless twelve hours or so? This has tempted many a cyclist. Indeed we could have got a train all the way from Aqtau! So – why not? Well, there is something important, magical even, about the purity of the continuous journey although we do admit that this doesn't apply in the same way to boats – after all, we can't ride on water. Unless prevented by injury, bicycle breakdown, visas running out or the police, we will ride. Illness and injury has stalled us but we have always got to somewhere we can rest. Our bicycles have been very tough but we have had threatening breakdowns – but we have managed to do DIY repairs or get to somewhere where it can be fixed. But, we have been forcibly shifted by the police – a story to come later. We were keen to get to the Uzbek border to maximise the use of our 30 day visa – it is a wide country to cross and there would be much to cause us to linger.

And so we left Beyneu with 26 litres of water, riding along a good asphalt road and wondering what all the fuss was about. We passed curious little white dried up lakes – salt perhaps – camels, sheep and workers with plant presumably working on making a proper road. The road followed a straight line, over tiny rises, each one giving more or less the same view. It was hot and dusty. There was a little traffic – trucks from Uzbekistan, Kazakhstan, Latvia, Russia, Turkey and some with letters BY on them which we couldn't work out (we later discovered that BY stands for Belarus). Kazakh and Uzbek cars passed.

After 58km we reached the village of Akzhigit where food and water were available – but we had enough of both. Then the road surface began to break up revealing wheel trapping re-bars. When we got to within 13km of the Uzbek border we decided that being shaken around in the hot sun had taken its toll, so we put up our tent – once more on the hard baked, cracked earth of the featureless steppe – and watched the sun set behind gathering clouds.

The next morning, on the way to the border, a Dutchman passed by on a Royal Enfield heading for the motor bike's home in Nepal. At the customs point there was a long queue of trucks waiting, the drivers standing around chatting. We skipped right to the front of the queue where we were kept waiting for ages whilst a young guard with an AK47 patrolled the other side of the huge iron gates. Then he let us through (before anyone else) and we were shunted around the grubby and tediously slow working border control operations. It took us two and a half hours to cross. The area of dusty earth around the crossing point was covered in trash and Uzbek people sold bottles of water and sold drinks from tatty old vans parked by the roadside.

Then just as we realised that we had no Uzbek money, we were accosted by a human ATM – Absolutely Truckloads of Money. A group of young men holding fistfuls of Uzbek Som gathered around Hugh. Hugh's exclamation of 'Oh my God' was immediately parroted back to him with more than a hint of jocularity. Hugh declined the first five rates of exchange offered until a good deal was struck at about 50% higher than the first offer and about 10% higher than the XE currency exchange rate quoted on the internet.

He was handed thick wads of notes – impossible to check, and impossible to fit into a wallet! He stuffed the notes into an empty dry bag. The highest denomination note was 1,000 Som, worth about 30p ($0.40). At the next *chaihana* we disposed of 18,000 (around £2.50 each) to pay for our lunch. At this point it became clear why the usual ATMs are rare in this country – they would need a safe the size of a room to store all the notes! The only ATMs were in the capital, Tashkent, and we didn't go there. Throughout Uzbekistan we exchanged cash dollars obtained at the bank for big bags of Som from street exchange gangs.

At the border village we found another essential commodity – water at a well. This is what we wrote in our blog about the first hours of cycling in Qaraqalpaqstan, the elaborate name of the autonomous republic of Uzbekistan which we had just entered.

> The temperature had dropped by around 10°C making for perfect cycling conditions. We sped along at top speed when the road surface permitted (it was mainly reasonable tarmac but with some rotten patches) and covered a good distance. The road shot into the distance – dead straight – I can't remember a single bend that day. There must be something longer than the Aussie 90 mile straight out here, but I haven't been counting. Little changed – the land became a little more arid, the occasional train ran like an ultra-long centipede along the track to our right and the odd lorry went by released from the barrage of the customs. It was pure cycling – a constant spinning of the wheels in the same direction, and with the wind making it so easy, even with a load of water on the back, it was good.

There was pretty much nothing in the 155km between the border village and the next village of Jaslyk which we passed through the next day quite early. So once again, we pulled off the road at a random spot and camped out on the flat steppe – something we had come to love. We watched the sun dip below the horizon and listened to the curious sounds of the night. The lights of the odd truck passed by on the distant road.

The next day was a National Holiday in Uzbekistan – celebrating the Russians clobbering the Germans at the end of the Second World War. The only evidence we saw of the occasion was on the TV in the *chaihana* displaying the grand show of military strength at the parade in Moscow. Churchill's photo appeared in a historical clip and a sombre faced Putin appeared for real in the Red Square.

In fact we saw very little all day – never had we ridden so far (131km) and seen so little change. The sky was the most variable aspect of the landscape and by dusk it had clouded over almost entirely, just leaving a thin line of brilliant red on the horizon as the sun set. I found myself wondering what would become of our camp if it rained – would the hard baked mud become a shallow waterlogged lake? A lorry driver stopped and told us that two cyclists were 10km ahead – we expected it was the French pair Anna and Guillain and we wondered if we would catch them the next day?

On the fourth day out of Beyneu we expected to reach relative civilisation in Qonghirat (Kungrad) and perhaps a hotel for the night with a shower. Passing once more over a great expanse of nothing with little to break the monotony apart from a huge open cast mine near Elabad, we reached smooth tarmac which took us swiftly towards anticipated comfort and a celebration of our triumph over the challenge of the steppe. Our first sight of Qonghirat was of the extensive, mud brick necropolis, tumbling down a small hillside topped with a blue domed masterpiece. The town itself was much less impressive having none of the comforts we were seeking and hardly worth the difficulty of access! A chest height, concrete barrier down the length of dual carriageway cut off our access to the turn off! We had to lift all our bags off the bikes and haul everything over the wall – just as the local cyclists were doing – only to repeat the process when we found that the only hotel in town was a pretty miserable place with no shower. This was not yet the time to celebrate our crossing of the empty lands!

Hugh found a secluded spot to camp just down the road on some strange white coated terrain which he was pretty sure must be salt, but I was not happy knowing that the cotton crops in the area were sprayed with all sorts of nasty chemicals and I didn't want to camp amongst it. A bit of an argument followed but Hugh won out because I had to accept that there was no other option. Throughout the night we heard curious sounds of life and howls that sounded like hyenas, which we took as a good sign that we weren't camping on poison. Our recuperation and celebration would have to wait until the next day when we reached Nukus, the capital of Qaraqalpaqstan around 100km away.

We set out along the divided dual carriageway, threading our way in-between a herd of skinny, horned cows walking in the opposite direction. They weren't the only road users going the wrong way. Locals walked nonchalantly down the centre and many stopped to chat over the concrete barrier. We wondered what the people with a mule and cart did if they wanted to cross to a track on the other side.

Just before Nukus we crossed the Amu Darya River, perhaps better known by its Greek name, the Oxus. The river – or what if anything is left of it, after the extraction of most of its water for irrigation – flows into the Aral Sea; technically not a sea but a 'terminal lake with no outfall'. It was once the fourth largest lake in the world. Becoming terminal in more than one sense, it had shrunk to a tenth of its former size by 1997 splitting into four lakes and by 2010 it had almost dried up. The region, which is also heavily polluted, has been called 'one of the planet's worst environmental disasters'. The valley of the Amu Darya is the most habitable area of Qaraqalpaqstan; the republic mainly consists of wilderness.

Nukus is the home of an important, curious and fascinating museum. The Savitsky Karakalpakstan (Qaraqalpaqstan) Art Museum houses one of the most important art collections in the former Soviet Union. Savitsky was an artist born in Kiev. He lived in Moscow and then fell in love with Qaraqalpaqstan when he visited the land as an illustrator for an archaeological expedition in 1957. He became the official curator of the museum in Nukus, housing a collection of Karakalpak artefacts. Then by various interesting means involving help from his friends he managed to assemble the works of Central Asian artists and then Russian avant-garde artists. Because of the remote location of the city, in those times virtually cut off from the rest of the world, he managed to amass works by artists who were forbidden, repressed or forgotten by the Soviet Regime – artists producing works not judged to be pro-Soviet in some extraordinary way. The huge collection of over 85,000 items includes works by Russians influenced by French impressionists and also items of Karakalpak folk art. The collection of paintings depicting picturesque fishing villages by the Aral Sea was particularly moving now that the area has become a dusty dry sea bed in one of the most dramatic man-made disasters ever to have affected the earth.

We wandered around the exhibits with fellow cyclists Guillain and Anna who we had bumped into yet again at the Jipek Joli Inn. They left that day and we hoped to meet again in a couple of days' time in Khiva. We headed off to find some money. If you want Som the bank isn't the place to go! We went to the bazaar and before long the people we needed found us. For our two, hundred dollar notes we got more than a fistful of 580 notes in Som from a very friendly bunch of guys. We didn't count every one – we just counted a random sample of two bunches and checked that the rest looked about as thick! We got our 'black' Som for the equivalent of 25p for a thousand rather than the rate of 30p at the bank. We then headed off into the market to spend a bunch or two. The problem with Uzbek money was that you can't get too much at once because it just takes up so much room!

Markets are often full of intriguing treasures. We found pastries which reminded us of Italian Cannoli – until we tasted them – they were filled with a kind of confectioner's cream rather than ricotta cheese. There were deep piles of noodles Uzbek style, like super long tagliatelle and flat, circular breads with floral and spiral patterns stamped on one side.

There was only one way to leave Nukus – on the main road carrying too much traffic across the arid sandy terrain. After a picnic in some shady trees by a deserted service station, we took off on a side road to Mangit, taking us less than 2km from the border with Turkmenistan – a country we would not be visiting although some intrepid cyclists do.

Boats go from Baku in Azerbaijan to Turkmenbashi in Turkmenistan as well as to Aqtau in Kazakhstan. Riding independently across Turkmenistan involves bashing across the country in the five days allowed by the transit visa – the desert dash. The 550km ride can be done in five days – it is flat – but that leaves little leeway for sightseeing or coping with the probable headwinds. Tempting though it was to visit this obscure country, we decided we didn't want the threat of being fined and deported if we didn't make it!

The rest of our day's ride passed through pleasant and fairly tidy farming country – big newly ploughed fields, acres of wheat and small household plots. We were following that strip of habitable land watered by the Amu Darya River. Large bill boards in the fields displayed what appeared to be propaganda posters showing flashy modern machinery, colourful produce and towns with shiny new tower blocks. In reality the workers were bending over the land using basic hand tools to plant and hoe.

It was flat, but it was hot. Little trucks loaded with gravel and earth plied the road chucking out smelly dirty fumes and churning up the dust at the side of the road. We ran low on water and found getting directions to a shop pretty difficult with our lack of language and with vague arm waves in response. However, later on we saw lots of people at little drinks stalls at the roadside, sat on their chairs next to fridges cum cool boxes, displaying gory coloured soft drinks.

A widely travelled cycle tourist (Alastair Humphreys) once wrote that you know when a country has a dodgy government when pictures of the leader are staring at you from bill boards everywhere. In our first couple of days in the country we hadn't seen any of that but we had already noted plenty of other tell-tale signs we felt would be worthy of listing. Internal road blocks in random places with far too many military/police officers hanging around; a currency which needs a special machine to count the notes when you pay the bill in a supermarket; petrol stations which are often closed with covers over the pumps; officials forbidding photos for no discernible reason and the need to collect registration slips to prove where you have stayed and to be presented on leaving the country.

We spent the night camped on the edge of a wheat field, hoping that the irrigation system wouldn't come on before we left in the morning. We moved on past tidy little bungalows with corrugated iron roofs and satellite dishes – many with neat rows of vegetables growing in their gardens. As we rode along the cracked paving the locals pedalled alongside us, old and young, kids with passengers – all waving and smiling. Children on a mule cart sat on a bed of hay and waved cheerily. We passed homes with intricately decorated brick work – patterns and symbols etched on the surface – and with clay tandir bread ovens looking like great pots, standing in the neat gardens. Women with colourful headscarves tied around their heads and wearing brightly coloured matching tunics and loose pants were working or resting in the little vegetable plots.

Children in neat black skirts and bright white blouses chatted on their way to school. This was our first experience of everyday rural Uzbek life and its people. We loved these parts of our journey, which took us through places not skewed by tourism – where you are just witness to the ordinary lives of the folks who live there and you are treated like a welcome visitor rather than a source of income. The journey across the largely uninhabited steppe was of a different world altogether. And now, we were on the doorstep of the first of those great Uzbek cities of the Silk Road which we would visit on our route through Uzbekistan – Khiva.

When Hungarian traveller, Arminius Vambery, visited Khiva in 1863 he was greeted by the sight of eight old men lying on their backs having their eyes gouged out by the Khan's executioner. In between operations he wiped his knife clean on each of his victim's beards. Similar gruesome treatment was handed out to punish slack slaves – their masters preferring to cut off an ear or gouge out an eye rather than waste their investment by killing their 'property'.

Today we were greeted by the magnificent sight of the city's minarets, mosques, madrassas and mausoleums – the brilliant blue and green tiles decorating the domes and facades glowing in the sunshine. For us it was a very moving and significant moment on our journey as we entered through the west gate and followed the line of the plain, adobe walls of the old city which towered above us and contrasted sharply with the intricately patterned architecture crammed into this tiny ancient city. It brought tears to our eyes to think that we had come all this way from home, a journey of nearly 10,000km taking us 231 days. However, it had taken Jon – a Kiwi living in London – just 30 days to reach Khiva! He was on the way to Cambodia. We spotted him standing by his British registered Toyota Landcruiser sporting a red T-shirt with an emblem stating 'say yes more'.

It was so easy to understand why the Englishman, Christopher Aslan Alexander, fell in love with the city whilst working there on a guide book in 1988. Known simply as Aslan in Khiva, he was adopted by a local family and decided to stay. He was born in Turkey, at one end of the Silk Road and brought up in war torn Beirut. An interesting thread of circumstances led him into carpet design and he set up a carpet workshop within the alcoves of an old madrassa. The story is told in his excellent book, *A carpet ride to Khiva*. We had just completed 'a bike ride to Khiva' and were enjoying the thrill of the achievement.

We found somewhere to stay and then headed straight for Aslan's carpet factory. He employs workers, mainly women, many of whom would otherwise find it difficult to get work – some of them handicapped in some way. We watched four women working on a carpet which would take eight months to complete. The piece, measuring 2.6m by 3.6m would sell to someone wealthy for $7,500 – cheap at the price considering the hours of skilled work which goes into a hand-made carpet. We were shown some of the old miniatures (illustrations) of the Timurid period. Aslan was inspired to bring to life some of the carpet designs depicted in the images. The dyes used to create vibrant reds, golds, blue and more are all natural. In manner redolent of ancient trading methods, Aslan made hot, dusty and potentially treacherous journeys to Mazar in Afghanistan, in order to procure ingredients of quality at a good price in the markets – madder root, oak gall and zoq! How we would have loved to take one home – but not on a bike! Aslan, also set up the Suzani Centre where the women embroider cushion covers and table cloths using silk thread. They are based on the same designs as the carpets and sell well being more within the average tourist budget. We bought a sample as a memento – not too cumbersome to carry home.

Once again we bumped into Guillain and Anna and over dinner we learnt a little more about them. Incredibly this was their first bike tour – what a route to choose! They hadn't done much cycling before. It isn't that rare for young people to embark on a bike tour with very little experience and some do it on a stunningly low budget.

The next day we spent hours wondering the streets amongst foreign and Uzbek tourists, locals and tour groups (lots of French), admiring the intricate carved doorways and pillars and taking in the views from many different angles. We found the turbaned, bearded figure of al-Khwārizmī, a Persian mathematician who lived from around 780 to 850, who is considered to be the inventor of algebra. Dressed in a loose robe the statue depicted him seated on a large stone block studying a manuscript. We climbed to the high points on the city walls to take in the whole picture and cooled down in the shade of exquisitely decorated courtyards. The places where students once studied the Koran or Khans once lived in their palaces are now often hotels, shops or cafés; some are quirky museums, and although exhibits of ancient costumes, weapons, stuffed wildlife and traditional instruments can be interesting to see there is not much helpful information to enlighten the visitor.

We found real coffee in the tourist cafés and inexpensive tasty *shashlik* in the little stalls just outside the east gate where we joined the fat mammas tucking into fatty kebabs and strawberries. Apart from being an architectural wonderland, the old city is clean, tidy and free of traffic. The Uzbeks, clearly used to a fair dose of tourists, showed no signs of being wary of us and were exceptionally friendly and helpful. Older women were out chatting as they hunted for bargains on the market stalls, dressed in almost ankle length, loose, gathered tunics and pretty patterned headscarves tied under the chin or round the back of the head. Many young women were wearing pretty, fitted cool dresses. There was no strict cover up in operation for women – one benefit of the Soviet era which promoted equal rights – and we were able to visit the mausoleums and mosques wearing our shorts, much to Hugh's relief. Attitudes to dress were far more relaxed here than in Tbilisi where Hugh was ordered out of a church for wearing shorts.

We had reached this gem of Central Asia after nearly two weeks of riding from Aqtau, much of it over sweltering semi-desert with camps on the open steppe. We now had three long days of similar riding ahead of us to reach the next jewel of the Islamic world, Bukhara and yet the same again to arrive at Samarkand – altogether a period of extreme contrasts – breathtakingly beautiful Silk Road cities interspersed with days totally out of the tourist zone in sparsely inhabited rural Uzbekistan. For us this was an agreeable mix, giving us time to wind down from the stimulation of a plethora of glorious treasure and tune in to the meditative turn of the pedals.

When Aslan was asked for his best piece of travel advice in an interview with a travel company, this is what he came up with:

> I was leading a group recently and we went through a particularly demeaning and rigorous security check in an ethnically troubled part of China, which included having the soles of our feet scanned and having to remove all battery-powered items from our hold luggage. "I find it helps," said one of the women in the group, "to remember that this isn't a holiday, it's travel. They're both wonderful, but they are different."

This connects with the way we feel about travel by bike – it's not a holiday (well perhaps in snippets), it is travel. It is these links in the chain between the 'destinations' and the encounters that it leads to that make it something very special.

We left Khiva heading east, aiming to avoid as much of the main road to Bukhara as we could. We passed through a fairly densely populated rural area. People worked in the fields and in their gardens and small round patties of dung were drying in the hard earth yards. Plenty of new homes were being built. Workers gave us a cheery wave as they hauled up buckets of damp mud for slapping onto the outside walls. Mud, being in plentiful supply, featured in much construction, old and new – homes for the living and graveyards for the dead. We commented on how tidy it was compared with other countries on our route. There was not much rubbish about and people seemed to make an effort to make their surroundings look good. It was busy in a pleasant sort of way and there was no shortage of little roadside shops to get the cool drinks which we constantly craved in the heat. We found a tasty lunch plov (pilau) and manti (a kind of large stuffed ravioli).

The road then crossed the Amu Darya River just a stone's throw from the border with Turkmenistan, using a bridge built in 2004 which the current President Karimov (in power since the Russians left) takes the credit for. He needs to have a look at the roads connecting with it – once over the bridge we were constantly dodging huge potholes. A few kilometres further on we were stopped at a checkpoint. Hugh took our passports into the little cabin whilst I stayed with the bikes in the dusty heat. Lots of information was messily written down in a little book and we were then free to go.

Then the landscape changed completely into an empty sandy semi-desert. We followed a muddy canal alongside a village of low adobe houses and rejoined the main road by a small garage where we picked up water from a pump

– they said it was good water.

The main road was much quieter than the same road had been near Nukus and the ride would have been pleasant enough but for the heat – still very hot at 5:30pm. We pulled off the road to the right, pushing our bikes through soft sand, up a gentle rise. We were surprised to find ourselves looking down on a wide sandy river bed with pools of water shining in the low sunlight. We found a lovely patch of soft sand for our bed, totally out of view of the road and with a great view. Just as we had got the tent up we saw two soldiers coming towards us – so the people I had seen earlier from the road weren't just shepherds after all. They were both very young and quite friendly at first – that was until they realised that we didn't want to move despite their ideas to the contrary. They repeated a word we didn't understand (sigale?) many times and talked about Turkmen, making gestures of firing a gun. We couldn't see any Turkmen on the sands before us although the border wasn't far away in the river bed. We had thought that Uzbekistan and Turkmenistan were friends. Radio communications with presumably their superiors followed, after which one of them started to try to take our tent down and move our bags. We realised the game was up at this point – Hugh was getting pretty cross with them which worried me – these were guys, no more than teenage kids really, with long knives and automatic weapons! It didn't seem wise to argue.

It appeared that we had chosen the wrong side of the road. We pushed back to the road where two friendly workers offered us a shower from the side of their dumper truck (which we politely declined) and helped us get our bikes onto the rough ground on the other side. The view wasn't the same but we were out of the sensitive border zone at least. By this time it was dark so we washed, cooked and ate by the light of a half-moon aided by our head torches.

Hugh spent the first 50 km of the next day feeling like – in his words – 'he needed either a splat or a yack' and the sight of the plate of fish that was served up at the first *chaihana* sent him on a rapid exit for both. The fish, almost as long as I am tall, came from a large tank by the tea house. A huge pile of curled up, deep fried slices appeared on a plate – all for me it seemed. We relied heavily on the *chaihanas* that day, having set out under-provisioned. There were several along the way although it was always very difficult to find out how far it was to the next one.

Miraculously we managed another 126km over a decaying, pot holed, sand splattered road before heading into the bush to camp surrounded by a garden of fascinating desert flowers. Nearby a large group of birds, possibly sand martins were flying to and from holes in a sandy bank.

The next day we arrived in Bukhara feeling absolutely jiggered having completed what we thought would be a four day transit in just three long days averaging 150km per day aided by a tailwind. The first priority was to find a cool beer and a good place to stay.

This is what we wrote in our journal on arrival:

> Entering Bukhara, Central Asia's holiest city, we now have a strong feeling of having arrived in the heart of Central Asia, formerly a land ruled by Emirs and Khans known for cruelty in war and fearsome punishments. In Bukhara, criminals were once thrown from the top of the Kaylon minaret, at 47m, the tallest building in Central Asia when it was built by Arslan Khan in 1127. In 1910 Khiva's Islom-Hoja minaret topped it by 10m.
>
> This is the land of the Great Game. In the nineteenth century it was a vast, empty, arid buffer between the great Russian Empire and British India, a land over which they were both keen to gain influence. Much of it was uncharted territory and the British needed to know if it was a route by which a Russian army could threaten their prize of India. Cycling across the steppe gave us a strong impression of this formidable barrier – even today between oasis towns there is very little. Some of the most brave and intrepid young officers of all time were dispatched into the region to unravel its mysteries and court favour with its rulers, talented men of great linguistic capabilities, frequently paying a dear price for their trouble.
>
> In 1839 Captain Arthur Connolly was dispatched to foster good relations with the cruel Emir, Nasrulla in Bukhara. For his efforts he was imprisoned in a vermin and snake infested pit. After three years Colonel Charles Stoddard arrived with the aim of securing his release, only to find he was thrown into the same pit. Following Britain's defeat in the Afghan war both men were publicly beheaded. Ultimately it could be said that Russia won the game, subsequently occupying all the Central Asian regions and dividing them up into republics, with a deliberate lack of regard for ethnic divisions.
>
> Today the old centre is smartened up for tourists, many of them French and many in groups. It is strange to find ourselves using French to communicate with the hotel staff – the place is run by a family who also have business interests in France and the young son speaks excellent French. We have found a gorgeous place to stay but we are inclined to agree with the Lonely Planet comment that you don't come to Bukhara for the food. However, we have enjoyed a few glasses of red wine from Samarkand.

Bukhara, Uzbek Bukhoro or Buxoro and also spelled Buchara or Bokhara was founded not later than the 1st century AD (and possibly as early as the 3rd or 4th century BC). It was already a major trade and crafts centre along the famous Silk Road when it was captured by Arab forces in 709. Alternative Latin script spellings abound in this region. Khiva may also be Kiva, Chiwa, Chiva, or Jiva and the region Uzbekistan which we first entered can be written as either Karakalpakstan or Qaraqalpaqstan and Aktau can be Aqtau. The Latin script versions appear to be different phonetic equivalents of the Cyrillic spellings. Bukhara fell to Genghis Khan in 1220, the legendary warrior and brutal ruler of what became the largest contiguous empire in history – the Great Khan or Mongol Empire covering most of Eurasia. In 1370 the city fell to the equally barbaric Turkic conquerer, Timur.

We stayed in the exceedingly charming Hovli Poyon Hotel, once the family home of a successful nineteenth century merchant, Bek. When the Emir was invited to the celebration of the completion of the building, he was offended by a mere merchant having a house more befitting an Emir, whereupon the Bek had to pretend that it was built in his honour. A rough ancient wooden doorway set into a high brick wall gave access off the street. The dining room was splendidly decorated with exquisite *ganch* work – a type of relief plasterwork which is carved on a pliable layer of a gypsum/clay mix and then painted. It is much in evidence in Uzbekistan. From the shower there was a great view of decorated brick minarets set against a clear blue sky. We enjoyed such treats all the more after days of hot riding and wild camping.

Over two days we visited many of the sights of the city including the pit where Captain Arthur Connolly and Colonel Charles Stoddard ended their days. We went for dinner at the home of Mumi who we met in the bazaar. He told us that in many ways things were much better in Soviet times – then everyone had a job and there was stability. Now, he said, there is a huge unemployment problem and a crazy currency. His daughter embroidered colourful Suzani cushion covers and table mats. Suzani is a type of embroidery specific to Central Asia – the name comes from the Persian word, Suzan which means needle.

In a café a man was playing a Tar – a long necked, waisted lute (shaped like an asymmetric figure of eight), a traditional instrument of Persia and the Caucasus. We had seen the same instrument in Baku. The translucent covering over the sound box is made from the skin of a cow's heart. We saw women on the street sat with their heads bowed and hands clasped in prayer. Men walked through the madrassas dressed in baggy beige pants with matching waistcoats and plain long coats with Indian style collars over pristine white shirts. Duppi caps, a traditional Uzbek skull cap, completed the outfit. These caps come in a variety of designs but the most popular is in black with a fine white embroidered design around the rim and over the four sections of the top. There are so many talented artisans at work in the city – silverware, miniature painting and fabric weaving. The distinctive brightly coloured traditional Uzbek design uses the warp rather than the weft to make the pattern. The silk warp threads are tie dyed and then the weft is woven in a single colour giving rise to a slightly blurry pattern with a look as if paint has run – but very pretty. This technique known as Ikat, has been used along the Silk Road for thousands of years. We saw many people wearing clothes made from this type of fabric.

And, of course, there was no shortage of stunning architecture to feast our eyes on. We had help with the hard work of sight-seeing from Aziza, a charming young woman who offered to take us round the city free of charge. She wanted to improve her English so that she could take tour groups. At the Abdul Aziz Khan Madrassah we saw the remains of a stork's nest. Sadly storks no longer come to Bukhara as the frogs disappeared when the Russians drained the disease ridden waterways and ponds, depriving the storks of their food. The portal to the Nadir Divan-Beghi Madrassah is unusual in that it depicts birds (happiness birds) and pigs (regarded as unclean by Muslims). The Chor Minor mosque is unusual for its four minarets which is what the name means in the Tajik language.

After a stay of four nights in Bukhara, we left the city riding through the arch of one of the ancient gateways. There is something magical about riding through the gates of an ancient city, feasting on the wonders of times so long ago, and then heading out once more, through another narrow archway into the present. Yet again, we had a ride of three or four days out in the sticks ahead of us. Time to digest what we had seen, and ready ourselves for the last of the jewels of Uzbekistan.

We were taking a back route to Samarkand, but our map wasn't up to the job. At a scale of 1:1,500,000 it was a little short on detail which we had to fill in with what we could glean from the locals in languages we neither understood nor spoke – neither Uzbek or Russian. We found ourselves in a police compound with a 'no entry' sign and an officer there to enforce it, but probably not being used to dealing with random non-Russian speaking cyclists taking bizarre back routes and not knowing quite what to make of us, they just let us through to where we wanted to go. A shop in the middle of nowhere, recognisable by the plastic carrier bag flapping at the window provided us with cold juice. Inside the concrete cube a lady watched television. The usual poster of two pious ladies in front of a view of Mecca decorated the wall behind along with a picture of tasty fresh food on the side wall – not the kind of stuff which was actually for sale. It was a day of uninspiring riding starting with an area of earth works and then through dull desert land, ending with a camp at the edge of a wheat field where a charming farmer came to visit us.

The next day was more entertaining. Rocky mountain ridges added welcome interest to the arid plains and there was even a decent, if gradual, climb – which we enjoyed. The road was lined with tall thistles which workers were digging out with long handled forks and loading into little trailers. Tortoises were crossing the roads in abundance, not all of them making it. Sadly, the shell is no match for the weight of a vehicle. We passed through isolated villages every 20 or 30km or so, their low, adobe construction pleasing to the eye. We chatted to many people along the way – within the limitations of language.

We approached the village of Tim, heavily laden with water as we had intended to camp before it. As we struggled up the gentle incline against the wind, I felt I had definitely done enough. We knew there was an interesting mausoleum to see in Tim, but discovering that it was 2km up the hill into the village, and off route, we felt it was too much – amazing how even 2km extra can seem a lot at the end of a long hard day with a headwind. However, we bumped into Akmal and he had different ideas. He had told us how far it was, and seeing us turn the wrong way he chased us on his old banger of a bike and offered to be our guide – 'it is 1000 years old' he told us. So we went – and saw the ancient village tree and old white mosque into the bargain. The mausoleum, dated 997, is on the UNESCO world heritage list. Intricate, but understandably weather worn designs, are etched onto the pale brown brick and plaster façade. Akmal then insisted that we come back to his home. We followed him down the road, along a dirt track, across a little stream and up alongside a field to his house. *Kurpachas* (quilted cotton filled mattresses) were laid on the kilim covered floor of the biggest room. Tea, bread and chocolates were laid out on a cloth on the floor beside us. His mother came to talk to us but soon got bored with our lack of Russian and left.

Before the meal, water was brought out in a small urn for washing our hands – there was no internal plumbing in the house. Chicken, salad and yoghurt arrived and then, the vodka! And then a phrase that Akmal seemed to know well. 'Let's go!' Three small glasses were filled with the spirit and he simply knocked his back all in one. Ouch – oh dear! At this point he told us how he had been a sniper for the Russian Army when they invaded Afghanistan. Then he dug out some battered old Russian school text books on English and algebra and then more interestingly some papers on agriculture in arid lands (all in English) – he was a teacher of agriculture at the college in Tim, which is a large village of around 10,000 people.

Akmal spoke little English, but he used what he knew well. He told us his salary was $115 per month. He had five children to bring up on that sum. His wife, also a teacher, didn't join us. He asked how much our bikes were worth and it was too embarrassing to give the truth. Such is the luck of the draw – like him, we earned our living as teachers and yet what a difference in circumstances – and yet, he was so generous in sharing what he had with us and taking time to show us his village. We talked about where we were going next, and he warned us that Tajiks are not good people. It is not uncommon for locals to warn of the dodgy people ahead, who will then warn you of the next dodgy people.

The next day should have been a great day's ride – small climbs giving good views of tightly clustered villages and rocky ridges. The adobe villages were charming and their inhabitants colourful. The problem was the wind. When you are pedalling hard to go down a slight incline, then it is bad. Going up a slight incline reduced us to our lowest gears. We wanted to cover more than 80km for a quick run into Samarkand the next day, but at times we began to wonder if we would make 60km.

Looking for a break from the wind, we asked a young man if there was a *chaihana* in Musakak; there wasn't but he invited us into his home for tea. Tea arrived and then some food was laid out – bread, biscuits, sweets and some lovely cherries. A great tea break we thought. Then salad arrived – cucumbers, tomatoes and onions. Having eaten quite a bit we made moves to go – but no, the meal was yet to come – what seems to be the traditional Uzbek meal of fried eggs and fried sliced salami sausage. This back to front way of serving food (to us that is) is a bit confusing. We politely declined the vodka. Bit by bit more of the family arrived to see us, including the women and children. The only furniture in the room was a low, metal chest with a beautiful, shiny, symmetrical design etched on the front and a dozen colourful patterned mattresses piled on top. We conversed as best we could in our little bits of Uzbek, and sign language, once again heads shook at our lack of Russian. As we left they took pictures on their mobile phones.

A long climb up into some pretty green rolling country finished us off. We found water in a deep village well. A helpful man connected up a very long wire to the power supply in his house to power a pump bringing up the water. We were told it was good to drink. Meanwhile, another chap decided to try out my bike. We pulled off up a dirt track and found ourselves in a wonderful meadow where we caught our first glimpse of distant, lofty snow covered peaks. Tethered cows munched contentedly on the grass. Having plenty of water, and a very private spot, we enjoyed a hot wash with the luxury of a

The driver of this car stopped and gave us 3000 som. People often think you are poor if you travel by bicycle

Lunch break inside an Uzbek home

whole pan of water each – luxury is such a relative issue! Later on a young woman came to collect the cows – she smiled and led them away. The sun set in a blaze of colour and a bright moon rose soon after. We were now a stone's throw away from our third iconic Uzbek Silk Road city, Samarkand, one of the oldest inhabited cities in Central Asia.

A statue of Amir Timur guards the entrance to Samarkand – seated on his throne, dressed in crown and cloak, his sword by his side planted in the earth with his hands resting over the top. We rode into town and stopped by the infamous warrior's mausoleum, its gleaming fluted dome catching the sunlight. 'From Sedbergh to Samarkand' we thought – a journey of a lifetime! We dropped straight into the haven of the Antica B&B with its gloriously rich and peaceful garden and traditionally decorated rooms. The Lonely Planet was right about some things – it was their top choice.

Samarkand (known as Самарканд by the Russians) became the capital of Amir Timur's great empire in the mid-fourteenth century and in its heyday was one of the most beautiful cities in the world. Amir Timur, otherwise known as Tamerlane (Timur the lame – a result of an arrow shot through his leg), built up an empire stretching from Russia to the Persian Gulf and from the Mediterranean to Delhi in India. This man can compete with Stalin and Hitler in his disregard for human life, building up his huge empire at a cost of around seventeen million lives – possibly more than Stalin and Hitler combined.

EXTRAORDINARY PLACES BY BICYCLE

It was only when we reached Samarkand that we realised the extent of the restoration which has produced the pristine architecture that we see today in these blue tiled cities. Before the renovators got to work, many of the buildings were just skeletons. The only hint of the lost colourful tiles was the faint tracings on the bare earth of the crumbling walls. The arches of the doorways had become narrow bridges in thin air. Work is still going on, providing employment for men and women skilled in the ancient crafts. However, the process of restoration is contentious. Had the buildings been left in their ruinous state, the cities would be very different places to visit. Some think that the city has been over restored – too aggressively losing the 'authenticity' of the monu-

Fruity and friendly in Uzbekistan

THE WORST ROAD IN THE WORLD

Arrival in Samarkand

ments. Many structures would have fallen down by now without some assistance abetted by the frequent earthquakes, but the worth of sprucing them up to as good as new is questioned by many. However, the result is more than an unquestionably stunning open air museum – it is also a living and breathing historic city centre where locals and visitors stroll, young boys bathe in the fountains, young women dance and school girls huddle in groups and chat.

There were many travellers in Samarkand – Silk Road adventurers, some heading east and others coming from China – by public transport, 4x4, motorbike and others like us by bike. There was even one who had come on foot from Europe. We either met or were aware of fourteen other cyclists in the city whilst we were there. Around the dinner table, excited conversations revolved around great places, visas, permits and personal destinations.

For us, Samarkand had provided both a welcome, luxurious rest and a chance to service the bikes in the comfort of Antica's shady courtyard. The loan of traveller Christian's 4x4 black box tool kit came in handy as did a borrowed chain whip from another English cyclist. After 5000km from Rhodes, it was time for new sprockets, chains and Rohloff oil. Our bikes were fitted with precisely engineered fourteen speed German hub gear mechanisms –

highly reliable and maintenance free apart from the oil changes. We were lucky that at least one postal delivery to Baku had worked – there was no chance of getting any of this stuff in Samarkand. As we jettisoned the old parts, Hugh's load became lighter!

It was also a time to think about the road ahead. Here we were, in the land of the Great Game, on the brink of setting out on a journey into the heart of the matter, along the Pamir Highway – tracing the slither of Afghanistan which forced a wedge between the great competing empires, the Wakhan Corridor where we hoped to be able to look across the headwaters of the Amu Darya River to the Afghan villages on the other side.

We had visited the great cities of our dreams – Khiva, Bukhara and Samarkand – and they had not disappointed. As for Tashkent – we decided to give it a miss having discovered that it is now a modern capital with little of the historical magic left to explore. The end point was still in discussion, new ideas of the Karakorum Highway had crept into our thinking, although this was probably not feasible considering UK Foreign office advice at the time. Having been steeped in the turquoise domes and blue tiled portals of the ancient cities, punctuated by long, hot, arid and empty expanses, we were now looking forward to the cool air of the mountains. Along with many other cyclists who had converged on this oasis, we were very excited about what lay ahead. Hugh went along to the bank to load up on US dollars for the coming months. At the next till a customer was paying in a suitcase full of Uzbek Som!

However, we were not quite finished with the ancient warriors and historical cities. Once out of Samarkand we were looking straight on at a high mountain ridge. After crossing a pass at 1700m, we descended to Shakrisabz, the birth place of Timur. This was one of those delightful little extras that fitted conveniently into our onward route. Timur stands proud on a high plinth behind the ruins of the fourteenth century Ak-Saray Palace (White Palace), Timur's summer home. Behind the Khazrati-Iman complex of mausoleums, where Timur's eldest and favourite son Jehangir is buried, lies a tomb in an underground bunker intended for Timur – only Timur isn't there as he died unexpectedly before the mausoleum was finished and was buried in Samarkand. The Kok-Gumbaz (blue dome) mosque behind it is notable for the palm trees incorporated into the patterns on the interior walls created by its original Indian and Iranian designers.

After a morning of sight-seeing in Shakrisabz we found ourselves once again riding along the flat in intense heat, the thermometer reading 48°C; the previous day's mountain terrain was short lived. We were looking for some shade when a friendly bunch of army chaps called us over and offered us tea – they said they didn't see tourists in these parts. Drivers passed us and tried to chat, hanging out of their vehicle windows and as usual many wanted us to stop and try to converse or take our photo. We wanted to keep going – desperately needing the breeze to cool us down, so we waved cheerily and carried on. One driver took exception to this and kept stopping further up the road to encourage us to stop – but we were determined to keep going and we didn't much like the look of him anyway. He was pretty determined and at his last effort he grabbed the bag on the back of Hugh's bike, bringing Hugh to the ground with the guy on top. I made it very clear that I was pretty furious, not at all mindful of possible retaliation. Luckily Hugh escaped with a few grazes and the man went away for good.

This incident is what often comes to mind when we are asked about 'bad' experiences on our travels. We have no scary stories of robbery or muggings, and few unpleasant encounters – we have many more tales of kindness and hospitality which gives us a heart-warming view of the nature of the human race in general. We ended the day at a pleasant, if hot, camp above a little adobe village where three young boys looking after the sheep were pretty surprised by the visitors to their pastures. They wanted to have a go on our bikes but we weren't keen.

We were ready to go high – our thermometer was topping out a 50°C in the sun. Three more days riding and two more camps got us over the border into the next of the 'stans' – Tajikistan. A landscape blighted by roadworks and powerlines changed into a contorted rosy beige rockscape, and then again, into the arable land of the plains where ladies dressed in colourful tunics offered us bright red cherries.

Thankfully we got through the border crossing in around an hour and twenty minutes as we were feeling excessively hot and dirty after three nights in our tent, and were keen to move on and seek a shower. The border zone was a complete mess of building works and road construction. They insisted on scanning our gear which meant hauling our heavy kit up several steps. We had been warned that getting out of Uzbekistan can be much more difficult than getting in, and medicines in particular can be heavily scrutinised. A very friendly lady looked through our vast collection of drugs, mostly unused, and she appeared to know what they were – no problem. The complete passage through the border involved about eight filters some of which were manned by camouflaged men with helmets and automatic weapons. There wasn't much international traffic at this border – no great queues of vehicles but lots of people on foot getting taxis on either side. We changed our Uzbek Som and $100 into Tajik Somani with money changers at the border – a sensible currency with about seven Somani to the Pound which would fit into our wallet!

Thirteen kilometres of roadworks led us to Tursunzade where several people had assured us there was a hotel. We would never have found it but for a driver who offered help. We followed his car, another car behind tooting the horn to draw attention to various turnings as we rode past decrepit apartment blocks.

We were relieved to find a very civilised modern hotel – not much character – but who cared? The room was palatial and the shower hot and powerful. After three days without a proper wash, the brown dirt in the shower tray had to be seen to be believed.

So a new country – but seeming initially much the same – the same trashy roads, road works, women in colourful dresses and people whistling to attract our attention. Another landlocked country but not doubly landlocked like Uzbekistan, as some of its neighbours have coasts. Tajikistan shares frontiers with Uzbekistan, Afghanistan, Pakistan, China and Kyrgyzstan. The man who took us to the hotel asked us if we had any problems in Uzbekistan and Hugh told him the story of the man who caused him to fall off his bike – yes, people always have problems with people in Uzbekistan he said. Pretty unfair really as our experience of the people had been overwhelmingly wonderful apart from the annoying honking of car horns (only meant in friendship) and the obsession with taking our photo which eventually became tedious. People often slight their neighbours – as with the British and the French!

As we ate dinner that night we heard crazy loud music coming from a room behind. We were invited to have a look at the proceedings – a wedding party! Some women encouraged us to join in the dancing, which we did with enthusiasm – perhaps too much enthusiasm – soon drawing a crowd around us. Before long we were quietly ushered out by a bouncer – what had we done wrong? The women serving our meal just laughed about it!

It took us one more day to get to Dushanbe, the capital of Tajikistan. It wasn't a pleasant day's ride. The paraphernalia and dust of extensive roadworks completely obscured the attractive landscape on either side – impressive high mountains to the north and pleasant farmland to the south. Our attention was totally absorbed with trying to find the line through the bumps, avoiding head on collisions with drivers who showed no sign of getting out of the way whilst heading towards us on the wrong side of the road and trying to keep out of the dust. We stopped to chat to three cyclists heading the other way and home to France. They were known as Solidream and had been on the road for three years spending an average of €8 a day each.

Dushanbe is an interesting city to spend a few days. We found a good Indian curry house which served proper Indian sweets and an excellent Korean restaurant where we shared a table with Jorge, a Spaniard from the Basque country, who was at the end of a six week cycling trip. Cafés served quality coffee and tempting cakes, flans and brownies. At the Public Pub they served cheap local draught beer and expensive foreign bottled beer. Old Soviet trolley buses, our main form of city transport, ran down the main drag. Craning our heads, as we walked along the streets shaded with tall sycamores, we could see the rock wall of an enticing mountain ridge way up high, the couloirs filled with snow.

Back when the city was called Stalinabad, former Soviet dictator Joseph Stalin reportedly took a personal interest in the greening of his namesake city.

THE WORST ROAD IN THE WORLD

A massive tree-planting initiative accordingly created a green canopy to shade the capital from Tajikistan's scorching summers. We strolled through parks and open squares cooled by fountains where monuments to the great and the good (and possibly the bad too) stood witness to the Tajik heritage. The statue of Ismali Somani stands on a huge red marble stairway pedestal flanked by two cross-legged lions in front of a monumental, art deco arch topped by a crown of pure Tajik gold.

The tenth century founder of the Samanid Dynasty (a Persian Empire which existed in Central Asia from 819 to 999) is known as the father of the Tajik nation. Pastel shades and white plaster columns are a classic feature of the city's Soviet era architecture. Mosques in the 'stans' are nowhere near as ubiquitous as they are in Turkey but the Tajiks are planning to build a new mosque with funding from Qatar – it will house up to 150,000 people and will be one of the largest in the world. We visited the 200-year-old Haji Yakoub mosque which can hold 3,000 people. Hugh was allowed into the courtyard in his shorts but I wasn't. The pretentiously grand presidential palace, also known as the 'White House' was built in the 1940s and is a classic example of Stalinist administrative architecture.

However, for us, the most interesting sight in Dushanbe was the 13m, sleeping Buddha. It has the distinction of being the largest Buddha in Central Asia, following the destruction of the pair at Bamiyan in Afghanistan, the largest of which was 53m tall and which we were fortunate to see in 1978 before the Taliban blew them up. The reclining Buddha lay in a basement for many years, carved up into 92 pieces and deemed too large for the Russians to shift to its 'rightful place' in what was then Leningrad. We were fortunate to see the Buddha reassembled in the museum of antiquities. It was excavated by Soviet archaeologists in the city of Kurgan-Tyube in southern Tajikistan, a site on the historic Silk Route.

However, we were mainly in Dushanbe to do essential business. We needed a permit for the Gorno-Badakhshan province – an autonomous region close to the Afghan border, which at the outbreak of the civil war in 1992, declared independence from Tajikistan. It is an area which has been claimed by China, Russia, and an assortment of emirs and khans but probably few of those living in this remote region knew that they were ever part of any empire. It makes up 45% of the land area of the country but only 3% of the population – sounded like a perfect area for cycling. We also needed a visa to enter Kazakhstan for the second time, after travelling though visa-free Kyrgyzstan. Visas can often only be obtained in capital cities and we wouldn't be visiting Bishkek, the capital of Kyrgyzstan.

The first was no problem – just a queue in a grubby office, a visit to the bank to pay in the 15 Somani each (£2) and a return trip in the afternoon to pick up a permit with all the details written on in messy Tajik handwriting. We didn't have the skill to check that the correct regions were marked on our permit and it was even indecipherable to a young woman we met in the tourist office who could read Cyrillic script well. However, the kind man in the tourist office assured us it was good for the Pamirs and the Wakhan Valley. We also picked up a 1:500,000 map of the Pamir in the tourist office – a luxury, especially as it actually indicated useful stuff such as homestays, interesting sights and availability of petrol (for our cooking stove). It was a map with contours and details of settlements, roads and paths – amazing. It was all so fortunate as we wouldn't even have spotted the tourist office were it not for the Dutch cyclists' bikes parked outside.

The second was not so successful – the embassy was shut on a Wednesday so we went back the next day, not very optimistic about getting visas before the weekend. A phone call to the Kazakhstan Embassy at 10am on the Friday produced the response – 'call back in ten minutes'. We left it fifteen and were pretty pleased to be asked to collect our visas. But it wasn't quite as straight forward as it sounds. The procedure goes as follows: open your bags for the guards to inspect outside the embassy, sign forms within the embassy, walk ten minutes to the Kazakh bank, wait while the bank clerks deal with the forms, pay $30 dollars each in cash, walk back to the embassy, hand over the receipts and then watch them being checked. It is then midday. 'Hand over your passports and come back at four' we were told – not a bad result when we were initially told that it would take a week. We returned at four and had to be pretty pleased to have got the visas in a little over 24 hours and before the weekend – we were ready to leave for the high Pamir.

The Pamir Highway

Through this world,
I am wandering, wandering,
A soft breeze blowing,
I am wandering now,
Through this world,
I am wandering, wandering,
These are the days I live now.

Kate Rusby song 'Planets' from
the album Awkward Annie, 2007

Pauline:

For 230km between Kalaikum and Khorog the narrow, coarse gravel road forged an improbable trail, etched into the base of the precipitous, crumbling mountain ramparts hugging the banks of the Panj River. The peaks rising abruptly to over 4,000m were barren, twisted contortions of bare rock, cultivation only being possible on alluvial plains close to the river, on occasional

June 8th 2013 to July 8th 2013
1300 kms

gentler slopes on the Afghan side, or where the valley of a tributary broadened as it reached the Panj.

We passed through pretty little villages on the Tajik side; people tended their vegetable plots and sold cherries, mulberries and ripe melons by the roadside. Colourful bedding hung out to dry on lines at the edge of the neat rows of onions, root vegetables, potatoes and beans. Just a stone's throw away across the grey, silty torrent we looked upon a different world. The compact, mud plastered, flat roofed mounds of Afghan villages were linked by a tenuous trail, at times degenerating to an undulating single track path across steep scree slopes. On the Afghan side there is no continuous road for motor vehicles. We waved and called to workers struggling to keep the route open – a small digger balanced precariously on the edge overlooking the near vertical river bank – a line of men with pick axes cutting a new passageway across a landslide. A man dressed in immaculate white baggy pants, a woollen waistcoat and a Pathan hat walked briskly carrying a small blonde child on his back. A couple nursed their donkey down a rock strewn slope.

Small dry-stone walled, cultivated fields and neatly pruned fruit trees formed a pretty picture and we found ourselves unable to resist taking photos

In Tajikistan above the river Panj looking across to Afghanistan.

THE PAMIR HIGHWAY

So far away.

– people going about their daily lives in these remote Afghan villages, cut off from Tajikistan on the other side by the wild waters of the Panj. We were transfixed by this life on the other side – like watching a film as we rode along. Looking at the map we weren't able to discover what linked these people to the rest of the world, or even the rest of their own country. They seemed to be living on a thread, a very fine one at times, of small communities, presumably to a great extent self-sufficient, sandwiched between the mountains and the river and with no clear route out at either end of the valley. But where did they go to buy new shoes, or fabric for clothes or a new bike? Later we were to discover that there were bridges and in places markets were held bringing the people together from the two countries.

We stayed in a homestay in Dekh, a pretty village of strong stone houses, neat vegetable plots and narrow dirt alleys. We had a room in the family house, with a carpet on the floor and acres of net curtains on the windows. They laid out comfortable beds for us on the floor and provided us with a bucket of hot water for a wash. There didn't appear to be any place for washing in private – a bit of a limitation for me! The loo was a little cabin at the end of the veg plot – a hole in the rickety floor boards and a long drop! For breakfast they brought us eggs with onions and herbs, home-made bread, a plate of mulberries and tea in a pretty little pot with matching cups.

The previous night we had camped in a secluded spot only to discover in the morning that there were mines in the area – the sign which we only saw on the way out, showed a figure in silhouette, the trailing leg below the knee detached and suspended above red spikes of fire. Another night a drunken old chap threatened to fall into our tent before he put his bottle of vodka away and went back to his cows. We found water in mountain streams and once at a village well. A partnership of various foundations was working to provide safe drinking water and hygienic latrines for the area.

We were travelling along the grandly named M41, otherwise known as the Pamir Highway, between Dushanbe, the capital of Tajikistan, and Osh in Kyrgyzstan. It is a highway in so much as it is used as a route for trucks, churning up the dust as they head for the Qulma pass leading through to China; but traffic is light and much of the road is unpaved. Huge boulders frequently tumble down onto the road and teams of hardy men work with crowbars to clear the route. Fuel was for sale by the roadside, stored in large rusty drums and transferred to vehicles using buckets and funnels with long spouts.

On 17 June, as we drew near to Khorog, the river broadened into a series of placid lakes, reflecting the magnificent mountains in their clear waters, reminding us of Wastwater in our native Cumbria. There was a frenzy of construction going on, new build using traditional techniques – stone walls and intricately shaped roofs formed with timber frames and topped with corrugated iron. We were hoping for a few days of rest and recuperation before the next stage of the journey which we expected to be tough.

We had cycled out of Dushanbe nine days earlier, keeping a close eye out for uncovered manholes, car doors opening in our path, vehicles jumping the lights and drivers exiting side streets looking like they hadn't seen us. We battled with an increasing headwind in temperatures over 40°C, but at least the road surface was good tarmac.

Two days later, just before the tarmac ran out, we set up camp on the gravel bed of the Vakhsh – a river which combines with the Panj to become the Amu Darya which we followed in Uzbekistan. We were both tired, suffering from the heat and still getting over the effects of stomach bugs contracted in Dushanbe. A dip in the water made us feel much better. Three men picnicking nearby invited us to a feast of freshly cooked river fish, chicken and lamb; oh, and not to forget the vodka which we took turns in drinking from a tea bowl. We learned about Tajikistan's relations with its neighbours – all countries *naz* (good) but Uzbekistan *ganda* (bad). A mime of gun fire accompanied the discussion on Uzbekistan. Stalin's blatant disregard for the ethnic composition of the population when drawing up boundaries has a lot to answer for. Ethnic strife continues to this day.

Our route followed the foaming chocolate mass of the Vakhsh River, climbing up the section of gravel road which we didn't have the energy for in the heat of the previous afternoon. Fortunately there were sections of smooth tarmac and we had some good downhill runs. At times we were high above the river, only to descend to the valley bottom later on. The waters were sometimes constrained between rock walls and at other times the river took a meandering course where the valley opened out. There was a real feeling of heading into the high mountains, the folds of the layers of ages displayed in an open geology museum! Perilously long, slender suspension bridges provided access to isolated settlements on the other side of the river. We passed the turning heading directly to Kyrgyzstan, continuing up a tributary of the Vakhsh and the traffic virtually disappeared.

A Tajik girl dressed to tend her garden

We picked up provisions piecemeal from several little shops en-route. They sold all kinds of goods – one had memory sticks. You could buy a new mobile phone, a pair of socks and any amount of sweets, biscuits, junk drinks and even ice creams – but proper food, not mouldy or rotten, that was a different matter! In one shop we picked up the best of the last of the carrots strewn across the floor along with a few sprouting spuds. We got rice and some sticky condensed milk. Then we found lentils. When we asked for bread, one of the children looking after the shop ran off to get us some, perhaps from home, and then gave it to us refusing to take any money. We bought honey from a chap by the roadside. At first we didn't realise what it was as it was stored inside a small plastic drinks bottles. The man made a few zzzzzz… bee sounds to make things clear. Water was no problem; we drank from small mountain streams which tumbled down the steep rocky slopes.

Eight days out of Dushanbe we reached the cool air of the Saghirdasht Pass at 3,252m where a man was working by the high snow banks shovelling bits of rock and earth to one side with a spade. We crossed mountain pastures where huge flocks of multi-coloured sheep were enjoying the recently exposed grassland. The *bergeries* were using the force of the mountain stream to drive the agitator which churned up the milk. We were invited into a shepherd's tent for tea and some very tasty yoghurt. Whilst we were sitting there a tour group from the Central Asian rally peeped in for a chat having seen our bikes parked outside. They were travelling from Budapest to Bishkek in eighteen days – unbelievable. We were surprised they had time to talk to us.

It was a spectacular 2,000m descent down a wild and wonderful valley to the town of Kalaikum. A short distance before the town we were stopped at a checkpoint. One of the chaps there did a little dance for us – he wanted us to join in, which I did for a few embarrassing seconds. It obviously wasn't enough as he asked Hugh for money for doing the paperwork – we didn't pay – we didn't need the paperwork! We found relative comfort at a homestay where we had a cold shower and a non-flushing loo that appeared to empty itself into the river. The town is a stop-over point for journeys between Dushanbe and Khorog – supposedly sixteen hours by car. We ate in a crowded restaurant with overelaborate ceiling roses and lighting, right next to the crashing river – too loud to converse at one of the outside tables.

We had entered the autonomous region of Gorno-Badakhshan – the boundary being the pass we had just crossed. Khorog, a town of 28,000 people, is the capital of this remote area. Under the USSR, the region, being inhabited by ethnic minority groups, was given special autonomous status which continued after independence. The privileges which came with this status included educational opportunities and the region today has a disproportionate number of academics, professionals and technicians. It has its own university and twelve schools.

However, the area is one of the poorest in Tajikistan, the only source of cash income being from the Aga Khan charitable foundation (and presumably a little tourism and black market drug trafficking). The town is surrounded by precipitous mountain walls and in June the temperature is very pleasant. At around 2,000m it is a good place to acclimatise. Many cycle tourists take a break there. At least twelve travellers were staying at the Pamir Lodge, six of them from our native county of Cumbria including Pete and Alice who had set off the day before us from Ulverston. Dave and Rich also from Cumbria (Morland and Ulverston) had, like us, left home by bike in September 2012. Yet again we bumped into old friends Guillain and Anna. Ben from Massachusetts who was exploring the Pamirs with a full suspension bike plus trailer sold us two very useful items – some new brake pads and a gas canister for our stove to be used if the bad petrol blocked it up.

From Khorog it is possible to continue along the border, following the northern edge of the panhandle of Afghanistan, known as the Wakhan corridor. Created in 1873 during the time of the 'Great Game', this narrow stretch of land between 16 and 64km across and 140km long, now separating Tajikistan and Pakistan, was created as a buffer zone between the great empires of Britain and Russia. It had been our plan to take this road. However, in Khorog, Hugh had been suffering from a bad tummy bug and also sciatica – he wasn't able to eat much for a few days and found it impossible to walk much further than the distance to the loo.

During the enforced rest we chatted to numerous travellers and discovered several difficulties in following this route – not the least of these being a large military presence in the area and stories of the Taliban causing trouble not far away over the border. The cross-border market at Ishkashim, one of the key attractions, was not happening because of security concerns. We heard US army military personnel talking seriously in acronyms over breakfast. Then to cap it all, we heard that the final 100km climb to the Pamir plateau is an impossibly rough track. Cyclists often push their bikes through long stretches of deep sand when going down the route we would be planning to cycle up. No place for semi-invalids we thought!

Instead we somewhat reluctantly decided to continue on the Pamir Highway – we were told the road was very quiet, had a good surface and most tempting of all, it passed through spectacular scenery. The right move for us but it left that irksome feeling of having opted out of the most adventurous choice, and a slight sense of regret still lingers. Just before we left, the cross border market in Khorog was also cancelled – security issues perhaps or disease – typhoid!

Four days of gentle riding on a well surfaced road took us up to an altitude of 3,550m. We were getting stronger each day and the calm pace enabled Hugh to recover from his ailments. We camped on grassy fields of clover with fresh, clear mountain water on tap. Wild roses and purple orchids bloomed all around us and the sun shone in a bright blue sky dotted with little puffy white clouds. Tall poplars grew in the valley bottom reminding us of similar scenes in Argentina. Women in spotless, bright tunics with matching pants tended the crops – dressed more for a party than for gardening!

Traditional Pamir homes blended in perfectly with the landscape – indeed they were part of the landscape being moulded from it. A young boy emerged from the courtyard of one of these low, rectangular buildings and invited us in for tea. Men were working on the roof light which was fixed into a shallow dome in the almost flat roof. The interior was a sight to behold. From below we could appreciate the very special construction of the roof light – four concentric squares in layers, each set at right angles to the one below and as a result getting smaller going up through the levels. The top square was topped by a tent of glass to let in the light. These layers are known as *chorkhona* (four houses) representing, respectively, the four Zoroastrian elements earth, water, air and fire, the latter being the highest, touched first by the sun's rays.

The people's home is also their temple, place of private prayer and worship for Pamiri Ismailis – the Ismailis (a sub-sect of Shia Islam) have as yet no mosques in Gorno-Badakhshan. It was a privilege to be invited into this special place. We were ushered into a rectangular room with a beamed ceiling supported by pillars painted in deep terracotta and turquoise. We sat on cushioned seats built into the edges of the room and a table was laid with tea, biscuits, sweets and bread and butter. Members of the family, two women and three boys, sat with us. Sleeping platforms were also built into the room along with a beautifully carved cabinet painted to match the pillars. Thick carpets were hung on the walls and family photos were pinned to the pillars.

Everyone removed their shoes and the women and children eyed us inquisitively as we drank our tea. We saw many homes like this, some with flat roofs of earth or tin which are used for drying hay, apricots, dung or mulberries. These were homes made by the people for the way that they live, blending perfectly into the magnificent landscape – mountains still of barren rock but not quite as harsh and forbidding as the claustrophobic walls alongside the road by the Afghan border earlier. We soaked in the beauty of our surroundings, relished in the measured ascent and we felt no regrets about our change of route.

On the second day out of Khorog we were surprised to see Thomas and Suzanna turn up on their motorbikes. We had chatted to them in the Serena Inn in Khorog – a smart hotel where we went for a good coffee and they were staying. Like us they had been intending to go via the Wakhan Valley and what's more, they were intending to stay in Khorog for another week for Suzanna to finish her work using the business centre there. Their reason for the change of plan was much more sinister than ours. Over the border in Pakistan, nine tourists had been killed by the Taliban; this was news to us. They told us that the reason for the Afghan market in Khorog being cancelled was because of increasing Taliban activity in the area. Moreover, they had seen Afghans across the river from their hotel, looking at them through binoculars and taking photos; these Afghans were not tourists taking holiday pictures.

The Serena Inn was built in a style suitable for visits by the Aga Khan whose foundation provides a lot of aid to the area, both on the Tajik and Afghan side. The Taliban detest this organisation which engages in projects they don't approve of such as women's education. It was not inconceivable that the Serena Inn could be a target; Thomas and Suzanna were not taking the risk of staying there any longer. This was another reason for continuing on the Pamir Highway being a good choice.

The next evening we set up camp in a meadow strewn with purple orchids and surrounded by bubbling springs. During the night I was troubled by the deep sound of rumbling boulders, but convinced myself it was just the clamour of the nearby river echoing in the night air. After riding barely a kilometre the next morning we found the road quickly degenerated into a cracked, rock strewn mess. Around the next corner we were in for a shock – a hundred metres

THE PAMIR HIGHWAY

Bridge over the Ghund (Tajikistan)

of the Pamir Highway had vanished; the river rushed by where the road used to be. The usual path of the river had been blocked by earth and boulders which had rolled down from the opposite mountainside. A digger on the bank above seemed woefully inadequate for the job of creating a new track.

Just as we were wondering how we would get around the blockage the situation was taken out of our hands. The locals picked up our bags and our bikes and carried the lot up the tiny, steep path that a man with a shovel was creating up the loose bank. Once at the top we were able to reload and ride down the rough track newly created by the little digger. We continued on our way past a long line of marooned traffic including many trucks, an expedition style German campervan and an old van with a cow's head in the boot. The truck drivers seemed happy enough cooking fresh fish caught from the river. We figured it would take weeks to create a new route which would take a car let alone the heavy trucks, but locals reckoned it would be open the next day! As it turned out the locals were closer to the truth. After only a couple of day's traffic appeared to be on the move once more.

Cycling on past women cleaning their carpets on the roadside we found a little track leading up to a hot spring where we were able to wash off the dust.

The water came out of the ground at a temperature of 98°C which is handy for the family living there for washing their clothes and dishes. Eight kilometres further on we reached the hot spring spa town of Jelondy which turned out to be a great disappointment. It is a windy place with half-finished buildings scattered around an alluvial slope. Rubbish strewn streams of natural hot water trickle through the stones. Hot water baths are hidden away all around town which had a sad and empty feeling. A friendly local pointed out the 'hotel' to us; there was no helpful sign to direct tourists to it. It is the most noticeable building in town with hot pools of its own and it is also known as the sanatorium. We got some soup and a sausage (just one) and mash for lunch, which was welcome. The loos were the attraction's real downfall – smelly pit communal loos. Hugh had to squat for his morning poo right next to the hotel manager! Natural hot water gushed out of a low pipe at a moderately convenient place for washing hands; we wondered if anyone had thought of plumbing it into a wash basin and providing soap?

We needed provisions for the remote route ahead and finding the shops was a challenge; they had no signs outside and we often needed to find the proprietor who had the key. With difficulty we managed to scrounge some vegetables (potato, onion, carrot) from the hotel and then on our way out a young boy

Getting through where the road had been washed away near Jelondy, Tajikistan.

showed us the way to a shop where we found some real treasures – halva, Snickers, a tin of tomato paste, a tin of chickpeas and a slightly rusty looking tin of fish.

We were now climbing up onto the cold, windswept and beautifully barren land of the Pamir plateau where snow storms are common even in June. The heat of the lowlands was well behind us. Much of the earth was bare and dry, but purple and yellow carpets of summer flowers gave some colour. Shepherds were out with their flocks. Snow streaked peaks on the horizon rose almost another 2,000m above us. At over 4,000m the air is energy sappingly thin but we were determined to keep riding up to the Koitezek Pass at 4,270m, partly because Sebastian from Slovenia who we had met five days ago told us we would be pushing our bikes up the pass! He was on his way home – a three year journey on a bike he put together in Shanghai. The tarmac ran out just as the going got tough and we hit the zig-zags. We did manage to ride it, mainly in bottom gear, but only with lots of stops for getting the breath back and with the help of a ferocious tailwind.

Just down from the top we were called into a house. Sheep and goats were crowded into pens outside. Inside it was comfortably warm by the stove on which hot milk was steaming. We drank it with butter mixed in and ate bread with thick cream. The family robustly refused any money.

We moved on over the naked, buff coloured landscape, past white salt lakes catching rays of sun escaping through the clouds, and arrived at Bulunkul – a little deviation off the Pamir Highway and reputedly the coldest place in Tajikistan. It reminded us of approaching a remote village on the Bolivian Altiplano. Bulunkul is a strange little collection of low, stone and mud buildings with a few yurts scattered over a large dirt yard, the cool wind blowing continuously across the open ground. There were piles of loose earth, soft areas mixed with bits of rubbish, little loo buildings here and there, dung laid neatly out to dry and lots of rough shacks. Cows and sheep grazed on the salty plain around the village. There are no trees to supply wood but people dig up the roots of *teresken*, a bush which takes 50-80 years to reach its modest height of around 30cm, but burns in minutes. Its removal unfortunately results in soil erosion.

A young boy took us to a homestay – a simple white square building with two rooms. The guest room was very cosily decked out with colourfully patterned carpets on the floor and walls. The other room had a dung powered stove where the food was cooked. It was the home of a Kyrgyz family and they were very charming. They brought us a jug of warm water and a tin bowl for washing and then tea, bread and butter and yoghurt to eat before we went out – a 45 minute walk to a view of Yashil-Kul Lake, at 3,734m. For dinner we had potatoes and salami cooked in an oily sauce and more yoghurt. Wires were connected to a battery (charged by solar power) to give us electric light. Later on they laid out mattresses and pillows for our bed on the floor – all very comfortable.

First thing in the morning there was a stark choice. There were two sides to the village communal loo block, presumably for men and women, but we didn't know which was which. However, the choice was really between a reasonably clean pit loo, with a great view to the countryside beyond the village, but in full view of the people taking their cows out to pasture, or the other side with a door you could close, but with the results of other people's use scattered all over the floor.

Not wishing to repeat the outward route from the main road we set out on a network of rough tracks; looking back on the village, it struck us how lonely it appeared sitting on a vast empty plain at the foot of empty hills with not a tree in sight. It took us all day to cover the 38km to Alichur. The tracks were indistinct, formed only by the passage of other vehicles – merely a gentle impression on the stony earth or dried out salt marsh and frequently threatening to disappear altogether. We made much use of our compass to keep us roughly in the right direction; this trip was before our use of digital maps. Shaggy long-tailed marmots – also known appropriately as golden marmots – popped up inquisitively from their holes, generally disappearing quickly as we got the camera out! A ruined village was testament to the harsh nature of life in this terrain.

A family and yurt on the move in Tajikistan.

By the time we got to Alichur we had done enough. It certainly was tough – but, well worth it – a challenge right to the end with the last kilometre on super stony ground and a steep little climb up onto the main road at a bridge. We called in at the 'Dining Room', where they served fish – cold, chopped into pieces and served with bread. Moving on with ideas of camping, Hugh spotted the Marco Polo homestay, which advertised a 'bathroom' – very tempting. And what a bathroom – a steaming room with hot water on the stove and cold water in a big churn. It was a blissful luxury to get a deep clean and wash our hair. Later in the evening the father of the house came back from ibex hunting. He washed his hands and feet and then, explaining that he is a Musulman and has to pray five times a day, he retreated to another room from where we could hear the sound of his prayers. We sat by the warm stove which was continually fed with *teresken* shrub and talked with the family (mother, father and daughter) helped by the smattering of English of the father and daughter. We learned a few words of Kyrgyz – the population of Alichur is half Tajik and half Kyrgyz. It was a wonderful place to relax our tired limbs. At dinner we all sat on thick mats around a cloth laid on the floor spread with plates of delicious ibex liver, thick chunks of bread and tea.

The next day we climbed gently up a wide valley dotted with yurts – the summer homes of the Kyrgyz people living in this part of Tajikistan. They are sturdy felt constructions held down with thick ropes laid over the domed roof. The wall, about the height of a small woman, forms a circle stretched over a wooden frame and held taught to the frame with more ropes. The single entrance is covered with a decorative hanging to keep out the cold or rolled up to let the air in. Some are quite plain and others have colourful decorations around the base of the roof dome. We reached the highest point of the day as a snow storm brewed up and the temperature dropped to 1°C forcing us to put our thick gloves on for the first time since Turkey. That night we stayed in a family yurt, warmed by a tin stove in the centre. Colourful, *shyrdaks* (felt rugs) decorated the sides and rugs covered the floor.

Sleeping mats were laid out for us at night time and at 6am a woman came to light the fire for us. I played my tin whistle to a captivated audience of two children. They blew us kisses when we left after a hearty breakfast of milky rice, thick creamy yoghurt and cream – produce of the yaks – and of course bread and tea.

It was a perfect morning to be cycling across the high pastures on the roof of the world and we remarked on how lucky we were. A small truck passed us, the deconstructed family yurt piled high into the cargo bed at the back and hanging out precariously over the rough wooden slats of the side walls and tail gate. Sat amongst the rolls of felt, ropes, raffia mats, wooden poles, wire fencing, plastic water bottles and other paraphernalia of the nomadic home was the father of the family, his arms around a beautiful long-eared goat with a shaggy coat of white hair. His smiling oriental eyes; neat, greying, goatee beard and suntanned face were framed by the dark upturned brim of his Kyrgyz hat. He looked so much at peace with the world and we felt just the same way. We stopped to make a picnic salad out of our remaining stocks, tomatoes, carrot, onion, cucumber and tomato paste, feeling the need to counteract all the thick yoghurt and cream which is a key part of the region's basic diet.

Forty-seven kilometres further on, we arrived in Murghab, the only significant town in the eastern half of Gorno-Badakhshan and at 3,650m above sea

Home for the night at Mamazair, Tajikistan.

level, the highest town in Tajikistan. The last significant town, Khorog, was nine days of riding behind us and the next, Osh in Kyrgyzstan, six days of pedalling onwards. Any places in-between these staging points could not be relied upon for supplies. The *Lonely Planet Guide* describes Murghab as 'not exactly charming' – true enough but having checked out the characterless Pamir hotel we found a charming guesthouse. Suhrab's guesthouse had one of those steamy bathrooms with lots of hot water to pour over yourself – I want one too! The loo was a hole in the ground but clean, without odour and even tiled where you placed your feet. The people were lovely, giving us tea, bread and a bowl of dried mulberries when we arrived. We were able to wash our clothes in hot water and despite what Lonely Planet says about the town's power supply being intermittent (the former is true) and low voltage, we were able to charge our devices. What more could you want? Internet please! Hugh wasted no time in enjoying a bottle of beer after an alcohol free week! I tucked into a bowl of fresh cherries – you can tell where our priorities lay!

A day off was in order to restock and recuperate. Feeling the need for meat we checked out the Pamir hotel for lunch. There we met up with the most extraordinary character sat on the hotel step, cradling the paw of his skinny labrador in one hand, his skin red raw with sunburn. In earlier times he may have made an intrepid Great Game player! Dave had walked all the way from his home in Germany, taking two and a half years. He set out with two dogs, but sadly one died in Turkey, and now the other was convalescing in the hotel with septic paws. Dave was contemplating stealthily crossing a remote border, hopefully unguarded, into China. He didn't have a valid visa and there were problems with quarantine for his dog, so he regarded this as his only option – seriously. We tried to fathom how he had managed to cross the great nothingness of the steppe between Aqtau in Kazakhstan and Kungrad in Uzbekistan – a journey which was challenging enough by bike with problems of getting enough water, although he had done it in November when it is much colder. He made what we are doing look like child's play!

We stocked up at Murghab's container market – not quite as jivey as the one we had visited last year in Christchurch, hastily put together to put some life into the city after a devastating earthquake – more functional but great for stocking up for the road ahead. The women there covered their faces with scarves – more about keeping off the sun than religious protocol we were told. Many of the men wore the *kalpak* perched on the top of their heads – a traditional tall, flat topped hat. They are made out of felted, white sheep's wool, with a curved up brim, often revealing a black lining. Traditional patterns, each with their own deep symbolism are embroidered on each of the four outer sections.

We didn't find any internet access in Murghab. We realised that our three children may like to know that we were still alive and kicking so we bought a Tajik SIM card and sent text messages. It was in Bolivia that we first woke up to the fact that our children may worry about their parents every bit as much as parents worry about their kids. The more we get used to fast, accessible communication, the more we worry when no messages arrive!

North of Murghab we reached the turning to the Qulma pass which the trucks take to get to Kashgar in China. The possibility of visiting China had always excited us and it was with some regret that we continued on the now empty road heading for Kyrgyzstan. It was difficult to know for sure if the pass was open for tourists and we had decided some time back that the hassle of getting yet another visa was one step too far given the remaining time we had available. We felt that our time would be better spent in more tourist friendly

Kyrgyzstan, where no visa is required.

As we climbed above the 4,000m contour we came within seven kilometres of the Chinese border. We put up our tent on the banks of a clear river, just 50m from a barbed wire fence which followed the line of the road – once a border fence perhaps but now no longer an effective barrier. The following morning we found many breeches big enough for Dave and his dog to get through. Approaching the Ak-Baital Pass, at 4,655m the highest of our journey, we were hardly able to pedal more than 50 meters in our bottom gear without stopping and gasping for air.

For the next few days we revelled in the magnificently empty high altitude landscape, shades of buff and grey being the dominant colours of the heavily eroded craggy mountains around us. We found idyllic camp spots on grassy banks by crystal clear rivers which tempted us to stop early, recuperate and revel in just being in such special places. Even after sunrise there was a thick layer of ice on pebble strewn patches of water near our tent and the water in our bottles was solid. Summer wild flowers lined the roadside with colour and snow covered peaks punctured the bright blue sky above.

There were few travellers along the way so we shared stories with all those whose paths we crossed. Jack from Connecticut and Eric from Montreal, both on bicycles had teamed up in Bishkek. Jack was on a 'short' trip from Bishkek to Dushanbe – pretty amazing for a 17-year-old. Eric had ridden from Shanghai and was heading for South Africa, towing his gear in a trailer. On a nightmare stretch of rutted gravel, reminiscent of our route across the Altiplano in South America, we met three Dutchmen on hired off-road motorbikes. These guys were on a short trip around Tajikistan and Kyrgyzstan. The deputy Norwegian ambassador to Iran was travelling with his girlfriend who lay sick in the back of their van, and two Kyrgyz guys. Olly from England and Mathieu from France decked out in donated Rapha kit, had been working in Shanghai and decided to ride home. They were raising money for operations for children with hare lips (*www.roadofsmiles.com*).

We were the first cyclists they had met since setting out, crossing their path near Lake Karakul. At an altitude of 3,923m it is reputedly the highest lake in Central Asia and the highest in the world if you exclude those in Tibet. A bowl created by a meteorite which struck the earth 10 million years ago has filled with salty water, creating a huge lake over 30km in diameter. Edged by snow topped mountains it shines like a pristine turquoise jewel under the bright blue sky. The tiny ramshackle village of the same name sits on the eastern shore in splendid isolation, the only sign of life in the area. This really felt like a harsh environment where it must be so difficult to make a living. What do the people of Karakul do? There are several homestays there and a traveller can get food but that can't provide much employment. We didn't see a shop but we didn't look – we bought bread from the place where we had lunch.

Between the villages of Karakul in Tajikistan and Sary Tash in Kyrgyzstan

High camp just north of the Ak-Baital pass (4,655m)

the only habitations are at the scruffy customs posts, a couple of tiny remote dwellings and a handful of Kyrgyz yurts. When we reached the Tajik customs the official went into his metal cabin, shutting the door behind him. He then shouted something unintelligible which we took to mean that we should go in and show our passports. Other officials came out and spat on the ground.

Twenty kilometres of no man's land lies between the Tajik border and the Kyrgyz border control. The rivers take on the rust browns and greys of the mountains, the contrasting colours showing up sharply at the confluences. Where streams crossed the road there were no bridges and the stony beds were too loose to ride. In a small, flower rich meadow a man tended his yaks, animals with impossibly long horns and long shaggy black or white coats. After exchanging money with a group of Aussie motorcyclists going the opposite way, we reached the Kyrgyz customs where we waited until they gave up trying to get a generator to start up, presumably to power their computer. They managed without and let us off the narcotics check, so we were soon away.

We arrived at the recommended Elisa's guesthouse in Sary Tash wanting two key things – power for the computer and a shower. Power came on after fifteen minutes and the shower was in a tiny outdoor cubical fed from a warm water tank above. The family were preparing for a big feast. The sheep had been slaughtered and the skin spread out. The head was being attacked with a blow torch – a curious way of cooking the thin layer of meat – and the ribs were boiling in the large round pot over the dung fire. The women were working with a bucket full of intestines.

Sary Tash is in a beautiful setting which must give great views of the high Pamirs to the south on a clear day; but it wasn't a clear day and only a vague outline of the magnificent mountains was showing under a cloudy sky. The town has a shop, a tin shack, which looks like an old railway carriage – common in these parts. We bought rice, tomatoes, chocolate, a Snickers bar, onions, eggs and peach juice. The woman outside was using the brush to mix up dirt with the fresh dung which had already clogged up my shoes.

So feeling a bit tired we set out to climb the 4.2km to the pass – the sign said it was an 8% gradient. Oddly, all the slopes we climbed were an 8% gradient! Over the double pass and down the other side the scenery was spectacular. We regretted passing through this stunningly colourful and complex mountain terrain so quickly, on a day with very little sunshine and some heavy rain, as lower down the valley it wasn't nearly so pretty. It was so different from the high Pamir plateau, with a wealth of good pasture and so many trees and bushes on the lower slopes which were dotted with the yurts of the summer shepherds. Down, down, down we went, on a paved route of switchbacks which was being repaired by Chinese workers, freezing with the lack of effort until we were finally down to 1,660m where it was considerably warmer. We hadn't been at such low altitude for four weeks. We put up our tent amongst willow trees on a big flat area next to the river. Storms raged around as we cooked dinner.

The next day we rode rapidly to Osh where we found agreeable accommodation in a yurt placed in the yard of the TES guesthouse. Osh is regarded as the end of the Pamir Highway. The beginning is less clearly defined, possibly being Dushanbe or Khorog in Tajikistan, Mazar-i-Sharif in Afghanistan or Termiz in Uzbekistan. The route was historically one of the Silk Roads. Between 1931 and 1934 the Russians built the highway linking the remote outposts of the Soviet Empire, a road which is now the second highest international highway in the world, the highest being the Karakorum Highway. It is said that much of it was originally paved; it is now deteriorating and looks like it has never been paved.

We had been sorely tempted by the Karakorum route from Kashgar into Pakistan. However, the visa problems, the antics of the Taliban, the issue of probably being forced to dump the bikes on a truck for a large section of the route (the Chinese moved the border control to a junction 142km beyond the border) and the certainty of getting very wet in monsoon rains at some point all added too much weight against it.

THE PAMIR HIGHWAY

The Soviets built the road so that they could transport troops and provisions to remote areas and towns such as Khorog and Murghab which really only exist as towns because they were Soviet administration centres. Khorog has a certain charm, but to be honest it is hard to see why Murghab, which is said to be an unsustainable community, continues to exist; people are reluctant to move from where they have been brought up. As with Pinochet and the Carretera Austral in Chile, the Soviets unwittingly created one of the great cycle routes of the world. It carries very little traffic; apart from the cyclists there are motor bikers, the odd independent traveller in a heavy weight camper truck, a few local minibuses, beaten up lorries moving yurts in summer and lorries going to and from Kashgar in China

Osh, the second city of Kyrgyzstan, with a population of around 500,000 and the capital of the south, is a place of little distinction with few attractions for the tourist despite its claim by some to be a city older than Rome. It is genuinely the site of an ancient town with a history going back at least 3,000 years, but virtually nothing of this antiquity remains and the architecture is unremarkable. The city sits by the Kyrgyz/Uzbek border, one of Stalin's most ridiculous divisions placed with the deliberate intention to divide and rule. Osh lies in the Fergana valley, with the lower valley, its natural hinterland, lying in Uzbekistan. The valley isn't so much a valley; it is more realistically described as an 'inter mountain depression' and some of it also lies in Kyrgyzstan. The area has long been the population and agricultural heartland of Central Asia, and since the collapse of the Soviet Union one of the most unstable areas in the region, not helped by irrational borders cutting through what is a natural geographic entity.

The population of Osh is pretty well divided between Uzbeks and Kyrgyz with a handful of Russians, Turks and Tartars thrown in. Ethnic clashes have been common; trouble in 1990 was followed by the 2010 riots resulting in 400 deaths, thousands of injuries and widespread looting. We wondered if the lack of a cheery countenance in the local people could be linked to tensions that are said to continue to exist. Little of the magnificent Uzbek dress we saw in Uzbekistan was evident here; women's clothing definitely tugged more in the direction of western style with a Central Asian twist.

The sights of Osh are limited and whilst the city is not totally without charm it wasn't the most delightful place we had stayed. There are parks and gardens, but they could be spruced up a little. Tall shady trees gave great relief from the hot sun and we found one restaurant that we liked, a log cabin style place built amongst the trees which served the local Hoff beer on draught and did very nicely cooked kebabs, 'potatoes in a rural style' and 'French salad'. The riverside around the centre of town is a lively amusement park with tiny kids shooting around in toy cars, balloons and ice cream on sale and karaoke cabins in abundance. The river was cleaner than you might expect for this part of the world and the kids played in it. However we saw rats jumping over the plastic bottles that collected in some of the town's open waterways.

We treaded our way through the huge bazaar strung out along the river where you can buy a great selection of dried fruits if you don't mind the fact that they have had flies all over them. Fat ladies sat hands on knees, legs wide apart, peddling their wares – tall sacks of sprouting potatoes, mountains of onions and cart loads of bright green cabbages. You could buy nuts, spices, brooms made of rushes, tripe, sheep's heads done over with a blow torch, piping, cables, bright *shyrdaks*, colourfully patterned long dresses, Adidas tracksters, cheap western fashion and traditional hats. The indoor Osh Market is a superb supermarket where we found most of the special things we needed – French wine, oats, dried milk, olive oil, couscous, honey, lentils etc. We also bought some jubilee clips for emergency repairs on Hugh's failing front forks.

Osh boasts a World Heritage Site, the only one in the country. According to UNESCO, the mountain is 'the most complete example of a sacred mountain anywhere in Central Asia, worshipped over several millennia'. There is a fine view of the city from the top. A shrine on the rocky outcrop supposedly marks the grave of Sulayman (Solomon), recognised in the Qur'an as a prophet and a divinely-appointed monarch. It is a popular place for local Muslims, with stairs leading up to the highest peak where there is small mosque originally built by Babur in 1510, although much of the mosque was reconstructed in the late twentieth century.

We were in need of some recuperation time, something different to eat and some good beer; Osh just about delivered. There was an eclectic mix of people staying in the guesthouse. A Czech couple were camping in the garden. Chris and Sue from Derbyshire were travelling around with a ton of flying gear in the boot of their heavy duty campervan so they could get a regular fix from looking down on unfamiliar territory from the height of their balloon. They had to take care not to land in dodgy places. We enjoyed the company of Yannick, Mureul and their sons, Victor and Robin over the evening's aperitif – beer, wine, olives, crisps with brie and camembert *à la boîte* coming in a tin from the supermarket. It was a pleasant surprise to meet up with Yannick who we had last seen making his way from Karakul to Dushanbe and back on his motor bike, on a five day mission to collect visas for his family who were at that point waiting in their camion at Karakul. The camion came a cropper short of Osh when the gear box gave up and they had to be towed to Osh. The Pamir Highway takes a heavy toll on vehicles; perhaps bikes fare better. The family had been in the other garden yurt for three weeks waiting for a new *boîte de vitesses* (gear box) to arrive from France via DHL.

Our guesthouse provided all the things which a weary cyclist needs, a strong hot shower, use of a washing machine and pretty reasonable wifi. Hugh made up his mind to make full use of the excellent facilities. Whilst I was sat outside enjoying a beer with fellow travellers he mysteriously disappeared for almost half an hour. When he returned he had turned the clock back at least ten years! The long greying beard, reaching below his neckline that had labelled him as a terrorist had gone, leaving in its wake a smooth, youthful fine boned chin. I have to admit that it was good; I was beginning to find the hairy fuzz something of an impediment!

Yurts, high lakes and mare's milk

*Only those who risk going too far can possibly
find out how far they can go.*

T. S. Eliot

Pauline:

We pitched our tent by a clear mountain stream at the foot of the 3,346m Moldo-Ashuu Pass in the Tian Shan Mountains, just before the road vanished into a deep cleft. Before long we had Russian neighbours, a mixed aged group of six, riding mountain bikes with suspension. They offered us mint tea with cognac and gave us a proper map of the Song Kul region – one with contours and lots of detail, the likes of which we hadn't seen since we left home! The mountains of Kyrgyzstan offered superb wild camping and we often had visitors – frequently children from shepherds' huts or yurts nearby. At one camp we had found bouquets of wild daisies amongst the panniers outside our tent – a thank you from the little boys with a flat tyre needing a pump.

One of the Russian cyclists was intently engaged in stitching a patch onto the inside of his Schwalbe tyre – sharp rocks can be wicked! We carry a spare tyre but some problems can't be solved that easily. Over 12,500km into our journey Hugh's bike was beginning to suffer – noisy bearings in the front wheel, broken front rack bosses shored up with jubilee clips, a hairline crack in a front fork and panniers with splits in the plastic backing. However, the rim on my bike used by Khvicha to rebuild my back wheel in Baku, was looking like it would make the end of the trip.

A series of tight switchbacks on the dirt road took us up 1,000m, above the tree line and over the pass to the high altitude lake of Song Kul. The level grasslands, scattered with flowering edelweiss in late July, provide perfect summer pasture for domestic animals – horses, sheep, turkeys, chickens and cows. The only permanent man-made structure was the narrow dirt road – no villages, no power lines.

We found good company in two sisters and their children occupying three yurts, one of which they offered for visitors. The roofs of the Kyrgyz yurts are supported by a magnificent wooden structure painted in bright red – a lovely sight when lying in bed. Close set, thin struts radiate out from a central ring called a tunduk. Three or four wooden bands are laid across the ring in two directions making the pattern of a cross. The tunduk can be left open to the air to let in light or to let out smoke from the fire, but in cold or wet weather a canopy secured by ropes is laid over it. The flag of Kyrgyzstan consists of a red field charged with a yellow sun that contains a depiction of a tunduk.

The sisters bemoaned the effect of vodka on the nation's men – we had seen plenty of evidence of it. The village shops have layers of shelves devoted to it along with huge boxes of junk sweets – the healthy stuff, ripe fruit and tasty

YURTS, HIGH LAKES AND MARE'S MILK

July 14th 2013 to August 18th 2013
1500 kms

vegetables, was often on display outside. We met many people well on the way to inebriation at all times of day. The Moldo-Ashuu Pass was littered with empty bottles, many of them smashed to pieces. One of the husbands was out working with the animals, the other ruined by vodka in Bishkek – we weren't sure if he was alive or dead but he was clearly useless.

The traditional drinks of the Kyrgyz are much more healthy, if not always more palatable to the average westerner. People make them at home and store them in reused plastic bottles. Koumiss is a popular drink made from fermented mare's milk – I found its fizzy sourness a shock to the taste buds but often felt it was only polite to put on a good show of drinking it with relish. We preferred the Ayran – a yoghurt drink, made from sheep, goat or cow milk, which we knew well from our ride through Turkey. We saw Kyrgyz women up on the summer pastures milking cows by hand – two teats at a time – quite a contrast to the machinery for milking 300 cows at a time, which we saw in Australia. The women make thick cream, butter and yoghurt but strangely we didn't see anything we recognised as cheese.

Horses are central to Kyrgyz culture – not only for their milk, but for eating, and sport. We often saw them, looking strong and shiny, standing on top of little knolls, presumably to catch the cool breeze. They pulled overloaded carts of hay, grazed in large groups in the fields and men rode them bareback along the roadside. The key horsey team game played in our country is polo – a popular sport with the sort who drink glasses of chilled champagne or pimms – a wild, but gentlemanly game in which a mallet is used to move a tiny ball between goalposts. Skilful for sure but nothing like as wild as the Kyrgyz version. In place of the ball is a dead, headless goat or sheep – stretched to its limit as riders grab it by the limbs in an attempt to gain possession. It was amazing that the carcase wasn't pulled apart.

On the way the body often fell to the ground, and riders displayed unbelievable dexterity in leaning right over the horse's side to grab its thick coat. There were no goal posts – just a piece of old cloth laid on the ground as a target. At the end of the game the animal was skinned and then, the presumably tenderised meat was put on the barbecue. We had seen the same sort of game played in Afghanistan in the mid-1970s which they called Buzkashi. Horse wrestling was another popular game. Two bare chested muscular guys sat on their horses, feet in the stirrups and locked arms in combat in an effort to throw their adversary to the ground.

Climbing out of the basin of Song Kul we bumped into four Czechs with walking poles and heavily laden rucksacs on a week's hiking trip. As the only one of the Central Asian 'stans' not requiring visas, Kyrgyzstan attracts a lot of visitors being particularly popular with the intrepid French. Flights to the capital, Bishkek, are not too expensive and travel inside the country is cheap so short visits are not a bad option for a fuss free holiday.

Just up the road we met a couple of Dutch cyclists, riding lightweight with a hired minibus with a driver and translator – useful for understanding questions from inquisitive visitors. Further up the road we spotted their van parked in a perfect place for camping so we joined them for the night. The next day they caught us up on the road having struggled to extricate their van from a ditch – possibly something to do with an over indulgence in vodka!

'Nice bikes' said Hugh, 'they must be worth 3 or 4 thousand Euros each.' He was in the wrong ball park there – Eef's Specialized S-Works (with 29 inch wheels and 'Brain' suspension) was a startling €8,000. We are often asked by locals how much our bikes cost and it is usually too embarrassing to tell the truth but ours are merely half the cost of Eefs. They invited us to stay with them in Amsterdam on our return journey. At the end of the trip we flew to Amsterdam and cycled back home, reversing our outward journey through a piece of England. There was something about the few days getting home slowly that brought the end of this long journey to a meaningful conclusion – a completeness – landing home suddenly would have felt so different. Eef and Suzanne met us at Schiphol airport, appropriately with their Audi, and took us, our bags and boxed bikes to their summer caravan by a lake on the outskirts of

Amsterdam – a perfect place for us to reassemble the bikes. It was so wonderful to have such amazing help from fellow travellers and cyclists.

We were on our way to another lake, Issyk-Kul, the second largest saline lake in the world after the Caspian Sea. We had a day's break in the little town of Kochkor, where we were lucky to find a real 'Pearl' in the form of a young lady called Bermet (which means Pearl). She took us to the Beeline Office where for an outlay of around £40 we bought a modem stick which enabled us to get on-line via a 3G connection – not great but much better than the local wifi.

Kochkor is a town of pleasant little single storey houses with corrugated iron roofs. Many of the people build their own houses out of mud bricks which they also make themselves. We watched men at work, sprinkling a little straw into the mould, piling in the mud with a spade and patting it down. They would then turn out a row of bricks which were left to dry in the hot sun. After washing out the mould in a muddy pool of water they repeated the process turning out bricks at quite a pace. Houses, walls and storage sheds are all made out of these bricks.

We stayed in many 'homestays' in Kyrgyzstan. Bermet's family moved into one of the outbuildings in the yard in order to vacate their house for paying guests in the summer. This house had the luxury of a plumbed in shower and washbasin. Often the shower would be a DIY affair in the garden with the water supplied from an old petrol tank on the roof which was filled up as required and heated by the sun. The loo, in common with most homestays, was a squatting long drop housed in a little cubicle in the corner of the vegetable garden where there were piles of dung fuel and some heaps of hay. Most were kept scrupulously clean and not at all unpleasant. Plumbing and sewerage systems were not the norm. There was one multi-storey block of flats in Kochkor. We were told that they have neither inside loos nor running water – not great for those who live on the fourth floor!

A charming common feature of many village and rural homes was in the use of the roof space. The wide triangle at the gable end of the gently sloping roof, and the front of the house, would be filled in with an ornate, complex construction usually made from wooden boards – sometimes painted, commonly in a light blue. They could be laid at different angles to create attractive patterns – sometimes a radial pattern representing the sun at the apex. The room in the roofspace would have a door leading to a recessed balcony protected by pretty wooden railings – little outdoor spaces of many different shapes, sunk into the gable end. The top of the recess was often much more than a flat ceiling, but a swirling arch tapering to a sharp point at the top which came in so many individual shapes. The gentle slope of the main roof would have a carved wooden edging, often with an interesting motif at the apex. It felt so uplifting to see such care being put into making everyday objects beautiful, contrasting sharply with the feeling induced by the sight of the rough, utilitarian, decaying Soviet blocks that were still miraculously standing in many towns, and which we had seen all over the ex-Soviet republics.

Lenin still remains the central feature of many town squares and city halls, where he commonly towers from above in granite or bronze with an anachronistic arm pointing the masses in the direction of a glorious socialist future. He stood in Kochkor coated in tacky, shiny silver – the coating missing in a spot suggesting that people may have been chucking stones at his balls! In many other towns he had been left to decay or evicted.

The craft centre in Kochkor is a wonderful place to see the traditional felt rugs or *shyrdaks* which create the warm, cosy feel to the interior of the yurts where they are spread on the floors and hung from the walls. They are decorated with inlaid swirling patterns in highly contrasting colours. On our way to Song Kul we had seen a family, including three young boys, having enormous fun using their feet to beat hell out of a long roll of cloth, tightly held together with string! Something damp was wrapped up in a reed mat inside it. They were kicking it along the road through Ak Tal. Later we found out that this was a stage in the making of a *shyrdak*, turning the wet wool into felt.

Hot, dry and dusty near Kazarman, Kyrgyzstan.

It was from Kochkor that the wonderfully contoured 1:200,000 map from the Russians enabled us to avoid 90km of main road. The alternative was a set of dirt tracks with grass in the middle, which turned to little more than faint imprints in the pasture, and occasionally vanished altogether. We found ourselves riding across close cropped grassland using our compass to try to confirm the route. There was a large element of hit and miss, and guesswork. Interestingly neither Google maps nor the Pocket Earth app that we use nowadays shows any through road. We had willing help from people at a yurt on the way who confirmed we were on the right route and they gave us some koumiss to help us on our way.

The folk in a yurt up the hill from our first camp came to help us in the morning, holding my bike while I clipped on the panniers. At our next camp a guy on a horse came to our 'sputnik' – his name for our tent! He brought bottles of yet another strange fermented brew – this one a mucky brown. He called it *shoro*. A company called Shoro branded the traditional Kyrgyz nomadic drink, Maksym, calling it Maksym Shoro. It is brewed from a selection of cereals and is one of a very large variety of healthy fermented drinks enjoyed by the Kyrgyz, generally with an undisputedly unique taste which we think takes some

Family fun making a shyrdak in Ak Tal, Kyrgyzstan.

getting used to.

We had to push the bikes through several little streams and at one point we realised we were on the wrong side of a river, which fortunately we were able to wade. When the track dumped us on rough pasture I was tipped off my bike hitting my head hard on a tough tussock. It's always good to wear the helmet as falls can be so unpredictable. We crossed several little rocky passes where the roadside was lined with many different colourful flowers – always hoping that we were landing ourselves in the right valley. This road/track/footpath/bit of pasture wasn't intended as any sort of through route – it is a thread in a maze of tracks which locals take to their yurts in summer.

It was a delightful little 'mini-adventure' and all the more special because it was all down to the map from the Russians. We landed on the shores of Issyk-Kul – the lake that never freezes. A Dutch family, with a six-year-old son, all on loaded bikes were doing a tour around the lake, which is so big it looks like the sea. There was a tacky resort along the shore where overweight holiday makers dressed for the beach walked past the shops selling blow up boats and buckets and spades. A drunk lay comatose on the earth at the roadside. This had been a popular vacation area in the Soviet era. We managed to find a quiet

spot for our tent on the shore where we enjoyed a swim. The name means 'warm sea' – it is fed by hot springs.

It was an easy ride along the lake shore – the blue waters stretching out on our left and mountains towering above on our right – beautiful. The drivers were not so beautiful. Some guys in a truck overtook me and then deliberately pulled in sharply towards the road edge. I had to pull off onto the grit to safety – they were within inches of my rear pannier. As they drove off I shouted out in anger – 'bastards'. Of course that was the aim – to wind me up – and they thought it was very funny. I saw the smirk on the guy's face as he hung out of the window. And the Dutch family were riding this road with a six-year-old, on his own bike – worrying! These experiences really colour your impression of a country and it is hard for it not to taint the whole experience.

Previous to this trip we had labelled the Kiwis as the worst drivers in the world – the Kyrgyz beat them easily – no seatbelts and often on the phone. They would play a game of 'chicken' with us, deliberately heading straight for us and then steering away at the last moment. We found long sticks and taped something bright on the end. We attached them to our pannier racks, sticking out a metre or more into the road. It worked and deflected the traffic. It was

Nearing the top of Akkyia-Ashuu (2,930m), Kyrgyzstan.

EXTRAORDINARY PLACES BY BICYCLE

tempting to attach a sharp knife on the end! Fortunately most of our route through the country was on deserted dirt tracks in the mountains where our experience of the people couldn't have been more of a contrast.

Our introduction to the country had also been atypical. The ride out of Osh was dull and busy with crazy drivers. The valley was flush with green corn and bright yellow sunflowers, and bordered by bare brown hills – pleasant enough scenery but not too inspiring following on from the wonders of the Pamir Highway. We weren't in the mood to camp – the area was inhabited and fresh water not easy to come by. We found a hotel five kilometres out of what we rated as uninspiring Uzgen, although had we made more effort we could have seen a beautiful twelfth century mausoleum. We found a simple hotel room at a kind of traveller's service area – a strip development along the road with lots of eating and drinking places – no charm but somewhere to rest, have a (cold) shower and eat – the basics.

The people who ran the hotel were very friendly and helpful. When I went to wash, I was a little surprised to find a nearly naked man stood in the corridor having just vacated the shower – in the room opposite a woman sat wrapped in a sheet. Soon afterwards the room was empty. It slowly dawned on us what the hotel was really about! Just up the road we had fish and beer for dinner entertained by two pissed locals sat behind us talking about President Tony Blair

Tasting fermented mare's milk high above Kochkor, Kyrgyzstan.

and Margaret Thatcher and singing out our alphabet – far from sober but pleasant with it.

As we closed in on the mountains at the head of the Fergana valley, the traffic thinned and the scenery became much more interesting. Fields had been cut for hay which was then piled up high and overflowed on ramshackle horse-drawn carts and small trucks. Little houses and outbuildings had a wild hairdo of hay.

Three days out of Osh, going north of Jalalabat, we climbed up into cooler air heading for the pass taking us to the next significant town of Kazarman, roughly half way to the high altitude lake of Song Kul. The road turned to dirt and the pattern of the journey across Kyrgyzstan was set. Empty, dusty tracks zigzagged up to high passes (*ashuu*) where vultures soared – Kaldamo-Ashuu 2,985m, Akkyia-Ashuu 2,930m, Moldo-Ashuu 3,300m and Kalmak-Ashuu 3,446m. Even in July, snow lingered in the cracks of the rocky summits. Lower down, conglomerate or mud cliffs were eroded into surreal formations, cliffs etched with close, vertical lines of gullies. The hillsides were often bare, with patches of scree and rock scratched out by the elements – or scattered with low trees and bushes. Taller trees grew where the streams ran down the hillsides and in the lush valley bottoms. Zones of red sandstone, multi-coloured layers of folded ancient sediments and naked, wrinkled mini ranges thrown into sharp

Topping up with fruit and vegetables in Baetovo, Kyrgyzstan.

relief by the light of the sun all made for a magnificent landscape, which at the same time could be harsh.

Semi-nomadic people lived in yurts, makeshift tents and mud cabins where they tended their animals during the summer. The children would come out and shout and wave excitedly as we went by. Bareback riders were rounding up multi-coloured sheep – reddy brown, shades of grey, off white and black – it was time for shearing. Heading up the first pass we were invited into a shepherd's shelter. He was busy making cream with a hand turned Russian contraption – he said he was processing 60 litres of milk! The thick cream ran out into a big pot and they scooped some into a small bowl for us to eat with bread – a practice which was also common in Tajikistan. We never worked out how they got the cream to market without it going sour. He camped with his family in the hills for the summer beginning in April – they had a small yurt. They kept twenty cows and chickens and grew some corn and potatoes.

Produce was frequently transported by donkey. Donkeys were a key element of mountain life – we saw people loading them up with metal churns full of water collected from streams, adults rode them and children liked to ride them

Playful kids near Jalalabat, Kyrgyzstan.

two or three at a time. We stopped at a tiny country shop for a half melted ice cream and the kids thought it hilarious when I briefly exchanged my bike for their donkey. Some travellers went for it big time though; French cyclist, Jipe had left France by bike over two years previously – he had picked up news about us from other cycle tourists – we met him and his girlfriend Justine near Kochkor, where for around $100 they had bought 'Dylan(e)' (*âne* being French for donkey). They planned to sell her (and her baby) after the walk, when Justine would return to Alsace and Jipe would get back on his bike – a much faster way of getting around. Donkey trekking in Asia is an 'experience' to savour.

However, most of the locals appeared to favour the Audi to the ass! The lady at our homestay in Kazarman explained to us why Audis plough the rough roads of Kyrgyzstan. They are driven over via the Baltic countries and they are popular because they have the clearance to manage the appalling road surfaces. We had one way back in 1981 and we know that spare parts for them are expensive, so we asked 'what do the people here do when they go wrong?' We were told that they use spares from even older Audis or cheap Chinese copy parts. Every little village has a garage which can repair them. So the Audi is the Kyrgyz Lada. They are fond of the ones with five cylinder engines. A young man with a 24-year-old Audi told us that a 10-year-old car counts as 'new'. It is a flourishing business – bringing them over from Latvia by train, transporter or driving. It could be a way to pay for your holiday – drive out an old Audi worth around $7,000 out and sell it for $12,000. He showed us his which had done more than 400,000km with no problems until the speedo broke – good for driving at speed up rough dirt roads he said, as we had noticed!

Kazarman is described in Wikipedia as having 'something of the sinister reputation of a tough mining town down on its luck' – it felt like it. The gold mine, which was its reason for existence, now provides little employment. The town is cut off in winter and although it has a small airport there are no flights. Getting anywhere from Kazarman is a rough journey. Our homestay was pleasant enough although we had been told that we couldn't use the loo because it was being painted – we could use the one next door but it wasn't as clean as theirs! A crazy driver went straight for us in the street and then other little things started to irritate – people just spitting on the street (a not uncommon practice); the incessant honking from passing cars; the bemused 'you must be an alien' stare from passers-by; and the lack of any vegetables in the shops. Perhaps we had been away too long!

Before we left heading for the Akkyia-Ashuu, we went hunting for a café. We found an intriguing building with wonderfully decorated ceilings and facades, housing a café on the ground floor. The pictures at the entrance summed up perfectly our experience of the ubiquitous dishes served in the simple eateries of Central Asia: *Lachman* – noodles with veg and bits of meat; *Samsa* – like an Indian samosa stuffed with various meats and/or vegetables and *Plov* – rice pilau with what was frequently a token serving of meat, usually lamb and generally regarded as a treat but sometimes little more than a mountain of greasy rice; *Manty* – our favourite – like a giant ravioli, filled with meat, rice and/or veg. Thin broth with pieces of meat and vegetables, plus miscellaneous meaty stews served with rice, completed the picture. Desserts didn't exist. We were often given just a spoon and a fork to eat with – just try cutting a fried egg with a spoon or fork! Knives were generally for tourists.

Once we passed the quarries beyond Kazarman, the road was almost deserted – no other tourists and no motor cyclists. The area really felt like the back of beyond – little visited – as remote as we have ever felt on the road. On the far side of the pass we put our tent in a flower meadow amongst the trees by a clear river and had a really good wash – I even washed my hair. I cooked a three course dinner – spicy lentil soup followed by cashew pilau and semolina with honey, raisins and jam for pudding. We had never seen such lush grassland, densely covered in a colourful array of wild flowers – a feast for the animals. No wonder they have such wonderful horses and the cows looked equally well fed.

In the tiny hamlet of Kosh-Dyube a man and his daughter invited us in for tea. Keen to communicate, they rang a member of the family who supposedly spoke some English but we couldn't understand a word he said. This was something that happened often in Turkey. Super strong tea was poured from a pot and then hot water and milk were added to make a weak milky mix. We ate home-made bread with cream, butter and jam (but not all at once) – all these things spread on the bread with a teaspoon. Before eating I washed my hands at the outdoor basin housed in a custom piece of furniture with a cupboard underneath – the water tub was filled from a bucket. They had a large fridge freezer but no plumbing in the kitchen. We noticed some German souvenirs on top of the fridge – one of the daughters had studied in Berlin. These people live so far from any significant town or city and any journey involves many hours bumping along a dirt road. We didn't pass any shops – the kind family gave us some bread refusing to take any money for it.

Our next camp was at the foot of a dry rocky valley where it was a struggle to find water for our camp – we ended up taking it from a milky river. We had seen blocks of mud for sale in bazaars – people actually eat it for the mineral content, just as we had seen in Beyneu in Kazakhstan earlier – so we hoped that the muddy water would be good for us!

In the valley bottom the river ran through a corridor with sheer walls of layered rocks – faint browns with a touch of rose – the mud walls of the semi-ruinous buildings near the roadsides were of the same colour – burial grounds and mausoleums made from the same earth, built of mud bricks and enclosed by mud brick walls. We passed many such buildings on the road from the Akkyia-Ashuu to Jangy Talap as well as new village mosques – attractive, diminutive buildings so unlike the monstrous constructions we had seen going up in Turkey. Scattered along the route were large, isolated mausoleums with domed roofs often in a state of collapse. They had little towers at each corner and a layer of decorative lattice work of mud bricks on the tops of the walls, enclosing open geometric shapes – rectangles, triangles and crosses. Some had archways or faux archways – tall and going to a point. One or two retained a layer of smooth plaster on the outside wall and remnants of white paint on the domes. Tombs crowded in the burial grounds, with short metal rods supporting metal stars and moons atop a stepped apex where the pictures of the deceased were on display. Outside walls had the remains of tiles in pale blue, faint reds and white. The only date we could find relating to any of these was on a plaque outside a particularly fine example near Jangy Talap, the mausoleum of Taylak Batyr, dated 1796-1837!

Jangy Talap is a tiny village but the *Lonely Planet Guide* listed a place to stay there. We struggled to find it. Finding a homestay was often a bit like a treasure trail – you ask lots of different people, some who look mystified and some who give you useful snippets of information, until you finally home in on the place. There are no signs to help you – not even a sign at the house indicating it is a homestay. We had heard stories about Kyrgyzstan being geared up for tourists but it wasn't always that evident on our journey. Cyrillic is used almost universally rather than the frequent dual script signs we saw in other Central Asian countries, which means that you really needed to learn your alphabet. We did eventually find the place from the man running the only shop in town which sold produce more useful than the usual million different types of vodka and large plastic bottles of beer. The charming family gave us a magnificent breakfast in the morning with a superb selection of the traditional home-made preserves – quite runny, containing whole berries and tasting very strongly of the fruit – blackcurrants, strawberries, raspberries and cherries.

We left with provisions bought in Ak Tal – a village just before Jangy Talap and a little larger – and fresh homemade bread and fruity preserves from our homestay. We reached the camp where we met the Russians the following night, passing many deserted farms – their occupants probably 1,000m up at Song Kul.

We spent two of our last three nights in Kyrgyzstan in Karakol, close to the eastern end of Issyk-Kul after taking a short out and back detour to Svetov Dolina (Valley of the Flowers). The valley is an area of striking red rocks which gave us a splendid night's camp complete with a natural stream powered Jacuzzi in an undoubtedly beautiful valley; even so we weren't convinced that the detour was worth it. Young men with falcons aggressively tried to make me take photographs (for money) – a strategy designed to produce the opposite effect – kind of summed it up. We had fallen for a falcon display a couple of days earlier in Kadji-Sai, an experience which we regret to this day and can't understand why we did it. In mitigation I don't think we realised what is was all about – we found the spectacle of watching a tamed, mainly tethered raptor swooping down on a helpless rabbit purely for our entertainment just made us feel sad.

In Karakol it was time to start thinking about the end game. With our daughter Amy's wedding in mind, it seemed a sensible decision to return home from Almaty in Kazakhstan. We had been sorely tempted to go into China but the intricacies of getting a visa and the limited time left to us weighed against it – China would have to wait. We booked flights from Almaty to Amsterdam for three weeks later, and then the ferry from Rotterdam to Hull. We had a contact in Almaty – Renat. The day before we left home at the start of the trip, we had visited friends near Kendal, who introduced us to Venera and John, a couple living nearby. Venera is from Kazakhstan and her family, including her brother Renat, live in Almaty. We were given their contact details and a sincere offer of help should we need it.

We walked around Karakol and found much of interest, including many lovely, traditional cottages with colourful windows in shades of light blue and green with pretty shutters and attractive moulded decorations above and sometimes below. Many had gardens full of flowers and trees – some wildly overgrown. In contrast there are also scruffy blocks of flats, the usual boring shop fronts and dirty streets full of puddles, heaps of earth and stones. With a little bit of tidying up it would be great – particularly with its wonderful backdrop of mountains – and there are little gems of interest well worth visiting.

Karakol was founded in 1869; in common with many towns and cities in the ex-Soviet republics it began life as a Russian military outpost. The population grew in the nineteenth century when explorers came to map the peaks and valleys separating Kyrgyzstan from China. In the 1880s the population surged with an influx of Dungans fleeing from warfare in China. They came from Xinjiang Province in north-western China, also the home of the Uyghur who are suffering badly at the hands of the Chinese at the time of writing this book; in common with the Uyghur they are a Turkic, Muslim people.

The unmistakeably Chinese and exquisitely beautiful Dungan mosque in Karakol was built in 1910. It was the work of a Chinese architect and twenty Chinese master carvers, and in order to conform to the Chinese architectural tradition, it was built without the use of nails. The style is very similar to that of a Chinese Buddhist temple. The undersides and rafters of the overhanging eaves are decorated with finely carved beams, painted in a delicate shade of blue with decorations highlighted in red and green and in classic Chinese style they curve upwards to a sharp point at the corners. The wooden minaret is constructed in wood and painted in the same blue. The main walls are of small, light grey bricks and all around the outside wooden pillars support the overhanging roof to provide a shaded perimeter. The Bolsheviks closed the mosque for ten years but it is now used as a place of worship by both Dungan and Kyrgyz. The apples for which the area is famous hung heavily on the trees around the mosque.

The Holy Trinity Russian Orthodox Cathedral is another very special building which suffered even more under the Bolsheviks. They destroyed its onion domes and turned it into a club. It has since been restored and is now very much a place of worship. The current wooden structure completed in 1895 was built on the site of the original stone structure which was destroyed by an earthquake in 1889. And heaven – we discovered a proper cake shop selling real sponge cakes (good ones too), baklava and various sweet croissant type pastries. We said *merhabe* to the Turkish guy from Antalya working at the counter.

Karakol is one of those towns which many travellers pass through and it is one of those bottle neck points where touring cyclists meet. Kate and Alee, an Australian couple travelling on a tandem from Amsterdam to Melbourne, like us, are very keen on their coffee. We thought we had it sussed with our smart mugs – a cafetière in a mug, but we were soon to find out that we were way off the mark. They demonstrated their $100 contraption which made perfect espresso using the power of a bike pump! We bought one, by post from Australia, as soon as we got home and it has been an essential piece of kit on our journeys ever since. Sadly they are no longer available so we need to treat it kindly.

Alice and Peter, the Cumbrian couple we had met first in Khorog and then in Osh were there too. It was the tandem that interested them. Alice was having on-going back problems so they had decided to get a tandem frame sent to them. Then they would fit it with bits from their solo bikes ready for a fast run through to the Far East.

Some way up the road to Kazakhstan from Karakol, we began to suspect that we were heading in the wrong direction; the compass confirmed it. We asked, 'Is this the way to Kazakhstan?' – 'No' was the answer! Eight kilometres up the wrong valley we put up our tent in a field of aromatic thyme next to the river. The bee keepers from over the road confirmed that we were en route to the little village of Jyrgalang, not to the Kazakh border! Surprisingly, given the simplicity of our navigation tools, this was the first time we had actually gone wrong. However, it was a very pretty valley and a great camping spot.

Our mistake was hardly surprising as the road to the border reared up ahead of us looking ridiculously rough and steep. It took us over the San-Tash pass (around 2,100m), down to the Karkara valley where we joined the main road from Karakol – still dirt – and went on to the border looking out onto a high level plain. Barbed wire fencing stretched out across the grassland in both directions.

We had spent 26 nights in Kyrgyzstan – fifteen wild camping, two in yurts, three in guesthouses, five in hotels and one in a brothel! Days of mountainous riding mainly on rough dirt roads had given us a window into the semi-nomadic lives of many of the people and we had received nothing but a warm welcome. We passed through the border quickly and were soon on the road to Kegen – once again in the ninth largest country in the world at the opposite end from where we first entered it.

We headed straight for the police station. Within five days of entering the country foreign visitors must secure a stamp on their immigration card. The first OVIR office (the Russian acronym for passport and visa agency) where this is usually done is in Almaty and we wouldn't expect to get there for around eight days or more. The plan was to persuade the police in Kegen to do it for us – we had been told at the border that this was possible. At first things looked didn't look good – 'Almaty, five days' was all they had to say, oblivious to our indications that we wouldn't make it. So we got our computer out and showed them the Russian translation of our plea, which Renat our contact in Almaty, had sent to us via email. This aroused some interest. The police officer tried tapping on the computer possibly thinking it would act as a translator – a pity it didn't! Then he got on the phone and after several conversations there were some thumbs up signs – promising! Come back in the morning at nine for the stamp was the final conclusion – brilliant – thanks Renat.

So we were left with two problems – finding a place to stay and getting some food. We had eaten only snacks since the breakfast porridge. We negotiated the minefield of broken vodka bottles around the back streets following up clues from passers-by to a *gastinetsa* (guest house) and only found two, closed and looking very uninviting. We decided to tackle the food problem and whilst investigating some loud music in a garden got ourselves invited into the kitchen where the food for a wedding was being prepared – this was after being filmed at the entrance. The guests were fascinated by our journey of 13,000km from England. A lovely lady made sure that our table was filled with yummy things to eat – paradise.

We considered cycling out of town and putting up the tent but then decided to give one of the 'hotels' a last go; some helpful chaps outside phoned up the boss who turned up about ten minutes later. It was a basic plyboard building with some windows covered in plastic. The room had hard beds and a glass window that nearly fell out into the room when I tried to open it. On the plus side the shower was hot (one of those Chinese made cabins in a huge room with no attempt at decor) and the loo was a sit down which flushed, actually inside the building. The room had a pretty lampshade and a rug on the floor. Not bad for around £15 for two. When it came to make porridge in the morning we found out that the water was off – luckily we had some in our bottles. The flush loo wasn't working so it was a dash out in the rain to the hole in the floor loo in the yard.

We arrived at the police station at 8:45 feeling hopeful of getting our immigration stamps – probably not at 9am – perhaps we would have to wait for an hour or so. We waited for three and a half hours, watching the rain teeming down outside, our mood increasingly matching the weather. At least it wasn't great weather for riding – surprisingly cool. Policemen came and went wearing their funny hats, lighting fags and spitting on the ground outside. The guy in a flak jacket with an automatic weapon seemed to have the most boring job – he kept taking his combat helmet off and putting it on again and pacing around the entrance looking completely ridiculous.

The chap who was helpful yesterday kept giving me a nod as he came and went suggesting something may be happening. In between times he did bits of paper work, fiddled with the lock on the door of what may have been a cell, and walked around the office doing nothing special. There was no suggestion of hard work or efficiency. Now and again one of them would come up to us and repeat the 'Almaty, five days' mantra and we would go through the 'not the way we are going on our bikes' response – we were not intending to take the main road. The scene alternated between hope and despair – exaggerated by our inability to communicate properly. I resorted to tears hoping this would embarrass them into action. At one point I was sent upstairs to talk to the boss. He flicked idly through my passport looking at nothing in particular – a favourite pastime of officials – whilst I tried to impress him with the story of how we had cycled from England and done 13,000km to get to Kegen.

Eventually a guy in Adidas tracksters turned up – the 'migration officer' no less – unbelievable. He took our passports and instructed us to follow his car. As we struggled to see where he had gone, I realised that we had just given our passports to a random guy who we might never see again. However, a miracle had happened. He led us off to another office where to our amazement he put the precious stamp on our migration cards, and the sun came out!

So – were the police being unhelpfully slow to help or did they do us a great favour getting our card stamped on a Sunday having tried hard to find the migration officer who was possibly out playing sport? Who knows? But, we were now spared having to explain ourselves in Almaty and being fined at least $100 each. We needed to recover from the stress of the morning so we put up our tent early close to a small mud built mausoleum. There was a stream in the little canyon below us and inspiring views of arid peaks and the huge flat steppe. So different from the green pastures of Kyrgyzstan – but we loved it.

Our 1:3,000,000 map of Kazakhstan had a picture of an impressive looking canyon on the front – looking a bit like a mini Grand Canyon. We realised that we were heading straight for it. On the road to the turn off we stopped to talk to a Belgian motorcyclist, heading for Kyrgyzstan and Bishkek having come from Mongolia where he said people try to rip you off all the time. Hugh is always quick to take advantage of an opportunity to change money, so we got some much needed cash in a mutually beneficial exchange.

We descended to the Sharin Canyon, the Valley of the Castles, a spectacular little side valley – the miscellaneously shaped turrets of red sandstone giving it the name; parts of the road were just too steep and rough to ride down –

never mind how we would get up again. At one point two massive boulders nearly blocked the road leaving a triangular gap that a chunky 4x4 would struggle to get through. A little grassy patch by the river in the bottom of the main canyon was our home for the night.

This little side trip was such a memorable spark in our journey, all the more because we had not been expecting to be near the location of that enticing image on our map and in addition it was such a contrasting environment to the barren steppe around – nothing hints at this sudden cleft in the earth until you are upon it and looking over the edge. It had also been a day of amazing

Sharin canyon – valley of the castles, Kazakhstan.

hospitality. We were given a bottle of iced water by a passer-by on the main road; several very welcome litres of water and some delicious water melon from the young chap at the entrance to the Sharin Canyon National Park; a modem stick which would work in Kazakhstan by a young Kazakh couple; beer, melon and cognac from Russian tourists; and bread, cheese and vodka from the threesome down at our camp. Would this happen in Britain we asked ourselves? It was a wonderful welcome to Kazakhstan.

Our route to Almaty deviated from the main road at Kokpek, where we planned to restock with provisions for several nights of camping – only Kokpek wasn't a village as such – more like a messy service station with a handful of little cafés. There were no village houses and nowhere to stay – no mobile phone or internet reception either.

Cyclists, Alex and Jana from Germany were in Kokpek, like us looking for provisions in the motley collection of little shops where as usual it was easy to buy vodka and sweets but not much else. They had just come over the off-road route across the Assy plateau – exactly where we were heading. 'It is hard' they said. 'You will have to push for three or four hours up onto the plateau.' I thought about this as I piled what food we could find into my panniers – more food means you can take longer but more food to carry means it takes longer! There was no way we were going to change our minds though. The main road had gathered more traffic after the junction with a road from the north and China – it would be a grim ride whereas Jana and Alex said that the hard way was beautiful; so that was the way for us.

It took us five days to get from our camp by a tiny stream just out of Kokpek to Almaty, the former capital of Kazakhstan. The Assy plateau was empty, rugged and rough tough riding. The track, entirely unpaved, frequently washed out and often strewn with rocks, stretched into the distance – a line across the close cut pasture land, curving with the contours of the hillsides, in and out of gullies and frequently taking the fall line straight up the rounded folds between the larger streams. We frequently had to push – I found it hard not having enough weight to counter the bulk of the bike. It took us through the depths of narrow, steep sided valleys with walls of cracked rock, where tall pines grew near the rushing waters lined with high grasses. The harsh, barren wildness of the landscape was tempered by bright outcrops of red sandstone, which shone in the sun's rays. There were rainbows and subtle evening light brought out the shades of colour and shadows in the creases of the lower slopes. The weather followed a routine – fine in the morning and rain with storms in the late afternoon. At high camps there was ice on the tent when Hugh went out for an early morning pee but it was gone by the time I emerged – only after Hugh had delivered the early morning tea.

Shepherds moved their animals in large flocks across the land. It was only near the end of the route that it felt at all like a plateau. Here yurts were scattered over a wide, gently sloping valley grazed by goats, sheep and cattle.

Somewhere near the middle of this final little excursion off the beaten track we reached a settlement called Assy. It seemed to be some kind of checkpoint as a barrier stopped cars and a man went out with a book in hand to note something down. We were invited in for tea – and bread, jam, butter and halva. They gave us some *qurut* to take away with us. These dried yoghurt balls have been enjoyed by Central Asian herders since the Middle Ages and were the nearest thing we saw to cheese – a passable imitation for parmesan when cut up finely and scattered on our pasta dish at camp.

We were following the valley of the River Assy, climbing gently through a valley dotted with yurts; the road crossed the river but there was no bridge. We took the panniers off the bikes and transported everything across in stages. We camped under a little crag further along the river and nearby there was a huge pile of empty vodka bottles – a sad legacy in all the ex-Soviet republics. A truck stopped on the road and offered us something out of a ten litre plastic bottle – it wasn't water but vodka. Even the dirt track across the *jailoo* (pasture) was littered with broken glass.

A clear fast flowing mountain stream accompanied us down the Batan Gorge and we found the perfect place for our last camp of the trip, surrounded by high grasses and forest with nature's bath on hand. We had a lazy morning watching the tent dry in the sunshine – it needed to be bone dry before we packed it away for the journey home. Lots of traffic including many chunky 4x4s were heading up the valley – families heading up to the plateau for the weekend.

We soon reached the asphalt road giving us a fast run down the valley. The bikes and panniers had picked up a lot of mud so we washed them in the river. The valley was lined with picnic spots – all numbered and named with little red signs. Families had set up yurts, tents and big tables under shade and were enjoying lunchtime picnics. We were hungry and looking for somewhere to eat but sadly no one showed signs of asking us over and although we passed several restaurants they were surprisingly all shut – everyone was doing their own thing – but we couldn't, we were out of food.

The lower end of the valley was guarded by the 'Golden Man' – replicas are scattered all over Kazakhstan, something of a national symbol. In 1969 archaeologists uncovered human remains along with magnificent gold-embroidered armour at the Issyk burial mound 60km east of Almaty. He was quickly dubbed the Golden Man, although some evidence suggests that the warrior who wore the costume may have been a woman – women warriors being common at that time. Little is known about the warrior, as researchers were so stunned by the rich find of jewellery that they largely ignored the human remains. A BBC report from January 2019 notes that 'The bones were only rediscovered recently at a forensic institute, stored in a cardboard box with a scribbled note reading: 'The Golden Man, May He Rest in Peace' – investigations continue!

We met Renat in the modern city centre of Almaty near Republika Alangy and the Monument of Independence, also known as the Golden Warrior Monument; the Golden Man again, standing on a narrow plinth which looks as tall as the nearby skyscrapers. It was a Sunday and there was wedding fever around the city – white stretch limousines decked with pink paper roses and netting;

wedding guests danced excitedly in the streets. We chased Renat's car for an unexpected 20km ride through the city to the family home. He offered to take our luggage but it didn't seem right. On the way we bumped into a couple of cyclists out for a spin on super light bikes. We couldn't remember when we had last seen people doing this. They said they were friends of Alexandr Vinokourov – the Olympic champion.

We had arrived in Almaty a little sooner than we anticipated, with ten days to go before our flight. It was a long time to depend on the hospitality of the family that we only knew from a fleeting contact with Renat's sister, Venera. However, they welcomed us warmly making us very comfortable and feeding us handsomely. We grew very fond of them and learnt so much from the stories of their lives.

Renat's parents, Farid and Flyura are Tatars from Ufa in Bashkortostan, Russia. In 1975 they were sent to work in Almaty, over 2,500km away to the south-east. They were sent – no choice – it was the Soviet Union then and you did what you were told. Almaty is now their home and they have built themselves a lovely large family house on the western side of the city where they live with Renat, their other son Eldar, his wife Galina and young son Emil. They have a beautiful garden with carefully tended lawns, fruit trees and a thriving vegetable patch. Farid and Flyura still speak the Tatar language between them at times and when they return to visit family in Ufa where Flyura's mother (83 at the time) still lived, but the family language is Russian. All over the former Soviet Union, families have been separated by thousands of kilometres as a result of enforced migration. People from so many different regions – Volga Germans, whole nations from the Caucasus and almost the entire population of ethnic Koreans living in the Soviet Union to name but a few were dumped in Kazakhstan amongst the native Kazakhs, where often there was neither work nor sufficient food for the new migrants.

Flyura was busy knitting and she showed me pictures of beautiful garments she had made for herself, her children and her grandchildren. She told me that back in Soviet times every women was a seamstress and knitter – you had to be – there was nothing in the shops. Fabric and wool sometimes came from factories – the workers stole it and sold it. Now the bazaars are full of cheap Chinese goods.

Almaty was previously named *Alma-Ata* meaning 'father of apples' – the apple originates from Kazakhstan. We had seen many wild apple trees in the mountains. The city is famous for the Aport apple which can reputedly grow as big as a baby's head and only a couple of apples can weigh up to a kilo. The Galyamov family house is surrounded by apple trees, including the Aport variety, although the apples are a little small because the trees are in the shade. Apples were drying on trays out in the sun, the lovely aroma of apples cooking wafted from the kitchen and delicious apple pies and cakes were served at tea time topped with homemade cream from Galina's family farm. We particularly enjoyed these sweet things having been deprived of anything resembling a proper desert or cake for some time.

Flyura also gave us delicious borscht, stuffed peppers and fish that Farid had caught in a nearby lake. The breakfast table was piled high with pancakes or bowls of porridge were served followed by eggs and more. The family make delicious jams from the berries and fruits that grow wild and in the garden. In common with homes of the more prosperous in Central Asia, the garden was enclosed within a high wall accessed by a sturdy gate – as were all the other homes around. There appeared to be a feeling that security is an issue, but it may be more of a statement of wealth than a real concern.

Galina also told us that in Kazakhstan mothers have three years' maternity leave – not three months as in England. Only one year is on full pay – but after three years they are guaranteed their job back. Extended family ties are highly valued in Kazakhstan and it was good to see the state supporting families too. It is not uncommon for newly weds to spend time living with parents.

In 1994 President Nazarbayev made the decision to transform an insignificant little village of the steppe in the middle of nowhere – Akmola meaning the white graveyard – into a surreal modern capital. It was named Astana, simply meaning capital. The move took place in 1997, and over a decade a spanking new city 1,200 km away from the old capital of Almaty was built at a cost of over ten billion dollars. In 2019 the name was changed to Nur-Sultan, after Nursultan Nazarbayev, the former president in office from 24 April 1990 until his formal resignation on 19 March 2019.

For all the talk of elections falling short of respected international standards and a conspicuous absence of an effective opposition, Nazarbayev may well have some respect from the people; in a sense he is of the people – the son of a poor family, at one time nomad shepherds, who in his youth went to work in the dangerous conditions of the foundry at the Termirtau steel plant near the infamous gulag town of Karaganda. There he personally felt the shock waves from the nuclear tests carried out by the Soviet regime. It is impressive that having been saddled with a large arsenal of Soviet nuclear arms hanging around after independence, the country has now become a nuclear-free zone.

The former capital, Almaty, a city shaded in summer by leafy trees sits at the foot of towering mountains which act as both a summer and winter playground. Astana sits on a dusty plain plagued by strong winds. The move was not popular. The streets of Almaty are busy with traffic and getting around by bus can be painfully slow – better to walk. There are cafés and bars in abundance selling great food and drink but it can be pricey if you don't eat the local food. It is a tidy modern city where a melange of peoples, the majority Kazakh with a large percentage of Russians and a smattering of Uyghurs, Koreans, Tatars and Ukrainians, dress in western style fashion. The dress code is very free – we were even able to visit the interior of the mosque and the cathedral wearing shorts and me with my head uncovered.

YURTS, HIGH LAKES AND MARE'S MILK

An earthquake in 1911 destroyed most of the city. The Zenkov Cathedral in the Panfilov Park was designed in 1904 by Andrei Pavlovich Zenkov and built entirely of wood, including the nails. It survived the tremors, only to be abused later by the Bolsheviks in common with the Holy Trinity Cathedral in Karakol. It was returned to the Russian Orthodox Church in 1995. In his excellent book, *In search of Kazakhstan*, Christopher Robbins describes watching the beggars in the park during winter, sharing their bread with the pigeons. He then realised it was a clever trick designed to lure the birds into a trap. After a quick death from a sharp wringing of the neck the birds were then stuffed in a plastic bag – collected for the pot! We did see beggars but not in action with the pigeons.

There was plenty to keep us busy – the Green Market, a Central Asian style bazaar; the Barakholka market which is over four kilometres long and spans ten bus stops where you can buy almost anything. There are posh malls all over the place and many grand buildings, described lucidly in the *Lonely Planet Guide* with the words 'Soviet Monumental architecture' or 'Soviet pile', including the 26 floor Hotel Kazakhstan, claiming to be the most earthquake resistant high rise building in Almaty – a Soviet era landmark built in 1977. There are fountains, statues and artists and buskers out on the streets. We took a gondola ride up to the ski resort of Shymbuluk at 2,260m – claimed to be the third longest gondola ride in the world at 4.5km – and walked up into a valley of bare rocks and glaciated mountains rising to 5,000m.

The time came to pack our bikes for the flight and we couldn't find bike boxes anywhere, including at Alexandr Vinokourov's shop in the super smart underground shopping mall next to the Republika Alangy. Eldar kindly found us a couple. We weighed the whole package on the family scales, allowing a little room for manoeuvre with the baggage allowance and we found ourselves weighing in light by quite a few kilos – especially Hugh.

For our last meal in the family home Flyura cooked us a classic central Asian dish – something I had been wanting to try – *Beshparmak*. The name means five fingers, which refers to the fact that it is traditionally eaten with the fingers. We used a fork and spoon. Flyura's version was a mixture of boiled horsemeat (including horsemeat sausage) and vegetables (onions, carrots, potatoes) served on top of flat pasta sheets; the stock was served in a separate bowl. Kazakhstan is the world's number two producer of horsemeat (after China) – and it certainly looked like it from the number of horses we saw up on the *jailoos*.

It was lovely for us to be able to treat the family to a meal out on our last-night. We had *kchini* – a kind of flat deep fried bread with a cheese and potato filling – and many different varieties of *shashlyk*. They selected a lovely place on what has become known as Shashlyk Street. We enjoyed our last taste of dining in the warm summer air under the shade of walnut trees before returning to a cooler Northern Europe.

When the taxi arrived to take us to the airport, the only way we could fit everything in was if I squatted in the back with the bike boxes – the driver wasn't happy at all and spent all the journey time on the phone – possibly trying to get another vehicle. We checked in at the airport just past midnight, central Asian travel inconsistencies following us right to the end. Hugh was asked to show his Kazakhstan police immigration document and it was placed on a large pile of others. I wasn't asked for mine – I keep it as a souvenir of the four hours we spent waiting for them in Kegen.

It was an emotional return home on 4 September, having been away for almost a year. We opened an enormous amount of post including some Christmas cards, which we put around the house. On checking our bank balance, we came to realise that the cost of living the life of The Great Game was less than that of living at home in England for a year.

4
CHEMO FOR CANCER BEFORE CUBA

It is by riding a bicycle that you learn the contours of a country best.
Ernest Hemingway

Hugh:

Shortly after our return from Central Asia and our one year bike tour, I started to get persistent pains in the abdomen. After several weeks of such pain I began to think that I had picked up a rare bug in Kazakhstan or one of the other 'stans' that we had passed through. Time for a check-up with our local GP. Oh dear. In a very short period of time, alarm bells were ringing and the word cancer was being mentioned. It turned out that there was no poison from a 'stan' but invasive bladder cancer which had probably got a grip even before we left home in 2012. The treatment took nine months and involved numerous

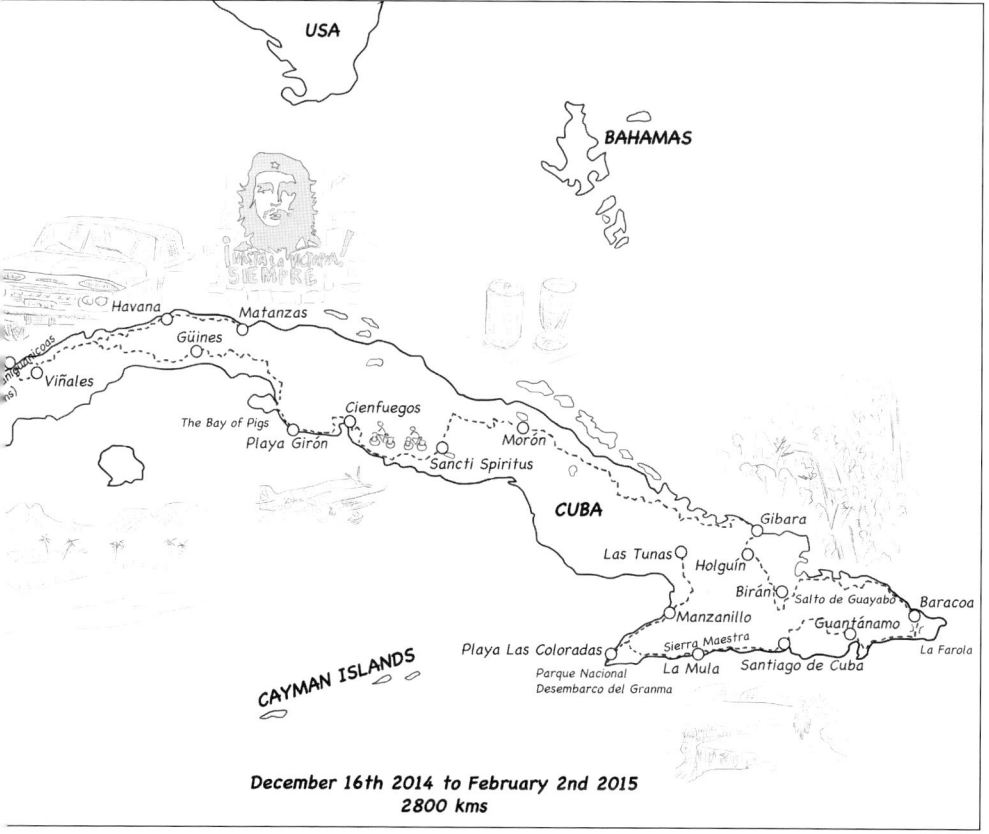

December 16th 2014 to February 2nd 2015
2800 kms

operations, the fitting and replacement of stents then chemotherapy and radiotherapy, sometimes both together. I continued to ride my bike most days except when I was hospitalised for general anaesthetics. I kept some sort of fitness but noticed that the treatment had affected my oxygen uptake considerably and so hill climbing in the Yorkshire Dales became harder. I kept trying and nearly keeled over one day whilst ascending the severely steep Coal Road near Dent station, so flatter rides were sought.

At one stage we thought that our touring days were over but we still had so many dreams of faraway rides. By November 2013 Dr Alison Birtle, my oncologist, said that the treatment had worked and that I was free to travel for a couple of months but then should return for check-ups and scans. We had had a lot of time to think about where to go next, and for a short trip in winter, Cuba seemed like an interesting option.

We now had to face the Cuban conundrum. It doesn't take long to realise that Cuba is a unique country with many distinct characteristics which make travel interesting but also puzzling. To take a tent or not to take a tent? Is camping legal? Money? At the time, there were two currencies. Are foreigners allowed to use the Cuban peso (*moneda nacional*)? Will you be allowed entry if your return flight is beyond the 30 day tourist card issued on arrival? One easy answer was the one about malaria tablets. The disease was eradicated decades ago and Cubans enjoy a thorough immunisation programme and a health system which is free for all.

Bicycles commonly have no gears and often no brakes.

An old beauty.

Preparations and actions before a trip are always exciting but nowhere near as exciting as simply riding bikes in a new country. Indeed, the action required to get to the start of a cycle journey can be quite stressful. Before our first retirement trip to South America we had bought rigid bike boxes to fly the bikes safely to and from Santiago in Chile. Such boxes give you greater confidence in the safety of transporting bikes rather than using cardboard. However, they are only useful if a trip starts and finishes in the same place and if you can find somewhere to store the boxes for months. With a little bit of research before we left home, we found a *casa particular* (family run bed and breakfast) in Havana which would store our boxes for two months.

As we approached Havana on our flight from London, we looked down upon endless palm trees and waves bashing the beautiful coast. We remembered the words of Columbus when he first set sight on Cuba in 1492. He had described it as 'the most beautiful land human eyes had ever seen'. Cuba is the largest Caribbean island stretching roughly 1,500 kilometres from east to west, the length of which we planned to follow. Below us the roads appeared to be almost devoid of traffic. Perhaps we had found a country where 'car is not king', unless you are passionate about vintage American limousines.

A few questions were asked at the customs desk. The most important one being whether we had been anywhere near an ebola area in recent months. We collected our kit bags soon enough but had an anxious wait of over two hours for our bikes. They arrived at the oversize baggage area along with car tyres, surf boards, TVs and air conditioning units. We changed pounds for CUCs (convertible pesos) at a *cadeca* (exchange office) and soon found help in finding a vehicle large enough to take us and our kit to our *casa* in Habana Vieja. Nilo and Marie Louisa gave us a lovely welcome at Casa Cary y Nilo. We went with Nilo through streets devoid of cars to Casa Miglis where a varied menu included Swedish meatballs, chicken nuggets, and *souvlaki* (pork, onions and peppers on skewers, a hot and a mild sauce and crispy sliced oven baked potatoes). Our first experience of dining in Cuba was good, as was the *Bucanero Fuerte* (strong beer). The chocolate tart and banana surprise (bananas and chocolate both Cuban) finished the meal off nicely. We slept well in the beautiful old colonial home before rising to a large fruity breakfast and then the streets of Havana.

We made for the sea where men were fishing, the waves crashing on the rough rocks just beyond the decaying concrete walkway of the *malecón*. The warm breeze was very pleasant – we thought of the snow falling back at home. The city was not quite as calm as the day before – more cars on the roads and people crowding the streets. The interesting and colourful buildings were in various states of decay, some in the process of demolition or renovation, and piles of rubble were left on many street corners. Workmen were digging trenches along many of the narrow roads with little obvious regard for safety.

An eclectic mix of people walked the streets. Big breasted and fat bottomed women in skin tight leggings, skimpy shorts or hip hugging skirts, weather beaten black men with fat cigars, Santería worshippers dressed totally in white, and tattooed men pedalling cycle taxis who constantly offered us rides. Bizarrely, many of the leggings were in the design of the Stars and Stripes. People offered us long thin paper cones filled with nuts, and rides in vintage cars (cars were so much more beautiful in the 1950s). Once in the tourist heart the touts emerged along with the odd beggar – an attractive pregnant woman in a tight mini dress stretching over a developing bump, asked for money for her baby. Fidel was once proud to say, 'there are no beggars in Cuba'.

We got money CUCs (convertible pesos – equivalent to the dollar) out of an ATM at 3% commission and went hunting for national pesos (1 CUC was equivalent to 24 NP). I joined an orderly queue at a *cadeca* where a dark suited man in a white shirt ushered the customers in one at a time. I changed £80 into national pesos and was told *mucho mucho*. This dual currency system is bizarre – both available to all but the CUC is used to pay for luxuries, such as shampoo and many of the pricier things tourists buy (accommodation and meals in restaurants) whilst the national pesos pay for some of the cheaper things the locals need. Street food, such as ham sandwiches cost next to nothing. At the posh Hotel Parque Central we found a pretty decent internet connection – but a bit pricey at eight CUCs an hour. Uploading photographs was no problem and we could sit in the comfortable cool foyer without even buying a drink.

We decided we would take a train to Cacocum, south of Holguín, to give us more time to meander about the more interesting parts of the island, particularly the mountainous areas in the east. The Estacíon Central is an impressive building from the outside but there is not much inside – a scruffy café, a couple of information desks, an area for dealing with baggage and nowhere obvious to buy tickets. It took us some time and questioning in our struggling Spanish to realise that the accommodating ladies at the information desk were telling us to go to another place 400m down the road to get the tickets.

Luckily once there, a woman stepped in to translate – we had to go back to the Estacíon Central to find out if the Sunday train to Santiago de Cuba took bikes and then return to get the tickets. No queues at least – just a Brazilian and a Ukrainian trying to work it all out too. We got tickets for 26 CUCs each – the train to leave at 18:13 on Sunday, sixteen hours (minimum) to Santiago (but a few less to Cacocum hopefully) and no sleeping carriages. We thought it would be an 'experience' but perhaps not exactly fun. Our expectations were not high given what we had heard about the state of the toilets and the unreliability of the timing.

"Nothing works in Cuba" said the wonderful man, jet black Carlos, who offered to translate the confusing messages from the baggage man at the station. He worked at the hospital and had to admit that at least the medical system worked. No carriage for the bikes we were told – it had broken down in Santa Clara – no way could we get the train with our bikes. Carlos offered to help us get our money back at the ticket office – it was shut. So we found ourselves back at Cary and Nilo's place – luckily there was a room for us.

The short ride through town whetted our appetites – it felt so good to be on the bikes, and the reaction of the people around was good too. On the way back to our *casa* the town was seething with life, music in the air, boys playing football in the street, women chatting. We realised for the first time that there are hills in Havana. So we confronted the dilemma – should we wait another two days for the Guantánamo train or should we ditch the idea of the train altogether? Trains to other provinces are infrequent. They told us that the same thing wouldn't happen with the Tuesday night train but who knows? This is Cuba. At least our bikes worked and the idea of just getting going was pulling at us hard. It looked like the next morning would see us riding off to the east, after another trip to the station to try to get our money back. At least we had been spared an uncomfortable night on the train.

We couldn't wait any longer. It had been sixteen months since we had lived life on tour on our bikes. We just had to ride. I thought of the words of Dr Alison Birtle – "we will do our best to get you back on your bike". So train or no train, wrong direction or right direction, we just got on our bikes and pedalled. After all the months of treatment I was like a coiled up spring. I just exploded out of Havana and we rode 110km to Matanzas east of Havana and on the north coast. From there we took an overnight bus to Las Tunas towards the east of Cuba. We knew that we wanted to pedal from east to west as that is the direction of the prevailing wind and so it proved to be. With quiet roads, beautiful scenery, good accommodation and a frequent tailwind Cuba was a wonderful country to make our return to cycle touring.

The first proper day of our tour of Cuba was flat. We passed by sugar plantations, grazing land for cattle and later on rice fields, irrigated by canals. Oxen are still used in the fields and horses for transport. Many people use bicycles in their day-to-day lives – kids on the cross bar, adults on the back rack and enormous amounts of crops strapped on to great heights often whilst the rider carries an umbrella as a sunshade. We entered the province of Granma – named after the boat in which Fidel Castro landed on Cuba in 1956.

It was a very pleasant day's ride in the warm air with misty, distant views of the Sierra Maestra. We were tired after a night on the bus with little sleep. In Manzanillo we met a friendly guy on a bike. Eugenio showed us to a *casa,* where four German cyclists were also staying. There we met Jens and Martina who told us that you can't get either inner tubes or puncture repair kits in Cuba. They found this out when they got eight punctures between them after pulling off the road to camp – ferocious thorns to rival those in Argentina. We had two spare tubes and fifteen patches. In Cuba the holes are fixed with a hot iron.

We were also keen to camp as we had bought a new light and well ventilated tent, the Hilleberg Rogen. We found a sandy spot close to mangrove swamps and next to the sea at Playa Las Coloradas. It was so hot and humid. Occasional sea breezes through the large area of mesh netting gave us some respite and protection from the multitudes of tiny biting sandflies. It was a challenge to cook and eat in comfort. Sometime in the night we became aware of a different type of biting beastie that was resting in our porch. It was a huge, bulbous, grey crab with a single extra-large pincer which looked like it could take off toes in one bite. We flicked it away with a stick guided by the light of our headtorches.

Our night time ordeal had been a drop in the ocean compared with that of Fidel Castro and his 82 campañeros when they landed nearby in December 1956. Outside Parque Desembarco del Granma stands a life size replica of the leisure yacht which was a virtual shipwreck in the swamp after its hazardous one week long rough and overcrowded sailing from Mexico. Today the park is a UNESCO world heritage site for its history and more importantly now for Cuba's best coastal landscape and plant diversity.

Castro had escaped the US backed military dictatorship of Fulgencio Batista in 1955. His life had been in danger after a failed attempt at an uprising against Batista's malignant Mafia-backed government near Santiago de Cuba in 1953.

CHEMO FOR CANCER BEFORE CUBA

It was a miracle that the Cuban revolution started at all as most of the fighters on the yacht Granma were killed by Batista's forces soon after they landed in the swamps. Three of the men who survived found each other again amongst a small group of other survivors in the mountains of the Sierra Maestra. The portraits of these three stare at you from walls, posters and rooftop water tanks all over Cuba. They are the portraits of the brothers Fidel and Raúl Castro and the Argentinian doctor turned guerilla Ernesto (Che) Guevara. It was both funny and strange that the only non-political or historical poster we saw in Cuba was an advert for Corona (Mexican) beer on the back of a delivery lorry.

Our route followed the base of the 2,000m high mountains of the Sierra Maestra along the southern coast of the island. Cuba has been bashed by the extreme politics of the far right and left and damaging long term trade embargoes. Along the route to Santiago de Cuba we witnessed a different sort of bashing. The road had been chewed away by hurricane blown high seas making it virtually impassable for cars but perfect for bikes as long as you looked carefully where you put your wheels. There was a bright turquoise sea on one side and the land rising sharply up to mountain tops dusted with cloud to the north. Small villages and pretty little cottages sit on the narrow strip of cultivated land at the base of the mountains, surrounded by banana trees, palms and flowering plants. The road is a joy to ride for cyclists – we met three coming the other way. One was a German on an electric bike which he said was 'the future' – his battery enabled him to do 80km and he was just changing to a new one. He said he could do over 100km this way – I thought, 'well that is possible with leg power too'.

We were expecting to get provisions on the way but found none. Whenever we asked about a *tienda* or *kiosko* we were told there wasn't one here but there was in a village ahead. We did the 75km on a few energy bars and some banana chips left over from the previous night's dinner. Asking locals about how far we had to go was equally confusing and the German cyclist only added to the confusion – our map seemed to be a bit out on distances.

La Mula is a campismo next to a pleasant enough shingle beach – popular with foreign cyclists, being a day's ride from Pilón, and used by Cuban tourists – we also met a Turkish tourist who had been coming for fifteen years. The cabins were not cute – inside they were a bit like a prison cell with bare walls and two basic single beds. The white tiled bathroom was fine although the shower just emerged from a pipe in the wall – good enough to wash the day's sweat off.

🚲   🚲   🚲

After Santiago de Cuba we didn't fancy the main road to Guantánamo so we opted for a less direct route on minor roads, hoping to find some good tracks and camping spots. The tricky bit was getting out of Santiago on the right road. As happens everywhere, the people we asked were too focussed on our end point rather than the means of getting there so they continually tried to drag us back to the main road, which also meant bits of *autopista*. It wasn't about the traffic really – there isn't much – it was about charm. So we stuck to it and ended up with a fine climb which gave us great views of the whole bay of Santiago – lots of charm. Heading north we spotted a signed turn off beyond La Prueba where there was a route east on our map on very minor roads. The stout ladies who we questioned about it said "no go", but then a man on a horse intervened and said we could get to Guantánamo that way – another chap agreed and then the ladies came to realise it was possible but the carretera was *malo* – not at all good – and up and down. Just our cup of tea we thought so we turned off onto the rough stony road to Jarahueca and Matahambre. It was lovely.

In Jarahueca we bought cold pineapple juice and tomatoes and we also got some water for camping, hopefully by the river further on. The river was in populated territory so we went on. Our first attempt at finding a site failed as we were spotted and told to ask at the nearby house if we could camp – the lady said 'no' – so we moved on. Just before the next village we found a steep rough track rising up from the road. It led to a nice open field where we placed our tent out of sight and with great views. There is a surprising lack of uninhabited zones anywhere along any kind of road.

We followed the beautiful route up and down, exchanging greetings and a

The hurricane bashed road south of the Sierra Maestra.

These rural folk helped us push our bikes up a steep and rough section.

little conversation with the jovial people along the way. For some time we were travelling at the same speed as an ox cart and the people on it were reassuringly going to Guantánamo – although not all the way on the cart. Here, out in the sticks, the young women were often dressed in tight tops and frilly skirts, as if they were going to a party. We got the impression that the countryside is extremely well organised. People were living in very simple homes but in a beautiful environment. I could imagine it being pleasant enough but for the year round oppressive heat.

Our intended route went roughly east, so we realised something wasn't quite right when we found ourselves going south. We unintentionally ended up in Costa Rica – the town not the country. Our mistake had been to keep asking the way to Guantánamo, rather than to a smaller place to the east. Directions led us to the autopista we had been avoiding. There was virtually no traffic on it but it was dull to ride compared with where we had been – but much faster. We turned off onto a parallel road after a few kilometres and soon finished off the last 20km into Guantánamo, having spent all morning doing over 25km on the rough track. But it's not about the end point – it's about how you get there and the places in between.

We found a warm welcome at Casa de Campos y Tatika and a comfortable 'blue' room with a hot shower and beers in the fridge. These *casas* are great, offering all the things a tired, dirty and hungry cyclist needs including Guantánamo laundry service.

The town of Guantánamo is some way from the US Naval base and detention camp. Some tourists make the trip to get a view of the base but there is nothing much to see so we didn't see any point in going. The US pays a lease for the 118 square kilometres of land occupied on Cuba – the lease agreement can only be terminated with the agreement of both parties. Fidel Castro never cashed a single rent cheque from the US government – they were just stored in a locked drawer.

There are areas of Cuba where *casas particulares* are few and far between and even if some sort of accommodation is available it may be rough or even illegal. A guestbook message on our *crazyguyonabike* website had said 'you will regret it if you don't take a tent'. Having a tent allowed us to be flexible about our route across Cuba and it also saved us from some nights staying in pretty rough places. Between Guantánamo and Baracoa our camp on a sandy beach below palms saved us from a cabin/prison cell at a campismo. It was so grotty that we decided to just use it as a bike and kit store. Paint was peeling off the ceiling and the windows were boarded up. The toilet was broken and the shower was a constantly running pipe.

Baracoa is the oldest city in Cuba. Until 1964 it was only accessible by sea and then Fidel Castro came to the rescue and organised the completion of the magnificent La Farola, regarded as one of the great infrastructure achievements of the Cuban Revolution. Sixty kilometres of winding road penetrate the Cuchillas de Baracoa mountains using eleven bridges and viaducts and reaching an altitude of 550m. The vegetation is dense and beautiful and the cyclist will never go hungry as there is no problem getting sustenance on the way up. Oranges, bananas, Baracoan chocolate and a sweet coconut and honey confection called *cucurucho*, ingeniously wrapped in a palm leaf cone doing away with concerns about throwing the wrapper away. Whenever we stopped to admire the view we were hounded by people trying to sell their produce. In Baracoa we were invited to join the family of our *casa* for New Year's Eve. The dinner was a traditional feast of roasted *cerdo* (pork), yucca (flavoured with garlic), salad of tomatoes, cucumber and cabbage, rice with black beans and two puddings – a flan and a sweet orange pudding flavoured with cloves.

We left Baracoa just as the heavens were opening. The rain came down hard. It was like a continuous warm shower and it soaked us to the skin but it was lovely and refreshing – no point in a waterproof. The road was unpaved and tacky. Mud stuck to our tyres and we had to scrape it off the insides of our front mud guards to let the wheels run free. After stopping for a lobster lunch by Playa Maguana we found a small patch of grass to camp by the sea in the lush Humboldt National Park. This enabled us to avoid staying the night in Cuba's most devastated area. The mining around Moa has covered the region in a film of dirty red dust. Without retracing our steps over La Farola this was the only way possible. Smelly fuming trucks rolling along the road accompanied endless hissing pipes and smoking chimneys. We moved as fast as we could on the damp slippery surface and soon returned to the more beautiful Cuba we had come to adore.

We entered the almost deserted Altiplanicie de Nipe climbing to 800m, and much higher than La Farola. We passed Salto de Guayabo, Cuba's highest waterfall, which drops 100m through cliffs with clinging Caribbean pines. It is surprising how only a small increase in altitude gives enormous respite from the intense humidity. The empty rough red dirt track gave us wonderful high riding affording distant views to the south over the province of Santiago de Cuba. The paradise was lost as we dropped altitude and returned to the cauldron below. A large poster of the smiling faces of Fidel and Raúl Castro marked the turn off to the *pueblito* of Birán where the brothers were brought up on their parents' large finca. There is a museum of artefacts and clothes and the smart yellow wooden houses of the Castro family can be glimpsed at through fences and cedar trees. Surprisingly there appeared to be nowhere for the traveller to stay so we looked for a place to camp by a clear running stream on the edge of Birán. Men on horseback had been working nearby at first but they cleared off before we set up camp. They didn't seem at all curious about us. Interestingly, on the way there we mentioned that we would camp to several people and none of them seemed to consider it a bad idea or in any way illegal. They were just amused.

With a little bit of administrative hassle, we extended our 30 day tourist visas in the provincial capital of Holguín before passing alongside the surreal rocky landscape of Grupo de Maniabón on the way to the picturesque fishing village of Gibara. Here the sea breeze was perfect for children to play the free and easy pastime of kite flying with kites made from old bits of string, plastic, sticks and anything else kids could get hold of.

We were now making big distances going west and near the centre of Cuba in an area which sees few tourists. We were heading for Minas, but the man at the 24 hour bar by the old sugar factory at Ingenio Santa Isabel told us that there were no *casas* there, so we asked if we could camp as the grass looked nice and it had a handy store for evening Bucaneros. It was a great camp until the party started at the bar – it kept going until 6am. Despite the lack of sleep, the following day we covered 174km helped by a following wind but also due to not being able to find anywhere suitable to camp. The scenery was dull, just endless sugar plantations, paddy fields and orange groves. Sometimes long lines of rice were laid out on the road to dry. We arrived in Morón in the dark and found a gorgeous *casa* to stay in, not having to wait long before the dining table was laid with an enormous buffet.

Morón has Cuba's oldest railway station dating from 1920. The times of trains were written on a white board. Ancient trains rumbled across the main road in the middle of town, often mixing with crowds of pedestrians and cyclists. The railway line points were operated manually by huge levers. Many of the town's streets are colonnaded and colourful but a little bit crumbly.

Besides the ubiquitous cycle taxi, Morón has many very smart looking horse-drawn cabs. We enjoyed one more beautifully wild camp before heading for a continuous succession of charming tourist towns. At Boquerón lies a canyon in the jungle perfect for a wash, swim and peaceful overnight stop if you don't mind the company of pigs and the calls of many species of bird. In Sancti Spiritus, Trinidad and Cienfuegos we enjoyed old colonial churches, good food, and comfortable beds.

For us the route along the coast westward beyond Cienfuegos was just asking to be done. As usual every Cuban we asked about it told us it was *malo* – rocks and sand etc., but it was perfect, a natural traffic free route along the coast. The hardest part was actually finding our way to it. Lots of people helped us – one even drew us a map. At the start we wasted some time riding around an industrialised area on the outskirts of Cienfuegos, near the oil refinery and looking across to an abandoned Russian project of a nuclear power station. We didn't take photos as signs of the military and lookout posts put us off. Once on the track, it was great. No problem at all to ride, and perfect peace. We added ten to fifteen extra kilometres to the distance with our messing around, but arrived in Playa Girón well before dinner time.

Playa Girón is famous for the 'Bay of Pigs', an event which severely embarrassed the US government of J. F. Kennedy. The battle took place at the height of the Cold War and preceded the Cuban Missile Crisis by one year. The story told at the Museo Girón is one of triumph of the revolutionary army against the mercenary forces of Yankee imperialism. In April 1961, a CIA trained force landed on Cuban shores in the Bay of Pigs. In less than 72 hours they were defeated. More than 1,000 prisoners and a whole stash of useful American weapons were taken. Prior to the invasion the American air force attacked various civilian airports in Cuba and many civilians lost their lives. This is yet another almost unbelievable story from Cuban history – first a meagre number of survivors from a small boat bringing revolutionaries from Mexico grew into an army which beat Batista and then less than five years later the same forces triumphed over the world's strongest power. Their portraits are on display in the museum. A film with English subtitles tells the story – the Americans would no doubt tell a different tale – that of Cuban exiles attempting to set their country free from repressive communist rule.

We were now heading to the far west of the island and yet again as the day dimmed we ran short of a place to camp or a *casa* to sleep in. We reached Güines at sunset and went hunting for a *casa*. We were directed to where there were three not far from the centre – but all were national peso *casas* – for Cubans and not foreigners. The first lady said her house was full, but it was clear from her face that she didn't want us in her *casa*. It isn't legal for foreigners to stay in these homes. A young man on a bike helped us out – he took us to a friend's house – again not a legitimate foreigners' *casa particular*. They asked us to take our bikes off the street quickly – before the authorities noticed. They gave us a decent room with a bathroom and beers in the fridge. Interestingly there was a mirror on the ceiling as well as three on the walls and condoms on top of the fridge. Not the first time that we think we have stayed in a brothel. Dinner was brought to our room, and in the morning we were ushered away from the house at a moment when it was thought we wouldn't be seen.

With broken clouds and relatively cool temperatures it was very pleasant for cycling. It was a beautiful route, with great views of the sheer sided, and forested Cordillera de Guaniguanicoas as we approached the Viñales Valley, a National Park and UNESCO World Heritage Site. As we rode through the centre of Viñales town we bumped into Steve and Sue, cyclists who we had first met a week earlier in Cienfuegos. They were able to rescue us from the clutches of women desperately trying to entice us into their *casas*. Sue and Steve had found a quiet place (Casa Boris y Cusita) down a dirt road where we took a room with a good view of a *mogote* (the name given to a limestone block that erupts from the valley floor). It was a peaceful location (apart from the overly vocal cockerels) in what seemed to us to be more of a busy town than the 'small village' portrayed in the Rough Guide – but we do come from a small market town in Cumbria. It was a great feeling to have almost cycled the length of the island and we looked forward to a day of rest in the good company of Sue and Steve. Viñales lies amongst a wonderland of rugged limestone karst scenery. Fields around grow large green leaves of tobacco which are hung to dry in steeply pitch roofed cabins. The area is speckled with many traditional farms and buildings and people work with and use horses in their day-to-day lives. People may have few material goods but their environment is rich.

The north coast of Cuba has several archipelagoes and low-lowing islands called cayos. Many of the cayos have been linked to the mainland by causeways and the islands have been turned into tourist destinations for people wanting gorgeous seas, beaches, palm trees and fancy hotels. Lots come to the cayos to escape freezing northern winters. What they see is a very different side of Cuba.

Thirty kilometres west of Viñales lies the small Cayo Jutías. We rode across the causeway knowing that this was a rare cayo offering just a restaurant and bar but no accommodation. We found a good place to camp in trees by a beach and almost immediately a man found us and offered to catch us a lobster and cook it on a barbeque – so tasty, and followed by coconut. We fell asleep to the sound of the lapping waves against the sandy shore. All was good until about four in the morning when we became seriously disturbed from our sleep. A light was shining around our tent and as the trees waved in the wind shifting shadows were cast onto our tent walls. I immediately got out of the tent as I thought it would be a bad place to be if someone was thinking of attacking us. Now I could see what was going on a little further away in the trees. Some other people were putting a tent up in the middle of the night. We left them to it and returned to our sleeping bags. In the night it is so easy for a little to make you feel uneasy – it nearly always turns out to be nothing. The pair in the tent were Russian and had left their camp at Cabo de San Antonio (at the end of the island of Cuba) in the night as someone had been taking too much interest in them.

Our journey now changed direction as we turned eastward to make the return to Havana. Crossing the causeway we could admire the rugged outline of the Viñales karst looking like the back of a giant prehistoric reptile. Rarely is there a dull day when traveling by bicycle. Things just happen. People, places and events just pass by. In the remaining five days to Havana we hadn't expected anything but we continued to find out that there is so much more to Cuba and Cubans than we heard from a saying we first learnt in Havana two months earlier. 'Cubans are good at two things – dancing and mending cars.'

We passed the port of Mariel and learnt that in 1980 125,000 Cubans left from the Mariel harbour for a new life in the USA. Fidel Castro agreed to this exodus, which began in April. Cuban exiles in the United States rushed to Key West and to docks in Miami to hire boats to transport people to the United States. It was ended in October of that year, following a mutual agreement between Jimmy Carter's administration and the Cuban government.

Between Mariel and Havana we passed one of the largest schools of medicine in the world. There are nine other schools of medicine in Cuba but this one, the Latin American School of Medicine, was established by the Cuban government in 1999 specifically to train people from other countries to be doctors and to apply their skills in countries of need.

Not much further along the road we entered the Marina Hemingway and admired the sculpture commemorating Ernest Hemingway's Nobel prize-winning book, *The Old Man and The Sea*. Hemingway enjoyed fishing off this coast and had lived in a villa outside Havana for twenty years until it was confiscated by the Castro regime. During the 1960s Castro had thought that the music of The Beatles was decadent and it had been discouraged in Cuba. However, in a dramatic policy U-turn, following John Lennon's social activism and opposition to US involvement in the Vietnam War, Castro rebranded him as a revolutionary. Our final kilometres towards the centre of Havana passed through the Parque Lennon where you can sit on a bench next to a beautiful life-size sculpture of Lennon. The statue was unveiled by Castro in 2000 marking the 20th anniversary of Lennon's murder.

On our final day in Havana we visited the Museo de la Revolución, housed in the former presidential palace where Batista lived, and hired an open-topped vintage car to take us to the beautiful Finca la Vigía where Hemingway had lived. With the last few notes of Cuban money, we bought two jars of Cuban honey at the airport before the flight home. Little did we know that the tops were not screwed on tightly. They became loose in flight. The taste of Cuba lingered long after our return home!

5
Cancún to Cornville

Hot chili peppers in the blistering sun
Dust on my face and my cape
Me and Magdalena on the run
I think this time we shall escape
Bob Dylan – 'Romance in Durango' from the album *Desire*, 1976

Hugh:

We had long since known that Northern Mexico, and in particular Sonora, has a reputation for being a dangerous place, and perhaps not one in which to be camping off-road. For that reason, we made an effort to not linger at the end of our hundred day journey across Mexico. We left the town of Nacozari early and made a dash of over 120 kilometres to the United States border at the large,

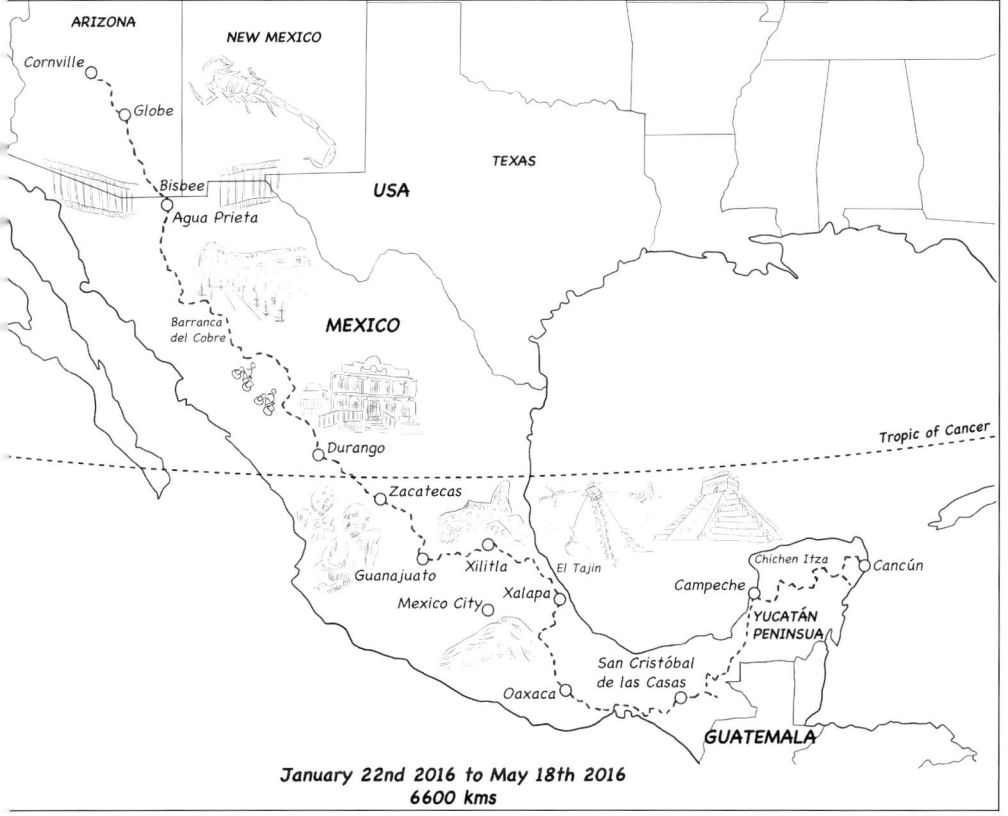

dusty and uninviting town of Agua Prieta. We found our way to a queue of cars waiting their turn to be processed by the border force. Standing proud across the high and thin blade of steel, which is 'The Wall' at this point, lay a tall flag pole carrying a fluttering Stars and Stripes. We awaited our turn to transit to the smaller town of Douglas in Arizona and this didn't prove easy.

"Do you have any narcotics or weapons?" demanded the border guard. "Well yes – I have a dog dazer," I replied teasingly.

"Let me see your tazer." Having rummaged through all eight of our panniers the guard disappeared with our passports not to return for forty minutes and when she did, she was accompanied by a security officer who gave us the Spanish Inquisition. The sight of full page visas for unpronounceable countries in our passports had raised alarm bells.

"What are the people like in Tajikistan? What were you doing in Azerbaijan? Where are you going in Arizona? Do you have a home address? Can you prove it? Are you married? What is your job?" Some notes were made and our mobile phone numbers taken before we were released. In all the rush of people coming and going, we had the chance to ask a question or two ourselves. We discovered that drug smugglers were caught regularly and that Trump was popular around here in the run-up to the next presidential election. Later on the same evening, in our comfortable old-fashioned Hotel Avenue in Douglas, the Trump question cropped up again and we learnt a new phrase from the friendly people at the bar – 'electile dysfunction'.

The final 600km north to Sedona was a delight. Bisbee, close to the Mexican border, is an historic mining town nestled in cactus adorned hills and now home to lots of trendy shops, bars, cafés, art galleries and one of the most interesting bicycle shops you could find anywhere. Ken Wallace's Bisbee Bicycle Brothel is more of a museum than a shop. There are lots of vintage steel-framed bikes such as Mercian, Holdsworth and Grubb from England. We chanced upon a Saturday night, with live American Roots music on the streets and in the bars, and got chatting with all sorts of interesting and friendly characters. Many people saw Mexico as a dangerous place to visit and several confessed to owning guns and even being prepared to use them.

We loved our journey north, the roadsides so much tidier than those of Mexico. The Arizonan landscape is intoxicating and the rough road through Cascabel was worth the effort for the chance to explore off road wilderness for a day and a night. However, we couldn't help but feel a certain level of animosity towards cyclists. On one occasion we were advised that we shouldn't ride the road ahead. It was said to be dangerous for cyclists and that if we had an accident then it would be our fault. A policeman ordered us not to cycle side by side despite the road being almost devoid of traffic.

A close encounter of a different kind happened when we stayed in Globe. I was awoken by a sharp pain in my back. At first I thought that maybe there was a thistle in the sheets. It was three in the morning and I had to turn a light on and take a look. Oh my god – there was a live scorpion in the bed. I had unknowingly rolled onto it with a bare back and it launched its sting. I soon jumped and swatted it but it took a few strikes to kill it. A numbness lasted for about six hours.

This had been unpleasant but at least not fatal. A bigger and more regular threat we felt in Arizona was the prevalence of guns. We passed big shops selling all types with signs inviting you to try them. Magazine shelves were stacked with copies of *Guns and Ammo*, *Ballistic*, *Black guns*, *Special Weapons*, *Recoil* and more. In one small country store we noticed the shopkeeper had a pistol in a holster. This gun culture is so peculiar and unlike anything we have seen in any other country. We reached the end of our four month ride by the red rocks of seductive Sedona, a fitting reminder of the wild lands of Mexico that lay behind us.

Like most of our journeys, we had started our Mexican one with little idea of the route ahead. One thing we did know though, was that we didn't want to cycle in the suburbs of the tourist city of Cancún. So we cheated and took a taxi from the airport to the seaside town of Puerto Morelos, avoiding the busy toll road down the coast.

We knew that Mexico had a reputation for violence in a few states and cities. We rarely enjoy cycling in big cities, so Mexico City was not on the agenda. When we left Puerto Morelos in January, we had very few places on any sort of destination list. This was simply another journey which would evolve.

This was the 28th country which we had cycle toured in, and it fundamentally differed from the others in its complete lack of other travellers, with the exception of a few honey pots, such as Chichén Itzá and San Cristóbal. It is easy to understand why countries have their honeypots. At Chichén Itzá, the thousand year old Mayan pyramids absorbed us for a day but every day we cycled through the Yucatán Peninsula we came across other equally enchanting Mayan ruins, many of which appeared to have few visitors.

The day before we arrived at Chichén Itzá we received a message from two cyclists who we had heard about but never met. Linda and Mike had been following our blogs for some time and when they noticed that we were in the same area as them, they suggested that we meet. They are really crazy guys. They had sold all of what they once owned apart from what was now on their bikes and up to this point they had been on the road for eighteen months in the USA and Mexico. They thought that they may carry on living as crazy guys on bikes for at least another ten years! *Crazyguyonabike* is an internet platform on which cycle tourists share their diaries, maps and photographs. Neil Gunton, from the USA, established the website in 2000 for his own use on a tour. It was designed for listing a day-to-day diary of his ride but following the tour he decided to widen its use to other cycle tourists. It is an excellent place to find and share information and to meet people if you happen to be close. Sadly, like most cyclists' tours in 2020, Linda and Mike's came to an abrupt halt. After five years cycling in many corners of the planet, due to the pandemic, their journey came to a rude ending in Spain and they had little choice but to

The pyramid of the magician, Uxmal in Yucatán.

fly home to the States.

It was a special day to savour for all four of us. The pyramids, columns, ball courts and temples are spaced out in peaceful grounds where it is delightful to wander about and wonder at the antiquity. It is not surprising that it is such a popular destination and it has the usual tourist touts at the periphery. Stalls selling carvings of curious masks, scary skulls, skeleton figurines, mini pyramids, embroidered clothing, brightly coloured rugs, keyrings, fridge magnets, sun hats, jewellery and much more line the paths between the areas of the site.

As was the case throughout Mexico, we weren't hassled. If you said 'no' then that was it. There didn't appear to be much bargaining or haggling for prices. Apart from a couple of cheeky children from Chiapas, we found the people friendly and welcoming, and we never witnessed the slightest hint of violence or aggression anywhere in Mexico. Having said that, there is a large armed police and military presence which we saw in all states and many towns. Coming from England, we were not used to seeing so many machine guns waved around.

The strong armed presence did not detract from the enjoyment of the enormous variety of towns and scenery in Mexico. The country is rich in history and colour. In early February we arrived in the beautiful old walled town of Campeche on the Gulf of Mexico. Five hundred years earlier the first expedition of Spaniards landed on this coast having come via Cuba. Founded in 1540 by Conquistador Francisco de Montejo, Campeche was terrorized by pirates and marauders until the city started to build defences in 1686. The city still has the appearance of a fortress. The military architecture of the seventeenth and eighteenth centuries was designed by the Spanish to protect the ports on the Caribbean Sea from pirate attacks. Many pedestrianised streets in the old town are lined with lamps and surrounded by charming colonial houses richly coloured in blue, red, yellow and green. The doors, windows and balconies are elegantly framed by friezes. It was easy to find a charming inexpensive colonial hotel to stay in and savour the history.

We turned south from Campeche to cross from the Atlantic to Pacific coast close to where Mexico is at its narrowest. As usual, a route was evolving, and we were heading for the ruins at Palenque and the city of San Cristóbal. Everywhere else on the way would just be another place in between. Tenosique was such a place. Entering the town, it was obvious that something mad was going on. Many streets were cordoned off and strewn with rubbish. There were wild and wacky costumes and hats, with some wearing lots of clothes and some very little. This was a town totally absorbed in its carnival. We found supposedly the best restaurant in town and ate a hot cocktail of prawns and octopus served in huge glasses. The owner wrote us a note: 'My name is Kevin. I hope you have a pleasant evening. Enjoy the carnival 2016, and not the last time you pass my restaurant'.

One hundred kilometres further towards the Pacific, we arrived at the ruins of Palenque, lying at the edge of thickly forested hills. Dating from 226BC to 799AD they are another Mexican delight where you can lose yourself for a day just wandering and admiring the pyramids, palaces, temples and carvings. Unusually, but maybe no longer, you were allowed to climb the steep steps of pyramids, risking yourself and your camera in the process.

Whilst crossing the mountains of Chiapas, heading further south, we passed through an indigenous region. This is an area of clear streams and freely flowing rivers, most beautiful at the waterfalls of Agua Azul. By the roadside men, and occasionally women, were working with machetes, clearing the verges or chopping wood. Here people carry heavy loads in the way of the Nepalese Sherpas, with a band around the head, taking all the weight on their necks. They carried wood and sacks of corn. Corn cobs were offered to us by children, ready cooked and hot in little plastic bags. They would block the road with a thin rope made from grass to persuade us to stop, but they laughed good naturedly when we said we had already bought some. We had two cobs each for a picnic lunch. The people looked like the Maya people of the Yucatán and some wore traditional dress colourfully embroidered. Women carried babies, or even toddlers in a sling over one shoulder and sometimes breastfed as they walked.

It was a beautiful route with great views, but highly populated and we passed through many *pueblos*. As we climbed higher, the people didn't seem too happy. Our waves were not always returned and children threw stones at me twice, one with a catapult. When we photographed guys crowded into the back of a Nissan pick-up they signalled their objection. We approached Oxchuc, a town known as a centre for the indigenous population of Chiapas, hoping to find somewhere to stay. We rode down into the centre of town and were shocked by what we saw. Oxchuc was a hell hole. Rubbish was strewn all over the streets, pouring out of black bin liners and it wasn't a carnival this time. In the central square the municipal building was covered in graffiti and the windows were smashed. Men queued to receive what looked like bowls of soup and tortillas. Others wobbled unsteadily around the streets. It felt incongruous to find that the people we approached, asking if there was anywhere to stay seemed normal, friendly and helpful and at odds with their environment. A girl who looked about ten years old showed us a room in a *posada*, one of those places that offer rooms at an hourly rate! This one had a heart with an arrow through it painted on the entrance. The windowless cell was not a place for anything resembling romance and not a place we would want to linger at all. Oxchuc was not a place to linger in either. We only took photos on the edge of town for fear of anger from the locals.

As we headed out of town armed with some bananas and drinking water, we passed a body lying in the gutter, face down with head on folded arms. Two girls walked by and looked

Carnival at Tenosique de Pino Suárez.

and laughed. We could only assume he was drunk. A young boy aimed his home made bow and arrow at us. I said a very firm 'no' and it stopped him.

We have seen some grim places but this was possibly the worst and so at odds with its beautiful mountainous surroundings. The recent history of the town shed light on its plight. It stemmed from the re-election of Mayor María Gloria Sánchez Gómez, who was accused of nepotic government. There had been unrest since the election in July. In January, some Canadian and American tourists travelling by bus were caught up in a violent protest involving men in balaclavas with machetes. Helped by police they escaped to safety. The mayor's house was pillaged and burned – no wonder the place was in such a mess.

Up the road we went and we chanced upon a small group of houses at the roadside where we were able to ask the family if there was anywhere we could camp on their land. Fortunately, they were lovely people, living in a tranquil environment in an extended family group. They gave us water and showed us a place behind the pig shed which was perfect. They watched with great interest as we pitched our tent, laid out our sleeping things and began cooking our dinner. They called themselves *campesinos.* They kept pigs, chickens and turkeys and grew corn. It was altogether a much better option than a grubby prison cell in Oxchuc. We even managed a fair amount of conversation with them in our broken Spanish. They told us that Oxchuc hadn't always been so bad. They wished us a good night and then left us to ourselves. Later some of the neighbours walked up the hill, the women dressed in the lovely local costume. They gave us friendly waves. We already felt that we were entering a more content zone.

Unbeknown to us, perhaps the presence of Papa Francisco had suddenly pacified the region. The Pope began his five day visit to Mexico by delivering blunt messages to political and ecclesiastical leaders. At the presidential palace, he denounced corruption and the drugs trade. At mass in Mexico City's basilica, he gave local bishops a dressing down, admonishing them not to waste time on 'gossip and intrigue' or 'trivial materialism'. He expressed sympathy for indigenous people who have often been ignored and exploited.

We descended to 2200m and rode into San Cristóbal de las Casas, the cultural capital of the state of Chiapas, and realised that something major was going on and this wasn't a carnival either. It just so happened that the Pope was passing through San Cristóbal on the afternoon of our arrival. We found a place to stand by the side of the road and watched him pass by in his Popemobile dressed in white robes, freely waving and smiling to the tens of thousands of well-wishers lining the streets.

It is well known that Donald Trump tried hard to prevent Mexicans crossing the border into the United States. What is less well known is that there are thousands of Americans who have moved in the opposite direction. We met several whilst in Mexico, one of whom was Richard from New York. A retired architect, he had left home eight years previously with a plan to travel south by land to Chile. However, he became absorbed by the charm of San Cristóbal and had been there ever since. He said that one day he may wake up and decide it was time to go to Chile. We understood why Richard had not gone further on his travels and was stopped in his tracks by San Cristóbal. Unusually for us, we stayed in the same place for four nights, partly because our home for the stay was not a hotel but the former residence of two extraordinary people.

We stayed at Casa Na Bolom – House of the Jaguar, the jaguar being a very important symbol in the mythology of the native peoples and a creature that still roams the jungle today. This was the house where Frans Blom, and his wife Gertrude lived from 1950. He was from a wealthy Danish family and she was Swiss. After living in Mexico working for an oil company, he became fascinated by the archaeology and went to Harvard to study the subject. He then returned to Mexico to work on the Mayan ruins, rejecting a more comfortable life back home. Gertrude was a journalist who was imprisoned in Paris for anti-Nazi sentiments. She went to Mexico when released and became fascinated by the indigenous cultures.

They met in Chiapas in 1943 and then took a few years to establish Na Bolom and their work in the community. They worked together for the preservation of the culture and history of the Mayan people, particularly the Lacandones. These people escaped the clutches of the Spanish by retreating deep into the jungle and are one of the most isolated and culturally conservative of Mexico's native peoples. The curious coincidence of the name Blom being so similar to Bolom, led to Frans being known as the Jaguar King, his striking blond blue-eyed appearance encouraging the tribute. Gertrude died in 1993 at the age of 92, thirty years after her husband. We stayed in what was Gertrude's office. Money from the tourists who stay at Na Bolom goes to fund projects to help indigenous people.

Despite more than 2000m of undulating descent, the ride to the Pacific from San Cristóbal took three and half days in which we covered 300 kilometres. We were discovering that Mexico is an enormous country, four times the area of Spain. The transition was beautiful as we descended, and felt like we were being blown by hot hair driers. As was normal in Mexico, we were constantly stopping to admire the landscape and colourful birds such as the striking vermilion flycatcher.

In the days spent approaching Oaxaca, the landscape turned arid, sometimes desert like with cacti on the hillsides. Another green spiky plant was being cultivated at the sides of the Caminos del Mezcal. We passed many places where men were busy making a strong alcoholic drink. Mezcal is made from the heart of the maguey plant, a kind of agave, related to the blue agave used to make the more popular tequila. Big stones, driven by horses, are used to crush the roasted *piñas*. The fermented mash is distilled in copper pots. In Oaxaca a saying goes: *para todo mal, mezcal, y para todo bien, tambien* (for every ill, Mezcal, and for every good as well). Oaxaca is centred around the Plaza de la Constitución, or *zócalo* which was planned in 1529. The plaza is surrounded by arcades. With the city having a wealth of historic buildings and museums, being pedestrian friendly and also having the reputation of being Mexico's culinary capital, it proved to be a good place to rest before heading through mountainous terrain on the way back north to the Atlantic.

For a couple of days our journey was dominated by the prominent volcano of Pico de Orizaba. At 5,636m it is Mexico's highest and the third highest mountain in North America. It is dormant but not extinct and despite being only nineteen degrees north of the equator it has nine glaciers. Approaching the town of Orizaba we were warned by a group of cyclists that there was a dangerous road ahead. We had little idea what they meant but having crossed a col and started a descent we saw the craziest road layout imaginable.

Sometimes on mountain roads in Mexico, the rules change as you 'go round the bend'. Like most countries of the world, in Mexico, vehicles drive on the right. However, on these hairpin bends near Orizaba the rules change. Large white painted arrows on the road instruct users to switch sides before and after the bends. The idea appears to be to give ascending traffic the more gently sloping outside of the bend, but we couldn't make sense of it, and it felt precarious as cyclists to be crossing from side to side before and after every corner. Fortunately the road wasn't busy.

Finding quiet roads between towns and cities was a challenge but, with some day-to-day research, we succeeded for the most part with the exception of our passage through Xalapa. This is one city which in retrospect we would have chosen to avoid but for its fantastic archaeological museum which houses 25,000 artefacts from the state of Veracruz. There are many bizarre sculptures and figurines in good condition and dating back to 1300BC.

Our route was now close to the Atlantic coast and we circled to the north east of Mexico City avoiding it by a good margin. The ruins of El Tajín, City of the Thunder God, were an obvious and worthwhile target. It was one of the largest and most important cities of the Classic era of Mesoamerica. As part of the classic Veracruz culture, El Tajín flourished from 600 to 1200AD and during this time numerous temples, palaces, ballcourts, and pyramids were built. The seven storied Pyramide de los Nichos has 365 steps, one for each day of the solar year, and at the top of the pyramid there are tablets framed by grotesque serpent-dragons.

The archaeological site is an obvious tourist destination, but there were very few there to pay the way of the entertaining Voladores. There are around

250,000 Totonaca speakers in Mexico, and the community is striving to preserve its language and cultural heritage. La Danza del Volador, the Dance of the Flier, is strongly associated with the Totonac people. Five dancers dressed in colourful embroidered robes psyched themselves up with a ritualistic dance to the mystical strains of a whistle accompanied by a mini drum. Then they all climbed the 30m pole! The music man went to the very top and stood precariously on a tiny platform. There was no protection.

Once up the pole, the other four tied themselves on with ropes which were wound around a bobbin below the feet of the musician. Simultaneously they all flew off and rotated round the pole whilst the ropes slowly unwound. They flew through the air, held by the ropes tied around their waists with feet hooked around the rope descending head first. In the final move, just as their hands touched the ground, they flipped over on to their feet before their heads struck the ground.

Serendipitous travel means that you inevitably miss places of interest but there are also random delights such as the awesome *pueblo majico* of Xilitla. Xilitla gave us a taste of the complex rhythm of Huapango music. The mayor introduced us, and invited us to join in and dance along with everyone else in the large outdoor square covered in wooden boards. Indigenous music styles influenced by American blue grass tones mix with Spanish and African touches and at times with some Irish hints. In the evening the town came to life again

Pico de Orizaba (5,636m) from Coscomatapec.

when the freshly painted white faces of the church were adorned with an amazing blaze of constantly moving colour accompanied by the deep beat of intoxicating music. The outdoor three dimensional vision gave a history of the town.

The natural beauty of Xilitla inspired eccentric British artist Edward James to create Las Pozas, The Pools, a garden in a subtropical rainforest just outside the town. It includes more than 30 hectares of natural waterfalls and pools interspersed with towering surrealist sculptures. James' objective was to create a 'Garden of Eden' at Las Pozas. Massive sculptures up to four stories tall punctuate the site. The many trails throughout the garden are composed of steps, ramps, bridges, and narrow winding walkways that traverse the valley walls. Construction of Las Pozas cost more than $5 million. To pay for it, James sold his collection of surrealist art at auction. It included paintings by Dali, Magritte, Hieronymus Bosch and Picasso. It felt very bizarre to spend an afternoon exploring a part of the Mexican jungle transformed by a British artist and poet between 1949 and 1984.

From Xilitla we went uphill almost continuously for 35km before freewheeling for most of 50km to the beautiful small town of Jalpan de Serra, the centre of Misiones Franciscanas de la Sierra Gorda de Querétaro. Many of the towns in the area are adorned with eighteenth century mission churches built of rosy pink stone which was delicately carved to make facades housing multitudes of statues. After leaving Jalpan we spent almost the whole day pedalling 50km uphill gaining 2,000m to camp on a col in forested mountains. The high camp was fortuitous as at the end of the day I became ill with a bad tummy bug which rendered me useless. It was a tough night with several moonlit trowel trips. The following morning, over the col, we left the forests for a rocky landscape covered in cacti and prickly scrub. All I could do was freewheel to the town of Peñamiller where we found a hotel for me to crash out in and recover. Fortunately the illness was short-lived and in the following two days we passed through more undulating arid terrain in heading for the state of Guanajuato and the city of San Miguel de Allende.

Nine weeks previous to our arrival in San Miguel de Allende, we had met Cheryl in Valladolid, on the Yucatán. She had invited us to stay with her, and her husband Dave, in their home in the town. It is estimated that there are roughly one million foreigners living in Mexico with 8,000 of them living in San Miguel. Cheryl and Dave, from the United States, had retired to their colonial home near the centre of the city. From their walled-in paradise we could hear the sound of cicadas at night, bird song from the inhabitants of the garden, the sound of church bells, music from the street and the ubiquitous bangs from fireworks at any time of day. There is a paradox that it seems fairly easy for North Americans to live in Mexico but it is pretty hard for Mexicans to migrate north.

By coincidence our time in historical and artistic San Miguel coincided with Semana Santa (Holy Week). Mexicans love an excuse for a celebration. On

Easter Sunday crowds were out waiting to see papier mâché effigies of their most hated demons blown to pieces. Victims were strung high across the street and then lowered for a fuse to be lit and then the effigy was raised again before sparks flew and smoke spread, as people waited in anticipation for the big bang which decapitated the bodies and sent limbs flying. And then it was the turn of the star of the show, the not yet President Trump! We realised that many of the crowd were expats when there were repeated calls, 'Trump, Trump, Trump'. He blew up in style to a great cheer, and on-lookers were eager to capture his head as a trophy. Another paradox is that it appears to be extremely rare to meet a Trump supporter outside the USA.

The Mexicans have an interesting relationship with death. Every year *Dia de los Muertos*, the Day of the Dead, is celebrated. It is an explosion of colour and life-affirming joy. Sure, the theme is death, but the point is to demonstrate love and respect for deceased family members. Colourful and skeletal models celebrating the day are sold at markets all over the country. Equally gruesome souvenirs are for sale outside the Museo de las Momias in the city of Guanajuato just 80km on our way further west. The bizarre museum starkly displays the corpses dug from the cemetery when relatives failed to pay the perpetuity

The Voladores of Papantla.

payments – no fee, no grave! The skimpy remains of bodies are displayed in cabinets. Some have clothes, some are naked. Some are frozen in time screaming and some look peaceful. One has the skin completely intact and many still have hair. Some are old and others as recent as 1965 – many will have living relatives.

🚲　🚲　🚲

North from Guanajuato our route became more and more remote all the way to Arizona. In our last month in Mexico we appeared to be in a gringo free zone both in terms of travellers and immigrants. For us, there was a gradual shift in interest, away from history and beautiful colonial buildings to the wild unpopulated lands of Chihuahua and Sonora. On one occasion, a farmer in a 4x4 advised us not to take the route we were following. It did indeed almost vanish in an indistinguishable track but it was the way we wanted to go. Strangely, on many back roads, the concrete cattle grids were aligned in the wrong direction, and not wanting to risk ourselves or our wheels, we had to push the bikes across.

With 2,000km to the US border we passed through our penultimate Mexican city. Typical of our arrival in many cities, at first, passing through the outskirts of Zacatecas, we wondered 'what are we doing here?' Once in the centre we realised that it was a city to savour. Zacatecas was made rich through the silver mines near the city. In 1540, The Spanish fought the natives, took the wealth of silver and built the many Baroque and religious buildings lining the paved stone streets and squares. Nearly 300 years later, on 15 April 1811, Mexican rebels fought forces loyal to the Spanish crown in the Battle of Zacatecas. It was one of the bloodiest battles of the Mexican War of Independence. Mexican-born Spaniards, Mestizos, Zambos and Amerindians were fighting for freedom from the Spanish colonial authorities. The Mexican insurgents won forcing another nail into the coffin of the Spanish Empire.

The desert burn of Bob Dylan's voice was ringing through our heads as we cycled towards our last Mexican city of Durango. Under an azure blue sky, the lines of Romance in Durango 'Hot Chili Peppers in the Blistering Sun' kept repeating as our thirsts became hard to quench. The lines – 'Me and Magdalena on the run, I think this time we shall escape' – hit a firm note in our heads that we wanted to keep cycling in this paradise for more and more months and perhaps we could continue north towards Montana. We dropped hints to our children; but wiser than us, they told us that we really should come home sooner rather than later as news had reached me that the checkup before leaving home had shown a small recurrence of bladder cancer and that some treatment would be required.

The laid back city of Durango has been the centre for a Wild West film industry. The surrounding scenery and low cost labour had made it a good location for the staging of over a hundred films including *Butch Cassidy and the Sundance Kid.* We walked the streets weaving amongst a plethora of famous film stars – John Wayne, Audrey Hepburn, Jack Nicholson, Kevin Costner – life size and cast in bronze.

North of Durango we found some of the wildest and most beautiful and peaceful cycling that we have ever enjoyed. Camping was now not only perfect and secluded but also essential as the distances between towns was often big. Without many flowing streams, typically one day, we carried fifteen litres of water between us, to a potential camp where there was an unlocked gate from where a little track led into the forest. It was another stealthy spot where we thought 'no one will ever find us here'. After dark, just as we were settling into looking at our photos of the day we heard what sounded like a gunshot!

Approaching Zacatecas.

Hunters? Was someone coming to get us? Had a drug lord just murdered a rival? We turned off our lights and talked in whispers. Then a vehicle drove up the track and disappeared.

The highlight of cycling in Mexico arrived the day we traversed the Barranca del Cobre. The combination of awesome scenery around every corner, a perfect blue sky with the temperature in the mid-twenties and a smooth road

Nothing but scenery for 100 km near Moctezuma, Sonora

virtually devoid of traffic gave us the most enjoyable day's riding ever. Around every corner there was a new view of a towering cliff face or deep gorge. Quiet roads give so much opportunity for thought and chat. We began to think about other great day rides and in our heads we began to create a mental list.

For all the plusses of cycling in Mexico, we met only twelve others on bikes and absolutely none in our last five and a half weeks north of Oaxaca. Inevitably there were some frustrations but the same sort of irritations that are found in other countries. Such as, plumbing that doesn't work properly, curtain rails that don't slide and wobbly toilet seats. Outside cities we found the food to be unexciting and we did our best to avoid tortillas when there was a chance.

The *abarroteros* (groceries) mainly sold crisps and sugary drinks but we found our essentials of *avena* (porridge) and powdered milk very easily. Drinking water is a major challenge for Mexico and for the most part it is driven around in trucks and sold in plastic bottles of various sizes. Pauline's stomach was good throughout the journey and I suffered twice for a few hours. We found it a challenge to avoid sugar in drinks as the Mexicans love it. Plastic is a terror and it would always take at least two calls of *sin balsa* to turn down a plastic bag when shopping.

We wondered about the level of education of the average Mexican as few appeared to know where England is. It often took a lot of persuasion to convince people that we were not from the USA. Many thought we had cycled from home, although many thought it unimaginable to even ride a bike from a neighbouring town. The straight line distance from Puerto Morelos to Agua Prieta is less than 3,000km. In fact, we had cycled more than double that on our wiggly route crossing the Tropic of Cancer. Except for the gunshot near our camp in the state of Chihuahua and for some bad traffic, we never felt unsafe in Mexico and we found it a wonderful and colourful country to explore.

6
CHENGDU TO PHNOM PENH

No Aliens Allowed

Wherever you go, go with all your heart

Confucius

Hugh:

Airports don't often make the best starting points for cycle trips. We have known some tiny airports in France, such as Bergerac, to be good, but when the airport is serving the sixth largest city in China with a population of ten million, almost half the population of Australia, then it is probably not going to be ideal. Traffic mayhem and huge amounts of infrastructure are the norm for city airports. At least the Chengdu one was on the south side of the city so we could hope for an escape that would not take more than a day.

The southern end of Chengdu is a totally uninspiring man-made environment in progress; a vast industrial estate with new high-rise accommodation sprouting up, linked by ridiculously wide streets. The air smelt bad and any wasteland vegetation was covered in dust. The place had a spooky air not helped by the gloomy opaque atmosphere. Things brightened up a little when we reached some more established suburbs. Men sat outside playing cards, women were sorting and cleaning big flat pans and others sold fruit and vegetables on the street. We bought some delicious oranges.

Things looked up even more when we escaped the edge of the city on a tiny, peaceful road following the Fu He River. People were busy working on the neatly and heavily cultivated land by the waterside. We were navigating using a map of Sichuan on Pocket Earth which we had fortunately downloaded before we left home as our experience of the internet was virtually non-existent for our first ten days in China. This was the first trip in which we used our phones for navigating. A Swiss cyclist we had met in Arizona the previous year had told us about the app called Pocket Earth. We found it to be mainly accurate and at times remarkable in its detail.

Entering Huanglongxi, looking for a place to stay, we were surprised to find it a historical place with charm, dating back 1700 years to before the Qing Dynasty. There were plenty of Chinese tourists around but no foreigners. The place was crammed with interesting but strange foods, beautiful colourful clothes and curious architecture. The town was vibrant on a Saturday night in December. We chanced upon a free show called 'Dancing with the Dragon'. There were many different acts performed to funky music, and the highlight was a vigorous dance where a man changed his mask by magic and breathed fire. Outside, music was everywhere. By the doors of open air restaurants, men flung long fresh noodles out of their pots into the air before serving them in bowls.

🚲   🚲   🚲

We had almost been put off going to China altogether, due to the seeming complexity of gaining visas. Our idea of taking a one way flight to Chengdu and just working everything else out later wasn't going to win us Chinese visas; we had to present evidence of eventual flights home. We were planning to return home from New Zealand – where our daughter was living – after continuing our Chinese tour through Laos and Cambodia. Trailfinders, the travel agent we used, came up with a brilliant plan. A return flight from Manchester to Christchurch via Singapore would show that we would be going home one day. We would break the journey on the way out – for a long time – and fly to Chengdu from Singapore. When we reached Phnom Penh we would fly to Singapore and continue to New Zealand – brilliant! We just had to write a letter saying we were leaving Chinese territory by bicycle at the border with Laos.

Also, hotel booking confirmations for all nights must be declared. How could we do this for a proposed journey of 2,500km over a period of nearly two months? Trailfinders came up with the answer again. In our formal letter we could pretend that we were transiting from Chengdu to the Laos border at Mohan in just two weeks by using a combination of bits of cycling and long sections of public transport. This would get us visas for three months and then we could take as long as we liked. It wasn't too challenging to fabricate two weeks of hotel bookings on the internet and then cancel them all once we left Chengdu. It worked and we gained the visas after paying nearly £200 each.

Our arrival at Chengdu airport was perplexing. Faced with an incomprehensible ATM, I tried a few strangers for help and eventually extracted a few hundred Yuan. The only booking we had kept was for the first night in a hotel near the airport. Sadly we discovered that not all strangers are there to help when a taxi driver tried to charge us a huge amount for the short trip. So, we had all our kit and some money, but it was now late in the day and we couldn't find a way of getting to the hotel. We thought of assembling the bikes and riding them but it was dark, confusing and we were pretty tired after 24 hours of travel. We needed help. Evidence was now gathering that there are more helpful people than unhelpful ones when it comes to being a stranger in need. We saw some airline stewards boarding a minibus and approached them cautiously. They spoke some English and immediately put us at ease. They asked if we had a hotel booking; we gave them the number, and then they told us that it didn't take foreigners. They called the hotel which they were going to and arranged a booking for us before loading our bike boxes and taking us there for free.

NO ALIENS ALLOWED

December 10th 2016 to April 4th 2017
6300 kms

It was December 2016 and this was our sixth major trip since leaving home for South America in August 2010. For this trip we changed our style by taking lighter bikes with rear panniers only and no camping kit. It seemed clear that accommodation is easy to find in China, Laos and Cambodia and terrain for camping is hard to find. Indeed, after the slight scare of Chengdu airport, our nearest night to sleeping in a hedge came a few weeks later by the Yangtze when it appeared that the hotel marked on Pocket Earth had disappeared under the dammed river. That night, all we could find was a basic truck drivers' stop, but even that was not without some character.

We had less than a handful of places which we knew we should try to visit in Sichuan and Yunnan. As usual, our journey was mainly one of serendipity. However Leshan was on the list. We found a hotel with a room on the fifth floor overlooking the murky Dadu River and then went to look for the Giant Leshan Buddha. It is 71 meters tall and was built between 713 and 803AD. It is the tallest stone Buddha in the world and the largest pre-modern statue in the world. It had been carved out of the red sandstone cliff face and stands at the confluence of the Min and Dadu, fast flowing muddy rivers from which by boat you can take a close look at the complete impressive Buddha. Apart from the main attraction there are many temples housing giant Buddhas in colour and gold, and with scary faces; hangings with bright colourful dragons; lotus flower shaped candles; burning incense; and patterned cushions for kneeling before the great statues. There were a handful of smartly dressed Chinese tourists armed with phones and selfie sticks and as was common throughout our time in China; we found ourselves the subject of their photos just as much, if not more so, than the sights they had come to see.

It appeared that the Chinese have as much of a problem with our language as we do with theirs. The footpaths surrounding the sights were adorned with signs in Chinese and English with advice such as 'You can enjoy the fresh air after finishing civilised urinating', 'Road is slippery be careful to fall', 'Not to parabolic' and 'Fire ext ingulsher box'.

There are days when you say to yourself, 'this isn't what cycle touring is about'. Although we are game for the warts and all view of a country as seen from a bike, there are limits. We had found some interesting little back routes but in the main we had been on wide roads with traffic passing through towns dominated by ugly apartment blocks. We were heading into the mountains – surely there couldn't be skyscrapers there! We wondered where are all the people came from to live in these huge blocks? Surely the one child policy had cut the population by now – was it migration from rural areas, and if it was then what did they make of these ugly, smelly and noisy cities? We would love to have known how they felt.

Looking for some kind of haven in the urban jungle of Emeishan we opted for a room on the tenth floor of the five star Century Sunshine Hotel (wishful thinking) which we got for a knockdown price complete with an enormous buffet breakfast. As had been the case with all the hotels so far, we had paid less than the advertised price (we could read the prices as they use Latin numerals). They also asked for a returnable deposit in case you trash the room. Looking out of our window, we felt more than ever before we were in a different, alien world and to be honest we felt sorry for the people who have to live in it, even those that are well off in material terms. The gloomy weather didn't help our mood.

The following day, just when we were thinking that we weren't really in control of this journey we passed a young policeman who beckoned us to stop. Unwisely we rode on but not for long. The policeman had brought reinforcements and a phone translator from which he showed us the message 'no aliens in this territory'.

We gathered that the area was not permitted for foreigners. We could travel through but not stay in the hotel at Jinkouhe – no way, no matter how much we tried to convey that we were tired. We had no idea where the next hotel was and it was getting dark. They weren't threatening or aggressive but they were very firm. We really didn't want to go back to gloomy Ebian. Their other option was to go on to Wusihe where they said we could stay. They would escort us out of the area. It would probably be around 40km up hill and too far for us to ride, especially in the dark. When it seemed like they would transport us we decided to ignore our usual scruples about taking lifts and accept. We jammed our bikes in the back of the police pickup truck and off we went. As we passed through Jinkouhe we saw the hotel – the name was even in English – and it seemed weird that we couldn't stay there – they wouldn't tell us why not.

A few kilometres up the road we hit a total road block which even the police couldn't get through – the road was being repaired. The old road offered a way round the blockage and vehicles were using it so the policemen suggested that we get on our bikes at this point. But how far was it? How high did the road go? Where exactly was the hotel they were suggesting? We briefly considered it but decided that it was mad – in the dark and with no tent. We tried our calm persuasion method and I even offered money which they firmly refused. After several phone calls and much deliberation they agreed to take us up the road. It was very narrow and climbed high above the river overlooking a huge precipice, fortunately on our left hand side. The traffic jams the police feared were a problem and twice they tried again to ditch us. I finally played the 'old' card – we were old and tired I told them.

We finally descended down a rough, muddy track around several hairpin bends and reached the main road. Getting over that in the dark after a 90km hilly ride would have taken a long time and there was still 20km to go to get to the supposed hotel. In Wusihe they tried to abandon us once more but we weren't having it – how were we supposed to find the hotel if they couldn't? After asking at the police station they turned round and took us three kilometres back up the road to Hanyuan where a bright red sign on a rooftop indicated something significant – it was a hotel. At first the guy in the lobby looked doubtful but once we were sure of a room we unloaded our stuff, put our bikes in the garage and moved in. What kind of a place will this be I thought to myself as we walked up the stairs? It turned out to be pretty decent and very cheap with a good hot shower, heating and wifi. If we had tried to ride the route, we would have arrived after midnight, probably not found the hotel and even then it would possibly have been shut for the night. We had travelled through a magnificent gorge that we only got hints of in the fading light. It would have been great to ride in daylight!

The following morning, we were cheered by the appearance of the sun and the low level of traffic, but the wholesale devastation of the valley continued. Dams were being built along the course of the river which was often muddy and not flowing freely. Vast works were going on to give protection from landslides in the form of cemented rock faces, huge metal nets and concrete retainers. All of this improvement of the infrastructure necessitated numerous cement works, quarries and gravel works. The river beds, river banks and mountain sides were all scenes of devastation.

The town of Ganluo buzzed in the evening. The streets were packed with families and the shops lit brightly displaying a wealth of consumer goods. We saw no other foreigners. One of the curiosities of cycle touring is how it lands you in random places where ordinary people are just getting on with their lives. We had become better at choosing food and we loved the Sichuanese hotpot – a bubbling stock, often very spicy but sometimes toned down for us. You choose your raw ingredients (meats, veggies, fungi, eggs) and chuck them into the pot. When they are ready you fish them out with chopsticks or a slotted ladle and dip them in a mix of coriander, garlic, chilli and other ingredients chosen from a collection on a side table. The restaurants were often very lively and often diners would sit in groups around a hot pot. The staff were incredibly helpful and several of the locals would take photos of us or offer us some of the local strong spirit. The people who inhabit these areas are so cheerful, so welcoming and keen to communicate. No one gave us cause for concern and they were so tolerant of our almost total lack of ability to communicate in their language.

Our journey was turning a corner. The sky had turned blue and we had met high mountains. A 35km climb to 3000m opened a completely new enthusiasm for our journey in China. It was one week before Christmas and much to the consternation of the people of Sichuan we were riding in shorts. We were now passing old, slated, stone-built houses and men and women dressed immaculately in traditional dress, many with spectacular headgear constructed from long rectangular embroidered cloths.

Approaching Xichang we joined a fantastic cycle way, lined with colourful flowers. The route at this point had us thinking, 'perhaps Xichang is a bit smarter than the cities we have been through so far'. Urban planning was very evident with the cycle way separated from motorised transport. A mixture of Chinese transport made its way into the city – cyclists, scooters, modern cars (you don't see old bangers) and little three-wheeled transport wagons. Buses and trucks added to the mix on most roads. As we entered the city proper we really did have the feeling that this was cleaner and smarter than the usual pile of drab skyscrapers which we had become used to. We passed the enormous

Yeucheng Plaza where men played cards at low tables, men and women played Mahjong and in the evenings large numbers of people danced and stretched to music, often performing Tai Chi.

We witnessed magic happening first hand; during our stay in Xichang the city performed magic on us. The city of half a million is a centre for the Yi people who speak a totally different language from the Han Chinese and also have different facial features. The old market was full of fascinating characters and the most bizarre collection of foodstuffs we had ever seen. There were curious fungi, a plethora of spices and chillies, dried fish and octopi, pulses and tons of things we didn't even recognise. Alongside the riverbank we chanced upon Yi people in traditional dress telling fortunes, performing dentistry, reading ancient manuscripts and mysteriously spinning eggs in bowls of water. Many women wore colourful robes and tall elegant headdresses. Men sported hats looking Cossack in style. Everyone looked very peaceful. Fortune tellers held people's hands and there was a strong element of trust in everyone's eyes. There was trust in the dentist too who looked to be inserting old teeth directly into a lady's gums whilst she looked skywards with her mouth wide open to the outside world.

We had been in China for ten days and using a VPN on our phones we had managed a small amount of communication and written a skeleton blog on the *crazyguyonabike* website. Our lack of access to the internet on the laptop came to the attention of other *crazyguyonabike* bloggers, Andy and Clare Evans, who had also passed through Sichuan and been picked up by the police as 'aliens' in the same place as us. They suggested that we try the Express VPN. The use of virtual private networks is common in China but illegal. We downloaded Express and were able to choose our location – Australia, UK, Hong Kong – anywhere but China. Hey presto! Everything worked and we were back in business and writing and publishing our daily blog freely. It seemed a small point but for us it had become important to share our journey with family, friends and strangers.

Whilst wandering the streets of both old and new Xichang we found the first church we had seen in China and a young lady named Amy gave us a warm welcome at the door. Many Chinese adopt English names. She had studied communications for a year in Leeds and spoke excellent English. She invited us to join her for a barbecue in the evening. Amy used her phone to call an Uber style taxi to take us to a modern part of town. As was common in this part of China, the meal was served over coals in the centre of the table. It is a brilliant way to keep the food and the customer warm with the coals often being by the legs below the table. We had crispy intestines, pigs' brains, a special Yi soup made with radish heads and leaves, chicken, beef and a stuffed aubergine – absolutely gorgeous! Amy refused any contribution to the meal and paid for it using her phone.

After a three day break we left Xichang feeling truly energised. Our last night in Sichuan was in a family home in the hill village of Yizuzizhizhou. Finding a good breakfast was often more of a challenge than finding a comfortable room and a tasty evening meal. We supped a bowl of something like a thin rice and corn pudding to the accompaniment of retching sounds coming from nearby loos. Shortly after a man arrived and sneezed all over the food. Apart from boiled eggs, breakfast food often consisted of noodles and dumplings. Tolerating Chinese dining and smoking habits could be challenging. Eating is often accompanied by a lot of slurping. We enjoyed eating out where we had the use of a separate dining booth!

It was Christmas Day when we entered Yunnan. We arrived under a blue sky by the turquoise Lugu Hu, which at an altitude of 2,700m is Yunnan's highest lake. It is extremely beautiful and astonishingly devoid of manmade structures such as pylons, dams and skyscrapers. By the lakeshore at the village of Lige a peninsula reaches into the lake. A narrow footpath connects the main part of the village to the peninsula and we managed to wheel our bikes to the end of the path. We had looked down on the peninsula from above and said to ourselves 'wouldn't it be beautiful to stay there?' Quite simply this was one of the most beautiful places we had seen anywhere on our travels and such an astonishing contrast to so much of what we had witnessed in Sichuan.

We found a gorgeous room with expansive views of the lake but it had a problem that we hadn't anticipated. It was freezing! There was no heating. As was common in many rural parts of Yunnan, there was just an electric blanket. The room temperature was seven degrees when we awoke. We wanted to stay longer and explore but we had to find a warmer room. We found another traditional building with a curvaceous roof just around the corner and still enjoying a view of the lake. It was small and cosy and had a heater. We watched from our window and saw fishermen and women come and go in their dugout boats and lots of large birds swooping high and low above the water. This was a mini traffic free paradise. We met some Chinese tourists escaping the pollution of cities such as Shanghai and in a local restaurant we met another young lady.

It was very special to be able to befriend someone who we could communicate with. Nancy (also an adopted English name) spoke good English – she had translated articles for the equivalent of the Chinese National Geographic – one of them being on Shetland. She was very knowledgeable about different areas of the world. She had been living in Lige for a month working in a lakeshore hotel and restaurant. She recommended that we visit the Zhameisi temple 15km north of the lake. It is a conventional Tibetan Buddhist temple and the largest one associated with the local Mosuo people. There are many different buildings, some of which date back 400 years and one of which was under construction. During ten years of the Cultural Revolution the site was devastated, as were so many historic buildings. Reconstruction started in 1986 and was still in progress. The head Lama, Luosang Yishi Rinpoche, was born on an island in Lugu Lake and he became a monk when aged six!

The Mosuo follow the Yellow Hat sect of Tibetan Buddhism. They are a matriarchal society. All property is passed down the female line and the women are in charge. They are known for their 'walking marriages'. Having multiple partners and children by different men carries no stigma. A Mosuo woman who is interested in a particular man will invite him to come and spend the night with her in her room. The man will walk to her house after dark (thus the description of walking marriage), spend the night with her, and return home early the next morning. Sexual partners do not live together – they live with their mothers' families. It is possible for a Mosuo woman to change partners as often as she likes and having only one sexual partner would be neither expected nor common. However, the majority of relationships are more long term and few Mosuo women will have more than one partner at a time. More than one anthropologist has described this system as 'serial monogamy'.

We left Lige climbing out of the basin which holds the lake and looked back at the impressive Lion Mountain which dominates the north shore. We continued climbing to reach a pass at 3,100m and for the first time on this journey we looked at a long line of high jagged mountains. We were now close to the south eastern edge of the Tibetan plateau. Settlements were scattered all over the mountains and high piles of wood were stashed outside their homes. There were people living and farming up there on a stretch of the road which undulated at around 3,000m before plunging down to the Yangtze River, which cuts an incredibly deep trough through the mountains. To reach river level we lost 1,500m of altitude enjoying one of our longest freewheels ever at 40km.

The Yangtze River, known in China as the Cháng Jiāng (literally: long river), is the longest river in Asia, the third-longest in the world and the longest in the world to flow entirely within one country. It drains one-fifth of the land area of the People's Republic of China and its river basin is home to one-third of the country's population. Another 1,000m climb out of the Yangtze took us to the beautiful ancient city of Lijiang. It was 31 December and from our cool room at the Moon Inn we could see and hear an almighty celebration of fireworks. The Chinese, the inventors of fireworks, get the chance to celebrate two New Years – the Chinese New Year in 2017 was on the 27 January.

When Lijiang was hit by an earthquake in 1996, the buildings constructed in the traditional Naxi (the local ethnic people) style held up much better than the modern constructions. Three hundred people died in the quake which measured seven on the Richter Scale. Impressively, the Government took note and put millions of Yuan into rebuilding most of Lijiang County in the traditional Naxi architectural style with cobblestones and wood. The whole county is on the UNESCO World Heritage list.

The old town is a web of narrow streets of stone setts, arched bridges, tiny alleys and small flowing streams. It was a pleasure to walk around because there was virtually no traffic. We enjoyed the chance to relax, eat good food and drink good coffee. Strolling around the old town there was the same selection of shops and all over town, doll like women were tapping on drums to the same ultra-repetitive tune. It did our heads in after a day of hearing it so no wonder the girls appeared to be like robots. There was a constant aroma of enticing foods, leather goods and incense. From the viewpoint of the pagoda high above the town, we looked down on a sea of beautiful tiled and curved roofs.

The town is dominated by the Jade Dragon Snow Mountain (Yulong Mountain). The highest of its thirteen peaks is 5,600m and it is sometimes incorrectly said that it carries the southernmost glacier in the Northern Hemisphere. Walking around the Black Dragon Pool just north of Lijiang gives serene views of the mountain and its perfect reflection below many storied pagodas and a classic arched bridge. Strolling towards the bridge we heard the mellow tones of a beautiful instrument and discovered a musician playing soothing melodies on a long bamboo vertical flute. She let Pauline have a go and she wanted to buy one but was told that you can't get them in Lijiang – only via the internet! The musical score she read from was incomprehensible to us.

For a couple of days our route deviated north for a purpose. In the village of Baisha we found a classic old guesthouse with a room adorned with intricately carved wooden furniture including a four poster bed. Down the small street we found the home of the legendary Doctor Ho. The 95-year-old is reckoned to have the best knowledge of Chinese traditional medicine. He wished us 'Happy New Year' (in English), asked us to sign his guestbook and showed us pictures of visitors including Michael Palin and Bruce Chatwin.

Sadly our ride past the Yulong Mountain had the view obliterated by a blizzard. We stopped to warm our cold toes and fingers by the open fires of people making tea by the roadside at 3,250m. Wedding couples had picked a bad day for their classic photos. The mountain which was to be the ultimate backdrop was in the clouds. We descended to the town of Daju at 1,800m and went in search of a boat to cross the Yangtze. After a couple of route finding errors we finally saw a boat on the turbulent waters below. The ferry ploughed into a mud ramp so that the handful of passengers could get on and off. There was no infrastructure at all. Like other beautiful wild rivers we have visited on our travels (the Río Baker in Chile and the Çoruh River valley in Turkey) the Jinsha River (the Chinese name for the upper Yangtze) has also been threatened by dams. After a public outcry the project was scrapped in 2007 but other projects are planned upstream. When you sit by the foaming mass of water at the bottom of the gorge and marvel at the power of the water, it feels like it would be sacrilege to rob the river of its life!

In the small village of Walnut Garden we found the Bridge Café and

Yulong mountain (5,600m) towers above the Black Dragon Pool – Lijiang, Yunnan.

guesthouse, run by a lovely Tibetan family. We enjoyed an extensive view of the steep sided gorge from our window and the sun warmed the room almost until sunset – and then it froze. Walnut Garden lies directly above the Tiger Leaping Gorge. We set out on a path going down – how far we weren't sure. It was very steep and clung precariously to the cliff. Some Chinese tourists going up warned us that it could be difficult to make it down and up before dark! When we reached the raging torrent below we were totally awestruck. We climbed down so close that we could feel the spray. We couldn't talk for the noise. The rocks were worn smooth by the passage of many feet so we had to be careful. In places there were sections of ladders, and fence which probably gave us a false sense of confidence. Some of the return path was carved out of a cliff face and a slightly scary, long, near vertical ladder returned us to Walnut Garden before dark.

The following morning we passed a far more touristy viewpoint overlooking the gorge. A warden tried to charge us to park our bikes whilst we glimpsed over the edge. A sign in Tibetan, Chinese and English announced 'no tossing'. Bashing and tossing rocks was what lots of ladies in colourful hats and aprons were doing at the roadside on this Friday afternoon in early January whilst we

Well dressed and well connected – Baisha, Yunnan.

were trying to find a quiet way to the 'First Big Bend in the Yangtze'. Roadworks are often awkward interruptions to a cyclist's journey. In China roads are frequently worked on in long sections and this one continued for 30km. The way was pot holed with pools of mud, smelly diggers every few hundred metres, and despite some mechanical assistance many jobs were still done by brute force. The ladies flung enormous axes and hammers at boulders, whilst men clung to rockfaces by ropes and smothered the surfaces in a honeycomb of concrete in an attempt to prevent cliff erosion. Invariably we were given friendly waves and probably asked where we were going – the Big Bend of course.

It didn't take long until we felt that we needed 'cleansing'. Not in the spiritual or digestive sense, but in the real physical sense. We were both impregnated with dust from the roadworks – our clothes, our skin, our hair, our bikes and probably our lungs. All the buildings, trees and vegetation were coated in it. In places the road had been sprayed with water to keep down the dust. We saw women throwing buckets of water on the road in front of their shops and houses. This added to the congealed mess coating our shoes, pedals and bikes. We looked down in horror at the state of our kit. We had an overwhelming desire to get rid of the mess but that had to wait.

NO ALIENS ALLOWED

At the old small town of Shigu we found – the Bend – literally the first big bend in the Yangtze River. The wide river flowing south from Tibet, makes a 120 degree turn to the north in a distance of one kilometre. The place was important militarily because big armies crossed the river at this point, and it was a place where Tibetans descended to trade with people living in the area.

Our journey was now heading increasingly south. We crossed the 25 degree line of latitude and were grateful for a little increase in warmth even though our altitude remained above 2,000m. The people were invariably lovely and did their best to help us, particularly when we stayed in those places in-between not normally frequented by tourists. Communication – or the lack of it – was hilarious! People seemed totally unperturbed by the fact that we didn't understand a word of their outflow of Mandarin and we took to responding in kind in English which people found funny! People looked very puzzled. Maybe it is because many of the westerners travelling in China are working there or married to a Chinese person and understand some of the language. When oral language failed people would expect us to understand the written language. They would write things down for us and present us with Chinese menus on which we could only understand the prices.

Happy people and happy fingers and feet by the pass (3,250m) between Baisha and Daju, Yunnan.

We won't forget the sounds of China – honking vehicles and the harsh sound in the throat as people built up to spit on the ground. We couldn't get used to these things! Then there is the sound of gravel being hauled out of river beds, cocks crowing and irritating recordings enticing you into shops. But the scooters are usually silent, electric, and it's easy to miss them. The people can be quite noisy when speaking to each other and family groups can be extremely loud. We didn't have a problem with traffic in cities which was neither dense nor fast but it was so common to see people driving while eating, drinking or using their phones. Overtaking seemed to be OK as long as there was no visible obstruction ahead regardless of the fact that it may be obscured by a bend, a dip in the road or another vehicle. We were frequently confronted by an overtaking vehicle heading straight for us and the escape was pretty unpalatable as most roads have a deadly deep gutter at the side!

However, there were many gorgeous days of riding past multiple layers of bright green terraced fields and overnight stays in ancient towns such as Shaxi where the market square has been restored and many of the old buildings have been protected by the World Monuments Watch list of one hundred most endangered sites. The town lies on the Tea and Horses Road which earned its

Boat across the Yangtze below the Tiger Leaping gorge, Yunnan.

name from the large-scale commerce between tea-growing regions of China and places with plenty of horses. Tea was traded to Tibet while war horses were brought to the south of China from as far away as Lhasa. The trading distance was 2,300km. The development of trade between the Chinese dynasties and Tibet dates back to the Song dynasty (960-1279AD).

A fundamental experience of slowly passing through Sichuan and Yunnan was that of the industry of the people. In many countries people are often just sitting by the wayside, chatting and passing the time of day, with apparently nothing in particular to do. We were constantly passing both men and women at work close to the roadsides. Welding sections of steel, baking bricks and roof tiles, carving wooden furniture and, over a 3,080m pass, crossing towards Erhai Lake, fields were being worked for cabbages, broad beans and garlic. Men and women leant over to the ground with large wicker baskets strapped to their backs. The aroma of garlic was overwhelming. Vast areas of concrete were completely covered in garlic drying under a blue sky in the clean air of high altitude. Thousands of large sacks were stuffed with garlic destined for export. When asked to guess China's main exports you think of electronics and machinery, however in garlic, China is a world beater, exporting three quarters of global production.

Close to Erhai Lake and just 20km north of Dali we chanced upon Xizhou, a gem of a traditional Bai town. The Bai are Yunnan's second largest ethnic minority. They have held on to their customs and traits. Xizhou used to be a major stop on the trade route to the north. The population included many rich families who built themselves exquisite houses. They designed their homes to have courtyards with delicately carved gates, brackets, doors and windows. We found one to stay in so we could take time to savour the narrow streets and old buildings and workshops of Xizhou before moving on to the tourist honeypot of Dali.

Dali, more famous than any other place we visited in China, deserves its reputation for the Three Pagodas inspired by the Indian Mahayana school of Buddhism. The tallest is 69m high, has sixteen tiers, and dates back to 850AD. Miraculously the three towers have survived many earthquakes and the Muslim revolt which destroyed the accompanying Chongsheng monastery. We entered the old walled town of Dali through the north gate and left through the south gate with its wood-carved struts and sloping roofs with curling corners. The inner town was crowded with many shops selling souvenirs, tie-dyed clothing and handicrafts. We didn't linger and continued south along the lake shore following a bike lane with some boardwalks built over hanging marshes at the edge of the lake.

We passed endless fields of vegetables, forests of eucalyptus and through villages where there were mosques and, from the headdresses people were wearing, we could see that the population was Muslim. Passing through another ancient gate we entered the traffic free town of Weishan. It is China's best preserved city of the Ming and Qing dynasties and dates from 1390AD. To us it was a puzzle after Dali, to find Weishan almost devoid of visitors and yet the place has far more charm and interest.

Weibaoshan, the mountain of Towering Treasures, 18km south of the city, hides fourteen Taoist temples along the ridges of its upper slopes. The mountain is swathed in thick forests of pine and cypress, the shrines and temples sited at intervals along paths that ascend to the summit. We could only find vague information about accommodation on the mountain so we chanced an out and back day trip from Weishan but ended up staying longer as we found a simple and otherwise empty hotel open. A walk amongst the temples is a feast for the eyes and spirit. Many have accompanying gardens, courtyards and pools. Enchanting sounds emerged and on closer inspection we found men and women in glorious and colourful costumes knelt over in prayer whilst bashing chimes and drums with sticks. We were alone on the mountain except for these residents who appeared to be from a different era. We felt guilty taking photographs but how could we not, when you see sights such as a man with a long wispy beard and moustache, and two pony tails dangling well below his shoulders? He had the courtesy to light incense for us when he saw us enter a temple festooned with vases, dragons, Buddhas and flowers.

The following morning we freewheeled down the hill and returned to Weishan. The city straddles Nanzhao Street, which is several kilometres long and punctuated by four tower gates. The street running from Gongchen Tower to Xinggong Tower is lined on both sides with red wooden shop houses with tiled roofs, and has the most traditional look and feel of any street in the city. They are all modest buildings, with the goods stored in the room facing the street, which may also serve as a workshop, and with the living quarters in the rear and in the attics. There are shops selling antiques, ethnic clothing and local food produce – their customers are not tourists so much as local ethnic minority people who buy the items to wear or the fresh noodles and wild fungi to eat. Many street corners are adorned with beautiful bronze sculptures depicting scenes of everyday life such as the playing of Chinese chess whilst in real life many men and women walk by smoking pipes of different shapes and sizes, long, short, fat and thin. The inhabitants of Weishan are mainly Yi and Hui some of whom are descendants of Kublai Khan's Central Asian Muslims. As if to reinforce the feel of a bygone era, people were travelling to the local market town of Dacang to the north by pony and cart.

Our last ten days in China saw a massive transition from mountain terrain to lush tropical forests. We had briefly met a cyclist in Dali. She had told us that it would be impossible to find a quiet way south to the border with Laos. She had travelled in the opposite direction with her bike on a bus and from her point of view she just saw busy roads with fast moving traffic on highways which trashed the landscape with their stilts and flyovers. Her thoughts had caused us concern but with some work you can usually find a way to travel peacefully. Historically most countries have an infrastructure of old routes through villages. With some research each evening we found a way south through charming villages and countryside on roads and tracks generally devoid of traffic. You have to be prepared to get dirty and lost from time to time and you have to be careful of what other travellers recommend.

At the heart of the journey lay the tea plantations of Pu'er, lying just south of the Tropic of Cancer. Some of the small lanes we took meandered through hillsides covered in neatly clipped bushes which followed the contours of the gentle hillsides. In the neighbouring towns there were cylindrical blocks of black tea for sale. In the south we passed some small areas where coffee was growing but it was hard to find a good cup of coffee. Coffee is an expanding industry in Yunnan and efforts are made to reward the farmers to support the claim that the coffee is 'ethically sourced'.

One of the things we love about cycling is your proximity to the sights and aromas of the surroundings and the ability to stop on a sixpence when something sparkles. Birds and butterflies often stop us, and snakes sometimes, but fortunately mainly when they are roadkill and they are dying or dead. On the steppe there were camels to admire and in Australia there were kangaroos but here in southern Yunnan, out of the blue, we were stopped in our tracks by an elephant munching its bamboo breakfast. We were aware that we were passing along the edge of a wild elephant reserve but we had read that the chances of seeing one were pretty small. You can pay to enter a park and see them in captivity but that was not what we wanted to do. Prince William had visited the sanctuary two years earlier, and apparently he appeared embarrassed by the show that is put on for tourists. Like a circus act, elephants have been trained to kick footballs and sit on tiny stools wearing spectacles!

Our route descended to the banks of the Mekong River in Jinghong at our lowest altitude since leaving Chengdu over six weeks earlier. Small for a Chinese city, with a population of half a million, it wasn't difficult for us to navigate our way along palm tree lined boulevards past thoughtfully designed skyscrapers built in the style of Dai pagodas. The Mekong was going to be a thread to our journey over the next ten weeks. The river rises on the Tibetan plateau and flows 4,350km through several countries before emptying what it has left into the South China Sea through its delta in Vietnam. The Jinghong Dam, the nearest Chinese dam upstream of the Thai border, has caused huge fluctuations in river levels, affecting people's livelihoods downstream by disrupting the river's natural cycle. It is impacting the ecosystem, disturbing the migratory patterns of fish as well as riverbank plants and agriculture. And this is just one of China's many dams on the river. Downstream, Laos, Thailand and Cambodia are also tapping into the bonanza without thinking of the long term consequences. At least with the dammed Yangtze there won't be water wars between countries.

The tail end of our traverse of Yunnan coincided with the Chinese New Year, an exciting time to be leaving China. There appears to be no regard for safety when it comes to the use of fireworks. It was extremely bright and flashy in the sky and exceedingly loud. Fireworks had been going off all day – people were still buying them late into the evening – but they upped the game after sunset. They set light to the end of what looked like a red rope and all hell was let loose! The super loud cracks shoot down the line and the ground is left strewn with red confetti. At times it sounded as if a car had exploded.

Our gloves, hats and warm clothes were now buried deep in our panniers. All we needed to pass through the Chinese frontier was our carefully guarded passports. We had been worried about the questions which we may be asked but there was no need for such fears. Our exit took less than five minutes and no questions were asked about the use of VPNs or where and for how long we had been staying. It had been beautiful and easy except for our police movement in Sichuan. The country had felt very commercial and capitalist and so unlike obviously communist Cuba where we had travelled two years earlier. And then we entered the one party socialist republic of Laos.

Into the Cauldron

Still, round the corner, there may wait, a new road or a secret gate.

J.R.R.Tolkien

Hugh:

Land-locked Laos has a similar area to Great Britain with less than ten per cent of the population. Most people live in river valleys with the Mekong running the full length of the country. Seventy per cent of the country is mountains and plateaus and two thirds is forested. With quiet roads and a friendly, rural population, Laos is an excellent country to cycle in during a northern hemisphere winter.

Arriving from China, the contrast is stunning. There is very little manufacturing in Laos. Agriculture, fishing and forestry occupy eighty per cent of working people. Sixty per cent of the population of China live in cities whilst in Laos only thirty five per cent live in urban areas. The country is poor with the average income being less than a third the income of someone from China.

We passed through rural settlements where wooden houses are built on stilts with circular stones at the tops of their legs. This prevents creatures such as rats from getting up and into the homes and food stores. Children playing by the roadsides with homemade toys would invariably wave, smile and call out *sabai di*. In between towns low cost accommodation, often in wooden cabins was easy to find but food to satisfy hungry cyclists was harder to get. Sometimes we just had rice and fried cabbage; we weren't keen to risk meat as there was often no electricity for refrigeration. We bought hard boiled eggs, waffles and peanuts to sustain us during the day. One evening we were still hungry so we went looking for another meal and somehow our needs got lost in translation and we ended up with a bowl of fried peanuts and Beerlao – a tasty ale brewed using rice.

From the first significant place over the border, Luang Namtha, we cycled two days west, 180km, to Houay Xay on the Mekong. South of China, the Mekong forms the border between Myanmar and Laos for roughly 100km before the river separates Thailand and Laos for another 100km. Looking across the river, Thailand appeared more prosperous than Laos. We had come to Houay Xay to catch a long, old, slow boat down the Mekong for a day. The night before we took the boat, disaster struck a family two doors away from the guest house where we were staying.

The day started almost five hours earlier than anticipated. Our dreams gradually turned to some neighbours' nightmares. Soon after two in the morning, I became aware of external crackling noises which gradually became louder and there was an acrid smell in the air. In my half sleep I thought that some Chinese fireworks were being ignited but the sounds didn't quite seem right. There were sounds of an intensifying commotion so I decided to get up and look outside over our balcony. Horrors! A nearby house was enveloped in flames and there seemed a real possibility that the fire could spread to our guesthouse. There was just one house between us and the fire but it seemed to be spreading rapidly.

I made sure Pauline was awake. We assessed whether we had time to pack up and go and within minutes we were outside with our loaded bikes. I helped the landlady confirm that there were no sleeping guests. By this time there were dozens of people, Laos and Western, on the streets staring at the inferno. There was absolutely no evidence of order, police or fire service. It was almost thirty minutes before a red engine arrived and who knows how long the fire had been burning before we were even awake. It took ages before the hose was in operation and then it seemed only minutes until it ran out of water. Meanwhile people were bravely pouring buckets of water feebly on to bits of the edge of the disappearing house. A few garden hosepipes were introduced but they were useless. When a second engine arrived it appeared to go down to the Mekong to get extra water.

By four in the morning we decided to look for another guesthouse on the opposite side of the street and well away from the smouldering and still burning wreck. Meanwhile throughout all the upheaval relatives and young tourists were tenderly trying to console a hysterical woman. Thankfully all the occupants had escaped and the fire didn't spread further than the one house but a family lost just about everything they owned that night. In the morning we saw the landlady of our guesthouse. She was cross that we had abandoned her hotel for another one even though we had paid.

The seven hour river journey by boat – really a kind of boat bus – was a totally new experience for us. There were more people than seats and more than would fit on a double decker bus. Most of the passengers were young western backpackers with a smattering of old hippy types and some villagers. It was fascinating seeing the countryside, villages and village life from mid-stream in the river. The river is a lifeline for local people, being the route by which they visit friends and places up and downstream, and their means of shopping.

We could have chosen to stay on the boat for another day after the overnight stay in Pakbeng. Most travellers take the two day Mekong journey all the way to Luang Prabang but we chose to explore the hilly terrain of wild Sayabouli – and in any case one day on the boat was enough!

The journey of 210km took six days and followed many roads marked as 'uncertain road condition'. For much of the way the road followed the steep bumps of the landscape – the 15% gradients were almost at our limit and we vowed to get smaller chain wheels when we got home. We passed through small villages with houses on stilts and schools or *lycées* with uniformed traffic police to control the children as they came and went from school. Hardly necessary, as not once did we see a school run done by car. Children travelled to school on foot or single speed bikes often carrying umbrellas to give shade from the fierce sun. Laos is the only country we have travelled in where all the kids in the school playground come running to see us calling and waving vigorously. The kids are often dirty and without shoes but always full of smiles and fun. They loved to clap hands with us as we rode past but that was often a very dodgy experience which threatened to tip us over.

The highlight of the section to Luang Prabang was the day from Hongsa to Xayaboury. The road led us through a mass of steep sided green mountains. For much of the way we could see the road ahead, unusually following the ridge line far into the distance towards the next village. The canopy of teak trees with their enormous leaves gave us shelter from the sun when we rested by the side of the road. Riding through a village was often like negotiating a farm yard with chickens, pigs, cows, goats and ducks all over the road. We stopped at a roadside market stall and struggled to believe what we saw for sale. Some guys had a good look at a porcupine and decided to buy it. They took it away in a cardboard box. There were squirrels, rats, a monkey, small colourful birds and large fungi laid out on display. The following day we crossed a bridge over the Mekong at Tha Dua. There were several barbecue stalls so we stopped for lunch. There were curious things on the menu. Little birds, rats and small fish! We tried the fish and the little birds which we could only hope were not any kind of rare breed. We felt bad about our choice and soon decided not to eat them again. There was not enough meat on them to make it worth the bother – better to leave them flying around.

The final day and a half's ride to Luang Prabang followed the east bank of The Mekong on a rough dried mud track passing through endless banana plantations. For five days we hadn't set eyes on any tourists and then suddenly, as we joined the road to the Kuang Si Falls for the last five kilometres, as it climbs gently into the mountains, we were on the tourist trail again. Tuk tuks and minibuses ply the road taking people on day trips from Luang Prabang. It was cool to find a cabin by the river and to stay the night. This gave us the chance for a swim and to see the falls in the late evening and early morning when the light is good and the area surrounding the falls is quiet. Before dropping away into the Mekong, the multi-tiered falls tumble over limestone into a series of turquoise pools, the scene appearing like a far eastern fictitious painting.

The last 30km leading to Luang Prabang was fast and easy on a paved road but the traffic level became threatening as we approached this small city on the Mekong. The contrast between our day-to-day lifestyle when riding through 'the places in between' and then staying in 'tourist honeypots' is extreme but we loved both. Luang Prabang was a gorgeous place to hang out, work on our dining deficit, enjoy Buddhist temples, balance across bamboo bridges crossing the Mekong's tributary, the Nam Khan River, and time to simply rest.

Travellers come to Luang Prabang from many parts of the world, but the place is understandably popular with French people due to France's historical influence in Indochina. The term Indochina was coined in the early nineteenth

On the way home from school near Hongsa, Laos.

century. It emphasizes the cultural influence on the area of Indian and Chinese civilizations. The term was later adopted as the name of the colony of French Indochina (today's Cambodia, Vietnam, and Laos). Wherever tourists gather, facilities pop up to cater for them. Some tourists like to visit exotic locations but still have many of the comforts they are used to at home. In Luang Prabang, you can almost be in a little bit of France and have good coffee, baguettes, almond croissants and immaculately prepared duck breast with red wine. No need to eat noodles for breakfast or cabbage with sticky rice for dinner!

However, this isn't exactly like France – amongst the clay tiled roofs and louvered shuttered windows are scattered wooden villas with pretty balconies built in the Lao style. Strolling around the streets you can't go far before stumbling upon a *wat* (temple) which bears no resemblance to anything European. By the confluence of the Mekong and the Nam Khan rivers stands the immaculate and beautiful Wat Xieng Thong (temple of the golden city). Built in 1560, it is reputedly the most historic and enchanting Buddhist monastery in Laos. The roof is formed of many layers of curved tiling and the rear outside wall features a mosaic of a tree of life. Inside lies a funeral chariot, a golden and saffron robed seated Buddha and a sanctuary with an elegant reclining Buddha.

Buddhism arrived in Laos in the seventh and eighth centuries AD. Roughly two thirds of today's population of Laos follow Theravada Buddhism. In 1975 the government of Laos became communist and some Buddhist spiritual practices were threatened. However it was recognised that Buddhist and communist beliefs shared some common values such as not promoting materialism. Today Laos is one of only five communist countries and it is curious to travel in the country and see so many monks and temples in rural Laos and in cities. An overwhelming feeling when passing by and meeting people in this beautiful country is that most are happy and it is rare not to be greeted with a beaming smile. Is this happiness, despite poverty, due to the unique blend of communism and Buddhism or simply due to the benefits of rural life or perhaps because the people never feel cold?

Four hundred and thirty kilometres of undulating terrain took us through a clear cut skyline of Karst landscape following one of the most popular routes for travelling cyclists in Laos. We met several from Europe and South America. It was so useful to compare notes with people going the opposite way. So often our route is influenced by others we meet on the road. As a consequence, we made the decision to deviate east to the Bolaven plateau after Vientiane, and later to take a route west of the Mekong to Si Phan Don – Four Thousand Islands. Riding along at fifteen to twenty km/hr is the perfect way to enjoy the serrated and silhouetted skyline of the limestone mountains. After six days from Luang Prabang, the beautiful transition came to a disappointing end in the uninspiring capital Vientiane.

The capital was a necessary stop to extend our visas. At the same time we learnt about a very grim tale of Laos' recent history. Our visit to the COPE (Cooperative Orthopaedic and Prosthetic Enterprise) centre made us feel both very angry and sad. Angry with the American government of the years between 1964 and 1973 and sad about the tragedies to ordinary people of this country not only during that time but continuing until now and beyond.

During the Vietnam War, Laos was a neutral country, and neither USA nor Vietnamese forces should have been in the country. Vietnam used Laos as a

Passing through a village near Vieng Phouka, northern Laos.

supply line, so USA forces bombed the route. But as ever, innocent people were the victims. In more than 580,000 bombing missions, roughly one every eight minutes, 24 hours a day for nine years, the USA forces dropped over two million tons of ordnance on Laos. It is the most heavily bombed country per capita in the world. They dropped cluster bombs which release a shower of little balls over a wide area. Thirty per cent of those bombs failed to detonate and they now hide all over land in the east putting local people, particularly the rural poor, in grave danger. Known as bombies, the orange sized cluster

Sunset on the Mekong – Luang Prabang, Laos.

bombs cause death and mutilation. Children play with the bombies they find, adults and children collect them and their casings for scrap and fishermen try to use them to stun the fish in the river. Forty per cent of those affected are children. Farmers have been unable to use their land because of the danger.

COPE, with the help of donations from multiple agencies including USAID is finding a way to help injured people. They can't give people their limbs back but they can provide good prosthetics which enable them to get their lives back. So impressed by the work of COPE, we decided to give regularly to their cause. A hundred and ten countries have signed the Convention on Cluster Munitions banning the manufacture and use of bombies but there are some notable exceptions to the signatories including the USA, Israel, Cambodia, Vietnam, Russia and China. A similar situation exists with a convention banning the use of so called 'anti-personnel' mines. There are more than three million active mines still in the ground in Cambodia.

After a good feast on international cuisine it was time to escape the capital and venture to find some cheer in the countryside. After a few days of low level hot riding we reached the cooler and higher Bolaven Plateau, a coffee growing area. Dried dirt track rides through lush vegetation took us past the succession of waterfalls named Tad Lo, Tad Yuang and Tad Fan. We found a peaceful log cabin in woods overlooking the fine dual falls of Tad Fan and spent a day scrambling through the branches and undergrowth linking Tad Fan with Tad Yuang stopping to swim in natural pools.

We descended nearly a thousand metres to return to the heat of the Mekong basin before crossing the 1.4km long Japanese built bridge to the west side of the river at Pakse. The bridge is one of only five crossing the Mekong in the whole of Laos. Completed in 2000, the designers incorporated a separate pedestrian and cycle way. Escaping the traffic of the third largest city in Laos, our route was now on quiet roads and tracks all the way for the remaining 250km to Cambodia.

Thirty kilometres south of Pakse we got our first taste of Cambodian antiquity to come. Wat Phou means 'mountain monastery' in Lao, and the Khmer ruins sit on the lower slopes of a 1,500m mountain. It was built between the sixth and twelfth centuries as a tribute to the Hindu Goddess Shiva but now it has become a Buddhist shrine. It is thought that the site may have been the precursor to Angkor in Cambodia.

We were so grateful to the Belgian cyclist who we met in the North of Laos. He told us that the west bank of the Mekong route was passable by bike and a

Amongst the karst mountains near Kiewkacham, Laos.

million times better than bashing down the busy main road. Boatmen and women in their little wooden craft provide a service for people on motor scooters and bikes wanting to hop between islands and river banks. Stopping for the night at Mounlapamok, just north of where Si Phan Don starts, enabled us to enjoy the ride through some of the many islands with plenty of time. It was slow going but good, the highlight being the ride down Don Som, an island

Island hopping through Si Phan Don, Laos.

totally without tourist facilities, without cars and not even mentioned in our two guidebooks. The track is used by people on scooters and offers wonderful cycling.

From Don Som we moved on to Don Det and then Don Khon where we found a floating room at the Sala Done Khone. It was lovely to be able to sit on the balcony and dangle our feet in the river. In the final kilometres before leaving Laos we deviated from the road to Cambodia to admire the force of the enormous Khone Pha Pheng Falls. The falls are the largest in South East Asia, and are the main reason that the Mekong is not fully navigable into China. They are only 20m high but at 11km it is the widest waterfall in the world.

We reached the quiet Cambodian frontier, paid $35 each for visas and were given a yellow document in return warning us that we were at risk of all kinds of diseases. The instruction was to hand in the yellow form to a doctor if we succumbed to some mysterious ailment!

INTO THE CAULDRON

We cycled on through the heat of the afternoon. The road was often stripped of its top surface and our sweaty bodies were showered with dust whenever a vehicle passed. Our thermometer read 38 degrees in the shade and we drank lots of warm water before escaping to an air conditioned room in a hotel in the city of Stung Treng.

Our route through Cambodia began to evolve after meeting a cyclist from Luxembourg in the north of Laos. He had strongly recommended a deviation to the north to visit the hilltop temple of Prasat Preah Vihear. But, he had also said, 'whatever you do – don't mention Pol Pot in the area of Preah Vihear or Anlong Veng'. He was right on both counts. Prasat Preah Vihear is a little visited gem and as far as Pol Pot goes – the people of the country smile readily and appear to have a strong desire to ignore or forget the traumas of the 1970s.

As soon as we arrived in Cambodia we became aware of a more modern day trauma – 'The Killing Fields of Trees' – meaning the burning of the forests. For the first few hundred kilometres in the north, in Stung Treng Province, the roadsides were blackened and the air was acrid. We cycled through scorched forest where new growth of bright green teak trees was taking hold. Habitation was sparse and we wondered what the people living in the dusty parched landscape did. There was the odd scraggy banana plantation and in places rows of what looked like pineapple but much of the land was wasteland. It dawned on us that the forest was being cleared to grow palm oil, a process which has caused massive deforestation and habitat loss in many tropical regions of the world. We passed many motorbikes carrying several enormous sections of tree trunks each, their back tyres heavily compressed, the riders barely finding room to sit on their saddles.

At a latitude of fourteen degrees north of the equator, the days were now really hot, approaching forty degrees. We got into a new habit of starting off before dawn and trying to find somewhere to stay before midday. It helped that much of the cycling in Cambodia was flat but this was not true for the final approach to the hilltop temple of Prasat Preah Vihear which stands 500m above the plain. We cycled most of the way to the top but were defeated in the last kilometre by gradients of up to 30% on concrete ramps. The effort was worthwhile. The site consists of a series of sanctuaries linked by pavements and staircases. Construction of the first temple began in the early ninth century and it was dedicated to the Hindu god Shiva. Curvy ends on the roofs are a distinctive feature and there are many exquisitely carved doorways and lintels. However, many of the buildings are in decay, and there are lots of wooden props supporting the structures.

The site is very close to the Thai border and it has been a scene of conflict. In 1962 the International Court of Justice deemed the temple to be on Cambodian territory and in 2008 UNESCO listed the temple as a world heritage site. The Thais have wanted to get their hands on the temple for a long time. It used to be possible for visitors to get day passes without visas from the Thai side.

But since tensions led to the deaths of troops on both sides as recently as 2011, this arrangement no longer exists.

Another easy and speedy ride took us west to Anlong Veng by midday. This was the ultimate Khmer Rouge stronghold and home to the notorious leader Pol Pot who implemented one of the most brutal restructurings of a society ever made. His goal was to convert Cambodia into a Maoist peasant dominated agrarian cooperative. Between one and two million citizens died between 1975 and 1979 as a result of the Khmer Rouge government. Many were tortured simply because they wore spectacles or appeared educated because they spoke a foreign language. The beginning of the end came in 1978 when Vietnam invaded Cambodia. It is a sad fact of random travel on the planet that scenes of evil history crop up remarkably often.

Deforestation by motorbike near Stung Treng, northern Cambodia.

One day further south we found happier places with happier histories. Twenty five kilometres north of the main site of Angkor we came to the tenth century Khmer temple of Banteay Srei. It was built largely of hard red sandstone that could be carved like wood leading to many intricacies. However, we hit an unforeseen problem in visiting the site. Tickets were only available from the main ticket office at Angkor. It seemed that nobody had ever arrived from the north before. The guards at the gate telephoned the head office and after quite a bit of discussion we were allowed in but we had to promise to go directly to the main office the following morning. We were very glad that we had made the effort to visit the temple. Some archaeologists rate the carvings to be amongst the best to be found anywhere in the world.

The Khmers were experts in wood carpentry and carving and these skills transferred to their work with stone. The site suffered from looting in the twentieth century. In 1923 French avant-guard author, Andrew Malraux tried to abscond with pieces of carving hoping to offset the losses he had suffered on the stock exchange. He thought he may get away with it because at that time the temple lay outside the Angkor park. He was later arrested in Phnom Penh and spent three years in jail before returning to France and eventually becoming Charles de Gaulle's first minister of cultural affairs.

Approaching the main vast complex of Angkor we were stopped by traffic police on a motorbike. Word had got round that we were on the loose without tickets. We were told to go straight to the ticket office to get our proper tickets with photos. That meant 'straight' there and not to stop and look at any temples we might pass on the way. When we finally reached the ticket office we were expected and welcomed. We bought five day passes back dated to the previous day. We looked forward to our biggest ever temple fest.

Angkor is Khmer for city. It thrived between the ninth and fifteenth centuries and only recently have archaeologists concluded that Angkor had been the largest pre-industrial city in the world, with a population of one million. To escape crowds and heat we left our hotel in Siem Reap by bike before dawn every day and enjoyed the peaceful roads and tracks linking over sixty temples, gates and statues. Many of the narrow tracks through the forest were deserted and a joy to ride. Approaching an out of the way relic felt like making a discovery. One of the joys of Angkor is that it is so vast, and there are so many antiquities to see, it is easy to lose yourself in a seemingly empty place.

During much of the twentieth century archaeologists made arduous efforts to clear away the jungle vegetation which was breaking apart and hiding the monuments. One of the finest monuments to be unearthed, cleared and exposed was the Bayon which had been built around 1200. There are more than 200 faces staring down from 54 towers and 1200m of bas reliefs incorporating over 11,000 figures. Being able to admire the original structures without the overgrowth of trees is awesome, but it is also fascinating to see the twelfth century Buddhist temple, Ta Prohm, as it has been deliberately left just as it looked when the first French explorers set eyes on it more than a century ago. Inside it is a maze of crumbling stonework with enormous trees enveloping the walls with their branches and roots. There is something irresistible about this mix of the work of nature and the work of man.

Our early morning rides to the temples in the pre-dawn light were short as the Treasure Oasis Hotel on the north side of Siem Reap was about as close to Angkor that we could find a place to stay. It was ideal for all the out and back trips that we did. Arriving by bike on the first day, the receptionist was concerned that we may not have much money – why else would we be on bikes? We were given a luxury suite at a knock down – 'walk in' – price. The hotel staff also helped us plan our onward route. The end game of how to reach Phnom Penh was a puzzle but the type of puzzle that we enjoy when you find an exciting solution. The key was to take a boat to Battambang with an overnight stay at the floating village of Prek Toal. The receptionist at the hotel showed us the possibilities and made the boat and homestay reservations. This looked like an interesting and far from direct way to Cambodia's capital, a route which would take us across the Tonlé Sap (great lake), along rivers, a couple of days in Thailand and then a final approach to Phnom Penh from the south via Kampot and Kep.

The boat left the small port south of Siem Reap and for the first part of the journey we crossed the north of Tonlé Sap, the largest freshwater lake in South

The deserted West Gate of Angkor Thom

The school run – kids only – near Prek Toal, Cambodia.

East Asia. For much of the year water flows out of the lake, down the Tonlé Sap River into the Mekong. However, during the monsoon the level of water in the Mekong increases rapidly, creating a unique flow reversal, filling the lake with fresh water. The lake swells and shrinks between 3,000 and 7,500 square kilometres. The vast toing and froing of the waters creates an exceptional degree of biodiversity.

The boat left the lake at the far north-west corner and entered a system of rivers leading through floating villages. The only way to get to the village of Prek Toal is by boat. We were dropped off at our homestay, a cute little floating house which moved with the river. It had a small outside bathroom where the river water was used to flush the loo and some cleaner water was there for washing. The river is totally intertwined with the life of the people. They wash in it, cool off in it, do the laundry in it and travel along it. More alarmingly all their waste goes into it too. The river is a highway and boats with noisy outboard engines continually plough up and down, some at high speed. Some boats are travelling shops selling vegetables and meals mainly of noodles. It is the water equivalent of living next to a busy road.

We escaped the noise and plastic waste pollution for a few hours and hired a small boat with a guide. We were taken to a different world; a world of birds in the air and on the river banks. The Prek Toal bird sanctuary is on a tributary to the main river thoroughfare and it is a protected area devoid of habitation and river traffic. The pilot had to steer a careful course and often build up speed to push through the growth of water hyacinth. It is attractive but an invasive plant which is very destructive, severely affecting the flow of water and reducing the oxygen needed by other water life. However, the bird life seems to thrive and we were treated to sightings of painted storks, darters, cormorants, adjutants, fish eagles, kingfishers, ibis, pelicans and openbills.

It took most of the following day to reach Battambang, Cambodia's second largest city. The water level gradually dropped as we moved further west. The river bank environment went seriously downhill. In front of every house lay a sea of plastic bottles and bags. Two boat changes were made to smaller ones to make it possible to navigate the low water. Each boat change was a stress for us as our bikes were precariously transferred from roof to roof. It was a relief to reach the edge of the city and return to our bikes for the final kilometre. We find it tough when we are not in control of our own journey but boats are better than planes.

We left Cambodia for a couple of days and enjoyed a tiny taste of Thailand. The country immediately felt cleaner and more prosperous. It also felt slightly oddly British to be riding on the left, and yet Thailand is the only south east Asian country not to have been colonised by a European power. There was no burnt forest as the area was probably cleared for agriculture some time ago. We saw cassava production, fruit trees, cardamom plants, papaya trees, rice paddies and banana trees. There were many pretty stilted houses along the roadside with hammocks slung underneath.

We lost the roadside rubbish of Cambodia, but sadly also the smiles. The people were friendly enough but didn't seem quite as chilled as the Lao and Khmer and there were few children running around waving and smiling. Further south from Trat, we were travelling along a very narrow strip of Thailand that hugs the eastern side of the Gulf of Thailand, sandwiched between the sea and the wild forested Cardamom Mountains of Cambodia. At times the country was less than a kilometre wide. We stopped by a beach for lunch. The soft white sand was clean and the turquoise crystal clear water was warm. There were times on our 260km spell in Thailand where we couldn't avoid the main roads but when we did the alternatives were often surfaced in concrete and never left as dirt.

We returned to Cambodia at Koh Kong before heading for 150km with only small villages and no hotels until Sre Ambel. It was too hot for such a distance in a day but Pocket Earth marked a homestay halfway, near Trapeang Rung. There were no signs for it so we asked some people by a shop before following a man on a motorbike. He showed us along a muddy track leading over a kilometre into the jungle. Here we found two lovely people living in their own paradise. It was clearly an official homestay with a sign indicating it as 'Homestay No 4', but how people discovered it was a mystery.

The couple lived a very simple life, having very few possessions, and they appeared to get much of their food from the land and the river. It was a traditional house on stilts and it was kept very neat and tidy. We were greeted with a plate of freshly picked sweet and juicy pineapple. There was a big bathroom where we could pour copious amounts of water over ourselves. After dinner of local fungi, pork, lettuce and fruit we were invited on a boat trip on the river. The local technique of rowing is to stand at the back of the boat facing for-

INTO THE CAULDRON

wards, pushing the two crossed oars rather than pulling them. In the morning we were given a heavy present for the road – three pineapples.

We had covered 6,000km from Chengdu and my back tyre had worn thin, so after five punctures in two weeks, it was time to change the tyre for the spare folding one tucked away in my pannier. We found substantial shade from the fierce sun, and even before I had extracted the back wheel, we had attracted an audience of several young boys. I replaced old for new and it became obvious that one of the boys wanted to play with the old tyre. He threw it high in the air, span it with reverse spin on rough ground so that it returned like a boomerang, and next he was using it as a hula hoop. We had planned to carry the tyre on to Kampot to dispose of it properly, but it was clear that the tyre had a better future than we thought. The look of pleasure on the boy's face was one of immeasurable delight.

The charming happy hippy haunt of Kampot, with its riverside location and French colonial architecture was a chance to refuel. It is a touristy place with abundant cafés and restaurants serving all kinds of delicious food. We had Kampot pepper burger and a steak with Kampot pepper sauce – not exactly traditional Khmer fair but Kampot is famous for its pepper which is often laid out complete with stalks on top of the food.

Riding east towards Kep, we passed through enormous salt pans where sea water is let into fields and then allowed to evaporate. Large, coarse salt crystals form which are then raked up into wicker baskets which are carried in pairs balanced across shoulders.

Before turning north away from the coast, we met the most

Jumping for joy with a new toy – Hugh's old tyre – near Kampot, Cambodia.

extraordinary cycle tourists. Denis and Tanja from Germany were not travelling light, this was extreme cycle touring with a big hairy dog in tow. They had been on the road for more than a decade with a trailer each. They had six Bosch bricks (batteries) each for climbing the hills with motors. The batteries might only last 30 minutes if the hills were steep. They were travelling journalists. For each day spent cycling, they would have three stationary days working on their material for Deutsch TV. For this work they were loaded with lots of camera and computer kit, not to mention the dog food and the walking boots which they were cycling in.

Kep is famous for blue crabs so lunch was one each with Kampot pepper. Two hundred kilometres remained to Phnom Penh. We broke the journey into two stages with an overnight stop below the eleventh century Khmer hilltop temple of Phnom Chisor. It was good that we had feasted well the previous day. All we could find to eat that night was fried crickets and roasted corn on the cob; however, we   enjoyed the crunchy street food.

Phnom Penh was founded in 1434 and succeeded Angkor as the capital of the Khmer nation. It was abandoned several times before being re-established in 1865 by King Norodom. The following year the Royal Palace was built and it is where the current king Norodom Sihamoni lives some of the time. Visitors can tour the immaculate grounds and gardens and admire the sumptuous buildings from the outside. Golden spires reach for the sky and beautifully tiled roofs glint in the sun.

The city of two million lies on the west bank of the Mekong at the confluence with the Bassac and Tonlé Sap rivers at the point where the waters from the Tonlé Sap lake come and go with the seasons. It is hard to understand the compulsion to visit a place such as the Genocide museum but we did. It is terribly grim. The visitor is faced with the sight of instruments of torture and vast numbers of portraits of innocent victims. Feeling that we had heard enough of Cambodia's history from the 1970s, we made a conscious decision not to visit The Killing Fields where the Khmer Rouge bludgeoned so many to death. The Foreign Correspondents' Club is a more cheerful place to see some photographs of the Khmer Rouge invasion of Phnom Penh. There are scenes taken by war correspondents who used to hang out at the club hoping that it was a place of safety. Large black and white photographs show action such as the Khmer Rouge entering Phnom Penh in 1975 and the storming of the King's Palace in 1979. Now the Foreign Correspondents' Club is an atmospheric hotel, bar and restaurant overlooking the Tonlé Sap River.

Our four months in Asia concluded with a day's stop in sweaty Singapore before we flew to a world of no temples, no ancient history, few diseases – a land of beauty – New Zealand.

7
WHERE THE BIKES ARE UPSIDE DOWN

Don't buy upgrades, ride up grades.
                                        Eddy Merckx

Hugh:

After our ride across Australia in 2011, we flew ourselves and our bikes to Napier in New Zealand where our daughter, Amy, was living and working. We explored sections of both islands and loved the East Cape of the North Island and many sections of the South Island. Three rides made it to our list of top twenty day rides. They are Opitiki to Motu (East Cape), The Banks Peninsula (Christchurch to Akaroa) and the Forgotten World Highway (Ohinepane to

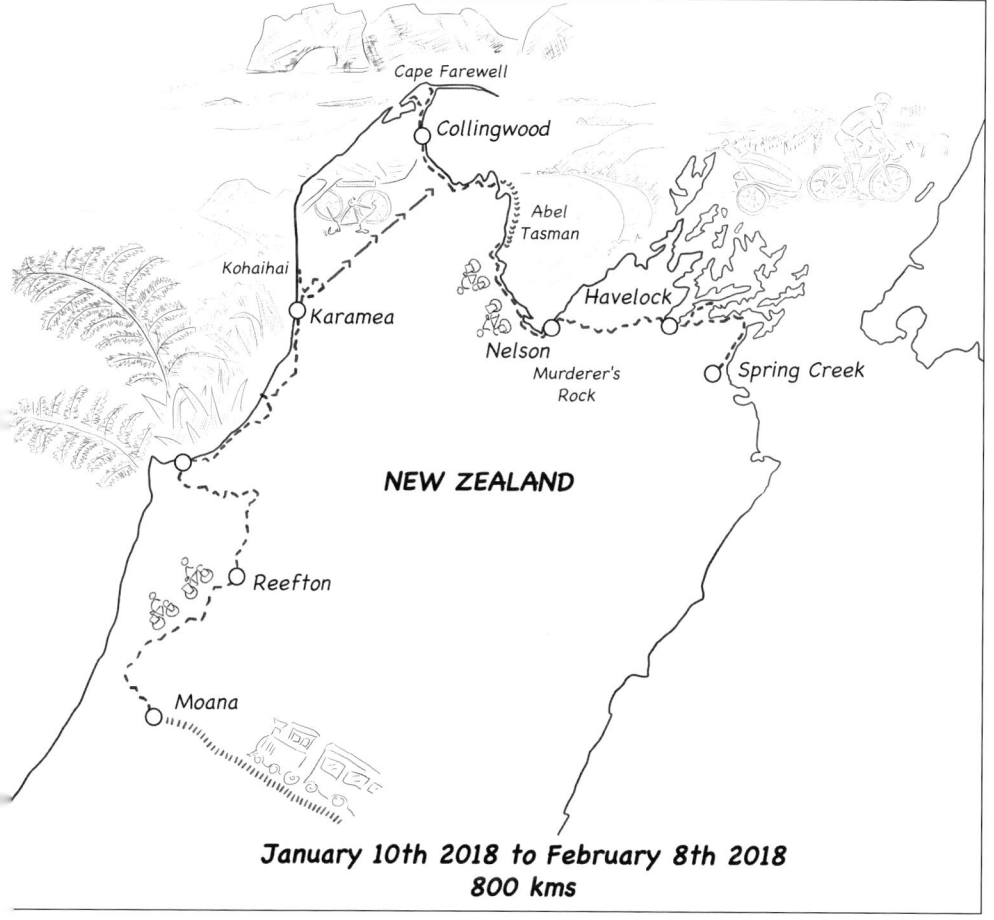

**January 10th 2018 to February 8th 2018
800 kms**

Whangamomona). These routes were on near empty gravel roads and often through lush tropical vegetation. However, we found it challenging to work out long continuous routes through the islands which at some stages didn't hit traffic bottlenecks.

New Zealand is ten per cent larger in area than Great Britain and it has just six per cent of the population. It currently enjoys one of the least antagonistic but strong governments in the world which has determinedly kept the Covid pandemic at bay. Considering the vast numbers of visitors to the country at any time of year, it now seems miraculous that their total lockdown and exclusion did the trick.

With such a low population it would be easy to assume that it would be a country of quiet roads. However, it doesn't have the vast network of tiny roads which many European countries have. Hence, the few roads linking towns are often not great for cycling as they may be narrow and harbouring wild drivers, fast cars and trucks. Unless you are a round the world record breaker following the antipodean rules, then it is almost impossible to find a suitable route from Invercargill to Auckland, a route which is often done by fast riders on fast roads in a handful of days. For this reason, our cycling in New Zealand has contrasted with long distance routes we have enjoyed in other countries. Cycle tours have focussed on particular regions, and we have not shied away from taking transport when the options to avoid unsuitable roads have seemed almost impossible.

So it was in the New Zealand summer of 2018 we sought an interesting and traffic free route around the north of the South Island. Avoiding what has a reputation for being a busy road, we took the TranzAlpine train over Arthur's pass to start riding from the small town of Moana on the north-west side of the Southern Alps. This side of the mountains has over 140 days of rain a year and this day was one of those days. Sadly, the views from the train were impeded by low cloud and wet windows. The climate along with all the space lends itself well to farming. The population of sheep in New Zealand is seven times that of people. Where the land hasn't been turned over to agriculture, rivers rush towards the Tasman Sea and forests thrive with much of the low vegetation dominated by ferns.

The day we met the River Buller, it was in spate, making the ride through the gorge all the more exciting. At times the narrow road is trapped between the river and the cliffs. For a tunnelled section there is a helpful set of traffic lights operated by the cyclist. In theory it gives the rider extra time to make it through, although a sign reads 'if signals not working proceed with caution'.

Most nights on this four week expedition were spent in our light and compact Hilleberg Rogen tent. We soon learnt to be careful with our food stored under the flysheet. One morning we awoke to a fruity aroma wafting around

Kahurangi National Park

the tent. The banana we had left in the porch had gone, along with our supply of fruit and nuts. All that was left was a thoroughly pecked banana skin. The local wekas are inquisitive flightless birds who run off with anything that takes their fancy – anything that can be carried in a beak isn't safe in the porch. New Zealand is home to more flightless bird species than any other country, the most famous being the kiwi, the kakapo and a few types of penguin. Some birds, such as the bellbird and the tui make their presence known through their beautiful songs.

Once north of Westport we were on a no through road for 130km to Kohaihai. On a whim we decided to drop into the Country Music museum in the little settlement of Hector – a place jam packed with CDs, vinyl and posters representing every country musician you could possibly think of. Just as we were leaving, the lady looking after the place casually suggested that we could ride up Charming Creek. Lots of cyclists go up there she said, it follows an old mining tramway.

So we went for it. Early on it was a bit tricky hauling the bikes up some steps and steep stony ramps. The damp, tramway sleepers protruding from the gravel track took some getting used to but the bikes rolled over them much easier than we expected. As we climbed, things got smoother and the rewards were well worth it – beautiful bush, a spectacular waterfall and curious old mine machinery. The track came out on a gravel road which took us into Seddonville, a short distance from the Gentle Annie campsite. The route probably isn't best done on a loaded touring bike but it is possible.

The campsite was a gorgeous place to relax by the coast, with the Cow Shed café offering great food and coffee and the bonus of an extra little trip up to a bush maze on a bluff giving great views along the coastline. To the north lay a wild and rough rocky coastline with stormy clouds and wild seas. To the south were long stretches of empty stony beaches.

A Department of Conservation campsite lies at the end of the road where the Kohaihai River tumbles under a pedestrian suspension bridge before meeting the sea at the wide shingly beach. The campgrounds provide simple, cheap and clean places to stay all over New Zealand, often by national parks. Like many, this one is unmanned, provides the basics of water and toilets, often compostable ones. There are honesty boxes to leave the few dollars needed for an overnight camp. Like many on the west coast, this site came complete with wekas and sandflies. The population of the South Island is a million but there must be over a million of the bloodsucking insects within a kilometre of the Kohaihai campground. Just like in Scotland with the midge, when the wind drops it is murder.

There are no showers at the site so we washed in the river at a distance from the sea's rip tides. Grim stories of people being dragged out to sea were recounted to us by Mike the mechanic who joined us at our picnic table. He introduced himself by saying 'tell me your story' but it soon became apparent that he was so drunk that he was incapable of listening to our stories. Every other phrase was accompanied by 'it is what it is'. With a little bit of encouragement he left in his ute and we again wondered about the safety of cycling on New Zealand's roads.

Most of the New Zealand landscape has been transformed; first by Maori and then more determinedly by white settlers. In a matter of little more than 700 years humans have destroyed most of the native forest and devastated the indigenous fauna (much of which is endemic to New Zealand) through the introduction of exotic predators. Much is going on now to preserve and extend what remains of the natural environment but it is an up-hill battle. Enjoyment of the wild side of New Zealand is controlled by the Department of Conservation who maintain limits on numbers walking the famous trails.

The Heaphy Track is one of many popular tramping routes in New Zealand. It leads 70km through the Kahurangi National Park towards Golden Bay, south of Farewell Spit at the far north of the South Island. A day's walk along the narrow track, sandwiched between the beautiful white sandy beaches strewn with sculptured driftwood and the lush green forest, offered us a taste of what once covered 80 per cent of the land. Between May and November mountain

Where the bikes are upside down – Karamea.

bikes are allowed but during the popular tramping summer months they are not. We wanted to get across to Golden Bay but didn't want to retrace our route to Westport and follow over 400km of road to Takaka. We had been told by our Kiwi friend Tim Mulliner that it is possible to fly bikes from one end of the Heaphy to the other. The service is provided by Adventure Flights Golden Bay so that walkers and cyclists can return to their starting points.

The landing strip was south of Kohaihai at Karamea. We had a day spare before the next flight so we explored further into the bush from Oparara. Having left our bags with a friendly farmer, we cycled along the Fenian track passing enormous limestone arches and caves. As for many wild places in New Zealand, there were signs prohibiting dogs. We weren't sure about access for bikes. We didn't see anyone, and but for a few sections, with large roots growing across the track, we rode most of the route deep into the lush bush. Native beech and podocarp forest is home to many native birds, insects and the short-tailed bat, the bat being the only native land mammal in New Zealand.

Mit from Adventure Flights strapped our bikes upside down under the wings and we flew across to the east side in forty minutes. We looked down onto the land of the Heaphy occasionally spotting the trail which typically takes four days to walk. Looking out of the small Cessna's windows, the view of our bikes hanging upside down above a landscape of coast, forest, mountain and puffy clouds was surreal and a little scary.

Off the plane and with NZD 500 less in our bank account, we cycled north to the end of another no through road, heading for Cape Farewell. There is little in the way of accommodation north of the village of Pakawau apart from the Wharariki campsite 20km further on. Remote and without services, the coastline and beaches near the northern tip are wonderfully undeveloped. Visitors need to walk a kilometre through sand dunes to reach the sea. Here the sand lay in smooth clean ripples and seals played in pools at the foot of enormous rock sea arches. From the high headland there were views of the 26km long Farewell Spit shaped like a giant Kiwi beak stretching east and reaching over the head of Golden Bay.

In 1642, the Dutch seafarer Abel Tasman became the first European to set sight of New Zealand. His ship anchored seven kilometres off the coast in Golden Bay. Smaller boats attempted to go ashore but Maori men arrived in more than twenty double-hulled canoes. Skirmishes erupted and four of Tasman's men were killed. By chance, Tasman had arrived at one of the most beautiful places in an extremely beautiful country. The Abel Tasman National Park was founded 300 years later.

Our challenge was how to traverse and explore the park when understandably bicycles are not allowed. The twisting, narrow, undulating coastal paths are no place for walkers and cyclists to mix. The park is carefully managed by the Department of Conservation. Except for the only lodge at Awaroa, accommodation within the park is at campsites. During the summer months these are often fully booked except for some which keep small areas of white sandy beach or grass for people arriving on foot who are allowed to camp for just one night whilst they are in transit. We thought that we may have to leave our bikes behind for a few days so we went to the iSite office in Takaka to explain our challenge. The advice we gained from this, one of New Zealand's official visitor information centres, enabled us to create a route through the park with our bikes.

The solution was one which we couldn't have imagined ourselves. Boats transport walkers and kayakers to bays between Kaiteriteri at the south end of the park and several other bays within the park. The very helpful officer at iSite made reservations for campsites at Totaranui and Apple Tree Bay. An enquiry to a boat company confirmed that our bikes could be transported along with the kayaks. The plan was to enter the park by bike at the end of the road 20km east of Takaka. Then there would be no pedalling until we left the park. Reservations were made for boats from Totaranui to Apple Tree Bay and for the following day from there to Kaiteriteri. From the camps in the park we savoured dawn and dusk and during the day we ambled north and south to enjoy the savage uncorrupted coast.

On narrow tracks and boardwalks we followed the Great Taste trail to Nelson using another small ferry to make the link to Rabbit Island. Just three weeks later the route was devastated and closed by cyclone Gita. Except for the threat of earthquakes, extreme weather and landslides, Nelson must be one of the most desirable places to live in New Zealand if not the world. It is the oldest city on South Island and with a population of just 50,000 would probably be called a village in China. In Nelson we found great taste. The cafés and restaurants are high class and the flat white coffees perfect.

It was great to catch up with an old school friend of Pauline's who has lived in New Zealand for many years. Lesley took us freshwater swimming in the Aniseed River and we enjoyed an evening meal where friends brought along tasty dishes. Lesley and Matt live in a charming wooden home in a lovely location close to our route out of the city along the Matai Valley. Life in New Zealand can be pretty good and we can see why friends and relations are drawn to it.

Besides the sunny climate and outdoor lifestyle, Nelson enjoys a strong arts culture. At the Suter Art Gallery, there is an ingenious depiction of the characters involved in the confrontation at Wairau which resulted in Te Rongo, the wife of the chief Te Rangihaeata, being shot. The affray, in 1843, the only serious clash between Maori and British settlers to take place on the South Island, resulted in the deaths of 29 British and four Maori. The argument was over a possibly fraudulent land deal. The creations of driftwood and cloth are compellingly realistic with the faces displaying the intricate tattoos of the historical characters involved in the fight.

In 2012 our tour of the South Island had passed through Nelson on the way to Pelorus Bridge and Havelock. We had found the ride scary as the busy and narrow road had a lot of logging trucks which often passed uncomfortably close. Six years later we looked for a better way and found it going via the dirt track up the Matai Valley, over the Maungatapu saddle to Murderer's Rock where a gang assaulted, robbed and killed five traders taking gold to a bank in Nelson in June 1866. The gang leader originated from London and had been deported to Australia where he continued his life of crime. He followed the gold rush to New Zealand. Caught and tried at the first ever murder trial in Nelson, he and two others were hung at the gallows simultaneously. We put our tent by the rock for the night and had few nightmares.

The key to staying traffic free after Pelorus Bridge was to cross the river on a suspension footbridge to join the Te Araroa (the Long Pathway). For a short way we followed part of the 3000km footpath which links the top and bottom of New Zealand. Our next town on the way was Havelock, nick-named the green lip mussel capital of the world. We ate a large panful each before leaving for the back roads around the sounds and bays leading to Queen Charlotte Sound by Picton, the port linking the South Island with Wellington, the capital on the North Island.

The final day's ride on our tour was from Picton to Spring Creek, just north of Blenheim. The obvious way would be along the State Highway 1, a route of about 20km. On close inspection of the maps we found an alternative on dirt tracks rising up and over headlands looking across the Cook Strait to the North Island. Touching the coast at Ocean Bay and Robin Hood Bay, following very twisty tracks, the route totalled 60km with 1500m of climbing. It was a fitting way to end a few weeks of New Zealand summer before returning to an English spring. It deserved a final fling with Amy and family, camping at Spring Creek and visiting and cycling between the wineries of Marlborough. We wondered about the ethics of riding bikes whilst over the limit having criticised Mike the mechanic. We guessed that at the speeds we were riding we were unlikely to do any harm but to ourselves.

We looked down on the beautiful islands as our flight left Christchurch and now, whilst writing this during the pandemic, we wonder when we or other visitors will return to Aotearoa – the land of the long white cloud.

8

BACK ROADS IN UNACQUAINTED EUROPE

But there are people in this world who don't think like you do
They don't think like you do
And some don't think at all

'Daisy' from the album *Scribbled in Chalk*
by Karine Polwart, 2006

Pauline:

After the war of 1992-5, Bosnia was peppered with around two million land mines. The breakup of Yugoslavia was ugly and Bosnia suffered badly. Between 1996 and 2019 nearly 700 Bosnians died and 2,000 were injured, by mines. Fifty five Bosnian de-miners lost their lives at work. Children were

March 28th 2018 to September 27th 2018
7500 kms

afraid to walk down the road and farmers were afraid to work in their fields. Whilst by 2019, 3,000 square kilometres had been cleared there was still about 1,000 square kilometres of contaminated land, just over two per cent of the area of the country. Bosnia and Herzegovina is reported to be high on the list of countries with the most uncleared landmines on its territory. There was a national plan for Bosnia to become landmine-free by 2019, but that did not happen and the deadline has now been extended by five years.

Heading towards Mostar – Gornja Dreznica, Bosnia.

This was roughly the situation when we crossed the border from Croatia, in July 2018. After a day of climbing and threatening dark skies, we were ready to peg down our tent, but wary of what might lurk under the innocent looking earth. Croatia suffers the same legacy but we only ever camped there on an official site. Hugh reckoned that a mined area would have warning signs; I hoped he was right!

The stony track, which was taking us quietly in the direction of Mostar, led us to a rough brick building with a large sheltered area under the overhanging corrugated iron roof. As the sky unleashed its load, water poured over the edge and I debated using it as a shower! An area around the hut was marked out with stones so we assumed it would be safe. It had been a relief to see tyre marks on the track. We pitched the tent on the grass and set up our kitchen on the large table under the veranda – luxury!

It was a treat to set out in the early morning light, admiring the reflections of the blue sky and roadside bushes in the still surface of the puddles spanning the track. It was delightful riding across pretty limestone hills with sparse habitation – the occasional hamlet and then, unexpectedly a line of smart new spacious homes; German registered cars were parked outside. A smooth paved road helpfully took us six kilometres up to our high point, by which time we were hungry after lots of climbing and fighting with the rocks in a wind that had blown me over on a particularly rough patch. The restaurant at the top was doing good business serving a hearty traditional dish known as *peka* – this version was mainly veal and potatoes – cooked in a pot with a bell shaped lid, in a cocoon of ashes and hot coals on an outdoor hearth.

We took off again on the gravel, winding down into the valley of the Drežanka River which slices through steep limestone mountains – forested where scree and sheer rockfaces allow roots to gain a hold. It was a view that is never forgotten, which says 'this is going to be a beautiful ride'. Then, on the first of many tight bends, our key question was answered; the sign showed the skull and crossbones in white on a starkly visible red background with the message, *opasnost od mina rizično područje*, 'mine hazard risk area'. The road looked newly upgraded, so we figured there would be no mines in our path – just best not to go for a pee off the road! Partway down we found another hut – a hunter's hut we were told by passers-by. They hunt wild pigs; surely a dodgy occupation with mines lurking in the forest. We put up our tent outside, although several people told us we were welcome to sleep in the hut; our tent felt more homely.

Stari Most (old bridge) – Mostar, Bosnia.

We just loved the ride down the valley; every twist and turn of the road brought a new inspiring view. We saw our first mosque in Bosnia, a substantial new building surrounded by a cemetery of new and old gravestones. The old were made of stone – thick posts topped with balls decorated in a variety of geometric designs and unlike any we had seen before. Then, a little further on, four stone crosses peeked out from the roadside vegetation; carved with human figures – fourteenth or early fifteenth century the notice said. This little necropolis, yet another war victim, had been broken and defaced – one tarnished by a crude Islamic crescent and star painted in black against the light stone. There are moves to protect this monument and many others but progress is slow.

We both have memories of the terminal fate of another, much better known victim of the war, the Stari Most (meaning simply, 'old bridge') of Mostar; a place that seemed distant at the time. Croatian units took two days to destroy the bridge – it had been built to last. On 9 November 1993 at quarter past ten in the morning, the stones collapsed into the river. The locals referred to it tenderly as Mostarci (the Old One). It had joined the east and west banks of the Neretva River for almost five centuries, spanning a distance at the time considered impossible with a single arch. It connected people, religions, ethnic groups, and different worlds. Over time, it had become the main symbol of the city; it was part of their cultural identity, an expression of Bosnian culture. It was almost beyond belief that it could be lost! This sacrilegious act was an attempt to clear the Muslims from Mostar.

We pushed our bikes up the shallow, stone flagged steps of the Stari Most, weaving between the crowds gathering there to watch a dare devil dive into

The aftermath of war – Stolac, Bosnia.

A memorial to victims of war, Bosnia.

the river. We struggled to get a grip on the slippery surface, already worn smooth, although this bridge was at the time only sweet sixteen. The tanned entertainer in his tight blue swimming trunks was so surprised to see us that he forgot to jump! There is something powerfully hopeful and moving about the rebuilt bridge; the symbol of holding people together triumphing over evil – too sad to imagine the space without it. It is a wonder that it was re-made so beautifully, in exactly the same style and using the same materials as the original with the help of people from many nations. Twelve out of fourteen mosques of Mostar were also destroyed in the war. Now many elegant minarets stand tall and at around 5am you hear the call to prayer from all directions. A handful of beautiful Ottoman homes were miraculously untouched. The heart of the old city around the iconic bridge has been lovingly restored attracting a fair number of tourists – we met a family from Saudi Arabia on our way in – there were many Muslim visitors.

Wandering away from the centre presents a different picture; dishevelled buildings pock marked with bullet holes, ruined facades propped up with scaffolding – some being renovated and on-going street repairs. We were told that 90 per cent of the buildings were destroyed in the war. Talk to anyone about it and they will tell you that they don't care about who is Muslim/Catholic/Orthodox or Bosnian/Croat/Serb; they just want to live in peace as they did before the war. So why did it happen? All this destruction for what? Now there is mass unemployment and a wrecked economy. A visit to the War and Genocide museum was an experience which brought us to tears. We have travelled so much of the world and found people to be universally kind and helpful. It is incomprehensible that the same people can inflict so much horror on those who were once their friends and neighbours.

For only €10 each we found a large room in a hostal on a back street, with a mountain view from the window and with wifi, air conditioning and a kitchen. Alica, was very keen to have customers – 'it is hard to earn a living' he said. We asked him about his role in the war – he told us that he had no choice but to fight, to fight those who otherwise would have been his friends, even married his children – he had to fight to protect his home. Such is the incomprehensible tyranny of war.

Leaving Mostar we stopped at the Zitomislici Church and monastery in Biletić Polje, where a notice, states, 'During the 1992-1995 war the church and *konak* (residence) were completely destroyed. The church and monastery were 're-habilitated' in 2005' – another meticulous reconstruction. Just replace the name on the information board and the same message stands outside so many historical buildings in the area. Hopping over a rough mountain track we entered Stolac to discover a mix of modern post war buildings, beautifully 'rehabilitated' older buildings and buildings pockmarked by shrapnel which looked like a bomb dropped on them only yesterday.

Leaving Stolac, a large roadside sign welcomed us to the Republic of Srpska, written in English and Serbian Cyrillic; what was this five consonants in a row 'republic' we thought? The tensions between Bosniaks, Croats and Serbs, predominantly Muslim, Catholic and Christian orthodox respectively, have been at the root of the problems of the region and all three live in Bosnia and Herzegovina (to give it its proper full name). In 1994 the smallest group, the Croats (15.4%), came to an agreement with the largest group, the Bosniaks (50.1%). The Serbs (30.8%) however were not happy, wanting to divide the state along ethnic lines and they took to armed resistance; many Serbs have a yearning for a Greater Serbia. Srpska was the answer to the problem. Bosnia was divided into administrative areas of roughly equal size but in sandwich style – the Serb 'bread' in the north where the country borders Croatia and in the east along the borders with Serbia and Montenegro, split by the Bosniak 'filling' and 'peppered' with Croats throughout.

Riding through Bosnia and Herzegovina we were constantly reminded of the troubles of the past – war damaged buildings and memorials to ones lost kept it all at the front of our minds. We were happy to escape across the border into Montenegro. We spent our first night there in the Yugoslavia Hotel in Nikšić (pronounced Nickschitch), the country's second largest city. From there we did a stunning mountain ride to the Ostrog monastery which is embedded at the foot of a high cliff, the façade being just about flush with the rock. It attracts 100,000 visitors a year, including Muslims, orthodox Christians and

Catholics. The present day building was constructed between 1923-26, after a fire which destroyed the major part of the original complex. There was a long queue of people waiting for the chance to pray by the body of Saint Basil of Ostrog (Sveti Vasilije Ostroški) in one of the little cave churches spared by the fire. There are some very special mosaics built into the cave walls and many pilgrims kissed them as they passed by. As we descended the zigzag road from the monastery we crossed paths with many pilgrims walking up the hill and a group of 100 Serbian cyclists riding up. It was quite a sight looking back on the white façade encased in the sheer limestone wall, and above, a white cross peering out through the mist above the tree covered cliff top.

Nikšić had a small town feel to it with tree-lined, café dense streets. It was relaxing to spend the evening in the square with a quiet beer – the board outside one bar read, 'nobody exists on purpose, nobody belongs anywhere, everybody's gonna die, come have a beer'. I suppose the corollary to 'nobody belongs anywhere' is 'everyone belongs everywhere' – so why did Serbs, Croats and Bosniaks need to fight and bring that inevitable death sooner?

It was pretty riding though mountainous Montenegro – pastureland, flower filled meadows, natural limestone architecture, and neat mountain villages. We had read about the Tara gorge, one of the deepest in Europe and decided to take the road through it going upstream from the Đurđevića Tara Bridge – a spectacular five arch concrete construction standing a dizzy 172 meters above the river. When it was completed in 1940 it was the biggest vehicular concrete arch bridge in Europe. In the Second World War it suffered the same fate as the Stari Most – blown up by a Yugoslav partisan raiding party and then rebuilt in 1946.

A German cyclist, Patrick, had also decided to incorporate the spectacular gorge route into his journey. He was riding around Europe, lightweight bikepacking style and stopping to climb the highest mountain in each country. His ultra-lightweight kit included a 900g paraglider – handy for a quick mountain descent. His life depended on a 100g harness! Our eldest son has recently taken up this seemingly life threatening sport – it seems that with care it can be brought within an acceptable risk level – 'we are all gonna die' but rather later than sooner.

Following three delightful camps we arrived in Rožaje where we found that the only hotel had been abandoned. We heard that the owner was involved in a Mafioso style drugs cartel and he had been put behind bars for fifteen years. A helpful local directed us to the Milenium Restoran, a restaurant serving excellent goulash and also offering cheap, comfortable rooms. We met a family there who had been living in Aleppo when the war in Syria broke out. They had escaped to Dubai and did not expect that they would ever return to Syria. The father was a surgeon and could earn a good living in Dubai. His wife was born in Rožaje and they were visiting family in the town. They had thoughts of moving to Montenegro one day and were staying in the capital, Podgorica whilst trying to get citizen's documents for their daughters.

A very pleasant climb out of Rožaje took us up to 1,800m from where a spectacular descent carried us over the border into Kosovo via the Radac falls – a bit of a touristy setup but well worth seeing for the impressive water power. We reached Peje, an interesting little town which instantly felt so very different from any Montenegrin town we had passed through. The people are of Albanian origin whereas most of the people in Montenegro define themselves as Montenegrins and a large minority as Serbs. In some ways Peje reminded us of China – a building bonanza of recently built flats; modern office and retail blocks; and crazy traffic just pulling out of turnings without looking. The clothing in the shops was more like what you might see in Turkey – elaborate eastern style gowns with ornamental belts and veiled headdresses. We should have stayed in Peje but we went on to Deçan.

We took a dead end road out of Deçan, hoping to see the fourteenth century Visoki Dečani monastery and then find a suitable spot to camp by the river beyond. The road led up into the mountains, where it branched into tracks zigzagging up through the forest. We were taken aback to find checkpoints by the monastery, three in total – KFOR (Kosovo Force) – protecting the monastery they said. The road was squeezed by monster concrete cones and surveyed by overhead CCTV cameras; signs forbade photography. Rated a cultural monument of exceptional importance, the monastery was placed on the UNESCO danger list in 2006 and in 2020 it was on Europa Nostra's list of Europe's twelve most endangered cultural heritage sites. I asked one of the military men if the area was safe, he just shook his head!

There was nowhere remotely appealing to camp – not in the messed up river valley, or at the advertised 'camp' site up the road, which turned out to be a restaurant with a few cabins and nowhere decent to put a tent. The monastery itself was surrounded by an old stone wall which was topped with barbed wire and metal spikes; we couldn't go inside as it was closed. We returned to Deçan, weaving in and out of the many pedestrians out for an evening stroll, people of all ages, families, taking advantage of the traffic free road.

Montenegro and Kosovo are in that tight group of non-EU countries in south eastern Europe, bordered by the Adriatic and the EU countries of Croatia, Hungary, Bulgaria, Romania and Greece – a region soon to be our saviour as places not included in the 90 day limit for British travellers post Brexit! Here was a part of Europe, so close to home, easy to reach and yet so unfamiliar to us.

Kosovo, in common with Bosnia and Herzegovina, still has the feel of a troubled country. Most countries of the world have recognised Kosovo as an independent state since it declared independence from Serbia in 2008 – but not Serbia! Along the road we passed many memorials with the Albanian, Kosovan and American flags flying and displaying pictures of the deceased all with the same year of death, 1999. The deep red Albanian flag, with the black double-headed eagle in the middle, was prevalent wherever we went in Kosovo. NATO bombing of 1999 in support of the Kosovo Liberation Army was the response to Serbian ethnic cleansing of thousands of Albanians in Kosovo.

Kosovo is also a poor country. The unemployment rate in 2018 was high at round 30%, being nearly 60% in the 16-24 age group. However, the scattering of large to huge luxury villas along the road to Prizren told of money although many were half-built and some looked abandoned. Closer to the city we passed monstrous, ostentatious resort hotels and restaurants, set in immaculately manicured gardens and couldn't help wondering where their wealthy clientele came from.

Many people from Kosovo have worked in other European countries, particularly Germany and Switzerland. The people tended to assume that we were German – we probably look German – so they spoke to us in German. Even when we told them we couldn't speak German they would often carry on encouraged by the fact a little of what they said made some sense to us!

The capital of Kosovo is Pristina, but Prizren is designated as the historical capital being one of the oldest settlements in the western Balkans – the sort of place we like to visit. However, significantly for us, there was a bike shop marked on our map in the centre of town, called Shimano XTR – it sounded promising. The bottom bracket on Hugh's bike was deteriorating badly and as he pedalled the cranks were wobbling alarmingly from side to side – it wouldn't make the end of the trip. Three previous mechanics in Croatia and Bosnia had been unable to remove the crank bolt from the chainset side – after 50,000km it was well and truly stuck. It needed a man with determination. It needed, Parim, the mechanic who never gives up, the man they call the 'Terminator'!

The normal method of extraction was not going to work, so out came a hammer and punch. His assistant Erdoğan held the bike down firmly whilst Parim ferociously whacked the offending bolt – again and again. Meanwhile Hugh looked on in horror at this abuse of his precious machine. It was brutal but it worked – the crank which had sat firmly in place for nine years moved and came free. Two more parts required hefty action but within twenty minutes a fresh Shimano sealed bearing bottom bracket was happily in place. Parim, only wanted paying for the new part (€35) but Hugh insisted on giving a generous tip; he celebrated by buying everyone an espresso and himself a new pair of cycling mitts. As with Khvicha fixing our split rim in Baku, we had found the perfect man for the job, just in time.

With that out of the way we were free to explore historic Prizren. It soon became startlingly clear to us why historic monuments needed protection. On our way up to the fortress we passed the fourteenth century Orthodox Church of the Holy Saviour. A Serbian man inside told us that the interior had been destroyed by fire in 2004; probably a case of arson. We later learnt that an Albanian mob did the damage during the unrest of that year. In the courtyard outside replicas of the blackened frescos were on display. Down in town, we found the Church of Our Lady of Ljeviš, heavily protected by barbed wire and with a sentry box and armed guard outside.

Our arrival coincided with another couple's arranged visit so we were able to see inside; there were many beautiful frescos, some intact or partially restored but others also blackened by fire or peppered with chiselled holes. So much of the heritage of former Yugoslavia has been lost in this way. The majority of the population in Kosovo is classed as Albanian – mostly Sunni Muslims. The rest, a diminishing minority group, are Serbians, mostly Christian Orthodox. We were able to go inside the seventeenth century Sinan Pasha Mosque and see the striking nineteenth century decoration inside – me without a head cover and wearing a knee length skirt – all that was required was a tip for the cleaner who let us in! KFOR vehicles were also in town; it is a NATO led international peacekeeping force responsible for establishing a secure environment in Kosovo.

We loved the food at restaurant Ambient from where we had a view of the minarets all lit up at night. Charming waiters brought us tasty local dishes – roasted peppers in a light cheesy sauce and stews of beef and lamb laced with many vegetables. A naan like bread came with the meat dishes. We found a wonderful bakery selling Turkish style sweets – *kadaif, baclava* and a type of rice pudding called *sutlijaš*. There seems to be much in common between Balkan and Turkish cuisine.

Leaving Prizren we headed up a ravine – delightful but for the constant stream of smelly trucks full of rubbish passing us. Near the top of the climb close to the border with Macedonia we found a little knoll just big enough for our tent – after we had used a rock to hammer down a metal peg sticking out of the top. It was a fortunate camp spot because when the heavens opened just as the tent was up and ready, the ground below became a river. The next day we found a wild stony track taking us down the bush clad mountainside towards Skopje. As I climbed down the hillside, after taking a picture, my camera flew out of my hand and the zoom stopped working – the end of my camera I thought! Fortunately we carry a camera each but as I had found out when I drowned my camera in a river in Laos, sharing doesn't work. I love my little Lumix TZ100 with its instant zoom – great for quick shots and pretty high quality too. Hugh has fancier equipment, which in difficult conditions will always get better quality pictures but it's all such a faff – not so readily to hand and then not always with the lens you want attached. And then, I have to ask, 'can I use the camera?' and I feel stressed that I might damage his precious kit!

In 1963 a massive earthquake destroyed most of the historic beauty of the city of Skopje. It was reconstructed as a modernist city. In 2014 the government of independent Macedonia – which was re-named North Macedonia in 2019 in order to keep the Greeks happy – decided that they needed to attract more tourists to their capital. They embarked on the Skopje 2014 Redevelopment Project with the aim of turning Skopje into a capital to rival the best in Europe, at a cost of around €600 million. A huge number of statues and fountains ate up much of this money. We were rather taken in by these statues, many of which are very beautiful. The monumental Warrior on a Horse, sits astride his horse on top of a marble fountain in the gigantic central square, looking like he is brandishing his sword at the Coca-Cola, Huawei and Halkbank signs on top of the pillared neo-classical building opposite. This dedication to Alexander the Great reputedly cost an extravagant €7.5m. The less grandiose, such as the Fountain of Mothers, had more appeal for us – a homage to motherhood with sculptures of pregnant ladies alongside those of women comforting their young children – one is said to be the mother of Alexander the Great.

But – did the plan work? *The Guardian* wrote, 'Skopje became Europe's new capital of kitsch' – about right. It also adds, 'but one thing is for sure: it has made the Macedonian capital a truly surprising and impressive spectacle' – which is also true. However, as with Kosovo there is much poverty in Macedonia. Most Macedonians considered the statues to be a waste of money from the start and now many think they are just a joke. More to the point, this money could have been spent on providing improved health systems and education rather than on a nebulous attempt to try to 'instil some national pride'. The money isn't there for maintenance – the job is unfinished and there are obvious signs of decay with sprouting weeds amongst the paving.

Some of the antiquity of the city remains however. There is the Ottoman architecture of the Turkish bazaar – a typical eastern market. Stalls along the stone flagged alleys selling dried fruits and nuts from large sacks; mountains of olives, black green and rose; spices; a huge variety of very fresh fruits and vegetables; and most other necessary things for living - we bought some duct tape! Up at the sixth century fortress we found a tourist city map lying on the turreted wall and picked it up thinking it might be useful. As we were leaving we bumped into the owner – a very interesting Australian, currently homeless and travelling the world! He was looking for the fourteenth century Orthodox Sveti Spas Church and together we found it. It was a stroke of luck for us to be directed there.

It doesn't really look like a church, which is the point. The building is sunk two metres underground so as to be almost invisible to the Mustafa Pasha mosque above. The Muslim Ottomans didn't want to see it! The little crosses on the roof indicating the building's purpose, could just as well be sitting on the roofs of normal houses – a common practice. The iconostasis inside is a wonder of craftsmanship, a three dimensional carving worked in walnut in the early nineteenth century. The carving is extraordinary, being 3D to the extent that the backs of figures are carved in full detail even when you can't see them without careful inspection. A mad but informative guide in there told us it was built in Lego style, the various pieces being attached with easily detachable wooden pegs. At the end of the Second World War, when under threat from the Bulgarian army, it was taken apart and transported to various places of safety and then reassembled once the danger was over.

Mother Teresa was an ethnic Albanian who was born in Skopje in 1910. At the Mother Teresa Memorial House we saw photographs of her childhood home and the church where she was baptised (destroyed by 1963's earthquake). Others showed events in her life, including receiving the Nobel Peace prize and meetings with people including the Queen, the Dalai Lama, Princess Diana and Yasser Arafat.

We stayed in a lovely Airbnb owned by a charming couple, in the bohemian quarter of the city. The owner, Igor had made all the furniture himself. They gave us advice on where I might find another camera. There was little hope of getting what I wanted as nearly all the cameras on sale were very expensive high end models; that was where the market was given that most people just use their mobile phones. However, the trail led me to a Lumix repair shop. 'Leave it with us and come back at 6pm' they said. I went back with little hope – in the UK it would probably have been sent away and then deemed not worthy of fixing. Not in Skopje – I collected a working camera for a cost of just €30.

Montenegro, Kosovo and North Macedonia are three tiny countries which emerged from the messy disintegration of Yugoslavia – we crossed them in just a few days. Our journey also took us through all but one of the other ex-Yugoslav countries – Bosnia and Herzegovina, Serbia and Croatia. Slovenia lies in wait for a future trip. All of these countries are also in a region known as the Balkans. The Balkan Peninsula is a geographic region – the most easterly of the three major peninsulas of Europe, the other two being the Italian and the Iberian. However, the list of so called Balkan countries is ill defined – as are the boundaries of continental Europe. From Macedonia we were heading for the largest countries of the region, Bulgaria and the biggest Romania – that is unless you count Greece. Greece, a tiny part of Turkey and even Moldova are also sometimes referred to as Balkan! Along with Slovenia we would miss out Albania – saved for another trip also.

It would take us six days to get to Plovdiv – a city which Hugh's sister Jane said we must visit – making our way across quiet, hilly countryside. Corn and sunflowers were cultivated in the flat valleys separating the mountain ranges and to our surprise, rice also. White storks nested on top of telegraph poles in little villages where there would often be a mosque with its elegantly tall minaret. Rough country cottages nestled amongst fields and pastures, many in a state of decay with render peeling off the outside walls and the undulating roofs with slipped or missing tiles. New homes were going up, often right next door to the old, probably financed by money earned in richer countries of Europe.

Horse-drawn carts carried farm produce and hand tools were used alongside machinery in the fields. People kept bees and sold honey by the roadside. We camped wild and no one seemed to mind. Road signs were in both Latin script and a Balkan version of Cyrillic. When our map sent us up an impassable path a man came to help and invited us into his house for coffee, juicy freshly picked plums and biscuits. His wife showed us pictures of their family – some living in the local town and others in Australia and Germany. We had no common language – just signs and pictures. There were vineyards near Vinica where we stopped at a little restaurant for a pizza. The menu was totally incomprehensible – hoping for a vegetable topping we found we had ordered one covered in ham and salami. Shopping was also proving interesting. I couldn't read the ingredients on labels of goods in the shops so I just had to go by the picture on the jar or packet. Sometimes no one spoke English and we just had to guess.

Over the border many things stayed the same – we were still seeing mosques. Most of the 130,000 or so Bulgarian Muslims – thought to be the descendants of the local Slavs who converted to Islam during Ottoman rule – live in the south-western part of the country we were travelling through. The first town over the border, Blagoevgrad was a laid back sort of place with a pleasant pedestrianised centre, an opera house, an American University and great places to eat and drink at very little cost.

We had selected a route which we expected to be a fairly quiet mountain road leading up to the edge of the Pirin mountains – but, frustratingly, it was very busy. The Pirin National Park is an area of outstanding biodiversity but our attention was drawn to the billboards tempting clients into a man-made paradise of luxury hotels and swimming pools. High in the mountains we went looking for a wild camp spot along a stretch of the old road, and landed in a camp site where we pitched next to a Norwegian couple in a 30-year-old Hymer van. The next morning we found another stretch of the old road, now degenerated to a track, which brought home to us how much the actual road we ride along matters. The scenery, no matter how wonderful, fades into a distant backdrop at the edge of your senses when vehicles are whizzing past your ears – a constant threat!

A deep dark valley where there was nowhere to camp, took us out of the mountains down to Pazardzhik, where we found a huge but hot hotel room. Pazardzhik is an interesting little town with some funky architecture, a cool shady park, a market, a generous supply of gambling haunts and its fair share of fountains and statues. From there it was an easy, flat and not particularly exciting ride into Plovdiv. A few kilometres out from the city we found a cycle track alongside the arena used for the 2017 World Rowing Championships.

Claimed by some to be the oldest continuously inhabited city in Europe, Plovdiv is to Bulgaria what Prizren is to Kosovo, the country's second largest city and a capital of sorts – in Plovdiv's case the cultural capital. It is also called the city of the seven hills, a geographical feature it shares with Edinburgh. In both cases tough igneous rock has stood proud above the softer sedimentary rocks worn away over time. The hills of Plovdiv rising above the Maritsa River, are formed from syenite, a coarse grained igneous rock similar to granite. One of the hills was used to build the paving for the city streets, so now there are only six hills. We ascended the rockiest for a fine view back to the old town. The slopes harbour rare protected plant species which are only found on the Balkan peninsula.

There are Roman ruins lurking underground all over the city, many still buried. Roman Plovdiv was known as Philippopolis. One of the world's best preserved Roman amphitheatres was only discovered around 1970. Many of the city's buildings had to be demolished in order to unearth it; the main road through the centre of the city goes underneath. It is now a venue for musical events; in the evening we could hear singers practising with the orchestra for a production of a Verdi opera. Only one end of the ancient arena has been exposed – uncovering all 240 metres of it would involve too much destruction.

In 1371 Philippopolis was conquered by the Ottomans and the city's name was changed to Filibe. Five centuries of Ottoman rule left a stunning legacy of colourful and now lovingly restored Ottoman houses, many of them previously owned by rich merchants and with lavish interiors that exude wealth.

We walked the narrow, stone paved and frequently stepped streets of the old town, shaded under the overhanging stories above. A cantilever structure enables the first and sometimes the second story to reach beyond the limit of the level below – a clever way of gaining extra space and possibly a way of avoiding tax which was based on the footprint at ground level. Apart from the practicalities this technique is an intrinsic part of the architectural appeal of these buildings. The luxuriant interior decoration was unlike anything we have ever seen.

Even though it was July the city's historic sites were not crowded. Plovdiv was flush with visitors for another reason – it was the weekend of Bulgaria's biggest rock festival; we had seen a huge stage being erected near the rowing arena. There was no mistaking the fans of heavy metal arriving in great numbers with their tanned skin; black T-shirts with fiery images which meant nothing to us; and crazy hairdos – overgrown, shaggy, close cropped, shaved or even plaited! Accommodation was in short supply and we had to resort to staying in the 'Boris' palace – the name that harboured bad connotations for us! The place was pretty smart with a lovely terrace view of the city but Boris lived up to his namesake!

As we moved on, Bulgaria was throwing up a bunch of mixed impressions. On the outskirts of Chirpan we stopped by a hamlet of rough brick built cottages, next to the rubbish tip. This was rough living. We saw a girl washing her hair at a water fountain below. A kid came up to Hugh asking for money. A man in a car stopped and told us that this was a 'dangerous area' – we moved on. In Stara Zagora, a town built in Chinese style with huge utilitarian apartment blocks, we found a fabulous restaurant serving very chewy pigs' ears for dinner. A beautiful tiny road out took us to a high point where a woman was collecting litter – she waved her arms around as if in disgust and said, 'my home'. She told us people left rubbish every night and apologised for the behaviour of her people. It is a problem in Bulgaria as in so many countries of the world to varying degrees.

We rode through forested hills and across flat valleys where fields were bright with sunflowers; 37% of Bulgaria is covered in forest. Old Ottoman houses were still standing in the pretty little village of Elena – much more modest than those of Plovdiv but enchanting nevertheless. A wild electric storm petrified us on the way to Veliko Tarnovo, a town with an impressive hilltop fort which attracts many tourists.

We were heading for the tiny village of Voditsa, for the simple reason that Kathy lives there and we very much wanted to meet her at her home, St. James' Park; Kathy grew up in Newcastle and declares she will always be a Geordie. When we met in the historic village of Shaxi, Yunnan, we had warned her that our journey could pass her place some day. A charming route through wild forest along cracked, overgrown roads led us through villages, quiet enough for the children to play in the street. However, most were in need of a facelift. Many of the houses looked beyond or in need of repair; abandoned fuel stations and decrepit relics from communist times added an air of melancholy. We learnt from Kathy that there is a depopulation problem in Bulgaria and many houses are unoccupied. The houses are literally held together with mud which washes away easily in heavy rains.

Kathy, along with a number of other intrepid Europeans have discovered that life can be good in the backwoods of Bulgaria. Around eleven immigrants, many British, live in Voditsa and there are little communities in many other villages nearby and around the country. For those game for some serious restoration work, houses can be bought for less than €10,000. Many come with land good for growing vegetables or cultivating vines. Trees abundant with fruit can supply apples, pears, plums, walnuts, peaches and more. Superb, fresh, local produce can be bought for very little, especially when it is in season.

Some with generous pensions come to live the good life, buying a cheap house and doing it up to be like a smart English home. Others, with less money to spare, come for something a little different; exchanging a hand-to-mouth existence in a dark corner of Europe with life lived the Bulgarian way. They live in homes that are 'projects' for sure – perhaps more of a project than many could face, and certainly so, if the aim is to create a home like an English home. But that isn't the aim. In summer they live outside. Their outdoor kitchens, with walls built in traditional style from mud, look out onto their leafy gardens; summers are usually hot and sunny. In winter, when temperatures can plummet to -30°C, they live in one room, heated to a cosy temperature by a wood stove. The loo may be a long drop in the corner of the garden, with perhaps an inside 'pee' loo. There is no sewerage system in the village. Homes often have no inside staircase and possibly no bathroom. These are hardyincomers – life like this involves more work, making an effort to get things done, but, perhaps that is what it is all about. There is a discernible sense of purpose – no sense of boredom amongst these pensioners. Kathy doesn't call it work; she says it is more real. There is also a community; we met many of Kathy's friends at her birthday party on the night that we arrived. Kathy has family living in the village too, including her ex-husband. Her daughter has married a Bulgarian and her son visits for long periods.

Then there is the wild country to enjoy. Low use of chemical herbicides in agriculture and large areas of forest mean that there is wildlife in abundance including wolves and no devastation of the insect population here. A friend of Kathy's says that 200 bird species have been spotted in his garden. There are paths through the woods where you can get lost and see no one.

It isn't hard to see why British and other nationals make the move; there is so much that is positive about the lifestyle. For us – well – we have problems with the decaying built environment. Voditsa now has a population of 500 but it was once nearly 4,000. Not only houses, but administrative, agricultural and public buildings which are no longer needed, are falling apart. As Kathy says, the country needs more people; the immigrants from Britain and elsewhere are helping to sustain the local economy.

We left Voditsa heading for Ruse and the Danube, passing through tunnels of wild forest, and pastureland where the verges were a feast of wild flowers and insects. All along the route we stumbled upon interesting relics from the past; the Kerpcha Rock Monastery carved high up into a roadside cliff, at 921AD, the earliest dated monastery with the oldest inscription in Cyrillic on the Balkan peninsula; the church and monastery at Cherven dating from 1220 to 1410AD where the ancient frescos still in amazing condition, are ingeniously protected from future decay; and the twelfth century St.Dimitar Basobovski monastery where we met Cristian, a tourist guide from Romania who told us we must visit the Happy Cemetery in the north of Romania. Inside devout pilgrims were kissing the icons as we had seen in other monasteries. Another community from abroad lives in Cherven.

We reached Ruse on the eve of the Blood Moon which we caught as if falling from the hand of the Liberty Statue in the main square. When the earth comes between the sun and the moon, preventing all direct sunlight from illuminating the Moon's surface, the red wavelengths find their way indirectly and the Moon takes on a red, yellow or orange hue. Following an afternoon storm that turned our hotel room window into the appearance of frosted glass, the skies obligingly cleared so that those gathered in the square could admire the spectacle. A city centre wouldn't seem to be the best setting for viewing an astronomical event, but in Ruse it was very visible and very special.

Ruse is termed the 'Free Spirit' city. We liked it – for its colourful and decorative 'neo-this and that' architecture (Baroque and Rococo in this case) which is so fashionable in Eastern Europe, the elegant fountains and statues, and opportunities to relax with a cool beer and a tasty dinner.

There are only two bridges over the 420km length of the Danube where it defines the border between Bulgaria and Romania. It is 190km to the next bridge downstream from Ruse and 90km to the next upstream crossing by ferry. You have to go over 300km upstream to the next bridge at Vidin! There were no customs checks as both countries are in the EU but there were long queues for passport checks as neither is in the Shengen zone; on a bike it is easy to shoot past all the cars and trucks so we were through in minutes. We stopped for coffee in the first Romanian town of Giurgiu and were surprised to find that we could understand the menu – Romanian is a Latin language with some similarities to Spanish, Italian and French and much more accessible to us than the Bulgarian Slavic language.

We took minor roads and tracks across the plains of Wallachia, a historical and geographical region of Romania. The Lonely Planet Guide states that, 'most travellers pass quickly through on their way to or from Bulgaria'. On a bike, you don't pass through anywhere too quickly and frequently the time taken is well spent. For two days we passed through a string of utterly charming rural villages where the people took a real pride in their homes – now I see a parallel with the pretty rural homes of Colombia. Cows, horses and donkeys grazed the wide grassy verges, which provided communal spaces along the roadsides. Colourful little cottages, mostly single story with roses, tomatoes and vegetable plots in the gardens, hid behind screens of flowering trees and bushes. The ordinary things – benches, fences and gates – were painted in matching colours; wells and water pumps were working, used and brightly painted too. It was all so tidy and cheerful, contrasting sharply with the decay of rural Bulgaria.

Nearly every home had a bench outside where we saw the young and old enjoying a friendly chat – surely no one could be lonely here. People waved as they passed by on horse-drawn carts full of fodder or in a covered family caravan. Every village had a colourful sign saying, *Bine ati venit* (welcome) proudly displaying the European logo. We bought *paine calda* – hot bread – and were given ripe tomatoes. We passed many newly built churches and monasteries; on our first night in Romania, a priest told us we were welcome to camp on the neat lawn by his monastery and he offered us food. It was easy flat riding so perhaps we did pass through rather quickly, doing 232km in two days!

After crossing the Danube we were on a gradual incline up to Curtea de Arges, known for its big white cake of a cathedral with curious twisted windows on two of the candle-like towers. From there we set out up the road to the Transfăgărășan, the second highest pass in Romania; a road, said to be entirely unnecessary, there being other much lower passes close on either side. It was built on the personal orders of Ceaușescu; some say, as a proud example of just what socialist Romania could achieve with its powerful leader – a status symbol! It would take some power from us to get up to 2,050m. However, the road does seem to have some purpose as there are mini-hydro stations on the river all the way up the valley and a massive pipe in the river bed.

We stopped for a picnic and realised that we were in the company of bears. A passing motorist warned us that the bears may go for our sandwiches and perhaps more. Initially the road takes a spectacular route clinging to the edge of a ravine, but then you hit the barrage at Lake Vidraru where a tortuous route takes you around the lake and up above the tree line. We climbed up into cloud and rain, under avalanche shelters and past waterfalls (several man-made) where people were taking selfies, culminating in a kilometre long, dripping, unlit tunnel which brought us out into an array of stalls selling local delicacies. Looking down on the irregular bends of the road snaking down the valley it can't be denied that it is an impressive road; on a clear day the views would be stupendous. But we were a little disappointed – there are so many scars on the landscape – electricity pylons and wires, large hotels, and the mark of the road itself.

Crossing of the Carpathian Mountains had brought us into Transylvania, known for its rich history, enchanting landscape – and Dracula but he wasn't on our agenda! We immersed ourselves in the enchanting landscape by taking the tiniest of tracks where we could. As for history – we were heading for Sibiu, built in the twelfth century by German settlers known as Transylvanian Saxons.

After crossing the Transfăgărășan, we stayed at a lovely rural campsite run by a Dutch/Romanian couple in the village of Carta – also an historic place. The monastery there is the easternmost establishment of the Cistercians and the Gothic style west portal was built by stonemasons after the Mongol invasion of 1241. To get from Carta to Sibiu by car it would take 45 minutes to drive the 50km along the E68. We set out on a stony track with grass down the middle and tall yellow daisies growing in profusion on the verges. A rickety suspension bridge, barely a metre wide took us across the Olt River, the loose boards clunking as our wheels rolled across.

A dirt path only just wide enough to ride, crossed a flowering meadow alongside a corn field leading to Noul Roman, a hamlet of pretty little cottages where a man with a wheelbarrow apologised for being in our path. He warned us that the road may turn to mud – it had rained heavily only two days ago. We gained a little height which gave views to the south of the extensive range of the Carpathian Mountains which we had just crossed. Continuing on dirt, alongside low wild forest, undulating through meadows of delicate whites, yellows and blues we reached some confusing junctions – guess work required. We landed in a marsh and just as we had been warned, the road turned to mud – impossible to ride.

Out of the marsh the track virtually disappeared – our panniers brushed against the wild flowers and tall grasses. It was quite a surprise to find that we weren't the only cyclists mad enough to take such an enchantingly crazy route. We bumped into a Czech cyclist who was taking his shoes off to walk round the edge of the mud bath. I decided to go for it and ride straight along the track through the water – it was fine – I was just a bit cross that Hugh hadn't taken a photograph! Our bikes and shoes were coated in mud by the time we emerged onto the paved road where we were lucky to find a car wash at a garage. All was spanking clean by the time we entered the huge central square of Sibiu, after five hours of riding – this was our idea of a good day's ride!

Sibiu, or Hermannstadt as the Germans who built it named it, was in the throes of an international traditional music festival so we were lucky to find a room at The Rabbit Hole. A huge stage was set up in the main square. A long line of men, dressed up in Morris dancing style costumes were dancing for all they were worth to the music of the lively, but rather raucous and repetitive band; limbs flying, high kicks, acrobatics, stamping feet and fast swirls made for a super energised show.

Walking around Sibiu there is a strange feeling of being watched! Eyes are looking down at you – narrow windows slit into the steep slopes of the roofs with small window openings at the centre – dark eyes with shingle eyelids sometimes staring in pairs. There are legends that they were built to frighten people but the reality is more practical; they were designed to ventilate attics where meat, cheese, and grain were stored without letting much sunlight through.

We left Sibiu heading for Aiud travelling along beautiful little undulating country roads passing fields of cultivated roses, rich sheep pasture and tidy villages with very distinctive architecture. Most gable ends were painted in a variety of colours. Circles, diamonds and Romanian Orthodox crosses added to the decorations. Many houses had roofs of shingle and a cross on the apex. Whilst Romania is secular with no state religion, it is one of the most religious of all European countries. The changing architecture is something that fascinates me as we travel – beauty in the everyday materials of a modest life being possibly more uplifting than the great and the grand. We passed though Aiud where there is an ugly but moving memorial to the victims of the communist regime and found a campsite which seemed more geared up for those wanting a Sunday picnic in the countryside – full of families having fun, kids playing, guys drinking beer and people sitting around tables chatting. The road took us through a land of steep limestone cliffs and little pointed peaks. The sign told us we were entering the village of Colțești. However, underneath a much more impressive name was written – Torockószentgyörgy.

We were heading for Rimitea, reputedly much loved by King Charles III, who has a keen interest in the preservation of the heritage of Romania. In Rimitea we met a Hungarian man sitting outside his summer house. He told us that nearly all the people in the village speak Hungarian – they are Hungarian in that when the land was carved up after the First World War and the collapse of the Austro-Hungarian Empire, many Hungarians found themselves living inside a country now called Romania. The towns and villages have Hungarian as well as Romanian names and frequently German names as well – hence the alternative name for Colțești. Rimitea is also known as Torockó in Hungarian and Eisenmarkt in German.

The eighteenth to nineteenth century architecture of Rimitea was different in many ways from any of the villages we had passed through earlier which dated from a much later time – the mid to late twentieth century. The one or two story buildings were painted in brilliant white with ornamented plaster facades – faux pillars and decorative window surrounds. Entry at ground level was through a stone framed rounded arch with a brightly painted or ornamental metal door. It was all so neat and tidy and totally charming. We found a room at a family run guesthouse Panorama Panzio where dinner was served family style with all the guests around a large table. We just love it when there is no menu – no difficult decisions – just what they do best. We had vegetables and meat balls in a thin broth for starters, then a pork dish with a tasty sauce served with pasta and for desert a delicious upside down plum cake.

Looking back on any trip there are always little regrets – places we missed and places we should have stayed for longer. We spent only one night in Rimetea – not long enough to get under the surface. One of the Hungarian family, staying in the same guest house as us spoke very good English and she told us that, as many of the people of Transylvania speak Hungarian, Rimitea is a popular area for Hungarians to visit and they like to come to climb up to the cross on the top of the hill – something we should have done, but sometimes we are afflicted with an irrational urge to move on! We moved on to the vibrant city of Cluj-Napoca (Hungarian name Kolozsvár), the biggest city in Transylvania, a place we had never heard of before – a university city, ten of them according to our student walking tour guide!

There were two fascinating areas we had heard about in Romania – the Painted Monasteries of Bucovina in the north-east and the wooden churches of Maramureș just to the north of Cluj-Napoca. We didn't have time to deviate to the east – Hugh needed to attend regular checkups resulting from his earlier bout of cancer – so we headed north to Șurdeşti where we found a place to camp amongst the haystacks – a simple rural site with toilets but no shower, so we took a bucket of water behind a haystack. Eneko arrived – a seasoned bike tourer who had pedalled through some interesting countries such as Japan, Cuba, Armenia and Tajikistan to name just four. It was important for him to give his home country as the Basque Country rather than Spain. We hadn't met other cycle tourists to talk to for long on this trip so we spent a lovely evening chatting with him about his country, his trips and his work with a cooperative company. When we meet other cycle tourists it is always good to compare gear – he had some really superb looking Arkel panniers with lifetime guarantees – must look into those I thought! Later I bought two for the front rack and they are great.

The wooden church in Șurdeşti is a UNESCO world heritage site, one of eight in the area. It was built in 1721 or 1766 depending on which source you take. It is, or was the highest wooden church in Europe and possibly the world, the slender, sharply pointed steeple rising to a height of 72 metres from the ground. A few years back a new church was built at the monastery of Peri in Săpânța which is 78m high (although this may be cheating as it starts off on stone blocks). Inside delicate frescos are painted directly on the wood – we were told that they are original and haven't been restored. In places the little gaps between planks of wood are covered with thin strips of cloth to give a level surface for the painting.

Perhaps I should confess that we are not religious people. Religion is so often incongruously at the root of discord and war – we had seen this in so many parts of the world and most graphically on this very trip in Bosnia and Herzegovina. Religion should be a force for good – indeed it so often offers a good moral code for life, a sense purpose and a caring community – so – there seems to be an obvious hypocrisy in killing in the name of religion! However, we do admire churches and the small, rural, not so flamboyantly flashy versions even more so, although there is no denying the impression of a magnificent cathedral.

Wonderfully crafted wooden churches are scattered all over the region of Maramureş most made completely of wood including the roof tiles. Some have carved gateways and this tradition has spilled over to the entryways of many homes. In Hoteni a man came to open the church for us and he talked a lot about the difficulties during communist times, particularly for Catholics. The Orthodox Church was tolerated but infiltrated with clergy sympathetic to the regime. In common with all the other churches we saw in Maramureş the icons at Hoteni were draped with colourful embroidered sashes made by local women. We visited many churches in the area, cycling through the cut meadows, dotted with tall hay stacks supported with sticks through the middle. Some people worked in the fields in the same way they had done for centuries gathering up the dry grass with wooden rakes and transporting the bales on a horse and cart, but tractors were at work too.

On our travels, we had been made aware of so many of the consequences of evil regimes in the name of communism throughout the world; Pol Pot in Cambodia, Mao in China and the effects of Soviet rule in the 'Stans' of Central Asia. There seems to be a kinder face to it in Cuba but perhaps we have been too taken in by the legend of Fidel Castro. As with religion, the principles behind communism have some merit – our capitalist society feeds a rich class who have far more money than anyone needs or can use sustainably. Passing through Sighetu Marmației on our way to the Merry Cemetery we visited the Memorial museum. One of its goals is the restoration of Romania's contemporary history, falsified during the years of the communist dictatorship. A very moving sculpture creation in the grounds, The Convoy of Martyrs, by Aurel Vlad, shows a group of eighteen naked human figures going towards a wall which closes their horizon, just as communism limited the lives of millions of people.

In contrast, the Merry or Happy Cemetery in Săpânța exudes joy where there is normally sadness – making fun of death in a good literal sense. We arrived on the road by the river Tisa which at this point forms the border with Ukraine close to the most northerly point of Romania. We had a brief incursion into Ukraine in 2009 when we were testing out our Roughstuffs during our summer holiday, prior to setting out for South America. We would like to go there again which may prove useful as we are now victim to a 90 day limit of stay in the European Schengen zone – a source of great frustration.

The graveyard in Săpânța is utterly unlike any other we have ever seen. The people of Săpânța have never been afraid of death, seeing it just as a gateway to eternal rest – death is not something to be solemn and gloomy about – even when the cause is tragic. One of the tombstones shows a child being hit by a car and another, a boy drowning in a river. They are not tomb 'stones' at all – the pictures are painted on solid oak – the dominant colour is blue but the decorations surrounding the images are in many different colours and the whole effect looking out over the graveyard is bright and cheery.

It all began with the local sculptor, painter and poet, Stan Ioan Pătraș who created the first tombstone crosses in 1935; he lives on in the cemetery, interned amongst nearly 700 of his creations. He used colours obtained from natural pigments – a special blue named by experts Săpânța blue and other colours, each with meanings: green – life, yellow – fertility, red – passion and black– death. It is not only in the bright, cheerful decoration that singles out this cemetery. The usual 'In loving memory of' and 'gone but not forgotten' are ignored and replaced by down to earth, truthful and often humorous verses that would make you laugh – if you could read them, which sadly we couldn't! Dirty secrets are revealed and the truth comes out. The epitaph below the tragic car accident reads:

The Merry Cemetery – Săpânța, Romania.

Burn in hell, you bloody taxi
That came from Sibiu.
Of all the places in this country
You had to stop right here.
By my house you hit me so
And sent me to the death below
And left my parents full of woe.

Many of the images tell the story of the person's life – at work, making hay, mending tractors, minding sheep the women often cooking, weaving and washing. They show people having fun and couples and families together. The cemetery attracts thousands of visitors, so many more it seems than the many beautiful little wooden churches of Maramureș which we often had to ourselves.

As we headed east towards Satu Mare women dressed like dolls came on the scene – gathered around a hillside monastery, walking down a track where smart new villas had just been built, chatting in the street at Bixad and gathering in large numbers by the church. They were wearing bright floral dresses with full gathered skirts, edged with a wide band of black lace, and billowing out like umbrellas above the knees looking like they might take off in a wind. Some had bulbous sleeves drawn tight at the cuffs, trimmed with the same black lace and a thick decorative belt tight around their waists. They wore colourful headscarves tied under the chin and black knee length boots. This was not what you expect people to be wearing on a random Wednesday in August.

But, this was the 15 August and the Fete de Santa Maria in Romania, a public holiday and one of the most important feasts in the Orthodox calendar which appeared to involve much dressing up in traditional costumes with singing and partying and gathering outside churches. The men were more restrained, going only so far as to wear a clean white shirt with black trousers and shined leather shoes. There were so many French registered cars about; we were told that the diaspora living in France come home for the event in great numbers.

Fete de Santa Maria, Romania.

We had left the Ukrainian border and were now heading back south, alongside the Hungarian border, heading for Timișoara from where we planned to cross into Serbia. It was a muddled five day ride – a five kilometre stretch of sucking mud that took us two hours to cross, a night in a beach resort without a beach in the middle of uninspiring plains and then the pretty town of Oredea with its church painted on the outside in the style of Bucovona's painted churches. In Oredea it was suggested that we go to one of Romania's best thermal resorts at Baile Felix – a place where crowds of bathers lounged around uninviting looking thermal pools. We did however enjoy the Hungarian goulash cooked in huge metal pots and the walk around the shady gardens with Lotus ponds and terrapins. The next night we were at La Foresteria near Galsa. The lady was delighted to have two cyclists to stay and she went to fetch a postcard which had been sent to her from Istanbul by two French walkers who had walked there from France. Mihaela said she would love us to send her a postcard from home – which we did!

An uninspiring and unexciting day of riding landed us in Timișoara. It had been one of those days when thoughts of 'what on earth am I doing this for?' lurk in the head. Twenty-five kilometres of traffic ridden roughed up paved road, relief coming when we lost the traffic in Arad – apart from the tractors – a frustrating track which lost itself in the fields where a tractor driver helped us out, more traffic and then a hack through the forest in an attempt to escape again; dull terrain and uninteresting villages.

On 15 December 1989, László Tőkés, a priest at the Hungarian Reformed Church in Timișoara, set in train events which would result in the fall of Ceaușescu and the end of the cruel communist regime in Romania. By Christmas day, Ceaușescu and his wife Elena had both been executed. Tőkés, an outspoken critic of the injustices of the communist regime was to be forcibly evicted from the city. A small crowd gathered at his house to protest. Hesitant murmurs of 'down with Ceaușescu' grew louder feeding the people's anger, leading to workers from factories all over the city coming out in protest in the following days. Despite the use of arms against them, and many deaths, the fever spread to many other cities all over the country where the vast central squares provided a perfect place to gather.

A museum, housed in the tatty building of an old military barracks, tells the story of the Romanian revolution and others in Eastern Europe. We watched a film, dubbed in English, which gave us a real feel for the events of the time. People coming out in huge numbers, cutting the communist emblem from the Romanian flag and calling out again and again 'down with Ceaușescu'; there was no giving up. This was also the year of the fall of the Berlin Wall and a fragment stands in the grounds of the museum.

At this point in our journey our cycling shoes were beginning to fall apart – mine were reinforced with strong black tape. We had realised that our shoes might not last out the trip but we were going to Europe, not the steppe of Central Asia or the Altiplano of South America; we could always get new ones – couldn't we? The problem was that we use shoes with cleats that clip into the pedals – known in a completely contradictory way as 'clipless' pedals because they were preceded by pedals with toe clips which then became obsolete. In this way our feet are fixed to the pedals and can't slip off. This may sound scary to the uninitiated but it feels safer than feet on the loose, once you get used to it; it also gives you more power – some say 30 per cent extra! In this city of over 300,000 we couldn't find anywhere that sold the type of shoes we needed, particularly in a woman's size. However, a very helpful assistant in the bike shop told us about a good cycle route along the Bega Canal, which would take us out of the city towards the Serbian border – a route which was destined to continue across the border only the Serbians hadn't finished their part of it.

We spent our first night in Serbia camping by a sluggish river populated by flocks of egrets. We had picked up water in the churchyard at the village of Idvor where Mihajlo Pupin was born – a physicist who devised a means of greatly extending the range of long-distance telephone communication by placing loading coils of wire at predetermined intervals along the transmitting wire. He died in New York in 1935. Shortly before reaching Novi Sad we crossed the Tisa River, a tributary of the Danube and the same river we had followed earlier along the border with Ukraine – but now much bigger after its long journey through Hungary. The Tisa joins the Danube just downstream of Novi Sad, our first Serbian city and Serbia's second largest.

Our first job was to sort out the shoe problem. We trailed around many bike shops but the smallest shoes available were in size 41 (UK size 8) – I am a 37! There was precious little choice in men's sizes too. The upper of my right shoe was separating from the sole all along the left hand side – this was the foot I unclipped most – when stopping. Something had to be done – Hugh decided on the repair route and went out to find a cobbler or get some strong glue. A lady in reception directed him to a nice lady who mends shoes. Come back at 4pm she said. Hope it goes the same way as the camera fix in Skopje I thought – and so it did – they kept us going until we reached home at least.

In April 1999, NATO forces shattered all three of the bridges crossing the Danube in Novi Sad, a Yugoslavian city at that time. Oil installations and any facilities with a military use were also destroyed. The aim was to stop the bloodshed in Kosovo. This was all part of the same issue of NATO trying to put an end to the ethnic cleansing of Albanians by Serbians, which had been brought sharply to our attention by the roadside memorials on our way through Kosovo.

An earlier tragedy in 1942 led to Serbs (700), Jews (800) and a few Hungarians drowning in the icy Danube. The Hungarian occupying units forced them to march across the frozen river only to perish when shelling from the shore shattered the ice. It was one of a series of fascist raids designed to get rid of suspicious individuals. The perpetrators were later tried and convicted by the Hungarian government. Four were given death sentences but they escaped to Germany before their executions. There is a memorial to the victims on the river bank – a moving sculpture in metal of an intimate family group – slender minimalist figures, three with arms linked and the youngest held in the father's arms with a hand on the mother's shoulder.

By this time we had spent over two months east of the Adriatic. We had learnt a great deal about the sad history of the region, and admired towns and cities which we had never heard of before we left home. I had little interest in history at school – the events of the French Revolution or the Peasants' Revolt of 1381 held little meaning for me. These things didn't have any relation to my own experience – and I didn't feel the need to know about them. Travel awakens the desire to know – to find out what has led to what is today – and nothing is more in need of explanation and understanding than the causes of conflict.

Yugoslavia had held together under the communist revolutionary Josip Broz, better known as Tito. He was viewed as a unifying symbol and some historians regard him as a benevolent dictator. After his death in 1980 there was no one to hold the country together. Nationalist groups throughout the region began to push for independence. In 1989 Slobodan Milošević became president of the republic of Serbia. His push for Serbian domination seems to be at the root of much of the ensuing violence. Piece by piece the region fragmented into many small countries, a messy and violent process in which so many were driven from their homes in a process of ethnic cleansing, including over a million Bosnian Muslims and Croats. Serbs suffered too – their capital Sarajevo was bombarded in the longest siege in history lasting nearly four years. Fighting between different groups continued until 1999 when Kosovo saw off the Serbs.

We stayed in Novi Sad for four days – partly to think about the route ahead. Our plan had been to go on from Novi Sad, to Pecs in Hungary, using the Euro Velo route 6 broadly following the Danube. This plan was getting kicked into touch; it would possibly involve too much flat riding through not particularly exciting territory. Instead we decided to cut straight through the eastern end of Croatia and head into Bosnia again, although we had no appetite for becoming entangled with the effects of war again – it made us feel uneasy. Hugh had worked out an interesting route but we changed it when we discovered that it passed though Srebrenica – we had no desire for our way to pass 6,100 gravestones of the victims of the 1995 massacre. The genocide had been commanded by Ratko Mladić of the Bosnian Serb army of Republika Srpska. It was the worst crime on European soil since World War II. People should know about these things, feel for those who suffered and try to understand why, but we didn't feel anything would be achieved by visiting Srebrenica.

Leaving Serbia (non EU) for Croatia (EU) was surprisingly simple; the checkpoint was very low key and the border seemed to be completely permeable with unfenced vineyards and cornfields running right across it. It was a one night stand in Croatia and the EU, wild camping by a little track off the road where the police turned up wanting us to move on. We didn't understand why – just picked up the word *zona* – but once we made it clear it was just for one night they left us alone. After sunset there was a curious dull thud around every thirty seconds coming from somewhere in the distance – like a muffled gunshot!

Our devious route across cornfields took us to the border with Bosnia and landed us on the wrong side of a serious fence – a bit of backtracking was needed. Once again we entered the Republic of Srpska, this time the northern slice. The immediately cheerful environment encouraged us – some smart new homes, neatly cut grass verges and enchanting old farm buildings with rows of arched windows. However, further down the road we saw some wrecked homes – concrete frames with a few bricks still clinging on and pock marks in the render. We picked up water from outside a bar and looked for somewhere to camp. A stark warning came in the form of a huge map by the roadside with 'mine, mine, mine…' written all across the top and various markings which we assumed to be the places to avoid – emergency marking, permanent marking and suspicious area (shaded in pink) is how it google translated the key, assuming the language to be Croatian!

A nunnery with a lovely patch of neat grass seemed like an obvious candidate for a mine free zone. The nun we communicated with was very happy to help but she needed to ring the boss – whoever that was – God? The answer was 'no' which struck us as very un-Christian. We settled for a nearby olive grove – people gathering the olives would have walked all around the trees, surely. It was lovely.

We were heading east to Banja Luka, the largest city in Srpska. It was mainly delightful rural riding – fruit trees, cornfields, forest and charming rustic, timber barns. Each village would have a board listing recent and future funerals and many a memorial to the 1992-5 war. We loved the traditional Balkan dish of Ćevapi – like a skinless sausage often made of lamb, served on fresh Turkish style bread with raw onions on the side.

Thirty kilometres before Banja Luka we turned into a forest campsite. We had a very friendly chat with the young couple who seemed to be in charge. They told us that it was a family business – developing the site on their land and it was popular with foreign visitors. The young woman spoke very good English which she said she had learnt from television. We talked about Bosnia and the contradiction between what the people want, i.e. to live peacefully together, and how this conflicts with the politicians' power grabbing instincts. The young woman was upset that all people know about the country is the war! Her country is Srpska she said, that is where she was born and she didn't appreciate suddenly being told she was in Bosnia. They offered us soup and bread which was brought to the table by our tent although we explained that we had already eaten and didn't really need it.

Amongst all of this interesting conversation, the young man was throwing in comments about returning our passports in the morning, at 10am – he had to take them to the police station sixteen kilometres down the road to register us. This set alarm bells ringing. When Hugh had taken the passports to his mother in the office, she had sat there in front of a huge leger filling in our details and she told Hugh she would bring them back in ten minutes. Now they said we couldn't stay without this registration. We made as if to leave although it was getting late and asked for our passports back. It made no sense, particularly as they reputedly had lots of foreign visitors. How could we be expected to let them take away our passports overnight like this – although we had let a young man run off with them in Kazakhstan?

Eventually it all seemed to be resolved – it was now OK as we were 'in transit'. Our passports were returned with apologies. We said we would be away early and offered to pay the fee there and then. The young couple told us no problem, we could stay for free and they would sleep in the cabin next to us just to make sure we were OK until morning – oh – and to watch out for the snakes!

We spent an uneasy night feeling that there was something suspicious going on. When we were ready to go in the morning the young couple had gone. The mother asked us if we would like a coffee so we accepted what we took as a friendly gesture. Then she asked us to pay – not just for the coffee but for the campsite too – a price three times the going rate at least. We told her that her son had offered us a place for free, but, never mind we would be very happy to pay a reasonable fee. She didn't accept this so we decided to go and then she threatened us with the police. Hugh said, 'let's just go, she won't call the police' – I wasn't so sure!

A few kilometres down the road we heard a police car behind us – after us. We explained the situation as best we could and the police appeared to have some sympathy for our point. They tried to persuade us to go back to the campsite, or one of us in their car, or to the police station – none very appealing. Meanwhile a lovely lady watching nearby offered us hazelnuts. The police called the mother and she arrived looking very officious with the huge leger in hand. The young couple, who had gone off for a holiday in Croatia, were telephoned and they denied all knowledge of their friendly offer – a mix up with language she said. We paid the extortionate fee – the only way out. It wasn't about the money at all – it was about deceit – or was it all one big misunderstanding? We would have happily given the money to the hazelnut lady.

We liked Banja Luka – like Cluj-Napoca, a vibrant university city with lots of young people about. We learnt more about the region's turbulent history in the museum there; about 'Ustasha', a Croatian revolutionary fascist movement, later supported by Nazi Germany and Italy's Mussolini, bent on creating a 'greater' Croatia. They were responsible for the deaths of 700,000 Serbs, Jews and Romani people who were executed at the Jasenovac camp in the years leading up to 1945.

The following night was a wonderful antidote to the campsite experience. As we approached the top of a climb we found ourselves in a wild storm with lightning getting closer and closer. We pulled onto a gravel track by a small house. A dog barked, and a lady looking out from a window beckoned us towards the field. We were soon sitting in Dara's garden shelter drinking hot

Bosnian coffee and doing our best with conversation based on a few words of German, Bosnian and English but mainly sign language! The storm looked set in for a while so we decided to ask if we could put up the tent in her field. We were made so welcome; Dara invited us into her home and gave us a tasty meal of a meaty, cabbagy, rice stew with bread.

We woke to mist covered mountains. Dara fed the chickens whilst we cooked our porridge under the garden shelter. An enjoyable undulating ride in damp but not stormy weather took us over a 1,200m double summit pass where we left Srpska and descended to an expansive high plateau at 900m. Elongated puffs of cloud floated below the surrounding summits rising above farmland and villages in the valleys. The fields on the plains were tended but many of the little houses scattered about looked abandoned. We passed a broken Muslim graveyard. A roadside sign told of efforts going on to rehabilitate dwellings in the municipality of Glamoč. This was a project of the International Rescue Committee, an organisation that began life with a plea by Albert Einstein in 1933, to help save anti-Nazi leaders targeted by the Gestapo.

We were looking for water and a place to camp but realised that we had to be careful after seeing another large mine map. We asked about camping near a village house but the lady said no. It was getting late and we just had to do something. Some people were working around a house up a short track so we went to ask them for water. The two men were a bit frosty and didn't seem keen to help at first. An old lady appeared – with brilliant sapphire eyes, wearing a full below the knee skirt, a black scarf around her head covering her hair and a baggy knitted waistcoat over her top. We eventually gained their trust and they warmed to us – filling our ten litre dromedaries with water from their well and drinking it in front of Hugh to show that it was good. We left with a gift – a bag of freshly picked plums. We think that they were just very wary of strangers – no wonder considering the times they had been through.

Further along we found a perfect camp spot on a little track off the road. There were cow pats around so we reckoned any mines would have been set off by the animals. We cooked as it was getting dark. It was a real surprise when a car rocked up at around 11pm coming from further down the track. Hugh looked out of the tent door and waved; he thought it may have been a police car. Anyhow, they left us in peace this time. The morning brought soft mists, hovering in the valleys below, veiling the ruined buildings along the track and forming a white backdrop to bushes in silhouette. The outline of the ridges above stood out sharply against a bright blue sky. A magical peace to be savoured – that was until Hugh got the stove roaring for morning coffee.

We set out along the lonely *strada bianca* winding across the plateau, heading for the village of Rore where we hoped to get water. After Rore there would be a long stretch of *nada*. The sink holes by the roadside reminded us of home – we had never seen them packed so densely – like bubble wrap in reverse. On the edge of the village the houses looked abandoned, roofs, walls collapsing and trees invading. Would we find water? We had very little and a long way to go before we expected to find more – no streams or habitation marked on the map! The main village was deserted. Any place habitable was boarded up. Then we saw a well near a decent looking house. There was no one around so we lifted the covers off and rigged up our kettle with two lines of string so we could lower it into the water and tip it so it would fill. The system worked really well and the water looked good. We took nearly four litres extra in addition to our four full bidons.

We went up and over a pass on a gently graded gravel road. We were on the edge of densely forested mountains with occasional glimpses of a valley below through the trees. There were tracks signposted to places below but they were not marked on our map. There was more water on the way down – no need to carry the four litres, but you never know! We emerged on a plateau at around 1000m. The distant mountains looked very Scottish. There were houses up there and some cultivated fields; a long way from anywhere. Where do these people do their shopping? Lower down sheep and cows grazed in fields bounded with dry stone walls also reminding us of home. The weather was fickle – soft sunshine filtering through thinning clouds and rainbows spanning the fields.

We reached Bosansko Grahovo hoping to find a place to stay. A guy on a motor bike offered to take us to a *sobe* (room) but we found the place depressing and decided to move on. The town is in a glorious setting but it basically needs rebuilding – although to be fair we didn't get to the actual centre.

Another little pass took us down to a valley of spectacular limestone crags and peaks. Torrential rain turned the paved descent road into a river – not a road to take too fast and not a time to have an accident. The sun came out turning the hillsides and valley fields to luminous green. It would have been wonderful to camp there but the ground was sodden, it was getting late and we were cold, hungry and in need of hot showers. We took the last free room in the hotel Mihovil in Kninsko Polje – the place was full of hunters. We had crossed into Croatia, having travelled much further than intended. We ended the day eating goulash with gnocchi and polenta washed down with dark Croatian beer.

The day's 90km ride was one of the best of the trip. We passed through such a variety of landscapes, much on good gravel tracks – high level plateaux of open pastureland with distant shapely mountains, steep mountainsides coated in dense mixed forest and dramatic, complex, limestone terrain. All of this in equally mixed weather; atmospheric mists, bright sunshine, blue skies with fluffy white cumulus and a torrential downpour.

The next day a four kilometre ride took us into Knin and we spent much of the day on a relaxing stroll around the impressive fortress, the second largest in Croatia. Yet again, the museum tells of the local history. This area, like much of Bosnia and Herzegovina, suffered ethnic cleansing at the hands of the Serb leaders' desire for building a Greater Serbia. There is no hiding from brutal

Balkan history.

We found a good place to stay in a room of Natasha's house, close to the citadel. Such a lovely lady. She did all our washing and asked for nothing, delivering it clean and dry by evening. Times were hard for her during the war. She left for Bulgaria, where she comes from, and where her mother still lives. Now all is fine for her living in Knin with her daughter but coming home wasn't easy with having to prove rights to her property.

Her son-in-law runs an auto shop and she thought he may be able to help us find the tool for changing our rear cogs, i.e. a chain whip. Hugh's was making lots of noise, especially when riding up hill. The son-in-law didn't have one, and although he gave helpful suggestions, such as a chain saw shop we weren't able to find one anywhere in Knin. There is a limit to how many tools you want to carry on a bike – the chain whip is heavy.

Our two day ride across peaceful, rural Croatia crossed the clear blue waters of the Krka River as it slides between forested cliffs of layered limestone and on through the pretty little town of Benkovac – a self-declared tourist free zone – landing us at the coast in Zadar on the Adriatic shore. On our outward journey, the boat from Italy had landed us 150km south in Split.

Croatia, or Hrvatska as it is called by its own people, is a bizarrely shaped country. The long tapering stretch down the Adriatic coast from its border with Slovenia to its 20km border with Montenegro is cut through by a bit of Bosnia at the city of Neum, giving Bosnia a token 20km strip of Adriatic coast and separating the region around the Croatian city of Dubrovnik from the rest of the country. Another, fatter strip trails east over the north of Bosnia.

The Croatian coast is a paradise – clear, blue, warm seas and historic towns of narrow alleys and ancient architecture that are a wonder to visit. No surprise that holiday makers flock to Split, Trogir and Zadar to name just the coastal towns that we visited – and loved. On the other hand we only saw a handful of foreign visitors in the inland town of Knin and also Sinj which was on our outward route from Split to Mostar.

On midsummer's day, our 43rd wedding anniversary and the day of the World Cup match between Hrvatska and Argentina, the cafés of Sinj were crowded with football supporters in their red and white chequered jerseys, looking intently through lines of bunting at the action on the television. Now I am not a football fan, and I find it curious that Hugh follows it to the extent he can have conversations about it, but, I have to admit that I was sucked up into the excitement that night. There was absolute uproar at each of the three goals which gave them the victory over a team unable to score! A second century tombstone of a Roman boy holding a leather ball, encased in the wall of a building on the main street, is claimed to be evidence that football began in this region.

The only place we could find to stay was the pleasant but unexciting Alkar hotel and although there were plenty of cafés frequented by locals there were very few restaurants. We found a quiet place in an interesting old building – wooden beams and stone arches – with statues of Adam and Eve on either side of the door. The young lad who served us told us that they get Italian and German tourists but generally the Croatian people find it too expensive. However, it was much cheaper than the restaurants in Trogir and Split. We had the traditional local dish of *sinjski arambasici* – some kind of meatball wrapped in very salty cabbage. Our appetiser was a version of prosciutto – similar in taste but cut more coarsely – with a hard, tasty cheese.

However, there are other reasons to visit Sinj apart from the football and the local food. The ancient fortress is surrounded by divine sculptures representing the way of the cross which makes for a peaceful walk through woodland and an extensive view from the top. In 1715, a tiny force on the fortress defeated a large Ottoman army. They believed their unlikely victory to be down to the help of Our Lady of Sinj, a beautifully delicate painting which was brought to Sinj in 1687 by Franciscans fleeing the Turks. After the defeat of 1715, the lady was adorned with a golden crown and it was placed in the church where it now stands.

Most of all, Sinj is famous for its iconic, UNESCO protected Alkar festival which takes place in August. Knights known as Alkar, participate in combatant tournaments linked with their turbulent history. The origins of this contest date back to 1784. The Alkars, dressed in elaborately decorated costumes ride at full gallop with spears in hand, ready to spear the Alkar, a ring made up of two joined concentric circles. Already they were setting up the area for the August event.

We found that once we escaped from the coastal strip the traffic vanished. We had investigated a route along the coastline, with the possibility of going to Dubrovnik, but talk of busy roads on the blogs of other tourers were off-putting. Island hopping would only solve part of the problem; we dabbled with this getting from Split to Trogir via Otok Čiovo – a bridge connects the island to the mainland at Trogir. The road was deserted and the land covered in lines of stones as if it had once been cleared for agriculture but it was now overgrown with low wild bushes. Getting on and off the little boat with engine fumes wafting around was something of a hassle and the idea of multiple boats didn't appeal; more to the point, not all of the islands can be linked. With any bike trip there is a need to tie in places you want to see with the pleasure of the cycling journey, which cuts out some seemingly obvious destinations whilst throwing in many wonderful surprises.

Discounting the little island boats, this had been a journey of six months and eight boats – four of them overnighters. We'd ridden from our home in Sedbergh in the Yorkshire Dales to the Lancashire port of Heysham, a strange direction for a tour heading for the Balkans. It was Hugh's ingenious way of avoiding the busy south of England. We sailed via the Isle of Man to Dublin and froze over the snow covered Wicklow Hills; it was the 29 March and supposed to be spring. We arrived, tired, cold and wet, at the home of Jackie and Mick, our warm showers hosts, situated on an elevated road out in the countryside. It wasn't only the shower that was warm – their welcome was toasty and the room was snug with the heat of the wood stove. Jackie cooked us a delicious dinner.

From Wexford we took the boat from Rosslare to Cherbourg and then crossed one of our favourite countries for cycling – France – spending ten days in Provence where our eldest son Andrew enjoys a charmed life in lovely Lagnes with his French wife and two children. We exchanged sunlit red poppy fields for the stormy forests of the Grand Luberon, descending to roads turned to muddy rivers and a flooded hotel in La Tour-d'Aigues. The wet restaurant was closed but they ordered us a take-away pizza which we ate away from the drips. We skirted round the limestone ridge of Montagne Sainte-Victoire and, after a night at a classic rural campsite where Ida was so impressed that she gave us a free stay, we descended to Marseille.

After a four kilometre ride through the docks to get to our boat, we set out across the Med to L'Île-Rousse. This would be our fifth time on Corsica, an island we could never tire of; the mix of mountain and blue sea is irresistible. For the first time we rode around the edge of the thumb at the north end of the island after crossing the Désert des Agriates, a limestone wonderland that we had only seen before through a covering of thick mist.

From Bastia we took the boat to Livorno in Italy and went east to Ancona from where we took the boat to Split in Croatia. On the return trip after a round of the Balkans, we took the boat from Zadar to Ancona and crossed Italy again, between the same end points but via very different points in between. We could cross Italy many more times and never get bored.

The regions of Tuscany, Umbria and Marche in central Italy are crammed with amazing historical towns, some very famous and some less known. Our outward traverse took 24 days taking us through Pisa, Florence, San Gimignano, Siena, Cortona, Assisi, Perugia, Macerata and Sirolo. The return journey was much more direct taking thirteen days via Urbino, Prato, Pistoia and Lucca. However, for nine of those 37 days we didn't move on, being stopped in our tracks – astonished by the wealth of amazing architecture, frescos, carvings, sculptures and paintings reaching its zenith in Florence, perfectly preserved and almost devoid of modern incursion.

BACK ROADS IN UNACQUAINTED EUROPE

Italy is the antithesis of the Central Asian Steppe. On our eleven day journey from Aqtau to Nukus across Southern Kazakhstan we moved on every day – there was nothing to stop for. We averaged over 95km per day even along the reputedly 'worst road in the world' – it was flat. In Italy our average daily distance for our days of riding was little more than 43km. The hills of Tuscany are short but can be punishing, with gradients up to 20 per cent. We are often asked, 'how far do you go in a day?' It is a question without a short answer. The furthest we went in an Italian day was 65km but in Uzbekistan we made 176km. It depends – on the wind, the terrain and the state of the road and how we are feeling. Short sharp hills can be more draining than long gentle ones. And then, is there anything to stop for? If we arrive in an interesting town or village early in the day we may stop or we may stop en-route to explore. We love the mix of delving into interesting towns and cities where we may spend two or three days and moving slowly across the landscape in between – however, in Italy temptations to stop can come a bit too often!

Pisa was pleasantly peaceful in mid-May – I had never been there before and I was totally bowled over by it. On the way in we chanced upon a beautifully decorated little Romanesque church, older than the cathedral of Pisa and built at the place where St Peter is said to have come ashore. When we passed through on our return journey in late September Pisa was busy with tourists, going through that bizarre ritual which takes place along the wall in front of the leaning tower – looking like they are doing some kind of ethnic dance as they stand with arms stretched out, hands bent back as the person with the camera attempts to tie in the pose with the lean of the tower. The same sort of ritual is practised on the Salar de Uyuni in Bolivia where Hugh played with perspective to capture my headstand on top of the tent!

A crazy hop over a mini mountain range near Pisa, in the interest of traffic avoidance, ended with a cramped camp high on a mountain path with a spectacular view. A day of using mainly tracks to get across a marshy area crisscrossed by canals ended at an over-priced campsite where we ditched the so called camping area – more of a car park designed for campervans – for a nice grassy spot next to an unoccupied cabin. Campsites catering for tents are slowly vanishing as campervanning takes over. Then four days of luxury in eye-watering Firenze, including several hours in the Uffizi, was followed by a camp in an overgrown vineyard before reaching San Gimignano, a hill top town of thirteenth and fourteenth century skyscrapers – at one time there were 72 of them, symbols of power and wealth, and some as high as 50m. There are fourteen still standing, tower houses of stone so high that Hugh had a field day with his fisheye lens.

Then we camped in the 'bush' near the lonesome twelfth century church at Marmoraia where we got water from a tap marked as drinking water on our Pocket Earth map – we had used it many times to find water. We reached Siena along the pilgrims' route, Via Francigena passing many walkers on the way. In

Siena we were told that we couldn't park our bikes in the iconic centre of Il Campo – we could only stop for a photo and then move to another piazza. The Restaurant Babazuf, had a special deal for pilgrims and we must have looked the part because we were offered the menu without showing our credentials.

In Cortona we learnt about the Etruscans – the fortified town dates back to the eighth century BC and the museum there is full of ancient Etruscan artefacts, the most famous being a chandelier dating from the sixth century BC, decorated with men sat on their haunches and swimming dolphins.

The next night we camped in an olive grove not far from Perugia. The old lady sitting outside the large villa seemed very happy for us to camp on their land – at least that's what we understood from our very limited Italian. Perugia was worthy of more exploration but we judged it would be an overdose to stay there before Assisi, the birthplace of San Francesco. So what did we know about Saint Francis before we arrived – not very much? Of course we had heard of Franciscan monks and had even met one in Mexico. He was a lover of animals, nature and above all, peace – we can go along with that. Staying in Assisi for a couple of nights meant that we could enjoy the peace of the early morning and the late evening when the daytime visitors had gone and when the light on the magnificent rose windows, carvings and statues is very special.

The day after we left Assisi we crossed into Marche. A climb over forested and fielded mountains dotted with pretty hillside villages and towns took us

Passing through Pisa, Italy.

Pieve Torina and the aftermath of the 2016 earthquake, Italy.

down a rocky defile towards Pieve Torina. We passed by some roadworks and then a building half reduced to rubble, cordoned off by concrete barriers and red tape, narrowing the road. Further along a bridge was being repaired. The memory of an earthquake in 2016 came to mind – could this be connected? We passed the church, the ancient tower thankfully intact but the upper walls braced with metal reinforcements and entered a ghost town. Just about every building was buttressed with thick wooden props and bandaged in planks strapped to the walls which were covered in sores of peeled plaster. Tall metal fences kept people at a safe distance. Just outside the village some simple accommodation had been built unobtrusively into the hillside – small dwellings with solar heated water. Later we saw many more little settlements like this, many with a field of solar panels nearby. Later we learnt that the government had built these for people displaced by the earthquake.

 We climbed out of Pieve Torina on a minor road in a very bad state and we hoped that it wouldn't turn out to be blocked later. Looking back down on the village from a distance it all looked so normal. Over the next days we found ourselves repeatedly descending into ruination, the extreme damage to the ancient architecture only apparent when we drew close. Cracked homes away from the villages often had a temporary construction in the adjoining field where the people were living awaiting repairs. The next day we descended towards the little village of Fiastra, hoping to find a shop. We did find a good shop, set up in temporary accommodation, as was the pharmacy and the bank. The old buildings were uninhabitable. A little further on, we found an open bar in Acquacanina. The place was eerily deserted and we weren't sure where customers came from. We bought cappuccinos and a pastry and sat under a new sun shelter across the road next to the strapped up town hall.

Leaving Acquacanina the road ahead was blocked for a very different reason. A cycle race was flying by; the Gran Fondo di Varano with hundreds of riders competing. The big climb of the day took us up to 1,300m, into the undamaged beauty of the Sibillini Mountains – flower meadows richer in different varieties than any we have ever seen. There were still patches of snow on the bare, moss green mountain slopes.

The experience brought back memories of Christchurch in March 2012 on our tour of New Zealand. We were visiting the Kiwi/German couple Tim and Tina who we had first met on the Carretera Austral in Chile. Two days after they flew home from Patagonia in February 2011 a major earthquake struck. Over a year later, their house was habitable, but full of cracks, parting walls, ill-fitting doors and uneven floors. Many of their neighbours had left after their homes were condemned. New Brighton where Tim and Tina lived had been hit badly. The road had sunk by half a metre and concrete barriers were struggling to hold back the waters of the River Avon. Lamp posts, telegraph poles and telephone boxes were inclined at unnatural angles. The old wooden houses stood up to the shock much better than the newer brick ones – just as the old wooden buildings in Lijiang in Yunnan, China, had stood up to the earthquake of 1996.

Whilst we were in Christchurch a walkway was opened up into the 'Red Zone' to enable people to visit the shattered cathedral, built of stone between 1864 and 1904 and repeatedly damaged by earthquakes over time. Some came to say goodbye – the plan was to demolish it – some just to see the damage for themselves and some, including the infamous Wizard, to give voice to the campaign to save it. Strong warnings ensured that visitors were well aware of the potential danger of entering an area of great instability where further aftershocks could result in injury or even death. We were asked to limit the time of our visit to 50 minutes.

The central business district of Christchurch was cordoned off, apparently frozen in time. A jivey container mall had become the new centre, injecting a good measure of cheer and colour into the place. When we left Christchurch we began to wonder when we would leave behind the crumbling garden walls, cracked homes, bumpy roads and leaning posts. Even years later in 2018 when we visited our daughter, who was living in Christchurch at that time, the city was far from back to normal. There were many vacant plots awaiting redevelopment and parts of the city had only just been opened up with cafés and restaurants.

So we began to wonder when we would reach an undamaged Italian town. We arrived in Macerata, a city which appeared unscathed. This was the home of Mirko, who we had met in the Sibillini mountains where he was out for a day ride with his friend Alberto. Alberto welcomed us to Macerata in the throes of an ultra-heavy downpour. We had dinner with both their families at Alberto's country house. Our Italian is pretty minimal but they could speak English as they had benefitted from the Erasmus scheme enabling young people to study abroad – the same scheme that had given our eldest son the opportunity to study in Grenoble, France, for a year and been instrumental in him becoming a fluent French speaker. Mirko's wife had spent a year at Manchester University and Mirko a year in Bordeaux. Our conversation with Mirko defaulted to French which we were both comfortable with – we found his French very easy to understand. We talked of cycling, travelling, family and, inevitably with Hugh around, politics! It was a lovely evening, we had wonderful pizzas and we were made to feel very much at home.

In the 82km between us and the boat to Split, in Ancona there was still so much antiquity to explore, not to mention the fact that we hadn't even done Macerata justice. There was the lovely hilltop town of Recanati where a relief on the 36m twelfth century tower in the piazza shows angels transporting the house of the Virgin Mary – devotees believe that they came by Recanati on their way from Jerusalem to Loreto. Perhaps more significantly on such a hot day we could get the best of Italian ice cream at a fraction of the asking price in Florence. We also went through Loreto and visited the magnificent Basilica della Santa Casa where the stones of the said house are enshrined behind an intricately carved marble entrance. We rode along the coast, littered with the trappings of holiday making – regimented rows of deck chairs and flaccid sunshades on the beaches. We stayed a night in the Pearl of the Adriatic as the colourful cliff top town of Sirolo is deservedly known. We ate wild *moscoli* (mussels) which grow naturally along the Conero coast and then headed for Ancona where we were surprised to see Amsterdam style cannabis stores!

Three months later we returned to Ancona for the reverse crossing and stayed in other historical towns which we didn't visit on our outward trip although we were so close – this was after all a cycling trip and we needed the buzz of the ride and a rest for the brain and senses. Prato, Pistoia and Lucca are all not far from Pisa and Florence – we loved peaceful Pistoia the most, with architecture like that of Pisa in contrasting white and black, serpentine marble.

From Livorno, we sailed back to our favourite isle. We approached Bastia in the early morning as shards of sunlight filtered through cracks in the grey alto stratus forming bright pools on the wrinkled sea. Unlike flights, sailings are a pleasurable way to cross the water – no boxing up of bikes required; burning sunsets and inspiring sunrises on the horizon, the feeling of leaving and arriving as one shore recedes and the other approaches; and space to move around, time for a beer and a comfortable cabin for sleep. The only plus to a flight is the view from the air – a crossing of Australia gives a first-hand impression of what an empty land it is and I will never forget the glorious view of the snow-capped Caucasus on our return from New Zealand.

From Bastia we could have sailed straight for Marseille but it seemed right to cross to the west coast first. We took a quiet mountain road up to the endearing little thirteenth century church of San Michele de Murato – built Pisa style in contrasting stone. We had camped there in 2012 on our way to Central Asia. Some restoration work had been done since and there was now a plaque with information for visitors. This time we camped further up the road near a pig farm!

The trip ended on a high; high on the rugged, empty and shapely mountain spine of the island. Narrow roads hug the steep slopes cut into the cliff sides or wind their way up from the valleys below to clusters of dwellings perched on the slopes above – church towers marking the centres of villages. A roadside fountain offered just enough of a dribble to supply water for our final camp at a cool 940m on wild open ground with 360° views to die for and a handy wall for parking the bikes – the best camp of the trip. The dawn light turned the mountains to golden etchings and the air to a cool 5°C. We descended in the company of red kites, the sunlight catching the light plumage of the head and the dark, long feathers of the wing tips spread out, contrasting with a clear blue sky. The Corsica Linea boat we would be taking to Marseille was nestled in the harbour of L'Île-Rousse. From Marseille we took the train to L'Isle-sur-la-Sorgue and cycled the seven kilometres to our son's home in Lagnes.

In this trip of six months, six ferries and no flights, we realised that there was a veritable playground, full of charm, history and scenery right on our son's doorstep. We decided to base our Roughstuffs there ready for future tours. Little did we realise how the games of the politicians would put us in a 90 day straight jacket and the world would shut down to travel for British citizens for an indeterminate time.

9
THROUGH THE RIF AND THE SIERRAS OF SPAIN

Miles from nowhere, guess I'll take my time, oh yeah, to reach there.
Look up at the mountain I have to climb, oh yeah, to reach there.

'Miles from Nowhere' from the album
Tea for the Tillerman by Cat Stevens, 1970

Pauline:

'I can't guarantee your safety'. These were the words spoken calmly, quietly, but firmly by the young police officer dressed in casual plain clothes, crouched at the door of our tent.

The ride up and over the heavily forested, rocky slopes of Mont Gourougou provides the ultimate scenic route to reach the Moroccan port of Nador and the 12.3 square kilometres of Spain sitting next to it, known as the Spanish enclave of Melilla. We thought that the terrain of the volcanic massif would offer a superb final opportunity to camp in Morocco, so part way up the mountain we started looking for a way into the forest where we could hide. We found a track leading off the road. A short way off the track was a neat, flat spot with a panoramic view of Nador and the sea and spit beyond. It was a bit disconcerting to have to cross ground covered in bits of broken glass and we had to clear away some of the inevitable litter, but it was nice enough on our patch. We didn't expect evening visitors but then a man came along who said he was staying in a *bergerie* (shepherd's hut) up the road and we could go there if we wanted. He seemed friendly enough but we politely declined, preferring our solitude. A young boy with a dog walked by and used the word *frío*; there was a cool wind. But, it was a real surprise when a policeman turned up, telling us we were not in a *touristique* zone and we shouldn't stay there. I was thinking to myself; that is the idea, not to be always in tourist zones. He put Hugh on the phone to the person we thought was his superior, and who also told us we shouldn't stay there and he would come to speak with us personally. Hugh didn't think anything would come of it, but before long there were torch lights shining on our tent.

Mohamed was in charge of local security. Explaining the situation with patience and a calm authority he told us that there are many people from all over Africa trying to get into Europe via the Spanish enclave of Melilla. They are often wandering around the area at night. We'd had dinner, washed ourselves and we were settled in our sleeping bags looking at photos, but it was clear that there was no choice but to pack up. This plain clothes police officer was not giving us orders but he made it quite clear that we needed to move. It took us around 25 minutes to take down the tent and put our things away. The lights of Nador twinkled below us and a starlit sky with a crescent moon poised like a saucer, shone down. The police were very patient and gave us extra light to help us pack our kit. We left with an escort of three cars and a moped, to make the short ride to a nearby four star tourist lodge. We had passed the Hotel Mont Vert on the way up and remarked on the heavy duty fencing around the compound.

We found ourselves in a spacious, comfortable room with a huge bed. From the balcony, there was an expansive view of lumpy, barren hills dotted with settlements of small scale apartment blocks in shades of pink and white. Our route earlier in the day had crossed this arid landscape. The police told us that the room would not cost us anything. Mohamed seemed genuinely sorry that he'd had to disturb our lovely camp and spoil our 'fun'. We were impressed with his concern for our welfare and his delicate handling of the situation but sorry to miss the morning view from our camp.

The next day we continued on the narrow road up the mountain, passing through a protected area populated by inquisitive monkeys. It wasn't long before we noticed that a car travelling very sedately behind us stopped at regular intervals. It soon became obvious that it was trailing us! Once we found an opportunity to talk to the driver, we found out that this was our police escort.

So what was it all about? We tried to find out. No, it wasn't dangerous but they were there for our security. The second police officer who took over just before the top of the climb said that the road was dangerous, meaning narrow with bends. We wondered if they thought we didn't know what we were doing as they kept asking if we were tired. Did we look too old for the job? It wasn't a steep climb and the road surface was far better than many we had ridden on this trip; perhaps they were just being considerate and wanted to make us feel safe. We didn't see any very dodgy looking people; unless you count a couple of very dark, obviously not Moroccan people walking along with plastic sacks. However, nearer to Nador, we passed a large encampment, which we thought was probably set up for refugees.

The road was very quiet; a few people who were obviously locals walked by and gave the usual friendly greetings and a few cars passed us. It was a brilliant way to end our ride across northern Morocco and well worth the effort of the climb. The road clings to the edge of the craggy mountain, winding its way down to the sea, with stupendous views of the rocky ridge and the ocean beyond. There were plenty of good camping spots higher up where in any other country we would be happy to pitch our tent. There was even a little stream near the top at 750m. Our escort didn't leave us until we went into the shipping office in Nador to buy our tickets for the boat to Motril in Spain. A spot of googling later revealed what we should have known already if we had researched

THROUGH THE RIF AND THE SIERRAS OF SPAIN

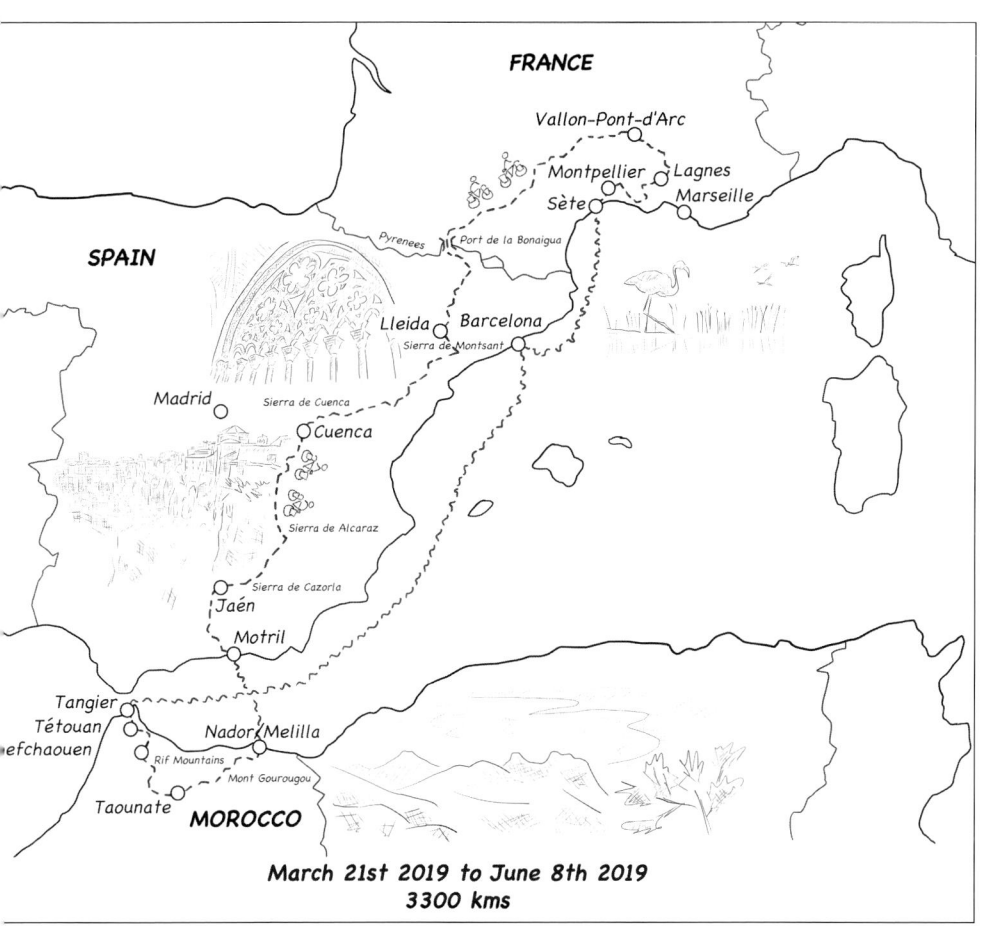

March 21st 2019 to June 8th 2019
3300 kms

our trip thoroughly. Mont Gourougou is the perfect hideout for groups of illegal immigrants. An investigation by Euroviews in 2018 found evidence of rough camps deep in the forest near the top of the mountain, but failed to spot any dodgy people, just hikers.

Opportunities to put up our tent in Morocco had been few with tempting locations being rare and accommodation being cheap. We only managed a full night's camp twice and this wasn't the first time we had been intercepted by the police in the attempt.

Earlier on in the trip, leaving Beni Ahmed with water picked up from a restaurant and a good supply of food, we set out hoping to find a secluded olive grove where we could hide ourselves. The supplies came in handy but not in the way we imagined. We hadn't even left the town when a police car intercepted us and escorted us back to the *gendarmerie*. There we were emphatically told that we should not be wandering around after dark; not that we ever do if we can help it. They would take us to a town hotel with panoramic views. The town was thoroughly grim but the weather was grim too, so a hotel didn't sound like such a bad idea. It looked smart enough on the outside with fresh white paint on the walls and bright blue newly painted doors and windows. Yes, once we had pulled the broken shutters from the window of our room, there was a view which could be called panoramic; half-built apartment blocks and tumble down houses strewn over the opposite hillside.

However, that was almost where the good news ended. We couldn't leave the room as there was no key for the door so we put our provisions to good use and cooked on a rickety table in the corner. The floor looked like it had never been cleaned and the luridly bright paint was flaking off the walls and ceiling, showering our bed with pink snow. The bedding wasn't to be considered so we used our sleeping bags. There was no shower and a squat loo with no flush housed in a room used to store cleaning materials. Luckily there was a bucket in there which we filled from a tap on a basin down the corridor and used in lieu of a flush. We took the bucket to our room in case we needed a pee in the night. It cost us 60 Dirham (£4:80) which was about all it was worth to be honest. To be fair the wifi was good and the young men working there were charming.

This wasn't our first encounter with the police on this trip. We had left our bikes and kit at our son's house in Lagnes, Provence, at the end of our previous tour and so that is where this tour began. We cycled through the glorious limestone crags of the diminutive Les Alpilles, truly an alpine landscape in miniature, and then across the flamingo speckled lagoons of the Camargue which sits between the arms of the Rhone delta and on to the historic city of Montpellier. Hugh had a problem with his camera lens and we were heading for a camera shop on the far side of the Place de la Comedie, when we encountered a situation which was far from funny. The square, one of the largest pedestrian areas in Europe, was smothered in smoke – tear gas perhaps. The sound of drum beats and loud cracks filled the air. Our way was blocked by a frighteningly, animated scene of battle between protestors, the infamous *gilet jaunes*, and the police. The 'yellow vest' movement, initially a populist movement resulting from clashes with the Macron government over raising fuel prices and tax reforms, had spread throughout the country often developing into violent riots.

Trying to find our way round the mayhem via the back streets, we found our way blocked by a line of police equipped with full riot gear; truncheons, metal shields, helmets with visors, gas masks, thick shoulder pads and strong, protective legwear from the ankle to above the knees. Despite their intimidating appearance we found them very helpful. They told us the shops would be closed but also gave us instructions on how to get around the battlefield. The city streets were crowded with *gilet jaunes*, police, ordinary folk just going about their business and street medics offering first aid should you find yourself at the wrong end of a nasty incident. We found our way to the camera shop just as it was closing and Hugh came out with a second hand lens bought at a good price.

The next day all was calm and we were able to enjoy the city's beautiful nineteenth century architecture, entertaining street musicians, excellent coffee shops and astonishing artworks in the Musée Fabre. The Place de la Comedie was host to yet another protest; this time Algerians wanting to oust their president who was old, sick and apparently not much use. There seemed to be a lot of dissatisfaction with leaders. The demonstrations of the previous day had left their mark in the form of cash machines either boarded up or sprayed with a cacophony of multi-coloured paint.

Before setting out from France we had been at home for around four and a half months, which felt like a long time. We had settled into a lifestyle which drew us away from home for much of the year, either on cycling trips or spending time with family in Provence where our eldest son lives and our daughter has a holiday home next door. This was causing difficulties with insurance. One of the first questions asked is, 'are you a resident of the UK?' The obvious answer is, 'yes, of course. We own a house in the UK and no other, we have worked here all our working lives and we pay tax here.' However, the definition of a UK resident requires that you have actually resided in the UK for six of the previous twelve months. For us this was beginning to become an obstacle. We were planning to go away again later in the year so we would have to make sure that we were at home long enough between trips to be legal residents of the UK. The other option is just to say 'yes' and assume that no one will check up on you.

When we set out for Central Asia we had only lived in the UK for four of the previous twelve months. In addition some companies didn't cover 'transcontinental' travel. On our first trip in South America we found that many insurance companies won't cover you if you go over 3000m of altitude and on that trip we went up to 4,800m. The length of our trips was a perennial problem as many companies only cover up to 60/90/100 days. We gave up on insuring the bikes as the cost was ridiculous. We invested in sturdy locks instead. Now we had two more problems to deal with. Hugh had turned 66, the magic age at which it is presumed that long trips are more risky so getting long term insurance is even harder. In addition his bout of cancer upped the price considerably unless you could find a company that would exclude existing conditions. So two very fit cyclists, with no claims for health issues to their name were on the verge of becoming uninsurable as stateless nomads of a certain age and it wasn't going to get any easier. For this trip we found that we slipped through all the hoops with Insure and Go. The whole process of contacting company after company only to find a barrier across the pathway is extremely frustrating. Some long term cyclists will travel without insurance but we felt that the possibility of incurring hefty medical fees in the event of a bad accident was too much of a risk although when we left for Central Asia we were close to taking that risk. Little did we realise how much more of a problem this was going to become in the near future.

Melilla was supposed to be at the start of our ride across Morocco, not at the end. Our ride across France from our starting point in Lagnes took us to the French Mediterranean Port of Sète. We had booked a boat to Nador (the Moroccan port next to Melilla), with the intention of riding to Tangier, over 400km to the west. Approaching Sète, Hugh received a text message telling us that our boat had been cancelled. Right away we found ourselves turning round alternative plans in our heads.

On arrival at the port, Hugh vanished into the mayhem of the booking hall; no orderly queueing at the ticket booth, just people pushing and shoving in a desperate attempt to get to the front. Police tried to calm the atmosphere but it was undeniably tense. Hugh shuffled around amongst hundreds of would be passengers, having to do a bit of shoving himself and eventually managed to get to the ticket office where he was able to do an exchange, for tickets to Tangier. He got verbal abuse for queue jumping when he eventually edged his way out of the crowds. The boat was cancelled because ferociously windy weather had made docking at Nador too dangerous.

There are great advantages of having loose plans with no bookings except the necessary, done at the last minute. Our plan had been to take the boat to Nador and ride west through the Rif Mountains which stretch along the north of Morocco, to Tangier. We would then take a boat to Gibraltar returning to southern France via Spain. That was it, and the only booking was for the first boat; serendipity intervened. In getting the boat to Tangier, we got across the Mediterranean and we could just reverse the direction of our trip through the Rif. The visit to Gibraltar was replaced by a view from the ferry and the route through Spain began further east along the coast.

However, our boat didn't land in Tangier; it landed over 50km away at Tangier Med. Strong easterly winds were churning up the sea and it took forever for the boat to ease its way into the harbour and dock. Light was fading by the time we rode down the gangway with the strong wind whipping up spray all around us. We were held up further because we hadn't filled in the right paperwork before leaving the boat and we had a hard time finding out what we had to do and where to go to get it done. Most of the passengers on the boat were Moroccans on their way to visit family who wouldn't be troubled by this bureaucracy, so we were soon the only people hanging around the dock.

It was pitch black as we headed out of the port looking for somewhere to get Dirhams (Moroccan money). We found an ATM and a guy at the exchange office there posed a question we are commonly asked on our travels; 'how old are you'? When I said 65, he said to me, 'I am 38 and I can't even ride one kilometre on a bike.'

The imperative was to find somewhere to stay so we headed for Ksar es Seghir, seven kilometres along the road to Tangier. There we were lucky to find the Le Petit Poisson, a cute little hotel where we had a room with a balcony looking out over the Mediterranean, a view which we appreciated at breakfast the following morning. We were just in time to catch fish in the little eatery over the road. It came with lots of tomatoes, raw onions, olive oil, homemade bread and the ubiquitous mint tea. We had made it to Morocco and were now to head east to Melilla and the port of Nador.

In the event we ditched Tangier too, opting instead to take what we hoped would be the less travelled route to Tétouan. This is how our blog recorded the first day:

Day 8: Ksar es Seghir to Tétouan

> Our first day's riding in Morocco was short but tough, battling with a wind of near Patagonian proportions; the same wind which re-routed our boat to Tangier and propelled us speedily to our hotel last night. As the road curved and the contours of the landscape changed, the wind would calm down a little and then hit us unexpectedly with its full force. It was a constant struggle to keep going and I had to stop twice. Fortunately it wasn't pushing us into the traffic. We learnt later that two ferries across the Strait of Gibraltar had been cancelled.
>
> We left the coast on a smallish road ducking under the flyovers of bigger roads and a train line. It climbed over a little pass and took us to the town of Khemiss Anjra, which was the highlight of the day. It was market day, the place was buzzing and the women wearing their beautiful traditional dress. The on-going route was less interesting, a little busier and the wind even stronger. For the last few kilometres we joined a bigger road and a view of Tétouan spread before us, all white, tumbling down the hillside.
>
> We found a quaint room at Riad Blanco, a little haven of peace hidden down an alley in the medina. We were told that there was nowhere to put our bikes in the Riad, but we could take them to a car park down the road where we were assured they would be safe. I had reservations when we met the rather vacant 'guardien', but we locked them up at the back of the parking area and hoped it would be fine – I can't say I was comfortable with it!
>
> We shared our dinner table with an interesting Canadian couple, Phil and Susan, travelling with their twelve-year-old son Heaton who they home school. They currently live in London, Ontario, but are looking for a home in Europe – possibly Spain, with a more temperate climate than Canada and a lower cost of living.
>
> We are finding the Moroccan people extremely friendly. They often wave as we ride past and say bonjour, hello or hola. We passed one guy who called out, 'hola, mucho frio'. I suppose cold is relative – the temperature is in the mid-teens. At least the medina is protected from the wind chill. There were even a few drops of rain today.

Khemiss Anjra, was one of those fascinating in-between places. The women were shopping and socialising at the busy market. They wore bright, stripy ankle length wraps in shades of red, white and black tucked into thick cloth belts around their waists. A group stood, peering into the hardware store, heads bunched close together. A range of mountainous wide brimmed hats, decorated with bobbles and sausages of thick wool, stood atop their delicately fringed white shawls which were wrapped around their heads under their hats, to keep their hair tidily out of sight. We never saw people dressed quite like this again in Morocco!

Tétouan is on the tourist radar although not in a big way. It is home to one of the smallest Moroccan medinas, but with the distinction of being one of the most complete and untouched by outside influences. A maze of narrow cobbled alleys thread their way under painted arches which link the high walls on either side. However, it was the chance meeting with Phil, Susan and Heaton which took us to one of the most fascinating places in the town.

They invited us to join them on a visit to the, the École de Métiers, a school where traditional arts dating from the fourteenth century are taught to school drop-outs (well mostly). A group of university students of architecture were there on a four day course to familiarise themselves with the ancient arts of the region; most of them women. One of them told me that out of 67 students in her class, 50 were women. On the other hand the school drop-outs are mainly boys.

The present town of Tétouan was established in 1484, by Muslims fleeing the re-conquest of Andalucía by Christians. Hence, the art traditions reflect a mix of Andalucian and Islamic cultures that is very special. The students create elaborate and stunningly beautiful artefacts from wood, plaster, ceramics, metal and cloth. Their starting point is an intricate and very precise drawing produced using the basic geometric tools of a sharp pencil, ruler, compasses and set square to design the pattern to be used. Using fine jigsaws and delicate chisels the patterns come to life in the form of table tops with inlay patterns made from shells, cabinets of delicately carved wood and iron vases covered with etched interlocking patterns. Even the hammer used to tap the inlay into the wood had a charmingly simple design etched in fine white lines on the handle. The embroidery, definitely regarded as a woman's skill, is particularly special, as a time consuming method of multiple stitching is used to fill in the shapes of the floral patterns producing bold, colourful and instantly striking designs.

Some of the masters who qualify from this school will go on to work on restoration projects in buildings such as the Alhambra in Granada, or produce works for the mosques of Morocco. Others will sell their wares in the markets or work for private clients. The school is funded by the state and students attend free of charge.

Before we left the next day, Sue and Phil invited us to stay with them in La Herradura, where they were going to rent a flat for several weeks. This was to determine our landing point in Spain; Motril being a port linked by ferry with Nador, is just a little way east of La Herradura along the coast. It is one of the joys of chance meetings on our trips; the way it often determines the flow of the journey. The journey is always flexible letting the wind take us where it will. Also those we meet add to our understanding of people and the world around us. Sue and Phil's son Heaton had 'problems' if you should call them that, in that he didn't readily fit into the world we live in and had difficulties at his school, despite being a highly intelligent young man. We had great admiration for the way in which Sue and Phil reacted to his sometimes unconventional behaviour. They were in the process of trying to find a place which would suit them all much better than their homeland in Canada, and they thought that somewhere in southern Spain may be the answer; hence the experimental stay in La Herradura.

From Tétouan, an uninspiring ride along the edge of the coastal mountains landed us in Oued Laou, an unattractive seaside resort undergoing an inexplicable building bonanza. The dull and damp weather muted the views of what would have been a beautiful, bright blue sea had the sun been shining. We realised that we would have to stay there but there didn't seem to be any open accommodation; it wasn't the resort season. Hisham, who saw us thinking about it on the street, came to our rescue and found us an entire flat owned by his friend Khalid, for 300 Dirham (around £24). The shower was hot and we had a kitchen for cooking our own dinner which was fortunate as there didn't appear to be any places to eat either. We bought food at the excellent market.

The next two days, heading for Chefchaouen, took us through spectacular scenery in the heart of the Rif Mountains. A well surfaced, quiet road threaded its way alongside dramatic gorges and terraced hillsides, with precipitous craggy mountains towering above us. This was riding at its best.

Chefchaouen, 'oh so blue', is without doubt a mega-tourist hotspot. It is a place where the camera doesn't stay in the pocket for long, as one alluring photogenic sight follows another; walls and stairways coated in a soothing pale blue wash, which is often echoed in the interior décor too. Bright turquoise doors with pitch black studs and decorative knockers are surrounded by exquisitely constructed porches with stylish arches painted in blue and white, sometimes topped with terracotta tiles. There are several possible reasons for all this blue, but it certainly attracts tourists from all over the world. We loved our three night stay there. Touristy sites usually attract tourists for a good reason; there are interesting things to see there and they are often places with charm.

Charm wasn't very evident in many of the places we would pass through later; indeed on the very night after we left we wound up in Beni Ahmed, the absolute antithesis of Chefchaouen. However, the hotspots often give little idea of how most people in the country live and travelling swiftly between them can give a very selective impression of a country. Superb traditional dishes are on offer but that isn't necessarily what you will find in the ordinary towns. The people catering for visitors are used to interacting with foreigners which is useful in that their command of English can make communication possible. People out in the sticks may react differently to strangers. Our slow pace of travel sometimes lands us in places we'd rather not be but always look back on it as an experience and we learn from it.

In Chefchaouen we met a Kazakh; he made his money through bitcoins and spoke English with a German accent. We saw Chinese tourists posing on an iconic blue stone staircase and there were several Chinese restaurants to cater

Buying fresh bread near Akchour

to their tastes. And, on our last night we ate at Bab Sour, where we were served *mrouzia*, an authentic Moroccan meat dish. It is sweet as it is cooked with honey. This one was made with beef and some small white beans. It was delicious, and generously complementary, the owner being the sister of Mohamed, a Moroccan who runs a tourist business in Marrakech. We had got to know him as he was once married to a friend of ours who lives in our home town.

We left in heavy rain taking with us a huge collection of enchanting photographs, heading through the mountains to the parts less travelled. In Dardara we had spotted a promising backroad on our map, which bypassed a stretch of the busy N2 highway. Just before the turnoff at the roundabout, a friendly policeman offered to help us with directions. As is so often the case he didn't know that we were looking to take a tiny dirt road which we expected to be both scenic and quiet, rather than the obvious way the car goes. As we left the roundabout at the 'wrong' exit he called out to us, pointing vigorously up the main road which we were avoiding! As is so often the case, our little route gave us twenty kilometres of delightful riding with many friendly locals calling out *hola* and giving us the thumbs up. Our journey is every bit as much about how we get there as opposed to the destination. Although the quiet dirt tracks may be steep and rough, we invariably enjoy them and this is often where the camera comes out the most. This was the day we ended up in the 'worst hotel in the world' in Beni Ahmed; not our intended destination at all although the getting there was delightful.

We didn't sleep well in our hotel. Dogs barked for much of the night and something was banging in the draughty building. The music downstairs went on for longer than we'd hoped. At least we were comfortable in our sleeping bags and the mattress wasn't too bad. The other good news was that even though the squat loo had no flush, it didn't smell, but there was no place to wash our hands.

As we left the town in miserable weather, we were amused by a bath propped up by the exit; so that is where the bathroom was. The Rif Mountains were proving to be wetter and cooler than we expected. We were using our full collection of waterproof gear and gloves. We heard our first cuckoo calls of the year but more important than that – we heard from our elder Scottish granddaughter, Ailsa, that 'Mummy's got a baby in her tummy'. Great news from afar. It was a pretty landscape. The mountain slopes and flat river valleys were cultivated; we saw green shoots of wheat, ripe oats and lots of broad beans. The road surfaces were very rough but it was easy to dodge the holes, grit and puddles on two wheels. We sat down by the roadside for a snack and to our astonishment a family appeared out of nowhere carrying a tray of

An enchanting alley in Chefchaouen, Morocco.

refreshments for us; fresh bread, olives, olive oil and tea on a little metal tray. They told us that they lived in Rabat but spend holidays up in the hills. They were staying in a house a little way off the road behind us. Such kindness to complete strangers is heart-warming and always memorable.

Our route took us to the shores of the reservoir, Barrage de Al Wahda, constructed for flood control, irrigation, water supply and hydroelectric power. It has been described as the second most important dam in Africa, after the Aswan Dam. It was raining hard when we hit the high point above the lake and so it was tempting to stop when we spotted the little coffee bar. In this part of Morocco coffee is every bit as popular as tea. The young man serving us was using a hand lever operated machine common in these parts and the coffee was good. As we sheltered from the rain he was very happy to talk. He told us how it was his dream to go to England; he viewed it as the 'Promised Land'. He refused to take any payment for our drinks and offered us a place to stay if we needed it but we decided to move on.

By the time we reached Ourtzagh we were cold, having been lazy about putting on more clothes. It's always tempting to move on and hope you'll warm up on the next hill. Ideas of camping by the lake had been kicked into touch so we asked about places to stay at a café in town. The result; we spent the night in the bedroom of Mohamed's children. His family were away in their rural gite way up the mountainside and he was happy to put us up at his home in the town and give us a tasty chicken tagine for dinner.

The riding continued to be delightful, the weather continued to be fickle and cool. I had brought thin, loose trousers with me for riding in thinking that my bare legs and lycra clad behind might not go down too well in this predominantly Muslim country and I had worried that I may find them too hot. That certainly wasn't the case!

Finding a route through the countryside on farm tracks, we were stopped twice by random events. First it was the sound of whistle playing shepherds herding their flocks of sheep to melodious music. And second it was a beaming farmer clutching the head of a sheep which he was about to blow torch for a feast. Our challenge came at the end of the day when we reached the turnoff to Taounate, the town being strung out along a ridge around four kilometres away and 350m above us. 'You can't climb up there on those bikes' said a young man standing at the bottom of the hill. So off we went, determined to rise to the challenge. It was steep but we did it.

We found a reasonable place to stay in Taounate but there was a major problem; where could we put the bikes? In the very smart hotel where we later stayed in Melilla there was no problem with putting them in our room. In Chefchaouen where the room was rather small, we stored them right by the reception desk, locked up to each other. Sometimes we stored them in a locked garage or in a hotel store cupboard. The hotel manager at Taounate wasn't offering any of these solutions, even though the corridor outside the room was a good place given that there was no one else staying there. He wanted us to put them in the TV shop up the road. Hugh demonstrated how they could be put on top of our tarpaulin laid over the spare bed we didn't need and this didn't go down at all well. It was developing into an unpleasantly heated situation but we needed a solution as there was nowhere else to stay. The two cleaning ladies stepped in with their brilliant negotiating skills. We didn't know what they were saying, but it worked and thankfully our bikes ended up locked together in the corridor.

After a leisurely start in the morning we went to the market to get some provisions as we were hoping to camp in the mountains ahead. The markets were wonderful places to shop as we could buy basics such as rice, couscous, pasta, lentils, dried figs and dates, and *ras el hanout* spice all from large sacks, cutting out the plastic waste. When we cook for ourselves we use fresh vegetables such as onions, garlic, peppers and carrots. However, this Sunday morning the market was deserted. A helpful guide came to our rescue. He told us he lived in Montpellier and also said that on Sunday the stall keepers prefer to stay in bed rather than get up and work. Who can blame them? He showed us the way to little shops where we could buy most of what we needed and by that time the market was livening up. It was a damp place with a muddy floor and we had to dodge the puddles in our sandals.

The next two days took us higher, up to 1,200m, through the most interesting landscape yet of the high Rif. Bright red poppies dotted the fields along with many other varieties of spring flowers and olive groves covered the lower slopes. Grain from the fields was stored in little stacks covered with nets weighed down with stones. Women were busy picking prickly, fern shaped leaves from the roadside and stripping the leaves from the stalks which they said were good with meat.

We heard calls of 'you want hashish?' We saw some stray plants growing on the edge of a field but that was all; the fields must be well hidden. Kif, a mixture of tobacco and chopped pieces of marijuana has been widely smoked by Moroccan men since the Spanish conquerors encouraged it to keep the peace. The Rif Mountains have been the focus of its production; Kif in the Rif. Chefchaouen is considered to be a haven by Kif seeking backpackers. It is strictly illegal to produce it, sell it or consume it but all this still goes on at some scale. Morocco is the world's biggest exporter of cannabis resin. Locals and travellers alike commonly consume it.

At the end of the day we were delighted to find a secluded little niche out of sight of the road with a clear stream running nearby and a striking view of a sharp, little rocky ridge. A shepherd appeared briefly but he wasn't interested in us. It was our first camp in Morocco and we were so happy there. Our spot was just short of the village of Thar-Es-Souk where we went looking for breakfast in the morning. We were getting into the habit of having a second breakfast or elevenses. Even in the small villages we would usually find a café serving erratically scrambled eggs, crusty flat rounds of bread, delectable olive oil, olives, sometimes a little fromage frais and tea accompanied by monster lumps of sugar. In Thar-Es-Souk we were guided by the hand to the best place – literally. Our helper took Hugh's hand and led us to his favourite café.

Leaving Thar-Es-Souk we followed a van up the hill which had a posy of large plastic bottles on the roof, hopefully for recycling. We were seeing so much plastic rubbish in the towns and by the roadside. Indeed it is a major problem throughout much of the world.

The next night we found a neat little spot in a tent sized clearing in a pine forest not far about the village of Boured. On the way up the hill we bought oranges at the roadside. We love this kind of shopping where we can buy some local produce just when we need it and provide a little income for local people, but in this case they wouldn't take any payment. Further on a couple of guys on a motor bike caught us up and handed us a photograph – a photograph of us! They had taken it as we passed through the village, gone away and printed it and then brought it to us as a gift. Once again we thought we had found a place where no one would find us but a young man went running by. He stopped briefly to chat with us, empathising with our desire for the peace of the forest.

We talked to people in English, reasonable French or partial Spanish. Whilst many Moroccans, particularly the older people, speak French as a result of the French colonial legacy, in the north, so close to Spain, we found many used Spanish. We knew only the odd word of Berber or Arabic. Fortunately, many of the road signs were in Latin script as well as Arabic.

The two consecutive camps and the mountain riding in between were the highlight of the trip. The next day we reached a pass at 1,450m where people had set out huge sacks of walnuts, almonds and mountain herbs. The RN29, a major but deserted road, blasted Chinese style through the mountains, took us swiftly down to the depressing town of Kassita. It looked like a grim and charmless place to live, particularly compared with the villages higher up. Unfinished concrete apartment blocks lined either side of the wide, dirty road and litter was scattered everywhere. The policemen controlling dodgy dealers on the road, stopped us, and were charming. They asked what we were doing and wished us well with smiles. They told us that there were plenty of motels in the next town, Midar, which sounded hopeful – a choice even. We were hoping for a hot shower and the chance to upload the journal. As we munched sandwiches in a litter strewn olive grove on the edge of town we debated how and why places get into such a mess. Why don't the people do something to sort out their immediate environment? Do they care? Do they notice? Are they just without the means to deal with it?

We headed off at good speed with the wind behind us. It was an effortless and unexpectedly pretty ride on what we expected to be a busy road. We noticed that there was less Latin script used on the road signs and a new script had appeared which we later found out is the script used by the Berbers. Neo-Tifinagh is a slightly modified version of the ancient Tifinagh script and it was re-introduced in the twentieth century. The Berbers are an ethnic group in Morocco considered to be the original inhabitants of the region; a pre-Arab culture with its own cultural heritage and traditions. They commonly live in remote mountainous areas such as the Rif.

The police had given us the impression that the town of Midar was a place catering for travellers with lots of accommodation and places to eat. Nothing could have been further from the truth. Helpful locals directed us to a hotel, the only indication of its purpose being the sign in Arabic which we couldn't read. The hotel check in procedure was ridiculous, reminding us of Indian bureaucracy of over forty years ago. Passports were photographed, two sets of forms each were filled in, and when Hugh made a slight error writing Huddersfield instead of Ajdir on one form it had to be scrapped and rewritten. Later in the evening a policeman arrived and my passport had to be produced again. Looking around for somewhere to eat we found that all the traditional tagine haunts were shut although there were plenty of cafés where men drank tea and coffee whilst watching football on the television – Spurs v Man City! With lots of local direction we found a pizza restaurant.

Our crossing of the Rif was nearly over. A dusty ride through bare, low hill country took us to the foot of Mont Gourougou where our final attempt to camp in Morocco was upended by the police. We would have liked to use our tent much more but we didn't encounter suitable locations. The route through the Rif in reverse to our original plan had worked well; in fact we reckoned that it was probably better than going east to west. After Chefchaouen we didn't meet any other travellers; no cycle tourists, just one or two Spanish and French campervans passing by. We had heard tales of cyclists having stones thrown at them and being pestered to buy hashish, but none of this happened to us. We didn't get any abuse and we were only offered hashish once. The people were invariably charming, helpful, respectful and welcoming. They would take trouble to make sure you could find what you needed; food, accommodation, the correct route, etc. We had no worries about going off the beaten track.

We loved the mountain scenery but some of the grubby, dreary towns got us down and the litter was shocking – amongst the worst we have seen anywhere, rivalling Mexico and Cambodia. In places people seem to be living in a garbage heap of mainly plastic bottles and bags. We try not to use water out of plastic bottles and this was surprisingly easy. We got water in cafés and occasionally people's homes. We didn't get ill. There seems to be much work going on with the water supply in Morocco. Water was only a problem in Melilla.

EXTRAORDINARY PLACES BY BICYCLE

Hugh bought our tickets for the boat to Motril in Nador. Our police escort waited for ten minutes outside the ticket office before driving off having presumably decided that we had reached safety and were securing a safe onward journey. We then made our way to the frontier with one of two flecks of Spain perched on the Moroccan coast. Melilla, an autonomous city of Spain is home to nearly 85,000 people made up of Iberian Catholics, Riffian Berbers, Sephardic Jews and Sindhi Hindus. Around 36,000 Moroccans cross the border daily to work, shop or trade goods. It is surrounded by a triple fence up to six metres high, including a thick tangle of looped barbed wire plus a 200m no go zone, all designed to keep out large groups of sub-Saharan Africans trying to get through this back door into Europe. Ceuta is another city of the same status, located close to Tangier.

The border fence between Africa and Europe, Melilla.

How can the Spanish object to Gibraltar? Morocco has requested sovereignty of both from Spain along with Perejil Island, and some other small territories. Spain does not consider them to be colonies as they maintain that the territories have been part of the Spanish state since the fifteenth century; for even longer than the cities of Pamplona and Tudela. It took us around fifteen minutes to get through the heavily guarded barricades, something which must be tedious for those living on the other side who work there every day.

I was very curious about how the territory paid its way. The principal industry is fishing and the territory receives Spanish and European grants. There is much cross-border commerce, both legal and smuggled. All fruit and vegetables are imported from Morocco as there is nowhere to grow anything inside the city. Alex, a young English girl working as a teacher of English there, told us that the city is an important military base. Also Spanish people live there because of the tax advantages. However, from our viewpoint, it seemed to be a very confined environment in which to live. Crossing the border is time consuming and there is only one crossing point. It feels a bit like a prison in reverse with huge fortifications keeping others out rather than people in. Nowhere exciting to go for a long run and to go for a decent bike ride you would have to cross the frontier – and many do. We had seen many groups of cyclists on the climb out of Nador as we descended.

There is a lot of traffic in the town and little pedestrianisation which seems odd for such a small territory. No one can drive far without leaving the country – wouldn't it be wonderful if they could create a car free city? There are a few parks, beaches and promenades for recreation, but it didn't amount to much for such a large population.

With so many people living in such a small space, there is obviously a water problem. As soon as I had a drink of the tap water I noticed that it had an odd taste, as if it was desalinated water, and it is. We learnt that the Cadagua water plant, installed around fifteen years ago, supplies 60% of the water for the city – the rest probably coming from Morocco in exchange for electricity. Ongoing projects are expanding this capacity. All the way through Morocco we had drunk the tap water and had been assured that it was good – it tasted good too, on the whole. However, in Melilla it appeared that no one drank the tap water but the reasons for this were unclear. Restaurants did not serve it. It hurt to think of all the plastic bottles going to waste every day as a result of people exclusively drinking bottled water. So what did we do? Drink beer? Well yes, but we did drink some of the tap water, we made tea from it, and in the restaurants we reluctantly took some water in glass bottles. Alex told us of a fountain in the Parque Hernández, where people who can't afford to buy water filled their bottles, but we didn't find it.

Having said all of that, I must add that it is a beautiful city and it was particularly striking after travelling through many scruffy little Moroccan towns. We treated ourselves to a large room in a posh hotel atop a hill with wonderful views from the balcony and we indulged in top class Spanish cuisine at La Traviata; well worth waiting for it to open at 9pm as is the Spanish custom.

The city was one of Francisco Franco's staging grounds for his nationalist rebellion of 1936, which started the Spanish civil war, and the only remaining statue of him in Spain stands below the walls of the citadel. There is a cute little cove below the citadel which gives access via the beach to the city. We wondered if illegal migrants could exploit this weakness. Further up the coast there is heavy fencing along the shoreline. Also we could see that Nador uses virtually the same port, with boats coming in via the same entrance but to opposite sides of the harbour.

It took us over 30 minutes to get back into Morocco and the port of Nador, even though we skipped the whole traffic queue by just riding past all the cars. The little sortie into Spanish Melilla had necessitated two extra Moroccan stamps in the passport and the filling in of the same information on two more each of the obligatory *fiches blanches* (white cards to be completed at each crossing). Every entry and exit requires these formalities, which means waiting in queues, all the time being somewhat unsure of exactly what is required. It was only when we reached the port and tried to board the boat, that we discovered we needed the third stamp and white card for exiting Morocco yet again. To their credit the officials were all charming and did their best to help although they were hopelessly slow at entering the information into the computer and producing the essential stamps.

The six hour boat crossing passed quickly. Before we knew it the Spanish coastline was so close, the coast road lined with apartment blocks and hillsides strewn with poly-tunnels. Soon we would meet and stay with Sue, Phil and Heaton who we met back in Tétouan. For a day we shared their experimental new lifestyle in a rented flat overlooking the sea at La Herradura.

From the moment we left the Spanish coast at Motril, south of Granada, we were in for a real treat. We were surprised by how green the land was and how much forest we passed through. The birdsong was constantly entertaining. We often saw large birds of prey high in the sky; vultures, eagles and kites. Our daily distances were quite short, but we regularly climbed over 1000m in a day. There was only one day that could be considered flat.

We deliberately went through all the sierras we could find in the vague direction we wanted to go, taking us in a line between 20 and 150km inland from the Mediterranean coast. Picturesque limestone crags and peaks rose out of swelling seas of olives in the valleys below – Sierra de Cazorla, Sierra de Alcaraz, Sierra de Cuenca, Sierra de Albarracín, Sierra de Montsant and more. Each sierra came with an historic hill town often of the same name, where we often stayed for a night or two – perhaps not as flush with artworks as those in Italy, but charming all the same and not quite so demanding. In between, almost deserted roads took us through breath-taking scenery and we found plenty of unfenced wild or semi-wild land ideal for camping. We usually found water from fountains nearby.

We had visited many of the better known historic cities of Spain before on trips in a VW campervan with our kids, so we skipped Granada and went to Jaén – interesting for its huge cathedral and hill top fort. It is said to be the 'olive capital of the world'. The province is covered by more than 60 million olive trees. That was not hard to believe – around Jaén we spent days riding through virtually nothing but olive groves which eventually became monotonous – 25% of Spanish and 42% of Andalucian soil is covered with olive trees. The extra virgin olive oil they produce is delicious but we worried about the impact of mono-culture over such a huge area. Herbicides are used to remove the undergrowth leaving bare earth beneath the trees – the result – four truckloads of soil are lost for every 100 olive trees.

The only other sizeable place we stayed in was Lleida, another city we had never heard of before and one of the oldest towns in Catalunya. The ancient cathedral along with its cloisters is quite astonishing. Like so many others in Spain, it was probably built over the remains of a mosque between the end of the twelfth century and the fifteenth century.

Five weeks of travelling along the backroads and tracks of Castilla-La Mancha, Aragon, Valenciana and Catalunya , took us to the Puerto de la Bonaigua, a 2,072m pass over the Pyrenees. It is a wild and beautiful ascent. The top is an extensive ski area and once down the initial zig-zags on the other side, we found ourselves passing through an area where the wealthy of Barcelona take their winter skiing holidays and escape from the heat in the summer. So much accommodation, nearly all with shutters closed in late May. The first place, Baqueira, is a huge resort – a jungle of apartments – attractively built for sure, in stone and slate, but just all too much. How much of the time are these places occupied? It does come across as pretty extravagant.

Following on from Morocco, Spain seemed very clean and tidy, particularly the towns and villages which were a welcome change from the dishevelled Moroccan towns. We did miss being able to stop mid-morning for a plate of eggs, olive oil and bread. We found the Spanish drivers second to none in their consideration for cyclists, giving us plenty of room when they overtook, often driving on the far left. Trucks, vans and cars would always wait patiently before passing. Once we crossed the border into France there was a noticeable difference in driver behaviour.

We have ridden a lot in France. We took many new routes, we revisited old favourites – returning to places we had been to with our children many years ago – and we visited old friends. Suzanne and Steve had given us excellent advice on the best, low traffic way to cross the Pyrenees in order to reach their home in Gouillou, near Aspet. We had first met them in Cienfuegos, Cuba, on our 2014/15 tour. They have discovered a real gem of a place to live in, surrounded by lush forest and magnificent mountains, with so many lovely cycling and walking routes on their doorstep. Like us, they love the outdoor life. Steve is kept very busy with his huge fruit and vegetable plot, so most of the meals at their place come straight from the garden. Although we have only met them a handful of times, they are amongst our most treasured friends. We had entertained thoughts of going the same way, going for the good life in France – we like La Drôme. However, our hard times during 2014 had brought home to us how much we valued friends in our home town of Sedbergh – friends built up over so many years.

In Vallon-Pont-d'Arc in the adorable Ardèche we went in search of old friends who we hoped still lived there – but we were not sure. Richard Crane has some incredulous exploits to his name such as Running the Himalayas and a Journey to the Centre of the Earth. When Hugh did his Mountains of Britain

Run it was the serendipity of Richard answering a phone call that led to our partnership with Practical Action (then called Intermediate Technology) which enabled us to raise quite a bit of money (£30,000) for the charity which teaches people in developing countries. 'Give a man a fish and you feed him for a day, teach him how to catch a fish and you feed him for a lifetime'. His wife Michèle runs a business making high quality films on the history of the region which are displayed in museums and other tourist locations. Their house looked deserted, but with the help of one of their neighbours we found their new home just down the road. It was wonderful to find them both living now in a house that Richard built. We had a lovely evening with them and for the first time learned how to eat artichokes. Our time together was short so we hoped very much to see them again before too long. It brings me great sadness to think of them now as in the summer of 2020 Richard died following a fall from his bike. So cruel that after all his risky exploits he should go this way, close to his home on a seemingly harmless local ride.

Just a short distance from our end point back at our son's house in Lagnes we stayed in a campsite in Pernes-les-Fontaines with our daughter Amy, her husband Steve and their son Oliver. What better way to spend the last night of the trip? A steep twist in the tourist road from Fontaine de Vaucluse to Lagnes is always a test, even on a skinny bike. After the Rif and the Sierras of Spain we got up it on our fully loaded Roughstuffs – just a little bit gassed. The Tour de France passed this way in 2021. Once again we left our Roughstuffs in Lagnes, awaiting the next trip – location as yet undecided, but certainly keen to spend more time in the wonderfully varied countries on our doorstep.

10
CARLOS' COLOMBIA BEFORE COVID

It is usually the roughest road that leads to the heights of greatness.
Ziad K. Abdelnour

Pauline:

The policeman said, '*No recomiendo esa ruta*' (I don't recommend that route). It was difficult to work out what his reasons were. We couldn't understand much of what he was saying and his phone translations were just turning out nonsense. Hugh picked up the word *guerrillero* in there somewhere. We were told that there were no people, no *pueblos*, and no traffic. Just the sort of route we love. The policeman drew a rough map of what he saw as a good alternative, involving two extra days of riding, reversing our previous day's route and taking a busy motorway. There was a strong incentive to ignore the advice. Surely no people means no 'bad' people.

Hugh had been very reluctant to go to the police, but I told him it was the sensible thing to do. Ever the optimist, Hugh is happy to assume that all will be OK and he didn't trust the police anyway. When we had returned to our lodgings after dinner the proprietor had told us quite firmly that on no account should we take the mountain road to Purificación. We had picked up the word *peligroso* (dangerous) and something about 'bad people' and 'not good for foreigners'. We had been given similar advice at the hotel we had stayed at the previous day and also at the first place we looked at in Cunday. What to do? Most of those directly involved in Colombia's recent violent history are still around and some are still not to be trusted, we were told. When several locals had come out with the same warning, it seemed foolhardy not to seek advice from those responsible for the people's security, the police. We had arrived early at the small town of Cunday in Tolima, planning a restful afternoon in preparation for the next day's ride. We were ready for the challenge of an exciting climb on a rough dirt road, but not the challenge of dealing with hostile combatants lurking in the fields and forests.

It was not the first time we had been warned about the road ahead. Santiago, a charming gentleman, who bought us excellent cappuccinos and giant cheese filled succulent croissants at a charming café in the town of Ciudad Bolívar had dealt us a similar warning of the route to El Carmen de Atrato in Chocó, with a similar roundabout alternative which was just as ridiculous for cyclists. In Charalá on Day 39, many of the locals did their best to discourage us from taking what they saw as an impossible route to cycle; this time it didn't seem to be about dangerous inhabitants. They just couldn't understand why we would want to take a dirt road, strewn with fat pebbles and sharp stones making the climb up to 3,600m slow and arduous, particularly when there was an easier alternative.

So, what to do? Local advice shouldn't be dismissed too readily. However there are complications. It isn't always easy to find out exactly what the problem is. What is the danger? The people? The state of the road? Did we look too old to manage such a tough route without having heart failure? Was the road truly impossible? In addition people would often give conflicting advice and some just laughed at the idea of guerrillas lurking.

When we arrived in Cunday, it was day 61 of our tenth trip, ten years after our first big tour through South America. We had found the Colombian people exceptionally hospitable and helpful. They had pushed our bikes up stony mud tracks, given us heaps of fruit, come to our aid when we looked lost inside supermarkets and presented us with cool glasses of fresh fruit juice just when we were running out of steam. Not once had we felt threatened.

It was fortunate for us that Abel was at the police station that day in Cunday. He had a *finca* (farm) up the road we were taking and he frequently went that way on horseback. He laughed at the mention of guerrillas and assured us that we would encounter the usual friendly folk. OK, bad things can happen anywhere but it wouldn't be foolhardy to take the high road to Purificación. He even offered to ride along with us but we wanted to set out earlier than he was able to. He told us that the police have to err on the side of caution. Perhaps the police hadn't even been along the road. Indeed, that may have been the problem for them – as often happens in remote areas (we realised later) the road wasn't patrolled.

As we set out in the morning we were more worried about being stopped by the police than the possibility of hostile people ahead. The proprietor of our little hotel was asking awkward questions about which way we were taking. I pretended not to understand and Hugh just said 'sí' in the appropriate place. I bought freshly baked yucca bread from the bakery across the plaza which opened at 5am. A guy who we met the previous night was waiting there to take our photos. He was so thrilled to meet two crazy guys on bikes heading up the Cunday to Purificación road; no safety concerns from him. We left town avoiding the police station and it was only when we had travelled well out of town that the fear of a police car rushing up in chase left us.

We headed up a picturesque valley, dotted with farms close to the river and heavily forested on the lower slopes of the hills. A couple approached us, both on horseback and towing a third animal heavily laden with hessian sacks. A welcoming smile shone from beneath the man's intricately patterned, wide brimmed, straw hat. His trainers were tucked into metal stirrups neatly engraved with an inverted fleur-de-lis style pattern. Three men on motorbikes passed us just before ploughing through a river and then a woman and child walked by carrying a bundle of giant palm leaves and a bunch of leafy twigs.

CARLOS' COLOMBIA BEFORE COVID

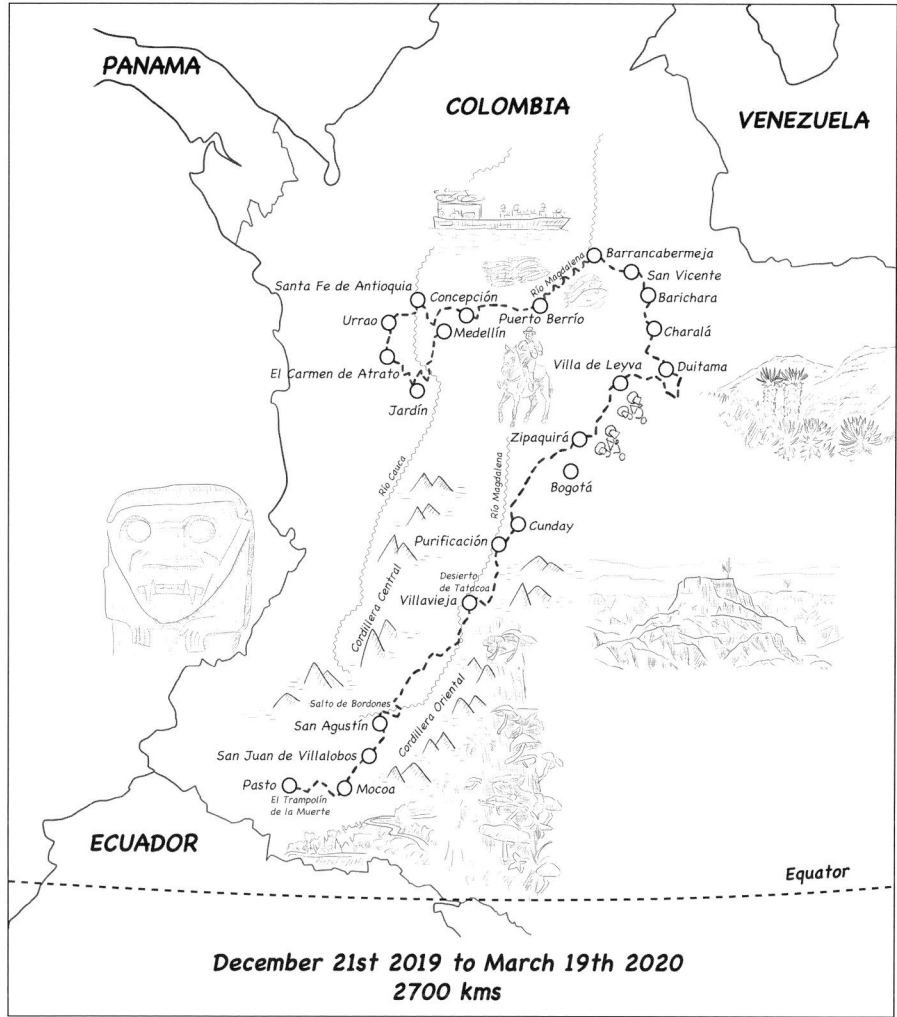

December 21st 2019 to March 19th 2020
2700 kms

People working in the fields by their *fincas* gave us friendly waves. There was no one sinister about, just very friendly country people going about their daily lives in their own little paradise.

We were captivated by the myriad of colourful butterflies flitting from flower to flower by the roadside – the dark Wallace's longwing with fluorescent blue and bright white patches on its elongated wings; the orcus chequered skipper with white and coffee patterned wings covered in fine, fluffy white hairs; the coolie with bright red and white markings on its dark wings; and the Gisella sailor with bright eye spots on the folded tips of its chocolate and white stripy wings.

Higher up where we were running short of water we spotted a lone, large purple orchid along the course of what would be a little waterfall in wetter times, but then the flow was just a dribble. There are more species of orchid in

Colombia than any other country in the world. A young woman walking down the road helpfully told us we could get good water fifteen minutes further up. We had started out on a dry, hard dirt road which later shrank to barely a path pushing through the long grass surrounded by forest and then later on broadening as we climbed, becoming stony and pierced by bedrock. This was no road for four-wheeled vehicles.

With Carlos leaving Medellín.

Close to the top of the climb we looked out on a rough dark sea of heavily forested bumpy ridges to the east and as we crossed through a deep cutting we found ourselves looking down on the Río Magdalena to the west, meandering along a wide, misty, flat valley. Rising in the Andean ranges in the southern department of Huíla and entering the Caribbean Sea at the city of Barranquilla, this great river runs much of the length of the country. On the descent as we passed beneath high cliffs we came to a blockage where huge boulders were strewn across the road having tumbled in the previous days' storms. The road was impassable to motor vehicles; difficult for the police to patrol! It would have been ridiculous to change our route. Our only concern had been the possibility of rain; a few drops fell on us near the high point. Heavy rain can slow down progress enormously when the road turns to sticky mud and also causes dangerous landslides as we had seen.

Fifteen kilometres of pleasant flat riding led us to the bridge over the Río Magdalena, just before Purificación. The last time we had crossed this river was on the boat from Puerto Berrío to Barrancabermeja five weeks earlier and nearly 400km further north as the crow flies or 1050km via Carlos's Colombian bike route.

CARLOS' COLOMBIA BEFORE COVID

We would never have been following this rough, renegade route if it wasn't for Carlos. It was all because of Carlos that contrary to our supposed intentions we had ended up in Chocó, and it was also because of Carlos that we had found ourselves in Charalá being strongly advised to take an easier route. In fact, our whole route, relying heavily on dirt roads, sometimes shrinking to single track and seemingly climbing every mountain in sight, was the creation of Carlos, an adventurous cyclist with an intimate knowledge of and passionate love for his own country.

We had met him ten years previously in San Pedro de Atacama, Chile, just after we had descended from the Altiplano; our journal describes him as 'the crazy Colombian cyclist!' When we left San Pedro, heading up onto the Altiplano once more we crossed paths several times. As we made our way up to Paso de Sico we teamed up with Carlos, and found him to be invigorating company, perpetually overflowing with the joy of the adventure. There was an instantaneous strong bond between us despite the fact that our Spanish was very limited and his English even more so. However, our stopping and eating routines didn't mesh too well – he seemed to survive all day on a muesli bar when we were regularly stopping for sandwiches and a brew – so we fell in and out of step with him over the next couple of days, finally losing him for good, as we thought at the time, when we stopped to melt snow to provide water for the night's camp. However, there he was again in San Antonio de los Cobres, the wild and high copper mining town on the other side of the pass. Way down south in Cochrane on the Carretera Austral, we found he had left the day before we arrived, but then he miraculously reappeared again in a supermarket in El Calafate, three and half months on from when we had parted ways in San Antonio de los Cobres. Eighteen days later we found ourselves taking the same boat from Punta Arenas near the tip of Chile to Porvenir on the island of Tierra del Fuego which is shared by Chile and Argentina. Carlos spent much of the time on the boat chatting to young Chilean women with whom he effortlessly struck up instant friendships. For the first time we spent a night at camp together which sealed our bond all the more.

Our next parting was a sad one. Carlos had been suffering from an inflamed Achilles tendon which ten days rest in Punta Arenas hadn't put right and he was in great pain whilst riding. We turned off on the road to Camerón in search of penguins whilst he had no choice but to take the easier option of sticking with the main road. In Torres del Paine a cyclist, Neil from Germany, had told us about an unexpected new penguin colony on Bahía Inútil (useless bay). These were not just any old penguins – they were king penguins, second only in size to the emperor penguin and every bit as beautiful. The possibility of finding them seemed even more improbable as we took the road round the bay to Camerón. A police car drove by and we asked them where to find the *pingüinos* – they told us to ask at the next *estancia*.

Then Hugh spotted a couple of cars by the beach, and some people; could they be looking at penguins we asked ourselves? We hopped over the fence and made for the shore, wading a small water channel on the way; and there, in a most unlikely place, proudly prancing on the grey sand, were four king penguins. Further up the beach were about twenty more. A man who had come from Ushuaia to look at them said that no one knew how they got there or where they had come from. At the time the temperature was 20 degrees in the

On the road from Cunday to Purificación

shade so perhaps it wasn't surprising that most of the penguins were going for a dip. A few days later we met a marine biologist at the museum at Estancia Harberton. She said that the king penguins should not be there and that perhaps they had been taken off course following their food. It was not known if they would settle for the long term.

I have now discovered that this colony that we visited in mid-February 2011 has since become the Parque Pingüino Rey as part of a project to protect the penguins along with the wealth of vegetation, other wildlife, and archaeological sites in Bahía Inútil. It was opened in mid-2011 as a managed visitor centre complete with footpaths and viewpoints – all necessary to protect this new habitat for the king penguins from the intrusion of too many visitors. For the first time in 2013, new offspring were born. You must now book a tour to view them from behind a wooden shielding fence and via constructed walkways. The website offers advice on being cautious 'driving' along the rough gravel

Roads impassable to cars are the best – on the way to Purificación, Tolima.

road and to be aware of the often inclement weather conditions. We were so privileged to be able to cycle there and walk amongst the penguins on the beach before the news of their arrival spread far. It remains the only king penguin colony in Latin America.

We were upset that Carlos had missed out on this wonderful experience which was one of the most memorable moments of the trip, all the more so for the serendipitous manner in which we had learnt about it and the unexpected nature of the event. Fortunately this was not our final parting. We met again in Ushuaia at the end of our South American journey. By this time we had heard so much about Carlos' verdant homeland where the people were amongst the most hospitable in the world and we realised that one day we should go there, not least because it would be so wonderful to meet Carlos again.

So, in the summer of 2019, when we were thinking about our next tour, it came to us that this was the time to go to Colombia. We were keen to trim down or cut out flying altogether and we thought that this might well be our last trip involving air travel. The country's violent and turbulent past and its reputation for drugs and danger contrasted sharply with the stories told by every cyclist we had ever met who had travelled there; all painted the same colourful, hospitable picture as Carlos. With the recent peace agreement with FARC and indications that the turbulence was calming down, we realised it would be now or never. We knew it would be a trip needing strength and a generous dose of energy; we were not getting any younger even though we were still feeling strong, so best to go whilst the going was good. Little were we to realise how right we were for more than one reason.

Of course, we asked Carlos for help with planning our trip. He now runs a business, Pedaleando Alma (Pedalling Soul), treating his clients to the

Bahía Inútil, Chile.

wonders of touring in his country and so has personal experience of the best routes. Moreover, he knows exactly what sort of route we like to follow from his time with us in Argentina and Chile and this matches exactly his own style; we share the same love of wild mountain areas and tranquil rural villages. Quite unexpectedly Carlos came up with a complete path through the country, in the form of a GPX file, starting in his home city of Medellín and finishing on the border crossing with Ecuador in Ipiales. From there on we would be left to ourselves. This was completely contrary to our usual approach where planning is generally minimal and we make much of the route up as we go along just bearing in mind a few key points which have caught our eye beforehand. We have never spent months before a tour meticulously planning every step, preferring to go where the wind took us; so how would it be to follow a totally prescribed route given to us by a beloved friend but who, nevertheless, we had only known for a brief and broken up time as we wandered down Chile and Argentina? Never mind, we thought, we can always change the route if we want – if it doesn't suit us.

CARLOS' COLOMBIA BEFORE COVID

It was such a joy to meet Carlos again. Our affection for each other had endured despite the passing of so many years and little in the way of improvement in our language skills. We were hoping to rather belatedly improve the latter with a week of intensive instruction at the excellent Toucan language school in Medellín.

We rented an apartment in Manila, a quiet area away from the dodgy red zones that still exist, although the city is not the den of drugs and violence that it used to be. Neighbouring El Poblado is the hip centre for gringos, where you can get excellent Colombian coffee brewed to perfection and super tasty meals in bars and restaurants often run by foreigners, typically Kiwis and French. Away from our quiet apartment the streets were busy with noisy, smelly traffic but we managed to find winding paths through bits of urban jungle – clumps of bamboo, huge eucalyptus trees and colourful strange flowers – where we could go for early morning runs to keep us fit for the climbs ahead. We got around using the fast, well used metro which runs the length of the city. It integrates with a cable car system which was designed to give easy access from the poor hillside communities to the city centre where many people work – incidentally providing a superb way for tourists to get about and enjoy spectacular views of the densely built-up valley below.

The museum, Casa de la Memoria, was created in 2006, as the plaque says at the entrance, 'to put a closure on old wounds so that out of death new life can blossom'. The area of the city which expresses this most graphically in two senses of the word is in Comuna 13, which a mere twenty years ago was possibly the most dangerous area of the most dangerous city in the world. It is now buzzing with tourists who come to see a plethora of highly symbolic, colourful and expertly formed graffiti. Another ingenious transport system of *escaleras eléctricas* enables easy access up and down the hillside. Afro dancers, musicians and the best in street food all add to an entertaining mix. These examples of the recovering city give a feeling of hope for the future.

Medellín is a city of art of all genres – we loved the Plaza Botero, created in a previously run down area of the city, where huge, bulbous, dark figures stand or recline on stone plinths. Fernando Botero was born in Medellín in 1932. The bulging thighs, thick necks and rotund tummies of his figures may look fat to us, but for the artist they are an expression of 'sensual, plastic volume' – or something like that which we didn't quite understand although we loved his art. Perhaps his most famous painting is *The Death of Pablo Escobar*, painted in 1999, depicting the 'king of cocaine' being cut down by a hail of bullets.

On 21 December Carlos guided us out of the city, taking the less major route along the west side of the Río Medellín. We left at 6am in an attempt to beat the traffic. There were many local cyclists enjoying a weekend ride, and they greeted us warmly. We were riding on a city highway surrounded by a forest of high-rise flats reaching up into the low cloud. Carlos assured us that very soon we would find ourselves in a completely different landscape, once we climbed out of the valley. He was loving it – he must have been thinking of the challenge ahead of us and the sense of achievement and pleasure he knew it would bring us.

Twenty kilometres of easy riding took us to Caldas where we stopped at a café, full of cyclists having breakfast. We had what was to become a familiar combination of scrambled eggs, an *arepa* (a small, thick, flat bread made with corn), a thick slice of fresh cheese, and a *pan de yuca* (a ring shaped bread made with *yuca* flour, egg and cheese). Hugh and I had a black coffee which they called a *tinto*. We thought this would get us up some of the hills which we knew were coming. Carlos warned us that we would only find tiny village shops on the rest of the day's route so we stocked up with fruit and vegetables.

The shop was full of unfamiliar produce and this marked the beginning of our love affair with the sumptuous variety of bizarre Colombian fruits. Being eager to try as many as possible, we started with a *granadilla,* a passion fruit about the size of a small orange with shiny smooth, pale orange, speckled skin. With a sharp slap of the hand the brittle skin split in two, revealing a murky, greenish-grey pulp that looked a little like frog spawn – not instantly appetising. However, the black seeds, with their jelly-like coating were a treat for the taste buds, both sweet and tart at the same time. Like so many of the native fruits they are full of healthy vitamins and trace elements – very tasty and consumed in great quantity by the locals.

It turned out that we needed all the energy we could muster. We were about to have a sharp introduction to Carlos' idea of a great route. We turned off on a steep dirt track heading into mountains coated in thick forest and we hadn't gone far when Carlos decided to let us go, to follow the route he had made for us. With our heavy loads he probably found us very slow although he showed no signs of impatience. It was an emotional goodbye, but we hoped to see him again soon as our route looped back towards Medellín in a few weeks' time.

Villages and *fincas* were dotted around the forest in steep-sloping clearings, where bananas, corn, fruit and coffee grew, and in the flatter areas, cattle grazed. Pretty little cottages by the roadside were painted in bright colours and plants hung in baskets from the rafters of the overhanging eaves. We stopped to pass the time of day with a family working outside their home and a lady gave us cold, fresh juice, pressed from many of the curious fruits we had seen in the shop earlier; she was wearing her Christmas pinny decorated with Father Christmas sleighs, Christmas trees, stars and holly – along with a big smile. We picked up water from a roadside spring – good enough to drink.

That first day gave us a strong taste of what was to come. After ten days in Medellín, we were not at full strength despite having taken short sharp runs in the cool of the early morning. On any tour, it takes time to tone up the body to the demands of turning the wheels on a heavily loaded bike, but given that a fair amount of exercise is built into our daily lives, it doesn't take too long.

CARLOS' COLOMBIA BEFORE COVID

After barely thirty kilometres of ups and downs on the gravel after leaving Caldas, we felt that we had done enough and started to look for a place to camp; we had climbed over 1000m on that first day. Carlos had told us not to be afraid of asking at a *finca* and so we did. We spotted an open field with a stunning view and asked at the house if we could camp there. The people were very happy to have us. There was even water on tap by the cow shed, and only a few cows in the field. Above us lay a large coffee plantation. We were about to get a taste of what the build-up to Christmas is like in rural Colombia.

By 6pm we had eaten and we were in our tent reading and writing the journal after enjoying the sunset. An early night was in order as we had arisen at 5am that day. However, the locals had a very different idea. We hadn't realised how many people lived in homes scattered around the hillsides until they all began to party; loud music and the ear-splitting bangs of fireworks came from every direction. Motorbikes rushed loudly around the hillside tracks well into the night and beyond. We got very little sleep. When I went out I could see lightning in the distance and Orion on its side in the night sky. I tried two different kinds of ear plugs (I thought I had come prepared) and neither worked. I think my ears are not made for plugging.

The first stage of our route was taking us on a tour of Antioquia. Having started with riding twenty kilometres south out of Medellín we would sweep around the city in a wide arc to the west before almost touching the city again on its north side. We were a little sceptical about this loop just short of a complete circle as it didn't fit into our idea of a continuous A to B journey. We would travel even more to the north and west of our starting point in Medellín before we would begin to make our way south towards Ecuador! However, we put our trust in Carlos and went with it.

The first week was our introduction to the astonishingly lush mountain scenery of Antioquia interspersed with days of rest from riding, spent in extravagantly colourful mountain towns, all geared up with wild enthusiasm for the Christmas celebrations – Támesis, Jericó and Jardín – all surrounded by spectacular mountain landscapes and overflowing with charm. Turned wooden window and balcony rails were painted in turquoise blues, bright reds, orange and many shades of green; door panels, window shutters, lintels and the rafters of the overhanging eaves were painted to match; and the pillars and walls of verandas completed the coordinated, vibrant picture.

As for the Christmas trimmings, it was a case of extreme decorating – tinsel, bright lights and colourful baubles everywhere, each central square ablaze with lights hanging from fine wires above, outlining nativity figures or illuminating motifs on the surrounding railings. The churches were festooned with lights and inside elaborate nativity scenes were on display – not small models but expertly made large scale creations. It is curious that the traditional winter icons which we are familiar with are adopted by countries all over the world, even when Christmas falls in summer or where the climate is tropical – snowmen, holly, snow-laden Christmas trees, etc.

We spent Christmas in Jericó. Serious festivities got under way early on Christmas Eve and continued undiminished until Christmas morning – loud music all night and the people going wild. Fortunately the population had burnt out by the night of Christmas Day and we got some sleep. We found a charming apartment in one of the colourful houses, with a kitchen where we could make our own meals. We tried out more of the fruits, as yet unknown to us. Many of them were claimed to protect against cancer – which, sadly, is very prevalent amongst our age group.

We scooped out the seeds of yet another type of passion fruit, the purple-skinned *gulupa* which is said to control tension and is rich in vitamin C. The *guayaba* (guava), round or slightly pear shaped with a pale green skin, is loaded with trace minerals – the pink flesh inside is soft and fragrant if sufficiently ripe. The *tomate de árbol* (tree tomato), a reddy orange egg shaped fruit, is a little tart and the skin too tough to eat. When buying fruit we would always ask if it was *buena para comer* (good to eat) – many fruits are generally only used for sweetened juices, offered mixed with either water or milk. The *lulo* (also called *naranjilla* in other Latin American countries or the golden fruit of the Andes), is widely cultivated in the area and mainly used for juices. It looks a little like an orange and grows on a sort of mini tree with a thick woody stem topped with huge leaves up to 60 cm long.

We were keen to try out a very traditional dish of the region, *bandeja*, which comes in many different varieties. Our first taste was in Puente Iglesias on the way to Támesis – a plate of scrambled egg, rice mixed with red beans, a piece of pork, an *arepa* and a slice of soft cheese – pretty much a variation on the basic breakfast. Our next version came with *frijoles* (casseroled beans), a fried egg, a slice of pork belly with sharp cuts into the crispy fat, rice, half an avocado, fried *plátanos* (a type of banana which is only good when cooked) and a slice of tomato with a bit of salad – this was definitely the up market version! To be truthful we eventually grew tired of the monotony of the simple traditional food and we made the most of the more varied diet available in towns with enough tourists to feed the market.

Nine days into the trip we arrived in Ciudad Bolívar where we met a charming fellow, who said to Hugh, 'thank you for visiting my country'. The next morning we went to the El Café de Don Edgar where we found superb coffee and sweet pastries. Santiago was there with a friend and they invited us to join them. We talked about where we were going – El Carmen de Atrato and then Urrao via a longish lonesome route. 'Muy bonita y no mucho tráfico' said his friend, basically *nada* – perfect, we thought. Santiago responded by shaking his head, and putting on a worried expression. 'Not happy about your security that way – guerrillas', he said and then proceeded to plot out another route on a rough piece of paper which he was much happier about but didn't suit us at all. However, his friend, who worked in security, seemed quite happy about it so long as we stuck with riding in the daytime.

Having cleared that one up we then went on to talk about our route further on out of Urrao (in Antioquia) through Caicedo to Santa Fe de Antioquia. Neither of them were happy with Caicedo – a dodgy place they said – but this seemed the only sensible way to get out of Urrao for us. We decided to consult Carlos by phone. He quickly reassured us: he had done the route ten times with no problems. He told us that often people who give out this sort of advice don't really know the road and don't have up-to-date information. Santiago gave us a big box of pastries to help us on our way.

After our leisurely start we set off up the 1000m climb on the road which eventually goes through to Quibdo, the capital of the Pacific coastal department of Chocó. We zigzagged up a steep-sided valley which was clothed in a mix of coffee plants, banana trees and many flowering shrubs, heading for the clouds which covered the mountain tops. The road was paved, apart from numerous places where it had been destroyed by landslides; signs warned of imminent danger – *perdida de banca* (sides of the road falling into oblivion), *transite con precaución.*

Shortly before the top of the pass we came to a café – it was raining, it was cool and they served a delicious hot soup. It was only then that we realised that our route was actually taking us into Chocó where the UK Foreign Office

Approaching Finca Café del Jardín, San Bartolo.

advises against all but essential travel. However, at this point our travel through the atypically mountainous, eastern edge of this lowland department had indeed become essential. The only other option was to retrace our steps which was definitely not on.

Christmas Day in Jericó.

Chocó borders Antioquia along the western edge of the Andes where the land slopes steeply down to a vast, jungle covered plain, before meeting the Pacific Ocean. This whole area, almost the whole department of Chocó, looks pretty empty on the map in that the only roads and towns are on a 50km north-south line topped by the capital, Quibdo. The rising air from the ocean brings mist and rain to this side of the Andes. Our route was following the headwaters of the Río Atrato. This river carries a huge amount of water fed by many Andean streams and on reaching the plains of Chocó takes an abrupt turn to the north, paradoxically emptying itself in the Atlantic Ocean, or more specifically in the Gulf of Urabá of the Caribbean Sea. We were curious as to what life in Quibdo would be like, but not curious enough to descend into the humid heat of this reputedly rogue department. So, we turned right off the R60 and followed the Río Atrato upstream to El Carmen de Atrato. And so it came to pass that we spent two nights in Chocó.

We approached the centre of El Carmen de Atrato via a very steep street. So many times we had been presented with this challenge at the end of a day when we had already climbed over 1000m. Often the streets were paved with setts demanding extra effort. We found a lovely room at Casa Lily – solid wooden floors, a beamed ceiling and balcony with a view of the hills and blue-grey tanagers perching on a moss coated tree. There was a bar across the road – the scene of a party on New Year's Eve – music at ear splitting volume blasting out well into the morning. Nora Sophia, who was running Casa Lily, said we could use a room at the back of the house if we wanted some sleep so we gathered up our bedding and moved. New Year's Day was a very pleasant rest day for us; we had a lunch of *sopa* and *tamales* at Los Balcones where we had a great view of El Parque festooned with decorations; they were brightly lit at night. The soup was often the tastiest part of a meal. The *tamales* was a flavoursome if rather stodgy mix of maize, pork, potatoes, carrot, an egg and a few other random vegetables all encased in a loose corn dough and wrapped in a *plátano* leaf which is then steamed for several hours. Fresh fruit juice was always on offer.

A large mural was painted on a wall along a side street displaying a dark-skinned couple and a humming bird hovering over a flower. We didn't really understand the message but there were references to El Carmen de Atrato, *pluricultural and miner*. Before the introduction of coffee to the mountains bordering Antioquia, the region was settled by gold miners. El Carmen de Atrato is unusual for Colombia in its ethnic diversity, including Afro Colombians and Amerindians. The motto of the municipality is *diversidad de cultura*. We saw a number of indigenous people in this town, mostly looking quite unhappy and one of their number seemed to be asking us to take his son away with us – he actually looked quite serious about the proposition. The warnings which we were given about the safety of the area stem from the recent history of the region. An area of rich biodiversity, the region is also one of Colombia's most remote and has in the past been plagued with violence and isolation due to FARC presence. The roads which we took both in and out of El Carmen de Atrato were roughly surfaced, prone to landslides and steep; these are the only viable routes for taking produce in and out of the area.

We went north out of the town, up the Río Atrato. The weather was grim and so was the road, particularly when six kilometres along the route we had to go right through a mining complex on a surface coated with a thick layer of grey mud. This was Colombia's only working copper mine – which also produces a small amount of gold – run by Minera el Roble, a subsidiary of the Canadian company, Atico. As happened so often in Colombia, the route took us up through hill pastures into a long section of virtually uninhabited virgin forest. Bright blue butterflies with luminous red markings on their wings gathered around spots of dung on the stony road along with others of the same taste for droppings coloured matt grey with luminous orange. There were bright red trumpet flowers, ripening blackberries and a curious swirling fungus with fuzzy stripes of pale green. The recent heavy rains left many sections of the road deep in mud and scattered with puddles.

We were ready to stop after just 36km. We were not covering great distances in Colombia – it was slow going and there were too many temptations to stop and admire the views, birds, flowers and butterflies. We approached a couple of women at a pretty little roadside house. It took a bit of effort to get across what we wanted but they were delighted to let us camp by the river – but – it would be *frío*. The river was actually warm enough to bathe in without much of a shock on getting in. There was a guy staying with them who showed us how to get to the best spot and he was so excited about us being there that he just couldn't stop frenetically chattering. Later he came back with a lovely ripe avocado for our dinner and promised *leche* (milk) in the morning. I was a bit scared when he took it into his head to demonstrate the whip he used to urge the cows along.

We were now out of Chocó and back in Antioquia – back in the safe zone. As we descended 20km of dirt road to Urrao we passed colourful little farmsteads with brightly painted fences and gardens full of vivid flowering bushes, a tiny white-washed church and a little school of three or four class rooms in a wide flat valley in the middle of nowhere. A guy stopped on a motorbike and gave us a big chunk of cheese from his sack. It was an area where we couldn't help thinking, the people must be happy to live in such a pretty environment and we felt content and relaxed.

We hadn't planned to stop in Urrao – we weren't expecting to be drawn to it but that is what happened. Urrao is a pleasant unpretentious sort of town in a picturesque setting – interesting and attractive but not ramped up for the tourist market – a town which is lived in and not dominated by hotels and cafés for visitors. We met so many people in the cafés, shops and the central square who wanted to talk – about what we were doing, and about the great Colombian cyclists. We were in the birthplace of Rigoberto Urán Urán, London Olympics road race silver medallist and grand tour rider. Colombia has so many successful professional cyclists, all great mountain climbers; we had no trouble understanding why. Sergeo Henao also from Antioquia, unusually raced in all three grand tours in 2019. There is Egan Bernal who was the first Colombian to win the Tour de France and the youngest in more than a century. Nairo Quintana, from Cómbita, Boyacá, once used a second-hand bike to cycle to school and sell vegetables in nearby villages. This world-beating Colombian cyclist is now a champion of the Vuelta a España (2016) and the Giro d'Italia (2014) and has twice finished second in the Tour de France.

The day's ride went like so many of our days in Antioquia: a climb of around 1000m, first of all taking us up through pretty farmland of green pastures, and little farmhouses with lush colourful gardens; then leaving habitation behind for the impenetrable forest dotted with flowering trees and home to

Heading towards Urrao from El Carmen de Atrato.

irresistible butterflies; and finally followed by the descent to the next town. The butterflies were attracted to our shoes, our handle bars and our panniers. There was a strikingly huge variety with iridescent wings of pale blue on the top and yellow underneath. I never managed to get a photograph because they were always fluttering. The road was usually dirt once we left the towns. The crops varied – this time it was tomatoes and avocados grown under large areas of netting. We reached the supposedly dodgy hillside town of Caicedo where we did some shopping – it didn't seem like a bad place at all.

We left the town hoping to find a good camping spot. Once the paving ran out, we found ourselves riding through a fairly poor area which was a bit untidy. It was getting close to nightfall so we had to stop. We saw a group of people near a little cabin, next to a flat spot of ground which happened to have great views and a handy tap for water. We asked them if it was alright for us to camp and if it would be safe. They were totally reassuring on both counts – the land belonged to an *amigo* of theirs who wouldn't mind. Although we were in view of the road we reckoned it would be fine.

However, the little cabin was the scene of much activity – motorbikes were parked inside it and the doors locked, whilst people went off to do things. Part way through the evening I decided to throw the tarp over the bikes so that the fluorescent tyres didn't show up when lights from vehicles shone on them – just so the bikes wouldn't be so obvious. They were locked to a stout wooden post. We were pretty tired and we went to sleep early, but then we heard voices and lights shining around us. No – not robbers – just the locals doing things at the old cabin and chatting as they worked. Cars, buses and motorbikes rattled up and down the road late into the evening and started again surprisingly early in the morning. It wasn't as peaceful as we had expected – no loud music but an insect sounding like a fire cracker buzzed around for a while and dogs occasionally barked. There are far too many dogs in Colombia!

Before daylight we heard the clip clop of hooves as someone came riding up to our cabin and then the sound of a tinny transistor radio. When I looked out of the door, I saw a man sitting on the bench outside the cabin – he gave me a cheery greeting. Just as we were getting breakfast a couple came along a ridiculously steep dirt path leading up from the coffee plantations below. The young woman wiped the sweat from her brow as she reached the top and once she had cooled down a bit, changed from her flat trainers into sandals with high cork heels. They were waiting for a lift to Caicedo, the town we passed through the day before. Their house was way below somewhere. The whole experience was an insight into people's everyday lives.

Once we left the habitation on high, we descended into a very dry and empty zone with scrub covered hillsides; it got hotter and hotter. We reached the banks of the Río Cauca, 1,200m down, and the lowest point so far on our journey at an altitude of 460m. This was the same river we had crossed nearly two weeks previously, at Puente Iglesias. The river had fallen just 120m in a distance of 100km.

We were heading for Santa Fe de Antioquia, founded by Mariscal Jorge

Urrao.

Robledo in 1541 and once the department capital. In common with many of the Spanish conquerors his statue is on prominent display in one of the town's plazas. The colonial centre of whitewashed houses arranged around beautiful courtyards and narrow cobbled streets attracts many visitors, mainly Colombians – some on weekend escapes from Medellín 50km to the south. On the way into the town we stopped at a garage. We saw a couple of cyclists loading their bikes into a car and wondered if they were pros, although they weren't quite as trim as the average pro. They were accompanied by several policemen.

Hugh went over to ask if there was anywhere we could wash our filthy bikes and admired the Colombian jersey one of them was wearing. It was a complete surprise to discover that he was Federico Gutiérrez, the mayor of Medellín. He was keen to know what we were up to and we were keen to let him know that we had heard of his work to improve the city of Medellín on a UK TV Channel 4 programme presented by Simon Reeve. Soon a crowd gathered all keen to have photos taken with all of us – we felt a bit like celebrities – and we found a nice shady place with water on tap to wash our bikes.

We struggled to find a place to stay – the hotels were all full – and then we realised why when a Canadian tourist, one of the few *gringos* we met in town, told us that the next day was a big national holiday. Día de Los Reyes Magos (Epiphany), is one of the major religious celebrations in Colombia along with Easter and Christmas. This holiday commemorates the presentation of the infant Jesus to the three wise men and is celebrated on 6 January. We were beginning to realise that religious ceremonies are big in Colombia. The long queues of cars blocking the narrow streets were not weekenders leaving but people arriving for the Monday celebrations down by the river.

After a weekend wandering around the historic sights of the town and making the most of the excellent restaurants and cafés, we left on a route taking us back south east towards Medellín. Five kilometres to the east of Santa Fe, the 291m long Puente de Occidente spans the muddy waters of the Río Cauca – the first suspension bridge to be built in South America. It has an upper surface of wooden boards, which has one or two holes in it – slightly alarming for the cyclist. The single suspension span is supported by four eye-catching pyramidal towers supported on attractive brick pedestals. At a distance it looks precariously slender hanging over the raging waters and sand banks of the Cauca. The cables and other steel parts were purchased from England, while the towers were constructed of local materials. Cars are not allowed across any longer but bicycles and tuk tuks can use it. There are pathways on either side for pedestrians. The Lonely Planet guide states, 'it's a boring and hot 45-minute walk downhill here. You're best to cycle or take a moto-taxi.' The beauty of Carlos' route was that this bridge was actually on our route – it took us across it, on our way to San Jerónimo, along a shady back road on the east side of the river. This was an area of resorts – escape holes for the people of Medellín searching for some nature and fresh air – first in a rural setting with grassy camping areas and enticing little pools, and later on large apartment blocks with huge water parks including big slides.

We climbed 1821m out of San Jerónimo, up all the way on the Antigua Vía al Mar (Old Way to the Sea) which hugs the hillside above the main highway and leads to a col at 2,500m directly looking down on Medellín. After around four kilometres, we turned a corner and the road came to an abrupt, jagged end on the banks of a river – the bridge presumably washed away and the water flowing rapidly down the river bed strewn with huge boulders. A mountain biker appeared from nowhere – to the rescue. He was just so super keen to help and he picked up Hugh's panniers, ploughing straight into the water and clambering over the boulders heading for a feeble looking bridge which offered a possible way over the deep, unfordable section of the river. He tripped and fell into the water, just about hanging on to Hugh's worldly goods. At this point I was determined that I would carry my bike myself – slowly and carefully. The little bridge was made from thick lengths of bamboo, stretching between big boulders sitting in the foam. It was no more than a foot wide with little strips of flat board pegged on top of the struts. Carrying the bike was a balancing act whilst struggling to keep the rushing waters below at the back of my mind. It took several journeys between us to get everything across.

Of course there was no traffic – just people raking out coffee to dry at the roadside. A delightful ride took us to the col where people by the little eateries

A chance meeting with a famous Colombian on a bicycle –
Federico Gutiérrez – the mayor of Medellín

The road bridge had been washed away near San Jerónimo, Antioquia.

up there helped us to find a secluded place to camp. We had extensive views of the bright lights of Medellín after sunset. In Santa Fe we needed air conditioning and a cool pool – nearly 2000m above we were in a different climate altogether, needing warm pants and three layers on top to keep warm in the evening. In tropical Colombia the climate is all about altitude.

The next morning we discovered that the ascent to the col was a popular early morning ride for keen cyclists and we got chatting with a whole bunch of them who stopped at the café for breakfast. We met Monica (from Medellín) and Dave (from Bromsgrove) who live in Cota, not far from Bogotá. They teach at an international school. The tour of Colombia cycle race was to pass close to where they live in February and they invited us to stay with them.

After a cup of sweet, dark hot chocolate and freshly made bread rolls from the café we set off down and then up again to St Felix, a big centre for paragliding. We stopped to watch tourists leaping off in tandem with the experts, to soar over the high rise of the city, heading for what looked like a clear grassy mound below looking impossibly small for a safe landing. This is controlled thrill seeking for relatively privileged travellers. But others, seeking the same adrenalin fix, go about it in a very different way.

On our way up we noticed that two or three young men on BMX style bikes were hanging on to the back of some of the small trucks which passed us. These were the infamous *gravitosos,* who hitch a lift up the hill and then let fly on the descent travelling at death defying speeds. These bikes have no pedals and are often put together from scratch by the 'gravity bikers' to produce a custom machine built for rocket descents – often with the addition of extra weights. Attempts have been made to outlaw the practice but the sport is addictive for some, and is often a way that kids from poor homes can put some excitement into their lives. Despite our heavy load we were never tempted to hitch a lift and our descents are usually pretty cautious.

We had now almost closed a circle to the west of Medellín, and were no nearer to the planned end point of our trip, somewhere in Ecuador perhaps. This is not what we would have chosen left entirely to ourselves but thanks to Carlos we had travelled through one of the most beautiful and interesting areas of his country – we wouldn't have missed it for anything. Moreover, we were now heading east, to Puerto Berrío on the Río Magdalena, the river which forms the border between Antioquia and Santander. We would not start to head south for another ten days.

The big attraction between us and the Río Magdalena was the colourful resort town of Guatapé, one of the top sights of Antioquia. We had talked to Carlos about deviating from his route to visit the town, *laguna* and famous, giant, granite rock. However, most Colombians (Carlos included) didn't particularly encourage us. Travel/tourism offers interesting choices and observations. So many people told us that the place was crowded, expensive and that the rock, Piedra del Peñol, was mutilated by a staircase. Moreover, we were further put off once we realised that the undoubtedly scenic *laguna* was actually a reservoir. We headed further to the north, to the diminutive, historic town of Concepción – not one of the most known and visited towns of Antioquia but on the route that Carlos had planned for us and by now we definitely trusted his judgement more than any tourist guide.

We arrived early having camped just a few kilometres out of town the previous night in the garden of an unoccupied house. The owners were in Medellín so one of the chaps at the little café nearby called them to ask if it was OK for us to put up our tent on their lush, flat lawn. In Concepción we checked in at the Hospedaje Donde Fercho where we found a cute little room for very little money with a view of the black vultures on the tiled roof opposite – very common birds and not at all pretty. We had lunch at El Ranchito, a popular restaurant oozing with rustic charm. I had *sancocho,* a traditional dish which comes in many variations all based on a large bowl of tasty broth – a sort of cross between a soup and a stew. Mine included a large lump of chicken, chunks of potato and some other yuca-like root vegetable. I was a bit surprised when I was later presented with a plate of extras – a mound of rice, *plátanos*, a mini *arepa* and some salad – a hearty meal to be sure.

Concepción was brimming with life in the evening; not the intolerably noisy kind where super loud music blasts out of every bar, but certainly lots of activity. There are bars and places to eat down every street, mainly catering for locals and Colombian holidaymakers. The shops were all open selling meat, vegetables and packaged goods by the score. Their fondness for hairstyling exceeds that of the French – as you walk up the street you can peer into barbers' shops and hairdressers, and see people getting stylish cuts – just as popular with the men as with women.

It was a delight to walk around the narrow cobbled streets lined with single-story whitewashed dwellings roofed with Spanish tiles – the half barrel sort which lock together and are also common in France. Painted designs in patterns of bold geometric shapes decorated the bottom third of the buildings using bright colours – sometimes a single colour on the white wall and sometimes two or three contrasting colours. The doors, windows and railings were painted to match as were the eaves which extended well beyond the outside walls. There were overlaid wooden designs on the doors, colourful shutters and pretty striped architraves. These were modest homes but such care had been put into making them beautiful.

It was common to hear the clatter of hooves on the cobbles – men on sleek

Entering Concepción, Antioquia.

horses, wearing wide brimmed straw hats and with pale scarves decorated with stripes of pale brown or grey slung over their shoulders – the standard dress of the men along with a pair of smart light pants and light cotton shirts.

We had our evening meal at our *hospedaje*; Fernando said he would attend to us as if we were royalty – what more could you ask? Just fewer chips and much more salad please. Oh, and some glasses for the wine *por favor*. He was just so keen to please. The trout came from a local fish farm – a common commodity in many parts of Colombia.

The next morning we found a superb café, popular with local cyclists where we could get the best of Colombian coffee beans expressed to perfection. The rustic room was hung with rural implements – horse shoes, axes, leather bags, baskets, saddles, pots, keys and an ancient radio. Then we followed the zig-zag path to a viewpoint above the town and looked down on a maze of weathered tiled roofs sitting in a bowl of pastureland surrounded by forest topped hills – the vultures liked to congregate there and fork-tailed flycatchers perched on the barbed wire fences. Fernando served us *sancocho* for lunch, but this time made with fish. It was accompanied by a salad and fresh *guanábana* juice. He told us that he and his wife had lived in London for four years previously, and their son is still there. They like it in Concepción, as it is *tranquilo* but they liked London too. He recommended that we visit the curiously named El Charco el Aguacate (The Avocado Puddle), a cool, clear mountain river a short walk away. We had it all to ourselves.

On the way up we had a look in the Casa de Cultura – many towns and

Just before finding a wild camp between La Argentina and San Roque

villages have such a place where visitors can learn about the local history. This one was mainly about José María Córdova, the general born in Concepción in 1799, who was instrumental in putting an end to the presence of Spanish troops in Antioquia. Córdova organized a small army of 700 volunteers, and on 12 February 1820, he defeated the Spanish army of General Warleta at the Battle of Chorros Blancos, in Yarumal, Antioquia. A huge mural on the wall depicts the ferocious battle – the wild charging horses of the Colombian forces, the flag carried with pride, bearing down on the fallen men and horses of the Spanish army. Córdova's statue stands in El Parque Principal Charco Los Payasos in front of the twin-domed, brick-fronted church in the centre of town. The International airport of Medellín at Río Negro is named after him.

We loved Concepción with its delectable mix of charming people, beautiful rural architecture, great local cuisine, a bit of history and the perfect place to cool off in a natural pool. We left refreshed, ready for the three day ride east to the sweltering valley of the Río Magdalena. We travelled along a dirt track with sections of horrendous cobbles and muddy roadworks, past beautiful waterfalls in glorious hill country before stopping at a *finca*. We asked if we could camp and after a family consultation they welcomed us and later joined us for a bit of a party in the field with a magnificent view. We gave them a taste of the Colombian tea we had bought in Medellín – they weren't familiar with it. We passed through Santo Domingo and then on to San Roque, still on the dirt. The next day it was downhill to the banks of the Río Magdalena all paved. Not quite as easy as it sounds though – whilst we descended 2,600m we also climbed 1,214m – an easy ride in Colombia is pretty rare.

The Río Magdalena, named for Mary Magdalene, is the principal river of Colombia and an historically crucial communications link, flowing 1,528km northward down a great valley where the Andes split into the subranges of the Cordillera Central and the Cordillera Oriental. We were about to cross from one range to the other. The extensive view of the great river that I was expecting didn't materialise – we didn't see the river until we passed through the centre of Puerto Berrío to the *malecón*, where there is a little port for small river boats. On the way down we had been cooled by the bike breeze and clouds had shielded the sun, but once we stopped in town, to ask where we would find somewhere to stay, we felt the full debilitating weight of the humid heat. Some lovely ladies sat out on the street came to our aid and offered us a seat by their fan and a drink of cold juice. Climbing out of the valley on the other side was going to be tough.

Airy eateries under palm-fringed roofs served fish landed straight from the river. We had bagre – a large, stripy catfish served with a tasty mushroom sauce. A fishy soup flavoured with coriander came with it along with some rice and salad. There are over 200 species of fish in the Río Magdalena and its tributaries, and new species have been found in recent years. Sadly, as with rivers all over the world, the harvests are decreasing drastically – by over 90% since 1975. Like so many great waterways, the river and the surrounding habitat is threatened by pollution from farming, mining, human waste, deforestation and hydro power. However, the good news is that in January 2020 the Enel Green Power company in collaboration with the Universidad Surcolombiana launched an ambitious plan to restock the river.

Puerto Berrío is a major port on the river, which is navigable by shallow-draft steamboats between Neiva in Huíla department and the sea, interrupted only by the rapids at Honda. However, we were about to discover how much the term navigable is stretched to include the hair raising slalom through the sandbars and giant floating logs that we were about to undertake on a journey 80km downstream.

When I tried to find information on the internet about the boat from Puerto Berrío to Barrancabermeja, there was very little forthcoming. However, comments of the nature, 'is the boat along the Río Magdalena safe?' cropped up frequently. Looking back on the trip, I think this is a very valid question. We shot out from the jetty heading upstream at breakneck speed, only to turn downstream in a tight banked curve. At one point we seemed to be heading directly for the opposite bank only to turn sharply away at what seemed like the last second. Much of the water is smooth but we did hit some alarmingly bumpy bits. You can only trust in the skill of the driver – he seemed to be enjoying himself immensely – a bit of a boy racer I thought. I wasn't too keen on his habit of turning to talk to the guy next to him. His knowledge of the river's traps must be amazing – hopefully. He steered a curvy course along the various branches of the river, hugging the deeper water. It looked like it would be so easy just to take the wrong branch and end up marooned on a sandbank. At times we came to a sharp halt – comforting to know we could stop quickly – not sure why, but perhaps to consider the options.

Our bikes and panniers were on the roof tied down with ropes; fortunately I had checked the knots before we left as a few were loose. I'd figured that if the boxes of eggs up there were expected to survive our bikes should be OK. I had been expecting a leisurely cruise on the calm waters; this was a speedboat with no chance of getting good photographs of the wonderful birdlife on the river – great egrets and flocks of cormorants sitting on the sandbanks. An alarm went off just before we stopped to pick people up – maybe to warn those on the bank to indicate if they wanted a ride. This boat was the equivalent of the local bus service to communities with poor or non-existent road access. They had no proper jetty – just a slippery mud bank down to the river. Little wooden skiffs were parked at the calm water's edge.

The trappings of the oil industry strung out along the river bank told us we had reached Barrancabermeja, the oil capital of Colombia. It was a relief. We loaded up our bikes and the other passengers helped us push them up the steep concrete ramp onto the quay where an impressive fish market was in progress – bagre, half the height of a man with their spotted tails and black streaks as if someone has dripped paint all down their plump bodies; flat fish gutted and spread out wide; and dumpy little fish with red fins and tails, and a rose scaled belly. It didn't look like the river was short on fish.

For the first time since Medellín we entered a big city, with lots of traffic to negotiate – Barrancabermeja has a population of 191,000 – many more people than the small, cool mountain towns we had been visiting. In our faltering Spanish we had a chat over dinner with Edward, a good friend of Carlos who works as a lawyer in the city – bagre once more, this time in a tomato and onion sauce.

It was as well that we had found a very pleasantly cool hotel for our stay, because, keen as we were to escape the oppressive heat, there was no way I could move the next day – our 7am escape was impossible after I had spent the night being sick. Leaving the hotel room meant entering an oven – the only way we would be able to escape the inferno was to leave as early as possible the following day. The buffet breakfast was served at the impressively early hour of 5:30am so we aimed for a 6am start.

Thankfully I woke up feeling fine. In the relative cool of the early morning, moving along at a good pace on *pavimento* we could just about convince ourselves that the air was refreshing. We hit the dirt and the climb after riding 26km on the level, mostly on an unexpected white elephant of a four lane highway taking us past oil drilling platforms tucked amongst the trees. We bumped into mountain bikers who had set out from the city at 5am – that's what you have to do if you want to survive a mountain bike ride out of Barrancabermeja. It was a pretty route heading up into the cooler mountain air but by midday we hadn't gained enough height to be comfortable and we were wilting. We spread our tarpaulin under the mottled shade of some tall straggly trees, drank lots of water and laid down semi-comatose. A host of colourful butterflies rested on our saddles and a saffron finch flitted amongst the thin branches of the trees. Luckily we found plenty of water – we got through ten litres that day – but we needed our Steripen to treat it.

We stopped at a café where we had *tinto* (inky water) – very cheap, basic, Colombian coffee, usually served with lots of sugar. Pinned to the wall there was a poster proclaiming in large letters *Niños y niñas por fuera del conflicto armado* (boys and girls outside the armed conflict) on a background of an armed figure in silhouette. In the bottom left hand corner, two young children were pictured hunched over a book. It was all about efforts to prevent young people getting drawn into armed groups – the potential for conflict in the area is not yet a thing of the past. Further up the road we came across an armed group. We had no idea who they were or why they were walking up the dirt track. Earlier on a guy on a motorbike had come up to us when we stopped for a picnic and said, *adelante* (move on) putting on a worried expression. He told us there were bad people nearby and we should move on to a *casa* half an hour up the road.

People we met always gave time and not distance to a place when they had no idea how long it takes us, particularly when climbing up a rough dirt road. We had our picnic – were we any safer moving up the hill at six kilometres an hour? The dozen men, many no more than teenagers and dressed in camouflage kit with netted helmets, carried rifles slung over their shoulders. They looked like the official military but how were we to know? Later we were told that if they are wearing leather boots they are probably not paramilitaries – these guys were shod in decent footwear. When we tried asking them what they were doing they just responded with sweet smiles. We moved on and felt comfortable enough as lots of normal looking local people were moving up and down the road. However, when we asked a lady about camping nearby she wagged her finger, shook her head and said 'no'. So we gave up on the camping idea and headed for a hotel up the road which turned out to be a scruffy looking sex hotel, leaving us no option but to end the day with a 500m climb up to San Vicente. There we bumped into a lovely young couple, Christian and his girlfriend Milena who instantly befriended us, showed us the way to a good hotel and took us to the best pizza place in town.

San Vicente is the cacao capital of Colombia and to make the point clear a giant model of a cacao pod stands in the main square. As we enjoyed yet another glorious climb on a deserted dirt road up into the forest, we passed many of the evergreen cacao trees. The pods or fruits of different sizes and colours hung on short stalks from the branches, shaped like elongated rugby balls with pointed ends. The sunlight accentuated the texture of the thick, crinkly skin of so many different colours – dark purplish browns, deep ruddy browns, golden yellow with red veins and deep greens. Colombian chocolate is rated amongst the best in the world – 95% of Colombia's cacao exports are classed as 'fine flavour' by the International Cacao Organisation and it is one of the largest producers of cacao in the world.

During our stay in Medellín we had been treated to the most bizarre chocolate experience ever at the restaurant El Cielo, which was featured in the Simon Reeve (Channel 4 UK TV) programme on Colombia. We enjoyed a thirteen course 'experience' menu – expensive but something which would cost five times as much in a rich western country. All the dishes were very small and delicate; each designed to titivate the palate in a particular way and all created to symbolize the development of the Colombian culture and landscape. A bit posy yes, and a bit over the top perhaps, but we loved it. We were quite taken aback when the waitress came and poured warm, thick melted chocolate all over our hands and told us to rub them together. 'What a waste of good chocolate' I thought, until she told us to go back to our childhood and lick our fingers. I licked mine almost clean!

CARLOS' COLOMBIA BEFORE COVID

After crossing the Río Magdalena we had entered the Department of Santander, having spent our time up to then in Antioquia apart from the few days' foray into Chocó. For a month we had been riding in and out of lush green valleys and over mountain passes clothed in dense native forest – the fertile land of fragrant fruits that Carlos had tempted us with so long ago had more than lived up to the enticing vision he had created in our minds. We were now heading towards the pretty little seventeenth century colonial town of Zapatoca, following a track above a rushing mountain stream taking us up one of the most beautiful and extravagantly forested valleys we had encountered so far. As we approached the pass, we turned a corner, and – bang – all change! First, large scale timber harvesting and then, as we crossed the pass, a view like no other we had seen so far in Colombia – looking so brown, so dry and so barren. Where had all the trees gone? When we asked about the reasons for this all that came back was the word, *fincas*.

In Zapatoca we found a room at the Hostal La Carmelina – a lovely old colonial house high up on the edge of the town with charmingly arty interior décor and managed by Luis and Cristian from Venezuela, barely 100km away as the crow flies. Like so many Venezuelans they had come to Colombia for work – they worked hard and were extremely helpful, finding us a hose so Hugh could give the bikes a good wash. Little did we realise at the time what a futile exercise this would prove to be. Luis told us that the owners of the *hostal* were away in their home town of Bucaramanga so meanwhile, he was in charge. He had left his home on a short term work visa after his father was shot dead in a violent Venezuelan conflict. His mother remained in her home country scratching a living. Luis' next move in life was to try to get a three month visa to Spain where he hoped to find more long term work. He had a motorbike which he bought for less than a hundred pounds but he had no papers for it and so could get into trouble with the police.

In Zapatoca they had taken beautification to the highest level. Everyday objects around the town had been transformed into colourful ornaments. It's amazing what can be done with a bit of paint in the hands of an artist; lampposts with flowering creepers reaching up to hummingbirds with outstretched wings; gas meters adorned with butterflies and dragonflies resting on open blossoms, scenes of waterfalls, stone bridges and pretty colonial houses and portraits of local characters; old tyres decorated in contrasting geometric designs and filled with flowering plants. Inside the town's delightful cafés, other everyday objects were put to novel use with lampshades made from upturned cups and teapots. Here for many times the cost of a *tinto* you could get top Colombian coffee turned into the perfect espresso or flat white using quality Italian machines. We often saw ancient copper and brass espresso machines in Colombian cafés and in the restaurant Esquina de Piedra, an 82-year-old German coffee machine was still in use.

It rained heavily the night before we left, leaking through the window in our room. The fine particles that in dry weather create clouds of dust as vehicles pass, and occasional depths of powder that slow you down, turn into something much more debilitating after rain. It becomes a thick, sticky glue that clings to your cleats, frame, tyres, mud guards and anything else in its path. The pedals became completely clogged and the cleats wouldn't clip in. Eventually the trapped mud becomes an all too effective brake and the wheels become stuck. The road turns into a slimy, frictionless surface which is unnerving on the flat, fails to grip going up and gives little control going down.

In the first few all too slow kilometres out of Zapatoca, I seriously wondered if it was stupid to continue. We were having to push the mud out from under the mudguards after only tens of metres of riding and our feet didn't grip the ground when we were forced to push. We had 1,000m of altitude to descend – possibly on a mud slide? A truck carrying chickens had come to grief on the road – the chickens didn't sound too happy. A bunch of guys had come to the rescue in an effort to get it out of the roadside ditch. Of course, we hadn't the heart to turn back so on we went. And fortune shone – the sun came out. The surface became rocky and less muddy.

We made it to Galán via the charming village of La Fuente and with clean bikes, as we were able to dip them in a river. We had not gone far but it had all been exhausting and we thought that the village looked like an interesting little out-of-the-way place to stay. As is often the case, in the shady park there is a statue of the hero of the town, Capitán José Antonio Galán Zorro. He was executed by the Spanish in 1782 after leading an insurrection. There is a beautiful sandstone church with a lovely wood beamed roof, open to the air on both sides which keeps it cool and airy. We were directed to the *panadería* which served us with their *kumis casero* by the glass – a sweet yoghurt drink made in-house. A room in the hotel Danny had cost us only £12 for two including dinner.

The next day we descended to a bridge over the Río Suárez – a river which is part of the great Magdalena basin – and then up to Barichara, claimed by some to be the prettiest town in Colombia and very much on the foreign tourist trail, accessed by bus from the city of Bucaramanga and then the large town of San Gil. The freedom of being able to approach these notable places on mountain dirt roads going through fascinating outlying villages, rather than by tedious bus journeys along busy main roads from big city hubs, is one of the major reasons why we love travel by bike so much.

Barichara is a town built of sandstone, atop a long sandstone cliff which gives great views over the Suárez valley. The buildings have attractive feature decorations of exposed stone. The roads are paved with sandstone and the walls of the fields around are made of big blocks of sandstone. It is a remarkably intact colonial town with virtually no noticeable modern additions. The houses, as in other towns, face straight onto streets lined with precipitous pavements. The walls are mainly whitewashed, unlike the colourful painted *casas* we had seen in Antioquia. Behind the walls lie open interiors with sunny courtyards adorned with plants and flowers. It is a lovely place to walk around, with little traffic and none of it too fast on the steep flagged streets. There were great cafés and restaurants where we could enjoy a tasty cuisine of interesting twists on local dishes along with Italian and French dishes – a welcome variation.

Possibly the least enjoyable riding of the whole trip through Colombia was during much of the next two days on a busy two lane highway between San Gil and La Vitoria. There were stunning views of the Suárez Valley on our right and we could see Galán where we had stayed but we always find that we can't appreciate the scenery with trucks squeezing us into the kerb. Carlos had a reason for sending us this way though – to visit the historic town of Socorro, which meant a lot to him and he felt it was a key part of our Colombian education.

It was here that the first steps towards independence from Spain were taken. In 1781 the *comuneros* took to the streets by what is now the Casa del Comercio – a beautiful colonial house which was the first toll station in Colombia. Two thousand townspeople led by weavers and butchers marched through the town shouting 'death to the regent and the prosecutor'. It is rare to see statues of female heroes but at the site of her execution by a Spanish firing squad in the Parque de la Independencia, stands María Antonia Santos Plata (1782-1819). She inspired, organised, and led the rebel guerrillas in the Province of El Socorro against the invading Spanish troops during the Reconquista of the New Granada. Standing with one foot forward, and arms raised, she carries a flag of independence in her left hand and points to the sky with her right.

Two hundred years ago, on the eve of Colombia's Independence, the country's three main cities were Bogotá, Cartagena and Socorro. Socorro has the distinction of having been the country's capital for a day. Today it is a small town, much less known than its bigger or more intact colonial neighbours; we didn't see any foreign visitors there. The architecture is a mishmash of different eras with wildly differing styles all mixed up in the same street. Our hotel had an art deco look to it. The cathedral built between 1897 and 1943 was one of the most beautiful churches we visited in Colombia.

After a brief stop at a superb coffee shop in town, we left via an attractive pedestrianised street and climbed up to a large cemetery. The guy looking after it gave us cold drinking water. We asked if it was for a special group of people as it seemed so smart and tidy. He responded by telling us that everyone is equal and special in God's eyes – a good answer. Back on the highway we rode amongst long lines of trucks – one with six guys hitching a lift on the back bumper – and not with bikes. It was an immense relief when we reached the turn off to the tiny village of Confines where we whiled away the afternoon visiting the Cascada de Barro Blanco, a pretty waterfall accessed by a tiny trace of a path through thick forest.

EXTRAORDINARY PLACES BY BICYCLE

We approached Charalá on an empty, rust dirt road climbing up through gentle hill country – a pretty mix of forest and agricultural land – and then crossing a plateau at 1,900m. As we descended on an increasingly bumpy road, the town came into view, the twin towers of the Catholic church rising above the red tiled roofs of the low whitewashed houses nestled amongst the forest and fields. Such a pretty little town, surrounded by streams and waterfalls and with a name that makes you think of happy songs. We fell in love with the place right away. The astonishing tree in the central park spread out so far that the branches, unable to hold their own weight, were propped up by metal posts. It was a place for locals to gather and chat, in the shade. One side of the park was dominated by the church, a big church for such a small town as was often the case.

It didn't take Hugh long to find the coffee shop. He was having great fun talking to the owners about his amazing coffee machine at home. It is incredible how all the good espresso machines come from not only Italy, but Milano. The lovely young couple who had just set up the shop produced superb coffee from Colombian beans. They were so meticulous about making each cup that they used scales to weigh the beans before grinding. Their tamping was a little extreme taking over half a minute. The furniture was made from wooden pallets and murals of coffee picking decorated the walls inside and out. There was a good store where we stocked up with provisions for the next four days. We had been told that there was nothing on our route to Duitama. The shopping done, we went for a quiet beer in a place on the park. The barman was interested in whisky so Hugh showed him where he thought the best comes from – the Scottish island of Islay.

We asked around about the road ahead. The guy in the bike shop told us it was very hard and we should take a different route with our loaded bikes. No bad people this time – just big, bad rocks. The couple in the coffee shop didn't know the road. The next morning there were even more attempts to put us off. Two alternative routes were offered, one by Joanna, at our hotel at breakfast time. So we decided to call Carlos for the guru's opinion – the rough road was 'the most beautiful' he said. Carlos had a feel for the beauty of cycling which those who only want to get from A to B often don't appreciate – and of course, he was right.

Riding past the bull ring on the outskirts of town, fourteen kilometres took us to the deciding junction where we turned right onto stones. We had been told that there was nothing along this route, but we soon passed a little rural education centre. There were ramshackle dwellings and the odd *tienda* but these country shops didn't sell much of use unless you wanted beer – you can always get Águila, a mild pilsner and the number one beer in Colombia. Fortunately we had stocked up in Charalá – pasta, quinoa, cereal bars, peanut butter, nuts, dried fruits, tinned *frijoles*, a little fresh fruit and vegetables and three bars of top class Colombian chocolate. We had been told that the route was rough *piedra*. It was strewn with rounded stones such as come from a river bed.

We gained height all day riding up a beautiful valley mainly given to cattle pasture – a tough ride but it was possible; we only pushed a few metres. Early on we cut into two *pitaya* (dragon fruit) – best to eat the heavy stuff first – and watched bright blue dragonflies resting on the roadside vegetation whilst we scooped out the aromatic seeds with a spoon. The road was almost empty. On a brief little descent we saw a neatly dressed young girl pushing what looked like a pretty decent bike up the hill from the village of Virolín, where there is a church, a basketball court, a school and a *tienda*. We got water from a house there and were told it was good for drinking. Fabian spoke some English which he said he had learned in Bogotá.

We put up our tent for the night by the red brown waters of a rocky mountain river at an altitude of over 2000m. This was the first time in Colombia that we had camped without asking permission – the first real wild camp, on a patch of flat grass out of sight of any habitation and shielded from the road by trees and bushes. We had been told that there are bears and pumas in the area so we hoped that they wouldn't take too much interest in us. As the last pegs were placed in the ground, the rain started, heavy and lasting for three hours. In need of a wash after a hot day we decided to just get out and into the river – with an extra shower thrown in; the water wasn't even cold.

We got up before daylight so we could get an early start up the great climb ahead; our route was still going up. We had breakfast by torchlight. The tent was sodden and the river was running high – far too high for river bathing. Fortunately we were a safe level above it. The road was wet but being very rocky, it wasn't one of those that turn into glutinous mud. It was a gorgeous ride, pedalling through the swollen streams which crossed the track, with the sun filtering through the trees as it rose over the mountain tops, illuminating the wet leaves and ferns. The early morning light is very special.

We had a little 200m climb ahead of us before a short descent into the headwaters of a different river system. Near the top we heard strange sounds which we found were coming from a speaker attached to a roadside shack. A poster pinned to the shack showed two bearded aesthetics above a list of negatives – no arms, no alcohol, no cigarettes, no drugs, no industrialised foods. This was the Gran Templo Vegetal Sakroakuarius, Tivet de los Andes – a Taoist village, the Tibet of the Andes. Further up the road a young lady by the name of Isobel approached us, walking barefoot from her house. She asked if we needed anything. We said we could use a bit more *comida* (food). She put on her shoes and led us up the road, lined with very distinctively designed homes made of wood.

We were led to the centre of the *pueblo*, but they didn't want us to go into what seemed to be the spiritual heart of the place. We were offered some homemade bread, 'natural' they said – it was delicious. Hugh offered money but they didn't take it. Isobel told us that they are all vegetarians. A very friendly guy talked to us about the *pueblo*. He told us that around 2,000 people live there, of many nationalities including people from Colombia, Peru, Germany, England, France, Japan and China. They like to do things 'naturally' and their houses are made without the use of concrete (although I thought I spotted some in the foundations). They can't grow much food as the soil is very thin and the ground rocky – we couldn't work out how they supported themselves. They shop in Duitama, the next town we would reach, which encouragingly suggested that the road to Duitama, even though it climbed up to 3,600m, would be an easier road than that from Charalá which is closer. From what they told us we understood that the road to Duitama from the top would be paved.

Further research on this community later revealed various threads, one stating that this religious commune professes an eclectic form of Judeo-Taoism and they sometimes refer to themselves as 'True Jewish Tao People'. The commune was the subject of Colombian police action during late 2004, in relation to accusations of the leadership's involvement in the assassination of former members, kidnapping, and involvement in the opium trade. The leadership is reported to have evaded capture, and there have been no direct follow-up actions against the group in the years since. Another site discusses how the community has been subject to violent persecution for many years resulting in several deaths. It also states that in 1995 the temple was fumigated with glyphosate and other highly toxic chemicals. These fumigations, that took place over the period of several weeks, caused the death of many monks, also provoking a miscarriage in a nun who was several months into her pregnancy. Among the victims were citizens from the United States and France. Whether or not these stories are true, it seems clear that much controversy has surrounded this settlement, and beyond that there have been many accusations of persecution of Taoist groups throughout Colombia.

We moved on looking down from our ever increasing height on the pastureland of the valley below and across to craggy mountains, forested right to the top. This was one of those days when we reached the point at which we were ready to stop but couldn't find a suitable place to camp – we needed water, flat land and privacy.

We had gone further than we wanted to by the time we reached El Carmen where there are a few houses, a school, a church and an assortment of abandoned buildings and sheds. The place had a pretty messy, semi-derelict look about it but the lady we talked to there was very friendly and said we could camp or stay inside a large empty hall. We preferred our tent and it was much warmer than the hall would have been. There was a nice grassy plot with trenches dug all around for protection against flooding from heavy rain. It wasn't the idyllic wild spot we had in mind but we couldn't go on up into the unknown. I asked about a *baño* and a guy showed me to a toilet block which was horrendously dirty and completely unusable – we would have to find a secluded place to use our trowel in the morning.

Whilst we put up our tent and cooked our food, seven-year-old Caterina who lives there, watched us with great interest and asked lots of questions. What were the clipits (little plastic grips for sealing plastic bags) for, what were we eating, what clothes did we have? She tried out the fasteners on our bags and had a look inside our tent with *dos puertas*. It was cool cooking outside (at 3,200m altitude) close to sundown and for the first time I used warm clothes that had spent the journey stuffed at the bottom of my pannier. It was cosy in our tent and the local dogs – which had often kept us awake at night – were thankfully quiet. It was an odd place to find street lights coming on after dark though.

We had a real surprise in the morning when we looked out of the tent door. Four large buses had arrived and lots of children were walking up towards the *colegio*. The older ones were dressed in smart school uniform – neat pale blue sweaters and white shirts, tartan patterned pleated skirts for the girls and neat long pants for the boys. A young woman, who introduced herself as the head of the school, came to talk to us. Ligia took us into three different classes to talk to the students and answer their questions: what animals are there in England? do you eat trout in England? why don't you travel in a car? They were currently studying the history of the indigenous people of Colombia. The little children said a prayer for us.

We were very confused about the school initially as the buses had come all the way from Duitama, a journey which takes one and a half hours by bus and all day for us on the bikes. Why were children coming from a large town, up into the mountains, over a 3,600m pass to go to school in a tiny hamlet? Some of the children did come from other villages nearby but not that many. Ligia told us that some of the children had 'problems'. Then later it came to light that there are big drug problems in Duitama, and the children come out to the middle of nowhere for schooling out of harm's way. To be honest we were still left confused. It seemed a bit harsh for the kids to spend nearly three hours a day on buses five days a week, much of it over a dirt road which must get in a bad state in heavy rain. We both enjoyed talking to the children who were very amiable and although they were initially reluctant to practise their English when asking questions, they did show quite a bit of interest. Most of the discussion was conducted in Spanish with some translation help from Ligia.

So we left a little late but it didn't matter at all – interacting with the children had been a great experience for us and it must have been a very unusual event for them too. We headed up the hill topping out in the moorland landscape of the Páramo de la Rusia, dominated by a curious, captivating plant, the *espeletia*, commonly known as *frailejones* (big monks). It is a type of giant rosette plant, a description which captures its looks perfectly. The succulent, hairy leaves which grow in a tight spiral from the top of a tall, thick stem are resistant to frost. It is a plant of the alpine tundra found in tropical zones above the timberline but below the permanent snow line, known as high altitude *páramo* ecosystems. This strange low forest covering the hillsides exudes an other worldly feel for those unfamiliar with this genre of vegetation.

It was then down to Duitama for the night, sometimes on paved surfaces where the names of Colombia's cycling heroes were inscribed – Chaves, Rigo, López, Nairo, Egan and Meta, sometimes going back to dirt – much of it in heavy rain. In La Ciclería Café Taller, the cyclists' café and shop of Duitama we were told that many foreign and Colombian cyclists come for the high altitude training in the area. The shop has lots of high-end kit.

We left the city on a busy highway lined with cute hotels in totally inappropriate locations; we were riding through the cement works of Boyacá, and the fine dust pervaded the atmosphere. This province of Sugamuxi is a region where amongst all the heavy industry, pretty little villages promote their craft specialities; in Nobsa, it was knitted and woven woollen goods – hats, gloves, rugs and particularly ponchos, for a climate that many Colombians but not a Brit would consider cold. Our day ended in Mongui, a beautiful little hillside town of whitewashed colonial houses with paintwork of dark green with a touch of red – a place which specialises in footballs. The final climb gave us bird's eye views of the surrounding hillsides scarred with quarries. It is a popular hill climb for local cyclists and there was a group of them in the huge cobbled plaza below the imposing Basilica Nuestra Señora de Mongui. It was the day before Hugh's 67th birthday and here were all the ingredients for a good place to celebrate the event – great coffee shops, quality beer in the bars, good restaurants and a gorgeous place to just amble around.

A sizable share of the footballs sold in Colombia is produced in Mongui. It is a very labour intensive process carried out by many artisans – some in their own homes. We popped into a football workshop where we could see how the hexagonal shapes were cut out from synthetic material of various colours. Guillermo Hurtado makes synthetic footballs and also leather versions of the kind which were used 50 years ago. He makes lovely replicas of famous footballs, including Manchester United and Chelsea. In the plaza there is a statue of a football cupped between a pair of hands and another showing an old lady stitching a football. Needless to say many tourist versions are on sale in various sizes and key rings come with mini balls. In October they have a *festival del balón*.

For lunch we had *cocido boyacense*, *cocido* being a Colombian stew which varies with region; this one came with a piece of pork, some sausage, and lots of tasty vegetables. There was a selection of corn on the cob, some tasty tubers of various types including *yuca*, peas cooked in the pods, broad beans, *frijoles* and whole potatoes in their skins.

The route out took us up on to the high *páramo* again where at almost

3,600m people were hard at work planting their staple crop in level fields between the rocky outcrops – potato planting is one of the main threats to this fragile moorland landscape. Other land was used for grazing but in places the special plant of the *páramo* was thriving in large numbers. We were following an intricate network of steep dirt tracks which didn't show clearly on our Pocket Earth map on the phone and when we hit a steep washed out single track path on the descent we thought we must have gone wrong – but no – it brought us out neatly onto the paved road with a full view of Laguna de Tota, the largest lake in Colombia. We marvelled at Carlos' intimate knowledge of the terrain.

At an altitude of 3,100m I was expecting a wild, mountain lake with little habitation – the sort of thing you might see on the Altiplano of Bolivia or Peru. As we pedalled around most of the lake close to the shore, the pervading scent was of onions. This is one of the major onion producing regions in Colombia; neat rows of green shoots filled the fields on either side of the road and in places people were busy gathering the crop. The area is also a popular tourist area for Colombians and there was an element of messy development going on to support this industry. We stayed in the only significant town on the lake, Aquitania – the pretty name raising our expectations. However, we were disappointed. We had dinner at Pueblito Viejo, which is in one of the few lovely old buildings of the town where Sebastian told us that the people didn't look after the old buildings, and that is why there is so little left of the town's colonial heritage. The restaurant served delicious creations using trout, which Sebastian said is a wild fish of Laguna de Tota. I was sceptical about this, as it reminded me of the abundance of non-native trout in Lake Titicaca. According to Wikipedia, the temperature of Laguna de Tota (13°C) was perfect for the introduction of trout, which led to the extinction of the native *pez graso* or grease fish, believed to be endemic to this lake. Something very similar has happened in Titicaca where the Lake Titicaca flat-headed fish (*orestias cuvieri*) is most likely extinct. On both these lake shores trout is packaged as a local wild delicacy, when its introduction has led to the extinction of the native fish.

The original people of the area, whose descendants are also under threat, are recognised in Cuitiva. Here the prominent statue in the central square is not of Jesus or a Spanish General or President, but of Bochica, the founding hero of the Muisca, the original inhabitants of this land of the Altiplano. According to legend they brought morals and laws to the people and taught them agriculture and other crafts.

We spent the night in the next village, Iza, the place of *postres* (puddings)! A whole line of little stalls on the main plaza were selling a vast selection of desserts – lots of sweet cream; fruits set in lurid coloured jellies of turquoise, bright green and brilliant red; trifles topped with deep red blackcurrants; and custards with coconut, chocolate chip and caramel toppings. We couldn't help wondering how they could possibly sell so much sweet stuff before the cream went sour and it was all contaminated by the flies.

We wanted to spend a day or two resting in Villa de Leyva, a beautiful colonial town, so we set out planning to get there in two days and avoid the weekend which would be very busy as it is a popular weekend haunt for Bogotanos in the same way that the people of Medellín escape to Santa Fe. Just out of Firavitoba we joined yet another popular cyclists' hill climb. The sign at the bottom advertised '8 kilómetros, cero estrés aire puro adrenalina' (eight kilometres of zero stress, pure air and adrenalin).

There were plenty of keen riders out on their skinny wheels heading up to El Alto de Curies – 400m of ascent on a paved but rough road going up to nearly 3,000m. They gave us lots of encouragement as they sped past us and we chatted to a few at the café at the top – a spot popular with the well-known Colombian pro-cyclist Nairo Quintana. In any populated area, local Colombian cyclists will make the most of any climb they can do on a light road bike. We even saw one or two on the descent on dirt. A huge poster at the top gave a wonderful education in the many benefits of *la bicicleta* for the rider and for the world, one of the best being, *hace muchos amigos* (you make many friends).

Over the other side, we met a huge group of cycling *amigos* – lean men and women dressed just like the professionals in their colourful lycra kit – all taking a short break just below the striking memorial to the heroes of El Pantano de Vergas (Vergas swamp battle). In 1819, Simón Bolívar's forces pasted the Spanish army at this key battle in the fight for the independence of New Granada. A chaotic mix of men charging on horseback with long spears in their hands, sculptured in black metal, has been scattered over one of the contrasting white points of the monument's frame creating a feeling of speed, terror and determination. Just a little way down the road we bumped into the real cycling pros – the Colombian branch of the UAE team taking advantage of the high altitude speed training in a pleasant climate.

Since climbing out of Charalá a week previously we had been at an altitude of over 2,000m and we wouldn't descend any lower for another two weeks when we left the region around Bogotá; it was a pleasant temperature for cycling during the day, wearing shorts and T-shirts but it could be cool at night. When we poked our heads out of our tent the following morning it was covered in frost. Although we had camped higher, this was our first camp frost. We had been warm in our sleeping bags but the top on our dromedary (water bottle) was frozen which slowed down the breakfast tea. We were in a field owned by José, a lovely gentle man who we'd met in the roadside bar. He was fascinated by our kit.

We were heading for Cota, on the outskirts of Bogotá, home to Dave and Monica who we had met on day eighteen of our trip on the col above Medellín.

CARLOS' COLOMBIA BEFORE COVID

Along the way we rested in the beautiful colonial town of Villa de Leyva built around the largest Plaza Major in Colombia – 14,000 square metres of bumpy cobblestones. We camped above Ráquira, another speciality village famous for its brilliantly coloured pots, passing through the hillside hamlets where the pots are made. A friendly craftsman with a large shed full of pots was happy to show us the kiln in his yard with a pile of coal nearby and tierra – special clay transported from elsewhere.

The next night our tent was by a pool of croaking frogs next to a hostel, our first official campsite, run by a lovely family who only charged £3.50 each for camping with breakfast – broth with potatoes and pork, fresh bread, two fried eggs and hot chocolate. A ride on a decaying road through an area of coalmining (dotted with posh houses – presumably for the rich owners) and on through tranquil cattle farming land took us to Colombia's rock climbing mecca at Suesca, with more than 600 routes established on a long line of cliffs. We followed a track along the railway line to a large flat camp ground and watched the setting sun turn the cliffs golden. There we met Euan and Nadine who live in Fort William and Glasgow respectively. They were enjoying a six month break from their jobs as a structural engineer and primary teacher, intending to travel around South America. Euan is a hill runner and we have several friends in common from Lochaber. Like so many other young people on travel breaks, their plans would be scuppered by the coming pandemic.

A cycle lane – fairly common in large Colombian towns – took us into Zipaquirá, famous for its cavernous salt cathedral, termed 'the first wonder of Colombia' in the Rough Guide. Zipaquirá sits on top of a great mound of solid salt that was once at the bottom of a vast ocean. The salt has been mined over time on three different levels. The indigenous Muisca people were the first to extract the salt, and mining on a small scale continues to the present day. The original cathedral was created around 1932. It was carved out by miners to enable them to feel protected when doing their dangerous work. It was replaced by the current version in 1995 when it became unstable. Visitors take a surreal walk along tunnels blasted out by explosives and lit with gaudy lighting constantly changing colour through purple, green, red and golden yellow, all giving it a bit of a theme park feel. It is home to the world's largest subterranean cross – although there can't be much competition for the honour. Most of all we liked the figures carved in sandstone by the Italian sculptor Ludovico Consorte.

We had dinner at La Carreta – steak coated in a little crystallised salt cooked in a cloth, *al cuarto* (rare). We were astonished to see all sorts going on with flames when it arrived, and much pouring of wine over the meat. It was delicious, but after passing through all the land deforested for cattle farming, I felt guilty eating it. Since leaving Antioquia the native forest had noticeably diminished but when we did pass through pockets of wilderness we saw an immediate change in the variety of birds, butterflies and flowers.

On the route to Cota going up another popular hill climb which turned to dirt at the top, I found myself watching a guy racing up the hill ahead of me. I noticed that he had artificial legs that were going really well. Mauricio told us he had lost his lower legs and his right thumb to a bacterial disease, but he was getting on with life and he seemed very cheerful. He said that it was good that at least he had his knees and he could still do the things he could do before the illness of three years earlier. Mauricio lives in Bogotá but he doesn't ride in the city as he can't unclip quickly enough in tricky situations, so he starts some way out on quiet roads. He has a driver accompanying him on his rides and gets out around four times a week riding between 50 and 80 km. Impressive for sure.

🚲   🚲   🚲

We had only chatted with Dave and Monica for around fifteen minutes near Medellín, but they treated us like old friends when we turned up at their home – one of the many impressively smart newly built houses in this developing satellite town of Bogotá. They met in a pub in Bristol and within six months they were married. Monica had been teaching French and Spanish in Bristol for over ten years at the time. She had gone out from Colombia on a cultural teaching assistant programme and miraculously managed to get an extended visa for long term work, which – for some strange reason – is not usually given to Latin Americans.

They moved to Colombia, seeking a healthier lifestyle and a better education for their kids – interesting! Bristol is a charming city but they didn't see it as the place to bring up their children. The local schools didn't look promising and the city is crowded and busy. Monica, as a Colombian who doesn't look English, found the children she taught were often rude to her. When a chance meeting threw a job offer her way at the Colegio Gran Bretaña in Bogotá, they jumped at the chance to move with their two-year-old twins Laura and Tomas.

They work at the Colegio Gran Bretaña – Monica is now the deputy head. Dave, whose degree is in acupuncture, has gone through a fascinating career change. He left a flourishing medical practice, and completed his MSc research in the nick of time before flying out to Colombia to take up a teaching post in the same school as Monica. He now teaches history and geography and loves it. Monica tells me he is a wonderful teacher – and I can believe it. The children go to the same school and all four get up at 4:30am on a school day and are at school by 7am. They return by around 6pm – a long day, but they come and go as a family and see each other during the day too. They all love the school and the kids get a wonderfully enlightening experience of meeting children from all over the world. Laura has picked up bits of many different languages from school friends. Unlike in England where new and sometimes different kids can find it hard to integrate, the children at this school welcome strangers with sympathy and help.

Dave and Monica train on the ridiculously steep mountain roads that head up from the wide flat valley around Cota – dead end roads with gradients that make our local challenging climbs seem tame. They must be super fit, especially given the altitude (2,600m). Yes, we have the steep gradients but they don't go on and on, at an unsustainable effort level for six kilometres or more. From their lovely, light and spacious house, they have great views of the mountain range to the west where the killer climbs head up more than 400m above the valley. The children can play safely in the enclosed area around the four houses where there is a strong sense of community and the neighbours help each other. It was a treat to have a taste of their family life.

We cycled to the Bioparque La Reserva, a privately run reserve where animals and birds have been rescued from illegal trafficking. Toucans pecked at our boots and great horned owls with impressively feathery ears perched in the trees, along with huge parrots from the Amazon which were not able to fly, as they had previously been kept in tiny cages which affected their wing growth. We saw tiny, bright yellow frogs which live in the jungles of Chocó. They have enough poison on their backs to kill two bull elephants – or around 30 people! They were kept in a tank, but they were harmless as they were not fed on the diet of poisoned ants which the wild ones find tasty. An area of the nearby mountainside was being cleared of exotic species – in particular the eucalyptus, which we had seen being cut down in many areas we had travelled through. Now we found out the reason: this tree is very damaging to the local eco system as it is a thirsty species. It is native to Australia and doesn't belong in Colombia. We had to work for our lunch, riding up one of the ridiculously steep hills to Ambrosia, a hillside restaurant. On the way back home we tucked into great cakes in a café in town where they insisted on storing all our bikes inside.

Our visit had coincided with the Tour of Colombia, a professional cycle race passing through nearby Chía on its way to Zipaquirá. In Chía there is a huge bike park for leaving bicycles – gated, ticketed and guarded, hence eliminating the need to carry a lock. We stood on a bridge and watched the stars shoot under us – after five stages, Sergio Higuita of Colombia was in the lead by twelve seconds from Daniel Martinez (Colombia) and Jonathan Caicedo of Ecuador. The winner of the 2019 Tour de France, Egan Bernal was at 50 seconds with it all to race for the next day when the final 183km stage rose to Alto El Verjon (3,266m) high above Bogotá. We watched the final few kilometres on a television in a smart shopping mall, an area of fast food restaurants and shops selling all you could wish for.

Dave accompanied us out of town on his beloved custom made steel bike (Medellín – Hincapie). We had hit lucky as Sunday is the day that anyone with any interest in cycling gets out if they can, and they take over the roads. The main road to Facatativá wasn't the sort of route we would normally use but it worked really well for us as a quick way of returning to Carlos' route after deviating to Cota. The roads weren't closed to cars as they are on Sundays in

Medellín, but there are so many cyclists on the road that the drivers of motor vehicles know that the day belongs to pedal power. We had lunch in Facatativá – a pretty run-of-the-mill Colombian town. Hugh and I had a local dish, *changua* – a Colombian egg and milk soup. Ours had a piece of round bread soaking in the bottom of the bowl.

We both felt a little tearful as Dave rode away when we reached the dirt road climb after Facatativá. They had been so generous to us and we had enjoyed their company so much. We hoped to be able to return their hospitality when they visited England the next summer, but that was not to be. We had so much in common, even down to Dave having been a distance runner like Hugh.

We were about to leave the environs of the country's high-altitude capital, Bogotá, a city which we didn't intend to visit, heading south and a little west in a fairly direct line towards the border with Ecuador. Little did we realise how things would pan out. After Cota we dropped off the Altiplano, losing 2,200m of altitude, descending once more into the cauldron of the Río Magdalena valley at an altitude of only 290m – once again in debilitating heat that we hadn't known since leaving Barrancabermeja, the lowest point in our trip at less than 80m above sea level.

It took us four days to reach Cunday, where we took the scenic route to Purificación on the advice of a local farmer in preference to the ugly, inconvenient route suggested by the police. We passed through places with no obvious attractions and not much visited by foreigners – the sort of places that travel by bike leads in the interest of finding pleasant, quiet roads, along the general line of a journey. On arrival, towns often seemed a bit messy, and not all that interesting. However, after a night's stay, because it was time to stop, you warm to a place and its people. You leave feeling that it was a *muy buena estancia* and find you have enjoyed being part of the everyday life of the town.

Walking around Anolaima in the evening we noticed people looking at us curiously, possibly wondering what on earth we were doing there. We found a very decent hotel but with absolutely rubbish internet. We had breakfast at an outdoor kitchen nearby – *changua* again with a glass of fresh orange juice. They also gave us a bit of sausage to try – it was soft, and very tasty. The town is dubbed the Fruit Capital of Colombia. We sat down for a snack in the plaza and shared our nuts with the people next to us.

There were many bizarre fruits on sale in the huge market, and some very friendly locals offered us a few and showed us how to eat them – it wasn't obvious. They handed us some huge green pods with rough crinkly skins – we split the pods and sucked the sweet white coating off the seeds inside. Another fruit looked like a large potato. We peeled off the skin and sliced off the yellow flesh from the big centre stone.

It had been a glorious day's ride, particularly the first part where the terrain was lush. We hadn't quite reached the hothouse of the lower valleys, but we had reached the point where early starts were essential as riding beyond lunchtime was too hot.

Moving onwards down the lower, more gentle valleys, we passed through a region which looked like a getaway area for the rich of Bogotá looking to escape the often cool, murky weather of the high ground – super smart new homes of monstrous size, spa hotels with rooms at sky high prices and condominios with grand entrances and secure fences. Many new ones were going up and adverts outside tempted those wanting luxury swimming pools and manicured gardens. We thought about the cost in cement/water/land – can we/the country afford such opulence? We stopped early to cool off in the pool at the more modest hotel Villa Chela in Carmen de Apicalá, where dogs slept in the air conditioned ATM booths and the shops sold the trappings of beach holidays – blow-up dolphins and rubber rings. It was here that people gave us the first warnings of our proposed route to Purificación – 'possibly a bit dodgy for foreigners'.

An early start took us comfortably up and over the 600m climb to Cunday, from where there was no going back. As we were searching for a place to stay, we met a lady who gave us some delicious fermented juice – we asked her about the road ahead to Purificación – she just laughed when we asked about guerrillas. Little did we realise that we would be grappling with a difficult dilemma before we set out on one of the best 40km rides of the trip.

Three days after reaching Purificación, we arrived at the Desierto de la Tatacoa, a remarkable arid region of ochre and grey clays which have been sculptured by the infrequent rain into a landscape of fine gullies, majestic towers and sharp ridges – remoulded with the passing of every storm. It was when we stopped to absorb the extensive fine view that I first noticed a slight pain in my right shoulder, making it a little difficult to lift my arm above my head. I thought little of it as it was only a slight impediment and didn't affect my ability to control the bike.

As ever, Carlos guided us into the region via the back door – a very minor road approaching from the east rather than via the road from Villavieja to the west. From Purificación we had taken the rough, mountainous route through the small towns of Dolores and Alpujarra passing through dense forests to the tune of glorious birdsong and under layered cliffs reminding us of Applecross in Scotland. We had been caught out in some heavy storms and the dirt roads were slippery with mud and strewn with puddles. As we descended towards Tatacoa, cacti started to appear in increasing quantities on the hillsides. The air was becoming hot and humid as we lost height. The night's storm had taken its toll scattering an assortment of boulders across the road, dislodged from the ochre cliffs. We picked our way around the rocks and the pot holes filled with pink, silty water and made our way down to the swollen cloudy waters of the Río Cabrera, a tributary of the Río Magdalena. In the village of Baraya we stopped for a fresh doughnut; at least that is what the man called it as he lifted it out of the hot fat. They were nothing like doughnuts as we know them but delicious all the same – very light and filled with *arequipe* (otherwise known as *dulce de leche*, a sweet made of milk).

Baraya was our back door, from where a narrow, gravel track took us through a land becoming progressively more barren and intricately sculptured as we approached the heart of this colourful creation of nature. We travelled through a landscape of changing colours, the sea of bumps and ridges at first in shades of buff, white and ochre dotted with dark green trees; then changing to light clays tinted pale green with a layer of sparse vegetation; and finally turning to a more deep ochre with fine fingers of water-cut gullies. This was our chance to immerse ourselves in the surroundings without the distraction of other tourists; a selfish desire, I know, but for us this is one of the joys of travelling through rather than in-and-out, linking these special places into the thread of our journey and passing through the places less visited.

We found a room in the Hostal Noches de Saturno which turned out to be a much better option than putting our tent up in the yard. The afternoon storm hit with a vengeance, turning the earth yard into a stony bottomed lake with raging mini waterfalls surging over the little terrace walls. The area is known for clear skies making it a great spot for star gazing, but clouds got in our way.

The road we were advised not to take (guerrillas?)

CARLOS' COLOMBIA BEFORE COVID

The next day when we set out on foot to explore, the ground had turned into a trap of sticky, wet clay which added extra soles of mud to our shoes – thick and very heavy. As we walked through it we realised that there was much plant life – cacti, towering above us as tall as trees and dumpy versions forming squat rings close to the ground. There were spindly trees and bushes rooted in the valleys and gullies. White goats roamed over the rocky ridges. In reality Tatacoa is not really a desert, but rather a dry tropical forest ecosystem and it bears the name used for the rattlesnakes in this region of the country. The area is inhabited by shepherd families who mainly keep goats and cattle. It was far from dry during our stay and the snakes had hidden from the rain!

Two young Italians were staying in the *hostal*. They were seasonal workers, spending the Italian summers working in the hospitality industry, and during the Italian winters finding summer elsewhere. They were beginning to get a little anxious about whether or not they would have jobs to go back to because of this new disease, Coronavirus, which had first been identified in China. In February the disease had taken hold in northern Italy, and eleven municipalities had been put under quarantine. We felt for the couple in their dilemma about what they should do but we didn't think seriously about the effect it might have on our own journey. In our relative ignorance and naivety we saw it as a Chinese/Italian problem. This was our first hint of what was about to hit the world.

We moved on to the town of Villavieja, the usual access point for Tatacoa, expecting it to be something of a tourist haunt, but it wasn't. Just a few travellers lingered there – most stayed within the desert, moving on to a larger town when they left. A Bohemian Paraguayan family had parked their big, blue, Mercedes bus in the Parque Principal, a vehicle which looked as though it had been places on rough roads. Café con Leche and Viajando por Sudamerica were written on the bonnet and a huge snake was painted above the windscreen. Their two little girls were coating themselves in sticky mango. They told us that they intended to travel around for years. We often think of them and wonder what they did when Covid began to change the world. We found a beautifully calm boutique hotel with a swimming pool, naturally ventilated rooms, delightfully colourful décor and an excellent breakfast.

The local garage did us a favour when they said we couldn't wash our bikes there – 'no servicio', they said. So we washed the Tatacoan clay from our bikes in the waters of the Río Magdalena, by a jetty from where a tiny ferry took pedestrians and small motor bikes across the wide river; the nearest bridges were thirty kilometres away in both directions. Nineteen-year-old Daniel came up to talk with us, an ambitious young man studying mechatronics in Bogotá and wanting to go and work in Germany where there are more opportunities and his family has contacts. He was very interested in our bikes and our journey. He asked how we had cycled here with no gears so we told him they are hidden away in the hub – fourteen gears going low enough to get up the steep and rough Colombian tracks.

EXTRAORDINARY PLACES BY BICYCLE

At this point we realised that we would need to extend our visas as our stay was going to go beyond the 90 day tourist limit. In theory this was a straightforward process which could be done online.

After two attempts we thought we had it sorted but it just came back with 'NO FUE APROBADA' because we didn't have tickets out of Colombia, which is a requirement. We were planning to cycle over the border into Ecuador. However, we had sent them a copy of tickets out of Quito which we had bought from a website specialising in onward tickets, one of many outfits through which you can buy supposedly genuine tickets for around $12, but which are then automatically cancelled after achieving the desired effect. At least this was close to the truth as we were planning to fly out of Quito in Ecuador at the end of the trip, but we didn't as yet know when. However, a flight out of Ecuador didn't count.

This had also been a potential problem back in December when we boarded the first plane on our way to Medellín. We were told that the airlines will sometimes refuse to take passengers without the required return ticket for fear of being landed with the responsibility of flying the passenger back to their starting point once it is discovered on arrival in Colombia. There were stories of this actually happening to people who would then try to quickly book a cheap flight at the airport checkin. However, in Marseille, there was a more immediate problem with getting our bikes in the small hold of the plane taking us to Madrid, which we think had been a useful diversion. Our bikes did make it into the hold and we were never asked about return tickets but we had been ready to book a quick fix if necessary.

Leaving Villavieja, we took the back road following the valley of the Río Magdalena going south on the east side of the river. We cycled past paddy fields in warm, light rain just wearing vests and shorts. Eleven kilometres along the road we came to a river, running in spate right across the road. The only hint of the concrete ford was the sharp lip where the silty waters surged over a two metre drop.

Cars were parked on either side, waiting for the torrent to calm down. Those in heavy 4x4 vehicles braved the current and a few bold motorcyclists gave it a go too. I just took one look at it and thought, 'no way'! I couldn't possibly guarantee being able to hold on to my bike with the force of the current pushing us both towards the drop and the consequences of being carried down the river holding a bike didn't bear thinking about. Riding it was absolutely out of the question. However, the idea of waiting didn't appeal at all either – it could be hours or even all day – and neither did the idea of turning back entertain us.

Seeing our dilemma, three strong young men came rapidly to the rescue. Hugh went first. The four of them pushed his loaded bike through the raging, knee deep waters and soon made it to the other side, thankfully avoiding a potential broken spoke when a small log became trapped in a wheel. They came back across and then with an optimistic two finger salute (not the rude kind) to Hugh across the river they helped me cross safely too. This was so typical of the way Colombians had reacted to us in times of need – offering help without hesitation and with great cheer – they loved to help. We rode through the flooded outskirts of Neiva, the capital of the department of Huíla and crossed the Río Magdalena once more, finishing the day at Yagurá, on the shore of the Embalse de Betania, a reservoir created by a dam on the same river. It may have been a sensible option to try to sort out our visas at the Migración office in Neiva but it looked like a very unappealing place and we didn't want to spend time there!

I was having more trouble with my shoulder, which was getting painful enough to disturb my sleep, but fortunately still not too bad on the bike. I found that I was unable to lift my arm above my head and Hugh had to help me undress. It felt like some tendons or ligaments were complaining. However, we wanted to press on and climb up into cooler air again so we kept going. We found ourselves on the same route as a Dutch couple, Robin and Celine, who we had first met on our way out of Tatacoa. They were travelling for a year. For several days we kept bumping into them at café stops or resting places for the night and at times we rode alongside them. They were a third of our age and very strong so they were generally moving faster than us. In fact Robin had been a professional cyclist and had once beaten Tom Dumoulin of the Netherlands.

We were passing through delightful rural terrain which compensated for the stress of the shoulder pain, but I was having to take increasing amounts of Ibuprofen to be able to keep going. We met Robin and Celine in the pretty little village of Íquira, which in common with so many villages had a neatly gardened central square, and a huge ancient tree in the centre with a canopy so wide that we had to use 'panorama' setting to fit it in for a photograph.

There was more paved road than usual which I found helpful but once we hit the rocky dirt roads in the mountains, the pain became almost unbearable. After La Argentina we hit a particularly steep, rough road which workers were fixing after a washout by heavy rains. The people don't wait for repair teams to arrive – they just get on with the job themselves. It was impossible to ride and I hardly had time to consider how I was going to get up it when several of the workers came to our rescue and helped push our bikes up. At the top the women were ready with cool, fresh juice. The following, jarring descent was agony and we realised that I couldn't go on like this.

We rode on through a stretch of native forest, always a joy for the variety of birds, butterflies and plants that live in these truly wild places. This one was home to the blue-necked tanager, a bird with a brilliant blue head, black body and straw coloured shoulders – and a fascinating collection of butterflies including the Latreille's 89 which has the digits eight and nine inscribed in black on its white wings (but actually in the form 98). On the edge of the forest, Hugh spotted a perfect grassy place for a wild camp where we could relax and think about our options. I needed rest at the least, but if that didn't work then perhaps we would have to abandon the trip and fly home to get treatment. Even at that point on the first day of March, it hadn't occurred to us that the trip

Helping hands crossing a river in spate between Villavieja and Yaguara, Huíla.

might be abandoned for a totally different reason! El Trampolín de la Muerte was ahead of us, a route with a reputation that lures those fond of rough adventurous rides, and we were resolutely determined to take this wild and reputedly dangerous road over the Andes to Pasto on the western side. There was no way I would be able do it with a handicap.

We arrived at the road junction in Guacamayo where we would have to make a hard choice. Straight on would take us mainly downhill on a paved road to Pitalito just twelve kilometres away, from where it would be a paved 34 kilometres the next day up to San Agustín – a good place for a rest. The San Agustín archaeological zone is said to be home to the world's largest necropolis and the largest group of religious monuments and megalithic sculptures in South America. There would be plenty to occupy us, lots of excellent accommodation and good places to eat. We only had nine days left on our visas so that would have to be sorted out too.

Carlos' route to the right would involve more days of hard riding, on unpredictable but probably rough, steep roads taking us up to the waterfalls at

Bordones and then down to San Agustín. After a spell of easy downhill riding I was feeling pretty good so Hugh had to take a firm line in making sure we did the right thing. It was so hard to pass that turning. Up to then we had followed Carlos' route almost to the letter so it felt like copping out. It was some consolation that the Dutch couple had come to the conclusion that enough was enough after days bumping over stones, and decided to take the easier option too.

So we descended and hit the main road into the place we shouldn't have gone through, breathing in the noxious fumes from trucks on the kind of route we always try to avoid, and headed for the centro where we found a decent place to stay and a pizza place for dinner. The next day we found a cosy little cabin at the Hotel Yuma at a *finca* on the edge of San Agustín. In the morning we opened our windows to listen to an eclectic mix of melodious bird song including the cry of the ibis strutting across the field. We received a message telling us that our daughter Amy, then 28 weeks pregnant, had just passed her medical examination in obstetrics and gynaecology – brilliant.

It was frustrating dealing with migración and our visa extensions! Paula, who was working at our hotel, kindly allowed me to use her phone and I was able to talk to a person at migración, in English. I explained that we were leaving the country by bicycle for Ecuador, which was why we didn't have a ticket out of the country. She suggested that I attach a document with our applications explaining that we were travelling by bicycle and to include evidence of it. We decided to include our blog address and a few pictures. Hugh thought about posting a couple of inner tubes too!

It took a few goes, as the migración website wasn't behaving that well and each time it crashed we had to fill in the entire form again. All the extra information had to be got down to less than 1mb in pdf files which took a bit of work too. This was the price we paid for honesty – it would have been much easier just to get a bogus flight ticket out of Bogotá. Two days later we had moved to Casa Nelly, a *hostal* just oozing with charm, a little up the hill from the Hotel Yuma. We lazed in the hammocks hanging in the lush garden watching bright, yellow-backed orioles in the trees. We were getting anxious – we only had four days left on our current visas. Harry who was running the *hostal* helped us out in contacting migración yet again. Later that day we both received documents which we then had to take to a bank – not any bank, but the Banco de Occidente – which meant a tedious trip to Pitalito again; we took a taxi to get it over with quickly. We left with stamped documents proving that we had paid for our visas, which we photographed and sent off to migración. We could only wait hoping that a document proving our legal right to reside in Colombia for another 90 days arrived quickly – at least we had proof we had paid for them. Penalties for overstaying were said to be severe.

The really good news was that my shoulder was mending during the days spent sorting the visas, looking round the town, enjoying Colombian coffee in the cool cafés and, of course, visiting the large site of the San Agustín archaeological park just a short, peaceful and scenic walk from Casa Nelly. I phoned my mother, who was living in a care home in Blackburn, Lancashire, and told her we were about to go and visit some archaeological ruins. Her response was, 'we're a load of archaeological ruins here' which I thought was a great witty response for a lady of 88 with dementia.

The tombs of San Agustín are placed on *mesitas* (small tables) – flat areas on the hill tops. The views of the country around are an added bonus to the walk around the park. Tomb platforms supported by curious stone figures, solid stone tombs, sarcophagi and burial mounds have been unearthed and surrounded by fenced enclosures, some with rain shelters to protect against erosion and all within an immaculately maintained reserve. Visitors can stroll along tidy walkways and across immaculate lawns to view the huge collection of impressive statues, depicting gods or supernatural beings. Their curious features carved into the light tuft and volcanic rock are so well preserved and clean – large eyes, flat noses, pointed canine teeth. It's hard to take in that they date from the first to the eigth centuries. Perhaps the most unusual shrine of all is the Fuente de Lavapatas, a religious monument carved in the stone bed of a stream, with figures and faces peering out from the damp, blackened rocks of a small waterfall. It was astonishing to realise how long they had survived the effects of erosion.

After five days of rest I was ready to leave. The part of Carlos' route which we had skipped would have taken us to San Agustín via El Salto de Bordones, the country's longest uninterrupted waterfall which freefalls for over 400m. This was something we didn't want to miss so we set out along Carlos' route in reverse, going north, following the line of the Río Magdalena which was meandering in a deep, dark cleft down to our right. We were so happy to be on the road again, riding over carpets of red petals, enjoying roadside snacks of fresh oranges and cheesy *arepas* and chasing the bright orange and yellow butterflies with our cameras.

We crossed the river at the Estrecho del Río Magdalena, a point where the mighty waters are confined within a spectacular, narrow defile – for us the highest point we would reach on this iconic river which we had met at so many points along our journey. Stalls were set up providing refreshing fresh orange juice to tourists with the time to explore the surroundings of San Agustín. As he cut up the oranges the man at the stall told us it takes four or five oranges to make a serving of juice. He also asked us if we were married, so we told him, 'yes, for 45 years'. In contrast he had been through seven wives. A lovely lady gave us four oranges to carry up the hill. We were often given generous quantities of fruit – nice but so heavy. On our way up to Támesis at the start of the trip we had been given eight fragrant, exquisitely ripe mangoes which Hugh put in his panniers – we ate them all within a couple of days. In Colombia mangoes are as common as apples in England.

We stopped in Orlando to look at the museum there – mainly a collection of tombs. There were also photographs on display taken during the excavation of the San Agustín archaeological park. It was interesting to see how the site looked when these statues were first discovered, scattered about the mounds of excavated earth looking so dirty. Looking at these pictures aroused that sense of antiquity which can be lost when the ancient is spruced up – the same goes for the intensely renovated architecture of the Silk Road cities in Uzbekistan. I'm not saying that things shouldn't be tidied up or restored but something is lost and gained in the process.

Hugh was feeling inexplicably dizzy and I wanted to ease my shoulder into the ride slowly so we stopped early at the Finca Agroturística San José where we could relax in the garden watching the tiny *colibris* (humming birds). The *hostal* made us an excellent dinner and a hearty breakfast: a plate of fruit, lightly scrambled eggs, fresh cheese, coffee and a *tamalito* (a banana leaf filled with rice, maize and potato and then steamed). In the morning the father, Dagoberto, took all his three children to school on a motorbike – none with helmets, which isn't legal but out in the sticks nobody bothers.

The next day we passed by the burial site at Alto de las Piedras, another site within the archaeological park but much less visited. One of the stone tombs still bears traces of ancient red and black paint showing that the monuments were once very colourful. From here on the paved road surface degenerated into the familiar rural covering of stone and grit. We passed a group of men who showed absolute astonishment at the sight of Hugh's loaded bike and they were even more amazed when they struggled to lift it. Further up the road a couple of ladies asked us where we had cycled from and when we told them, 'Medellín', they just stared in amazement.

We arrived in Bordones where we treated ourselves to a room in the Hotel Bordones, a charming modern building full of interesting works of art and with a terrace giving a fine view of the sunlit spray of the waterfall tumbling down a cleft in the hillside – 400 metres may be an over estimate and the uninterruptedness is possibly questionable but it is an amazing waterfall without any need of statistics in support. This was a place to linger so we booked a large room with a view of the *salto* for two nights.

We walked to the waterfall, at first by a rough dirt road which would have been fine to ride; but we like the change of activity and it removes the problem of leaving the bikes somewhere safe while you take the final steep, narrow track down to the falls. It was a pleasant scenic walk and it took us around an hour to get to the *casa* where the narrow trail down to the falls takes off. We were offered a guide and given plenty of warnings about the possibility of slipping on the steep, muddy path, but we took off on our own. They charged us 4,000 pesos each for access but we only had a 10,000 peso note – they didn't have the change. We gave them the note and told them they could give us change when we came back. On the return he was going to give us our money back (around £2) saying he couldn't find any change so we told him to keep it.

They told us to turn left at the first *casa* down the hill, which turned out to be just a shelter, and we found the trail easy to follow and not too problematic if you are used to that kind of thing. We were surrounded by fluttering butterflies for most of the way as we walked through the forest, the most stunning specimen being the *Rhetus Dysoni* (Dyson's blue doctor). There were many flitting amongst the rocks and we had to take care not to fall whilst chasing them with our cameras. They have an iridescent blue sheen across the black, upper surface of the wings, which curve out to a point at the back where they are splashed with a touch of bright pink. We reached the viewpoint where we had seen people the day before, far below and across the valley from our hotel, but then we saw that the track continued further down. It was well worth continuing to get a view of the full length of the falls.

It was just wonderful to spend two nights at the Bordones Hotel; it is one of the best places we have ever stayed, perhaps our favourite place anywhere, closely followed by El Pilar Hosteria under Cerro Fitz Roy in Argentinian Patagonia. We had breakfasts and dinners on the terrace where the views of the falls and surrounding mountains are very special in the early morning and late evening light. They offer camping in the pretty little garden which is home to many *colibris*. Being the only guests, we had the full benefit of the warm hospitality of the staff who couldn't have done more to please us. We were told that more people come at the weekends. Cyclists had stayed there before, from France, Germany and England.

We saw no tourists on our walk but a friendly group of Americans did turn up at the hotel for lunch and we had a pleasant chat with them. In 2019 there had been a plan to pave the road and the hotel may have been built in anticipation, but the route remained rough – fun on a bike but not on four wheels.

Our visas had still not arrived by the time we left and we had reached the end of our permitted 90 day stay. We left the village of Bordones as the local schoolchildren, all dressed in the same light green sports pants and bright white shirts, were gathering in an outdoor sports area which was covered to provide shelter from sun and rain – these were common feature in the villages. We had to retrace our route for fifteen kilometres but then we joined the Ruta Nacional 20, a highway linking the city of Popayán on the west side of the Andes with Pitalito. We enjoyed a smooth and fast descent – a rare experience on this trip – to the Río Magdalena, which we crossed for the fifth and last time. Passing the turning we had taken up to San Agustín we re-joined Carlos's route once more, repeating a small section of the RN20 which we had ridden on our way out of Pitalito.

However, Carlos as ever had found a way off the highway and after only ten kilometres we turned off on a beautiful little back route, where people passed by on horse and cart, village houses nestled amongst a burst of colourful

Dyson's blue doctor, 'rhetus dysonii' – Bordones, Huíla.

flowering plants and flaming red flycatchers perched on telephone wires. From Bruselas the only route south is the RN45 and we would have to ride 115km along it to reach Mocoa, the gateway to El Trampolín de la Muerte. Even Carlos hadn't been able to find a ridiculous, steep and rough dirt road avoiding this one, but thankfully this highway in the far south of the country didn't carry much traffic.

We were almost out of food when we arrived in Bruselas. Hugh had spotted Finca Turística Bella Vista, marked on the map five kilometres down the RN45 which offered accommodation and a restaurant serving fish. The guys in the square verified this too but I decided it was best not to trust in it and bought enough food for an evening and the next day. Five kilometres up the road there was no sign of anything *turística* and the people we asked were very vague about it, one woman pointing up a very steep dirt track, and offering us a camp spot in her garden.

Hugh was determined to pursue it so we went up the track and parked part way up. Hugh walked 50m up to investigate and found a *finca*, but not operating as a tourist place at the time. He struggled to talk to the young lady because of the barking dogs but the outcome was that the owner wasn't there and she couldn't give us permission to camp. We had experienced this reaction before from people who were not the actual owners of the land – they fear getting in trouble with the owner. Hugh returned to me and suggested that I give it a try. A young man had passed me on a motorbike whilst I was waiting for Hugh. I went up to talk to the man and the lady Hugh had spoken to, and I remarked how beautiful the *finca* was and that we only needed a little space for our tent. We would be off early in the morning and we had all we needed except for water. Soon they were showing me where the *baños* were and the water supply of *agua potable*. It was fortunate that they hadn't seen Hugh kick one of the dogs which was threatening to attack him. We were soon pitched on a lovely grassy plot, just in time to cook dinner before dark. The dogs soon got used to us and went away with some encouragement from the dog dazer.

In the morning, the *proprietário* (owner) turned up, just when I was thinking that perhaps we should have left before he found us out. However, he was absolutely delighted to see us, and more than happy that we had enjoyed his hospitality in his absence. Javier then spent about twenty minutes creating a video featuring Hugh and Pauline's camping experience. Hugh of course got out the coffee making kit. He asked us lots of questions and we gave answers as best we could; when he plays it back later he may well have a good laugh at all those answers resulting from misunderstanding the questions. There was no sign of the supposed fish restaurant indicated on Google, but it is a coffee producing *finca*. Javier Sanjuan Gomez produces BosCafé.

We had been told that there wasn't much along the road to Mocoa – true enough – little in the way of *pueblos*, just little settlements here and there, one or two restaurants, fruit stalls, fish farms and the odd shop – but lots of dense tropical forest reaching to the very top of cloud-capped mountains, and heavy rain. The mountains are scarred with the bare tracks of landslides which have obliterated the forest and in one place the slipping earth had crushed a beautiful wooden, roadside house. There were many sections of *banca perdida*, where great bites out of the road had just fallen down the steep banking. It was an enthrallingly savage landscape, being constantly and rapidly changed at the hand of nature with no regard for the creations of man or woman. But the fight to keep life on the move was on-going; the locals took to DIY repairs, filling in potholes with thick clay and rocks, and attempting to extract donations for their labour from passing motorists. Fallen trees were rapidly removed by teams of men with saws.

We stayed at the less than salubrious hotel Gilvar in San Juan de Villalobos, the only significant place on the route at the half way point. A German cycling couple, Harold and Elke, were also staying there having come in the opposite direction from Ecuador.

As we entered the streets of Mocoa, choked with smelly, noisy motor bikes, we immediately felt that we would prefer to stay somewhere more tranquil.

CARLOS' COLOMBIA BEFORE COVID

Hugh got this across to a worker from a bank, who came out to help us as we stopped at the roadside wondering what to do. He recommended the Suma Wasi out on the south-west edge of town. It suited us just fine. It was such a surprise to find that the group of mainly Americans, who we had met at the hotel Bordones three days earlier, had just arrived too. We discovered that they are actually mush-roamers, or alternatively known as the Fungal Fellowship; they wander the forests of the world looking for fabulous fungi. Daniel is the inspiration behind these trips. Titiana, an ecologist, was their expert Colombian guide. We had a chat with her in the evening and she tried to persuade us to go to Ecuador via a flatter route to the south – we gave it some thought.

We were so pleased when they invited us to visit El Fin del Mundo with them the next day – they had spare seats in their bus. The End of the World is a wonderful little nature park. A path takes you through the forest and then along the line of a small river which tumbles over several picturesque waterfalls into clear pools, delightful for swimming. Then, without warning, the waters vanish over a monstrous drop. These are falls which you view from above – below is difficult to access through the thick forest. In the interests of stopping unwary tourists sliding over the edge, harnesses are provided – compulsory and included in the ticket.

However, without the mush-roamers we would have missed one of the other main attractions of the park. During the walk to the plunging falls we were introduced to an amazing variety of growths sprouting up from the leaf covered earth, colonising decaying logs and decorating the base of large trees – translucent growths like branches of jelly; fine white stalks bending outwards from the tree bark with wide white caps; little beige balls standing on short stalks, covered in long, thin white hairs; huge, stripy brackets; little caps in blue, yellow and red; and white fingers with grey anchors on the fallen logs. These North Americans are going against the grain of the normal line on fungi in their country which says that the only safe mushrooms come in a can. Not only do they hunt them and photograph them, but they also eat them. Their enthusiasm was infectious and it was such a privilege to be made so welcome as part of their group.

Chatting with Titiana that evening, it was clear that she had been reading the news on Coronavirus, and was concerned about what was happening. We had decided to stick to our original route – in any case the border with Ecuador had just been closed. We needed another day to rest and buy provisions in preparation for the hard route ahead and also to communicate with our family. However, our children had a better handle on what was happening in the world and the message was, 'if you want to get home, you'd better get out now'! It began to look like we might need all those magical immune-system boosting properties of Colombia's exotic fruits.

We considered the options. Did we want to return to a disease infested Europe? Would it not be safer to sit it out in Colombia where there were so few infections – only 22 recorded cases? Should we head straight for Bogotá from Mocoa and try to fly out as soon as possible – the airports could close any time? Could we fly to Madrid and cycle back to our son's house in Provence where our touring bikes are usually stored? However, we were at the foot of the infamous El Trampolín de la Muerte, the start of our route to Pasto. A good reason to turn around you may think, and yes, that probably would have been a sensible thing to do, but, the urge to ride it was so strong – it would be our final adventure in Colombia – much more of a draw than a dreary bus ride to Bogotá.

So, we began to seriously think of returning from Pasto – we would arrive there in four or five days' time. Would this be too late? Would the world's airlines have shut down by then and would all borders be *cerrado*? Would there be provision for repatriation? We didn't know the answers but we decided to take the chance. However, we did want to get home; we didn't like the idea of getting sick with the virus in Colombia where we had no idea how the authorities would react if the disease really took hold (mind you the same could be said for our own country).

In the space of a single day we had gone from thinking of Coronavirus as something not of immediate concern – of thinking we would still be crossing into Ecuador – to realising that the trip would be truncated and that the adventure over El Trampolín de la Muerte could cost us our flight home, should Colombia decide to go the way of Ecuador and close all land, air and sea borders. We sat by the pool with cool piña coladas, thinking about what lay ahead – would we regret our decision? We needed to book a flight out of Pasto, probably four days ride away, but we couldn't yet be sure how long it would take so reservations would have to wait. The good news was that I had got my extended visa but the bad news – Hugh's still hadn't arrived.

El Trampolín de la Muerte sometimes also called El Trampolín del Diablos (the Devil's Trampoline) is the name given to the 79km passage cut into the dense, mountain forest slopes of the Andes between Mocoa and San Francisco in the valley of Sibundoy. It isn't a road built for tourists or adventure cyclists – it is an essential transport route plied by trucks taking produce over the Andes. The next route over the Andes is over 130km to the north – the RN20 from Pitalito to Popayán. To the south, you have to go over 200km into Ecuador to cross the mountain chain.

There was eleven kilometres of paved road at the start, and then, to use the words of fellow *crazyguysonbikes*, Linda and Mike, 'the road turned to crap'. Vehicles passed in clouds of dust. The bends were tricky as they were often steep and heavily cambered – and sometimes very loose at the edges where the gradient was less demanding. We passed a couple of restaurants; there were enough places on the way to keep a cyclist well fed but we had sandwich stuff with us just in case. Rivers ran right across the road of grit and stone, adding their own collection of rocks to the mix. We ploughed in and hoped for the best. I tried to follow my daughter Amy's advice – just let the bike find its own way – but then the bike got it wrong and tipped me over. No harm done – the panniers took the shock.

The road zig-zagged up the near to vertical slope and way above we watched a truck moving along the ledge above. Sometimes there was a safety barrier – and sometimes not, where the ledge was narrow and there was no room for supporting posts on the abrupt edge. Thin waterfalls tumbled down from the cliff above. Higher up we found ourselves in the clouds, waterproofs on and passing trucks lit up brightly. As we approached the summit at 2,264m, clouds parted and formed magical shapes – a landscape of their own. Views of distant mountain ridges opened up through cloud, framed by trees of the forest – it was very special.

We had our work cut out to reach Los Cristales, marked on the map as a camping area and restaurant. We had considered camping a few kilometres above it but we would have been easily visible from the road and we weren't sure of the security in the area. Los Cristales is a messy place and noisy with the television from the bar, passing and stopping trucks, and music playing. We decided to pitch our tent on the grass over the road next to a pig sty. It was a shame not to have the wonderful mountain scenery to ourselves in a quiet spot. We cooked and ate just as it was getting dark and then had a facecloth wash in the tent – better than nothing but we still felt a bit sweaty. We had climbed nearly 2,000m on an energy sapping surface. The next day we were pretty tired but the thrill of the epic mountain journey kept us going. The state of the road improved a little and miraculously my shoulder was holding up. All minor worries were now beginning to pale into insignificance against the backdrop of a world becoming gripped by Coronavirus. The idea was to enjoy our last days of riding in Colombia and forget about the unbelievable state the world seemed to have got into so suddenly – but we found it just wasn't possible. We had been very fortunate to get so close to the end of our trip before it all started.

We continued rolling over the wet stones, riding through areas of landslides where slices of the hillside had recently sheared off creating a bare earth patch, starkly visible against the dark green backdrop of the forest. Passing under overhanging foliage, we clung to the inside of the road to allow trucks to pass – our eyes following the curve of the track tucking in and out of side gullies as it made its way up the steep valley side and our ears tuned into the sound of rushing water. Three times we stopped to dry the tent and each time spots of rain made it a pointless exercise. Finally a view opened up of a wide open valley and we could see San Francisco, the end of the rough road, and the straight line of tarmac leading to Sibundoy where we would stop for the night.

In Sibundoy, the heladería, la Gata Golosa caught our eye straightaway – that delectable mix, of ice creams as good as those in Italy, the most delicious fruit in the world, the ultimate chocolate sauce and crispy light rolled wafers. The proprietor, Carlos, sat with us and we chatted for some time. He told us a reason why the road is called El Trampolín de la Muerte. Not infrequently, trucks fall off the narrow bends of road and bounce down to the road below, and below and so on! To be honest we didn't feel in danger – on a bike you are in control of your own destiny to a great extent although there is always the unpredictable danger of landslide. It would be much scarier in a bus, truck or car. I had been worried about the possibility that the route would be overrun with trucks but it wasn't. Also, the truck drivers mostly know the road, are generally experienced and are very courteous to other road users including cyclists – and they travel slowly – the road demands it. These truck drivers are something special; it's not like driving down the M6 in England.

Nearing the top of El Trampolín de la Muerte, Putumayo.

We found a comfortable room in the Hotel Turistíca where there was good wifi – now essential as we couldn't wait any longer to book flights home – and we were still waiting for Hugh's extension visa. In the evening a guy came to ask us a few questions related to Covid-19 but we couldn't work out what the purpose was. He said it was for the government and seemed mainly interested in when we arrived in the department of Putamayo. We could have used a day of rest in Sibundoy but we were now feeling that we should get to Pasto as soon as possible.

The next day, Wednesday 18 March, was the day when what was happening in the world hit home hard. Talking to our children and booking our flights back home brought it all into focus. The best we were able to find was with Avianca from Pasto to Heathrow via Bogotá on Monday, 23 March – all earlier flights were fully booked. We were just thankful to have a flight. Our daughter's au pair had gone home to Majorca for a short break and then had been unable to return. We found out that a good friend of ours had just had his cancer treatment cancelled. Our son Andrew and family in France were effectively under house arrest, although he had been able to go out for some short runs. Our son Joe's wife was home schooling the kids and they had been self-isolating as a result of having coughs which were probably not Coronavirus but could be. At times like this you do have to be at home near to family.

With all of this on our minds we didn't much enjoy the day's ride. We were tired and although the road was paved, it was uncomfortably steep in places. The scenery didn't match up to the drama of the previous two days, although to be fair much of the mountain landscape was very pretty and there was a fabulous area of *páramo* landscape at the top of the climb. On the way out of Sibundoy we were stopped and questioned by the police – in the nicest possible way – about how long we had been in Colombia and Putamayo, and where we were going – all in relation to Coronavirus.

We ended the day in the curiously twee village of La Cocha on the *laguna* of the same name. It was a total surprise to us that it turned out to be a resort of sorts, mainly run by indigenous people living in pretty little timber houses, built along a water channel leading to the lake and lined with colourful small boats. We had the local delicacy of trout at the Restaurante San Francisco. We were the only people eating and the television news was dominated by Coronavirus. We chatted with a charming young Colombian couple who were in a dilemma as to whether or not they should return to Bogotá which was about to go into lockdown.

Our last day of riding in Colombia was a lovely climb through virgin forest, mainly in sunshine with views of Laguna de la Cocha and then the cultivated hillsides above Pasto on the descent to the city. We both felt very sad that our trip should be ending this way, although we had been very lucky to get so far. I felt quite tearful as I descended through the beautiful, lush forest and thought of the amazing journey we had taken – all thanks to Carlos. We tried to enjoy the ride but our minds were full of the troubles of the world and we were thinking of friends back home who would be hit hard by the situation. We were thinking of family and whether we would be able to help them. We were wondering what kind of England we would get back to if we were lucky enough to get back.

Getting a hotel in Pasto turned out to be more of a mission than expected. We wanted a nice place for the next four days so we went to the San Blass Boutique hotel which had a charming, spacious room. However, at this point we were told that we would not be able to leave the hotel on Saturday and Sunday – but we would be able to get a taxi to the airport on Monday morning. Pasto was going into lockdown as from the weekend. So we went looking for alternative accommodation at a place with a restaurant so at least we wouldn't go hungry.

That came to nothing, as yes, places had restaurants, but there would be no staff to run them at the weekend. So, back to San Blass. But, there were then more complications as it became unclear whether or not they could accommodate foreigners – especially from virus ridden Europe. What were we supposed to do then – sleep on the streets or in our tent in the park? After a long wait while the receptionist phoned whoever called the shots, we were granted permission to stay. She was very interested in the date of our arrival in Colombia – sufficiently long ago to make us virtually no risk! In addition we still had the issue of Hugh's visa extension, despite repeated emails to migración. The last thing we wanted was any extra complication as we made our escape.

It was clear that we only had the rest of Thursday and Friday to do what needed doing while the city was in operation – looking pretty normal in fact. First of all we went looking for bike boxes, tape and string. A small bike repair place pointed us in the direction of Bicimania which had a whole stash of boxes in pretty good shape.

First thing on Friday morning we read a message on our guestbook telling us that Avianca had cancelled all international flights and 84% of internal flights – as from Monday – the day we were due to fly. Checking on the Avianca website listed our flight as cancelled, although our flight to Bogotá from Pasto was still up and running. We had booked the tickets through Trailfinders, as they are usually helpful and very easy to get hold of on the phone. They told us that their live information was that our Bogotá/London flight was still going. Moreover, if it went pear shaped then they would do their best to get us home. They had been very successful at getting people out of Ecuador which was encouraging.

Our hotel receptionist gave us face masks. Even though at this point there were no recorded cases of the dreaded virus in Pasto most people were wearing them. Hand washing seemed to be the best prevention and there was hand gel all over the place. As we went into the supermarket looking for provisions for the weekend, a guy at the entrance squirted some on our hands. We found a lovely little shop selling nuts, seeds, dried fruits and oats, and we stocked up on fruit from street stalls. All workers in restaurants and cafés were wearing face masks and plastic gloves.

The other priority was to get Hugh's extension visa sorted. We went to the office in Pasto and after a lot of conversation, which we couldn't make head or tail of particularly with the masks on, and much use of Google translate, we managed to find out that the problem was a fault in the system. We persuaded them to give Hugh a sort of replacement document from the office – not quite the real thing but hopefully good enough. We really felt for the Haitian youths queuing outside the office and wondered what would happen to these people in such a crisis – and all the Venezuelan workers and refugees we had seen earlier on in the trip, particularly Luis who we met in Zapatoca. We saw quite a few people around the city lying on the pavement, sleeping, twitching and looking despondent. The people at the bottom of the pile were going to be hit so hard.

After doing the chores we needed to do whilst we had freedom, we went on a walk around the city. We couldn't get into any of the interesting buildings or churches – all were closed. Even some of the cool cafés had shut early but we made the most of what was open. Later, when we went in for dinner at the Volcafé the young women at the next table quickly donned their masks. When we explained that we were not fresh from Europe and had been in Colombia for 100 days, they took them off again.

The hotel San Blass was the limit of our horizon for the weekend. We began to piece together what the receptionist must have been discussing on the phone on Thursday night. If we were to stay for the weekend, someone would have to be there with us – they had not been expecting to have clients. Paulo, a member of the family who own the hotel and a dentist by profession, took on the job. He came just to look after us and he was so helpful. If we needed anything he would get it – provisions or takeaway food; he told us that we could use the kitchen on the roof terrace if we needed to and he booked a taxi for us to get to the airport on the Monday morning. Each evening a cup of aromatic tea complete with floating strawberry slices arrived in our room. In the morning Paulo made us a good breakfast.

We couldn't have found a better place for a weekend of confinement. The roof terrace had 360° views of the mountains and the nearby volcano; the pretty white and pale blue Templo San Felipe; the towers of the Iglesia Santiago Apostol; and a large extent of the modern city. We could at least get outside. Our room was luxurious with a comfortable sofa, tasteful artworks and ornaments plus a great view from the bathroom shower. We realised that we had just missed getting to the Equator which was one degree to the south.

Our first priority was to pack the bikes in the boxes. Then we got in contact with family and heard stories of how life was changing at home. We contacted Trailfinders and they gave us the same story but our flight still showed as being cancelled on the Avianca website. Sunday brought even more frustration over our flight – Trailfinders saying they would let us know straightaway if it wasn't going, friends in Bogotá telling us that Bogotá airport was closing as from Monday, the Avianca site continuing to show it as cancelled and a friend in the UK telling us that the flight was shown as going. All extremely frustrating and anxiety inducing. It was so good that we had Paulo to cheer us up – and a good supply of beer and wine.

Monday morning came with the predictable news. I persuaded the guy at

Trailfinders to look at the Avianca website – and – yes – finally – he had to agree that the flight was probably cancelled. We arrived at Pasto airport in two separate taxis with the bike boxes protruding from each boot, thankfully secured by ropes. It wasn't even clear that we could get on the flight to Bogotá at first, but after some moments of anxiety they took us. It was very clear that we would get no further. I was angry that Trailfinders had strung us along for three days when we could have been looking for an alternative.

At Bogotá airport the only people around were the lucky ones in the queue for the KLM/Air France flight to Amsterdam; I made enquiries but they told me there was a long waiting list for all KLM flights which were the only ones operating. The only help came from officers of the German Embassy. Tino told us – yes we could leave the airport and return as necessary; we could go out to get food and for twenty minutes of exercise, one at a time. He gave us a list of *hostals* and hotels which were open to foreigners – Europeans were not popular. I felt we needed to go around with headbands on saying we had been in Colombia for 100 days and were uncontaminated.

We decided to make the most of a bad job and head for Candelaria, the historic centre of the city, so we took a taxi – a big one this time – to the Casa de la Vega, a beautiful old colonial hotel. The staff were extremely helpful in letting us use their phone to contact the British Embassy, but the embassy staff were no help at all. Hugh managed to email them and got an emergency number to ring – in Chile. The next day I managed to get an email address which enabled us to send our details and then request repatriation. This came, not from the embassy website, nor from the Foreign Office website but on the embassy twitter feed. So having shunned both Facebook and Twitter, I had to sign up to the latter to get crucial information. However, it wasn't really a repatriation flight that was under discussion but a commercial flight with Avianca which would only run with enough demand and in addition could cost around $1,800 each.

Meanwhile we received a WhatsApp message from Harold and Elke who we had met briefly in San Juan de Villalobos. They were staying at the Cranky Croc *hostal* nearby, a place run by a helpful and friendly Australian married to a Colombian. Our decision to move there turned out to be our saviour. The place was full of mainly young people, all desperately trying to find a way to get home and some were well clued up on the options. Flights were operating in a highly unpredictable manner, mainly through Air France/KLM, with last minute alterations common and information on the airport departures list and airline websites erratically changing. We heard that the Avianca flight to London was likely to go ahead in a couple of days' time. At least we were in the best place to make a last minute move – we were thankful that we had at least got to Bogotá.

On Wednesday, 25 March, we booked a flight to Manchester via Cartagena and Amsterdam – leaving at 16:30 on Thursday 26 March (our grandson

CARLOS' COLOMBIA BEFORE COVID

Elliot's eleventh birthday) with KLM. This sounded good – Manchester being much closer to our home than London and an easy train ride to Oxenholme, near Kendal from where we could cycle home. Interestingly some of the inhabitants of the Cranky Croc, including Harold and Elke, had decided to sit it out in Bogotá, hoping to continue with their travels later. Celine from the Isle of Man had also decided to stay for the duration as she had nothing to go back to, no job back home and staying in Bogotá would be much easier on her bank account. There were also three Swedes who had turned up after a fourteen day curfew was imposed on arrivals. They were living in strictly enforced isolation in their room with food left at the door – now and again police came to check on them. There was also a German guy who had put himself into self-isolation pending the results of a test as he was showing some symptoms.

We saw what we could of Bogotá whilst on permitted shopping trips. We surreptitiously took photos – behaving like a tourist was definitely frowned upon as was being out without a mask on. The Cranky Croc was a cheerful place to stay with good food and coffee on offer, interesting company and a little live music which we made a small contribution to.

On the day of our flight Hugh woke at 4am and was on to his favourite app FlightRadar24, which shows the status of all aircraft in the world. He was straight on to our flight number (KL749 – KLM) and was initially dismayed to see it was cancelled. Then all changed. We watched the little red plane on the screen boarding and then take off along the runway and head for Bogotá from Amsterdam's Schiphol. However, it still wasn't listed as arriving at El Dorado airport, Bogotá – but by 9:30 it appeared. We set out for the airport – again in two taxis – and then joined the queue to get our temperatures checked. Help – what if we had a fever? There was a check by migración and they noticed straight away that our entry stamps showed we had been in the country for more than the permitted 90 days. We handed over our documents, including Hugh's makeshift extended visa document. The officer looked at it for a long time but finally he waved us through. That visit to the office in Pasto had been well worth the time.

At the last minute I got called up for a random hold baggage check. We had put our panniers into hessian sacks to get around the limit on the number of luggage items allowed. We were just in time to stop them cutting the sacks open and destroying them. It was a good job we had the extra tape and string to do them up again. No problem and we got some exercise walking miles through the airport. It was a relief to find that they weren't interested in the bike box – or so we thought.

We were treated to a glowing early evening view of the high-rise of Cartagena as we landed to fill up the other half of the plane and pick up a new crew. The original crew changed to plain clothes and continued with us. This was the last KLM flight out of Colombia for an unspecified amount of time. As we taxied away from the gate, there was a heart-warming send off from the ground crew, waving Dutch and French flags. The airline must have flown so many stranded tourists out of the country in those last few days. Many aircraft on the runway had covers over their engines – they were not expected to fly anytime soon. Bogotá airport was to close until 1st May at least – or longer. We knew we were so lucky to be on our way home.

After a sleepless night we landed in Amsterdam. Almost every flight on the departure list was labelled cancelled – but ours was going. We were surprised to see the airport shops open – all was closed in Bogotá. Some passengers were taking the virus super seriously though, being dressed in full body suits with hoods, masks, gloves and goggles.

When we collected our baggage in Manchester, Hugh's bike box turned up with a completely open top. Thankfully nothing was missing. My baggage sticker must have been on his bike box. We assembled the bikes in a near empty airport. There were no checks or advice at the airport. We rode to the station and took a train heading for Windermere – there was only one other passenger on board. We got off at Oxenholme and relished the ride home, which is always a joy – particularly when the sky is blue and the lanes are lined with a profusion of bright yellow daffodils. We were so happy to be back and very grateful that we live in such a beautiful part of the world where there would be no problem making the most of our daily ration of exercise as decreed by Prime Minister Boris Johnson.

The final entry in our blog reads: Saturday 28 March 2020. *Últimas Palabras: Mil gracias Carlos - fue maravilloso*:

> As we flew out of Cartagena we both had tears in our eyes. Colombia, we didn't want to leave you so soon. Not in our wildest dreams could we have believed it would happen like this. I was thinking back over our journey – one like no other and like no other will be. It had been the most amazing ride, and all thanks to Carlos. He had given us a most precious gift sharing with us his intimate knowledge of his wonderful country and the roads less travelled. All that time ago in Chile and Argentina he had told us his country was beautiful, its fruits were exotically delicious and its people so warm and welcoming – and so it was. We can never thank him enough. I would so much like to give him the biggest hug. I hope one day I can, but, perhaps we will never meet again. We will always keep in touch in the digital world.
>
> We took a chance, going as far along the road of Carlos as we dared, and it was close at every turn. We were nearly trapped in Bogotá – but it is over-dramatic to think of that as the end of the world! We wish those who chose to stay back at the Cranky Croc well and we're sure they will have lots of fun – like so many others making the most of their more limited world.

We kept in contact with a few people from the Cranky Croc – they finally returned home as it became clear that the virus could be around for a long time. At the start I would not have believed we would do this, but we followed very nearly every twist, turn, energy sapping climb and bone shaking descent of Carlos' trace as it soon became apparent that there was a good reason behind all his selections which turned our trip into something magical, way beyond the possibilities we could have worked out for ourselves. How lucky we were to be able to almost complete this journey before the whole world changed out of all recognition.

Epilogue

Put me back on my bike

Tommy Simpson

Pauline:

My mother frequently gave out the advice, 'do what you can, whilst you are able to do it.' We went for it and we have no regrets.

In 2020/2021 there was a three pronged setback to our travelling lifestyle, creating a cloud of uncertainty over the possibilities for the future. We looked back on ten years of fascinating journeys by bike, and realised how fortunate and privileged we had been, to have spent more than half our time away from home, on journeys of between a few months and almost a whole year. Several crucial elements combined together to make it possible – some under our control and others down to good luck. We had been able to give up our jobs at a relatively early age (56 and 57). We had sufficient funds for what we needed in life. In any case, bike touring need not be expensive. We had the health and fitness to take on a very physically challenging activity – excepting one significant hiccup! And, the world was very open for travel excepting a few countries where travel was not advised by the UK Foreign Office and others which threw in the hassle of visas. Perhaps, most significantly we had the motivation – and who knows where that comes from? It was something that we were both very keen to do, together.

There were some sacrifices. We went long periods of time without seeing our close family – particularly significant when we had young grandchildren growing up quickly. I have to admit that there were times when I felt that I should have been around to help my mother but I left it up to my younger sister who was always supportive. I tried to make up when I returned home.

This book was written during a global pandemic, beyond our control, predictable by those with insight, but totally unexpected as the event that would curtail our trip to Colombia and restrict the possibilities, possibly for the foreseeable future. So, in late 2020 we took to travelling by proxy, re-living our wonderful journeys of the past in the process of writing – indeed, without the pandemic keeping us grounded, this book may never have come to life. Moreover, the joy of putting our story into words helped us a great deal through the hard times of the pandemic and other unfortunate concurrent events in our lives.

Our travel had been interrupted in 2014 when Hugh underwent extensive treatment for bladder cancer, which included six weeks of radiotherapy. The success of the treatment had enabled us to undertake seven more extensive journeys around the world, but at the end of 2020 unwelcome late effects of that radiotherapy took a nasty turn when it came to light that Hugh had

EPILOGUE

developed 'radiation cystitis' – a condition in which blood loss can result in severe anaemia. It made for a very stressful January in 2021, including Hugh picking up Covid-19 whilst in hospital for seven days of treatment on the bladder. Hugh also had treatment for two outbreaks of melanoma – too much time in the sun perhaps! On Christmas Eve 2020 my bike slid on hard black ice and I broke bones in the pelvis. However, this turned out to be the least of my problems when a tumour was found on my left kidney leading to removal of the kidney, in June 2021. Fortunately, at the time of writing, we are both mending and are keen to get on the bikes again soon.

With medical issues to be added to the list for both of us, it is clear that in addition, travel insurance is going to be a nightmare even assuming the resolution of some conditions. We are very slim and exercise is endemic to our lifestyle. We eat very healthily and we have never smoked – but this had not been enough to protect us and the positives don't seem to hold as much weight with the insurance issue.

The third setback came from Brexit – that archaic nationalist action taken by our government just when a world of global problems requires nations to work together. It had been our idea to cut or eliminate air travel and explore more of the varied cultures and landscapes of Europe and the neighbouring countries. We would now need health insurance for the EU and even worse, we would be restricted to 90 days of travel in the EU Schengen zone within any 180 day period. We had reached this limit on our previous tour of Europe but would have overshot it substantially had we not spent a good deal of time in the countries of eastern Europe which are not in the Schengen zone – although some are very likely to join before too long.

All that can be said about the future now is that it is uncertain – but it is always uncertain. We have done what we can whilst we can and will continue to do so as the vagaries of life allow. Shorter trips closer to home and shorter distances perhaps, but hopefully still that free-form travel that we love, incorporating fresh air and exercise that we are addicted to. Meanwhile we have been making the most of mini-adventures close to home – bike rides, gill scrambling, seeking out hidden gems that we have never been to before. We are so fortunate to live in a beautiful place that we have always been happy to return to.

Whatever happens in the future, the experience of so many years of serendipitous travel will always be with us, deeply colouring our outlook on life. Whilst in many ways the world is controlled by the rich, the powerful and the greedy, the normal citizens, trying to make the best of their lot are overwhelmingly kind, helpful and generous. We struggle to think of any bad experiences with the people we have met on our travels – we have never been robbed, mugged or left in distress. It is so much easier to recall times when we have been offered help – food for the road, a home for the night, help in getting things fixed, directions on where to go – in places where we were total strangers from a different culture with minimal knowledge of the local languages.

INDEX

Abel Tasman National Park 260
Abercrombie River 54
Acquacanina 300
Afghanistan 129, 140, 143, 146
Aglientu 64
Agrigento 67
Agua Azul 209
Aiud 281
Ak Tal 170, 171, 179
Ak-Baital Pass 160, 161
Akhaltsikhe 102
Akkyia-Ashuu 173, 175, 177, 178
Akzhigit 123
Albarracín (Sierra de) 320
Alberobello 70
Alcaraz (Sierra de) 320
Alghero 65
Alichur 156, 157
Almaty 180, 182, 187, 188
Alpine Way 53
Alpujarra 365
Altiplanicie de Nipe 201
Altiplano 16, 19, 26
Altofonte 67
Amsterdam 168, 385
Amu Darya River 125
Ancona 296, 301
Andes 25, 28, 38, 336
Angkor 248, 249, 250
Anlong Veng 247
Anolaima 364
Antigua Vía al Mar 342
Antioquia 333, 335, 337, 338
Apple Tree Bay 260
Aqtau 113, 114, 115, 116
Aquitania 359
Aragon 321
Aral Sea 125, 126
Ardahan 100
Ardèche 321
Argentina 17, 25, 26, 27
Arica 11, 26, 36
Arizona 206
Aspet 321
Assisi 296, 298
Assy plateau 185

Australia 38, 39, 40, 44
Aysén 25, 31, 32
Azerbaijan 103, 109, 110, 111

Baetovo 175
Bahía Inútil 327, 328, 330
Baile Felix 286
Baisha 230, 232, 233
Baku 107, 111, 112, 113
Balakan 110
Balkan 271, 274, 275, 276
Balladonia 41, 42
Banja Luka 290
Baqueira 321
Baracoa 200
Baraya 366
Barichara 352
Barrage de Al Wahda 314
Barranca del Cobre 218
Barrancabermeja 326, 348, 349, 364
Basilicata 69
Bastia 62, 63, 296, 301
Battambang 249, 252
Bayburt 92, 93, 94, 95
Belgium 60, 61
Bell 56
Beni Ahmed 305, 311, 313
Benkovac 294
Beyneu 115, 116, 118, 119
Biletić Polje 268
Birán 201
Bisbee 206
Bishkek 143, 160
Bixad 285
Blacktoft 59, 60
Blagoevgrad 275
Blenheim 261
Blue Mountains 53, 54
Bogotá 343, 353, 363, 371
Bolaven plateau 243, 245
Bolivia 9, 10, 16, 17
Bonifacio 64
Bordones 371, 372, 373, 374
Borjomi 102, 103, 104
Bosa 65
Bosansko Grahovo 293
Bosnia 263, 265, 266, 267

INDEX

Bosnia and Herzegovina 268, 270, 274, 293
Boured 316
Boyacá 338, 358
Brindisi 71
Brugge 60
Bruselas 375
Bruxelles 60
Bucaramanga 351, 352
Bukhara 122, 130, 131, 132
Bulgaria 274, 276, 277, 279
Bulunkul 155
Bunda Cliffs 46
Burdur 80
Burra 51

Cagliari 65
Caiguna 43
Calabria 62, 68, 69
Caldas 332
Camargue 306
Cambodia 98, 222, 237, 247
Camerón 327
Campeche 209
Campo Alacaluf 30
Canal du Charleroi 60
Cancún 207
Candelario Mancilla 34
Cape Farewell 260
Cappadocia 78, 84
Cappella Palatina 66
Carmen de Apicalá 365
Carpathian Mountains 280
Cartagena 353, 385
Cascabel 206
Caspian Sea 103, 115, 116, 120
Castiglioni di Sicilia 69
Castilla-La Mancha 321
Catalunya 321
Caucasus 105, 109
Çayıralan 88
Cayo Jutías 203
Cazorla (Sierra de) 320
Ceduna 38, 48, 50, 57
Central Asia 58, 85, 103, 129
Central Asian Steppe 297
Cero Fitzroy 36
Charalá 323, 327, 354, 356
Chefchaouen 311, 312, 313, 314
Chengdu 221, 222, 223, 237
Cherbourg 296
Cherven 278
Chía 363
Chiapas 208, 209, 210, 211

Chichén Itzá 207
Chihuahua 217, 220
Chile 19, 26, 27, 29
China 221, 222, 223, 224
Chirpan 276
Chivay 13
Chocó 323, 327
Christchurch 255, 262
Cienfuegos 202
Ciudad Bolívar 323, 334
Cluj-Napoca 282
Cochrane 327
Cocklebiddy 43, 45
Colca Canyon 13
Colombia 326, 329, 333, 337
Colțești 282
Coñaripe 27
Concepción 344, 345, 346, 347
Confines 354
Conguillío Park 27
Cordillera Central 347
Corsica 62, 63, 65, 75
Corte San Carlos 32
Cortona 296, 298
Çoruh River 95
Coscomatapec 214
Cota 361
Coyhaique 30
Crete 72, 73, 74
Croatia 264, 289, 293, 294
Cuba 192
Cuenca (Sierra de) 320
Cunday 323, 324
Curtea de Arges 280

Daju 230, 233
Dali 235
Danube 278, 279, 280, 288
Dardara 312
Darling Causeway 56
Dead Horse Gap 53
Deçan 270
Dekh 147
Désert des Agriates, 296
Deustua 15
Divriği 87, 89, 90, 91
Dolores 365
Don Det 246
Don Khon 246
Don Som 246
Drôme 62
Dublin 296
Duitama 354, 356, 357, 358

Duomo di Monreale 67
Durango 217
Đurđevića Tara Bridge 269
Dushanbe 142, 143, 148, 149

Ebian 225
Ecuador 364, 368
Eğirdir 82
El Alto de Curies 360
El Bolsón 28
El Calafate 36
El Carmen 356
El Carmen de Atrato 323, 334, 336, 337
El Chaltén 35, 36
El Fin del Mundo 377
El Poblado 331
El Sosneado 26
El Tajín 213
El Trampolín de la Muerte 375, 378, 380
Elena 277, 289
Emeishan 224
England 168, 296
Erhai Lake 235
Erzincan 92
Escuela la Jaula 26
Esperance 41
Eucla 46
Exploradores Valley 31
Eyre Highway 38, 48, 50

Fabrizia 70
Facatativá 364
Farewell Spit 258, 260
Fenian track 259
Fergana valley 163, 175
Fethiye 69, 79, 94
Fiastra 299
Firavitoba 360
Firenze 297
Flinders Range 50, 51
Florence 296, 301
Fontaine de Vaucluse 322
Fowlers Bay 48
France 22, 61, 62, 81
Fraser Range Station 42

Galán 352
Galsa 286
Galston Gorge 56
Ganluo 226
Gent 60
Georgia 93, 95, 99, 100
Ghund river 153
Ghythio 73

Gibara 201
Gibraltar 308, 309, 318
Giurgiu 279
Glamoč 292
Globe 206
Golden Bay 258, 259, 260
Göle 100
Gölhisar 80
Göreme 78, 79, 84, 86
Gori 104
Gorno-Badakhshan 143, 150, 152, 158
Gouillou 321
Goulburn 54
Gran Templo Vegetal Sakroakuarius 355
Granma 196
Great Australian Bight 44, 46
Great Dividing Range 53
Greece 71, 72, 73
Green Hammerton 60
Guanajuato 215
Guantánamo 199
Guatapé 344

Hanyuan 225
Hasan Dağı 83
Havana 193, 194, 196, 204
Havelock 261
Hawkesbury River 56
Heaphy Track 258
Heysham 296
Holguín 195, 201
Hongsa 241
Hoteni 283
Houay Xay 239
Huanglongxi 221
Huíla 348, 369, 370, 375
Hull 58, 60, 180

Idvor 288
Imata 13
Ipiales 330
Ireland 22
İspir 95, 97
Issyk-Kul 169, 179
Italy 66, 68, 69, 70
Iza 359

Jade Dragon Snow Mountain 230
Jaén 320
Jalalabat 175, 176
Jalpan de Serra 215
Jangy Talap 178, 179
Jarahueca 198
Jardín 333

INDEX

Jaslyk 124
Jelondy 154
Jenolan caves 54
Jericó 333, 334, 336
Jindabyne 54, 98
Jinghong 237
Jinkouhe 225
Jinsha (river) 230

Kadji-Sai 179
Kahurangi National Park 257
Kaiteriteri 260
Kalaikum 145, 150
Kampot 250, 253
Kangal 89
Karakol 179, 180
Karakorum Highway 140, 162
Karamea 259
Kashgar 159, 162
Kassita 316
Kazakhstan 116, 118, 123, 143
Kazarman 177
Kegen 181, 182
Kep 254
Khemiss Anjra 309
Khiva 122, 126, 128, 130
Khone Pha Pheng Falls 246
Khorog 145, 148, 150, 151
Kissamos 73
Knin 293, 294
Kninsko Polje 293
Kochkor 169
Koh Kong 252
Kohaihai 257, 258
Koitezek Pass 155
Kokpek 185
Kolympia 75, 76
Konya 84
Kosovo 270, 271, 272, 273
Ksar es Seghir 309
Kuang Si Falls 241
Kungrad 122, 125
Kurucaova 83, 84
Kyrgyzstan 148, 149, 158, 159

L'Isle-sur-la-Sorgue 302
La Argentina 346, 369
La Cocha 381
La Farola 200
La Fuente 352
La Herradura 320
La Joya 12
La Mula 197

La Ruta de los Siete Lagos 28
La Tour-d'Aigues 296
Lagnes 296, 302, 306, 308
Lago del Desierto 35,36
Lago Nahuel Huapi 28
Lago O'Higgins 34
Lago Umayo 15, 16
Lago Yelcho 26, 29
Laguna Amarga 32, 33
Laguna Chaguay 25
Laguna de Tota 359
Lake Karakul 160
Lake Titicaca 16
Laos 239, 241, 242, 243
Las Tunas 196
Les Alpilles 306
Leshan 224
Lige 228, 229
Lijiang 229, 230, 231
L'Île-Rousse 302
Lindos 75
Livorno 296, 301
Llao Llao 28
Lleida 321
Loire 20, 62
Loreto 301
Los Cristales 379
Íquira 369
Luang Namtha 239
Luang Prabang 241, 242
Luberon 62, 296
Lucca 296, 301
Lugu Hu 228

Macedonia 272, 273
Macerata 300
Madura Pass 43
Mallku Villamar 17
Mamazair 158
Mani 73
Manila 331
Manzanillo 196
Maralinga 47
Maramureș 282, 283, 285
Marche 296, 298
Mariel 204
Marlborough 262
Marmaris 75, 76
Marmoraia 297
Marseille 62, 296, 302
Matai Valley 261
Matanzas 196
Matera 70

– 393 –

Mawson Trail 51
Medellín 326, 331, 332, 333
Mediterranean 79, 81, 94, 117
Mekong (River) 237, 239, 240, 244
Melilla 303, 308, 314, 318
Mendoza 26
Messina 69
Meulebeke 60
Mexico 205, 206, 207, 208
Midar 316, 317
Minas 201
Mirador de los Torres 33
Mirador de los Volcanes 13
Moa 200
Moana 256
Mocoa 375, 376, 378
Moctezuma 219
Moldo-Ashuu 166, 167, 175
Monemvasia 73
Mongui 358
Mont Gourougou 303, 305, 317
Mont Ventoux 62
Montagne Sainte-Victoire 296
Montenegro 268, 269, 270, 274
Montpellier 306
Montsant (Sierra de) 320
Morgan 51, 52
Morgantina 68
Morocco 303, 304, 305, 308
Morón 201
Mostar 264, 265, 266, 267
Motril 304, 310, 318, 320
Mounlapamok 246
Mount Etna 68, 69, 84
Mount Victoria 56
Mtskheta 105
Munda Biddi 39, 40, 54
Mundrabilla Station 41
Murato 302
Murderer's Rock 261
Murghab 158, 159, 163
Murray River 51, 98
Mystras 73

Nacozari 205
Nador 303, 304, 308, 319
Napier 39, 255
Neiva 348, 369
Nelson 260, 261
Netherlands 61
Neutral Bay 56
Nevers 62
New Zealand 255

Nikšić 268
Nobsa 358
Norseman 38, 41
Noul Roman 280
Novi Sad 288, 289
Nozières 62
Nukus 125, 126
Nullabor 43, 53
Nundoo 48

Oaxaca 212, 213
Olympia 72
Oparara 259
Oredea 286
Orizaba 84, 213, 214
Orlando 373
Osh 148, 158, 162, 163
Ostuni 70, 71
Oued Laou 311
Ourtzagh 314
Oxchuc 210, 211

Pakawau 260
Pakbeng 240
Pakse 245
Palenque 209
Palermo 66
Pamir Highway 122, 140, 151, 152
Pan American highway 11
Panj River 145, 146, 147, 148
Papantla 216
Pareditas 26
Parque Nacional los Arrayanes 28
Parque National Villarrica 27
Parque Pinguíno Rey 328
Paso de Pino Hachado 27
Paso de Sico 327
Pasto 370, 378, 381, 382
Patagonia 26, 28, 30, 31
Patras 71
Pazardzhik 275
Peje 270
Peloponnese 72, 73
Pelorus Bridge 261
Peñamiller 215
Penek 101
Penong 38, 49
Pernes-les-Fontaines 322
Perth 39, 40, 46, 54
Peru 11
Perugia 296, 298
Phaestos 74
Phnom Penh 250, 254

INDEX

Piazza Armerina 68
Picton 261
Pieve Torina 299
Pilón 197
Pirin mountains 275
Pirin National Park 275
Pisa 297, 298, 301
Pistoia 301
Pitalito 370, 371, 374
Playa Girón 202
Playa Las Coloradas 196
Plovdiv 275, 276
Polje 268
Popayán 374, 378
Port Augusta 50
Porvenir 327
Posof 86, 87, 100
Prasat Preah Vihear 247
Prato 296
Prek Toal 249, 251
Prizren 271
Provence 62, 296, 306
Pu'er 237
Puente de Occidente 341
Puente Iglesias 334, 340
Puerto Berrío 347, 348
Puerto Bravo 34
Puerto de la Bonaigua 321
Puerto Montt 25, 30
Puerto Morelos 207
Puerto Natales 36
Puerto Río Tranquilo 30
Puerto Yungay 34
Puglia 69
Puno 15
Punta Arenas 36, 327
Purificación 323, 324, 326, 328
Putamayo 381

Qaraqalpaqstan 124, 125, 132
Qonghirat 125
Queen Charlotte Sound 261
Quibdo 325, 336
Quillacas 16
Quito 368
Qulma pass 148, 159
Quorn 50

Radac 270
Ráquira 361
Rawnsley Buff 51
Recanati 301
Reggio di Calabria 69

Renmark 52
Rhodes 74, 75, 76
Rhone 62, 306
Rif 308, 311, 313, 315
Rimitea 282
Río Atrato 336
Río Baker 31, 32, 33
Río Cabrera 366
Río Cauca 340, 341
Río Magdalena 326, 344, 347, 348
Río Ñadis 31
Río Suárez 352
River Darling 53
Romania 280, 281, 282
Rore 292
Rosslare 296
Rotterdam 60, 180
Rožaje 269
Ruse 278
Ruta Cuarenta 26, 27, 28
Ruta Interlagos 27

Sagalassos 78, 80, 81
Saghirdasht Pass 149
Salar de Uyuni 18
Salto de Guayabo 201
Samarkand 134, 135, 137, 139
San Agustín (Bolivia) 9, 10, 17
San Agustín (Colombia) 370, 371, 372, 373
San Antonio de los Cobres 327
San Carlos de Bariloche 28
San Cristóbal 209, 211, 212
San Francisco (Colombia) 378, 380
San Gimignano 296, 297
San Jerónimo 341, 342, 343
San Juan de Villalobos 376, 384
San Martín de los Andes 28
San Miguel de Allende 215
San Pedro de Atacama 17, 19
San Roque 346, 347
San Vicente 350
Sansange 61
Santa Fe de Antioquia 335, 341
Santa Lucía 13, 14
Santa Teresa di Gallura 64
Santander 344, 351
Santiago de Cuba 195, 196, 197
Santo Domingo 347
Săpânța 283, 284, 285
Sardinia 64, 65
Sary Tash 161, 162
Satu Mare 285
Sayabouli 240

Sedbergh 58, 296, 321
Seddonville 258
Sedona 206, 207
Serbia 268, 270, 274, 288
Serra San Bruno 70
Sète 308
Shakrisabz 140
Sharin Canyon 183, 184
Shaxi 234
Sheki 110
Shetpe 115, 117, 118, 119
Shigu 233
Si Phan Don 243, 246
Sibillini (Mountains) 300
Sibiu 280, 281
Sibundoy 378, 380
Sichuan 221, 224, 226, 227
Sicily 65, 66, 67, 68
Sidonia 74
Siem Reap 249
Siena 296, 297, 298
Sierra Maestra 196, 197, 198
Sighetu Marmației 284
Silk Road 73, 94, 110, 116
Singapore 222
Sinj 294
Sirolo 296
Sitia 73, 74, 75
Skopje 272, 273, 274
Snowy Mountains 54
Socorro 353
Soğanlı 85, 86
Song Kul 166, 168, 170, 179
Sonora 205, 217, 219
Spain 303, 304, 308
Split 294, 295, 296
Spring Creek 261, 262
Srpska 268, 289, 290, 292
St Felix 343
Stara Zagora 277
Stari Most 265, 266, 269
Stolac 266, 268
Streaky Bay 49
Stung Treng 247, 248
Su Nuraxi di Barumini 65
Șurdești 283
Sydney 56

Tad Fan 245
Tad Lo 245
Tad Yuang 245
Tajikistan 141, 142, 143, 146
Takaka 259, 260

Támesis 333, 334
Tangier 308, 309
Taormina 69
Taounate 314
Tara gorge 269
Tatacoa 365, 367
Tatacoa (Desierto de la) 365
Tbilisi 104, 105, 106, 107
Te Araroa 261
Tenosique 209, 210
Tétouan 309, 310, 311
Tha Dua 241
Thailand 250, 252
Thar-Es-Souk 315, 316
Thredbo 54
Tian Shan Mountains 166
Tierra del Fuego 36, 327
Tiger Leaping Gorge 234
Tim 134
Timișoara 286, 287
Titicaca 16
Tivet de los Andes 355
Tolima 323, 329
Tom Groggin 53
Tonlé Sap 250, 254
Torres del Paine 32, 36
Tortel 33
Totaranui 260
Transfăgărășan 280
Transylvania 280, 282
Trapeang Rung 252
Trat 252
Trevelin 26
Trogir 294, 295
Turkey 77, 78, 79, 80
Turkmenistan 126, 130
Tursunzade 141
Tuscany 296, 297

Uçhisar 79
Umbria 296
Urbino 296
Urrao 334, 335, 338, 339
Ushuaia 28, 36
Uxmal 208
Uzbekistan 122, 123, 124, 128
Uzgen 174

Vakhsh River 148
Valenciana 321
Vallon-Pont-d'Arc 321
Veliko Tarnovo 277
Vientiane 243

INDEX

Villa de Leyva 360, 361
Villa la Angostura 28
Villa O'Higgins 34
Villavieja 365, 367, 368, 370
Vilque 15
Viñales 203
Vinica 275
Virolín 355
Voditsa 277
Volcán Llaima 27
Volcán Villarrica 27

Wakhan Corridor 140, 151
Wallachia 279
Walnut Garden 230, 231
Warren Gorge 51
Wat Phou 245
Weibaoshan 236
Weishan 235, 236
Wentworth 52
Westport 257, 259
Wexford 296
Wharariki (campsite) 260
Wicklow Hills 296
Wilpena Pound 51
Windsor 56
Wusihe 225

Xalapa 213
Xayaboury 241
Xilitla 214
Xizhou 235

Yalata Aboriginal Lands 47
Yangtze (river) 229, 230, 232, 234
Yashil-Kul Lake 155
Yeşibaşköy 80
Yucatán 207, 208, 210
Yugoslavia 263, 268, 272, 274
Yulong Mountain 230, 231
Yunnan 224, 228, 231, 232
Yusufeli 95, 97, 99

Zacatecas 217, 218
Zadar 294
Zapatoca 351, 352
Zeebrugge 60
Zelve 78
Zipaquirá 361, 363

REVIEWS

"*Extraordinary Places by Bicycle* is a rich and rewarding free-wheeling journey for anyone with a dash of true adventure in their blood. Hugh and Pauline Symonds have shared the highs and lows of truly remarkable two-wheel odysseys to the wildest and most beautiful corners of the planet. Through the rugged Pamirs, across the deserts of Australia, exploring the lesser known byways of Mexico, China, New Zealand and Georgia, these are authentic accounts of great charm and humour – with an occasional moment of drama and peril.

"The photographs are absolutely stunning and are inserted into the text where they have most impact. The background to this intrepid couple's everyday world at home is also woven into the journey in a candid way: a life threatening health scare and the ups and downs of family dramas make this a satisfying autobiographical experience as well as an outstanding series of genuine adventures."

Matt Dickinson, author of *The Death Zone* and *The Everest Files*

"A decade of adventure that inspired so many of us, me included, to hit the road and explore the world by bike."

Alastair Humphreys, author, keynote speaker and
National Geographic Adventurer of the Year

"Most people's idea of retirement doesn't involve cycling to some of the world's most inaccessible and inhospitable places, on some of the roughest roads imaginable, while wild camping in a small two-person tent with only a thin layer of fabric protecting them from the elements. But Hugh and Pauline are not your typical retirees. Retirement to Hugh and Pauline simply means dedicating their life to their passion for adventure, travel and physical challenge - 100%.

"*Extraordinary Places by Bicycle* chronicles their increasingly ambitious journeys across landscapes and environments as diverse as the back roads of Europe, the Australian Outback, the Patagonian Andes, communist Cuba, and the mountains of Tajikistan, including year-long cross continental odysseys

REVIEWS

."Bicycle touring can be one of the most rewarding and enlightening ways to explore the world. The narrative illustrates and takes the reader through the history and the beauty of the areas they travel through while detailing the many trials and tribulations of life on the road. Notwithstanding the incredible physical and mental feats, Hugh and Pauline's journeys offer a unique insight into the culture, way of life and generosity of the many people they meet along the way, as well as the shared comradery from fellow travellers in remote corners of the world.

"Among the many books about cycle touring and intrepid, adventurous travel, Extraordinary Places by Bicycle stands out with its depth and breadth and beautifully written prose. It's sure to sit up there with the best."

Tim Mulliner, environmental scientist and author
Long Ride for a Pie and *Me and my Hero*

"This isn't just a book about extraordinary places, it's about extraordinary people. The pragmatism and gentle humour employed to deal with improbable situations make this pair of adventurers a true inspiration to anyone, cyclist, or otherwise. Essential reading for anyone contemplating a long distance cycle journey, there is a lot to be learned from the Symonds' experiences, both the scrapes they get into and how they get out of them! It is a book that will open your eyes to the world's possibilities and foster a belief that even the furthest flung corners are no more than pedal strokes away. It will leave you with the irresistible urge to get on your bike and pedal, wherever the road may take you."

Hannah Reynolds, journalist and author
France en Velo and *Britain's Best Bike Ride*

Read More...

by Hugh Symonds

Running High: The First Continuous Traverse of the 303 Mountains of Britain and Ireland, (1991, 2004, 2009, 2017), 978-1-904524-15-X